OPEN SYSTEMS ENGINEERING

How to Plan and Develop Client/Server Systems

Wendy Rauch

Wiley Computer Publishing

John Wiley & Sons
New York • Chichester • Brisbane • Toronto • Singapore

Publisher: Katherine Schowalter
Editor: Theresa Hudson
Text Design & Composition: Integre Technical Publishing Co., Inc.

Designations used by companies to distinguish their products are often claimed as trademarks. In all instances where John Wiley & Sons, Inc. is aware of a claim, the product names appear in initial capital or all capital letters. Readers, however, should contact the appropriate companies for more complete information regarding trademarks and registration.

This text is printed on acid-free paper.

This publication is designed to provide accurate and authoritative information in regard to the subject matter covered. It is sold with the understanding that the publisher is not engaged in rendering legal, accounting, or other professional service. If legal advice or other expert assistance is required, the services of a competent professional person should be sought.

John Wiley & Sons, Inc. is an accredited member of the IBM Independent Vendor League.

Library of Congress Cataloging-in-Publication Data:
Rauch, Wendy.
   Open systems engineering : how to plan and develop client/server
systems / Wendy Rauch.
     p. cm.
   Includes index.
   ISBN 0-471-13038-9 (paper)
   1. Client/server computing.   I. Title.
QA76.9.C55R38   1996
004$'$.36—dc20   95-50773
                                             CIP

Printed in the United States of America
10 9 8 7 6 5 4 3 2 1

To Eric,
My son, friend, and sometimes mentor

Contents

Chapter 4   Phase Three: Develop an Architectural Model   73

Chapter 5   Phase Four: Infrastructure Planning Tasks   83

Chapter 6   Phase Five: Standards Selection and Prioritization   113

Acknowledgments

It is difficult to provide appropriate acknowledgments to individuals in a book that was written with the cooperation of many people. One person, Harvey J. Hindin, stands apart from all others who gave their time and advice, and I am at a loss for words to thank him adequately. An authority himself on distributed open systems, he read and criticized every chapter of this book. I owe him a great intellectual debt for making many comments and suggestions that improved the book.

I would also like to thank the folks at Alcoa, particularly Jerry Speakman, Mike Reidenbaugh, and Bob Holtgraver, for their influence on this book and for being warm, wonderful (as well as smart) people to have a relationship with over the years.

Although the book bears the name of a single author, it has been influenced by many people and would not have happened without their help, ideas, and cooperation. Some of these people are not aware of how much I have learned from them over many years. So it is my pleasure to publicly acknowledge and thank Jim Isaak, Alan Hankinson, Nina Lytton, John Stanton, George Gunn, Jim Thompson, and all the active participants in the IEEE P1003.0 Group.

I extend special thanks to Joe Howard, Manager of Customer Service at ANSI, for his extraordinary help in locating and standards information, in a timely manner, whenever I needed it.

My very special thanks also to Pat Scalice for performing the logistics work and preparing the art and manuscript for submission.

I am grateful to many of the Paradox technical support people at Borland, without whose help I could not have developed the software accompanying this book in the time allotted. First and foremost of these, I must thank James Arias-La Rheir, one of the sharpest programmers it has been my pleasure to know. Other very special Borland people I am grateful to, both for programming and other types of help, include Rory Bannon, Andrew Bennett, Corrine Cottle, Ralph Galentine, Chris Levesque, Ben Matterson, and Janet Perry. And I would like to extend the most special thanks to the unknown person at Borland who chose the best of the classical music war horses to play on the telephone, and played it at just the right volume.

Finally, I extend thanks to Terri Hudson, my editor at Wiley. She is gracious and genial and it has been a delight to work with her.

My apologies to anyone who has been inadvertently left out. Needless to say, any error of fact, interpretation, or emphasis that may have crept into the book is mine.

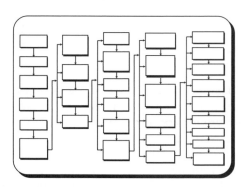

Chapter 1

Introduction

Introduction

Though barely understood, not yet complete, and its products have only recently begun to appear, a new kind of computing has burst onto the business, industrial, and government scene. Many organizations believe that this computing is indispensable for competing in national and international markets, or in running organizations with national and international presence. Called *distributed computing* or *Client/Server computing*, it allows users to easily access the data and information they need when they need it. But Client/Server computing goes further than just allowing timely data access. It also allows users to process the data, analyze it, combine it with other information, update it, and take actions based on the data. Consequently, users can take advantage of opportunities as they arise, respond to events in a timely manner, and generally perform higher quality work. Client/Server computing stands in contrast to traditional centralized computing (common since the 1970s), which required users to request data and other information from overworked MIS professionals, and to wait on a long backlog queue to obtain that information. Moreover, once the data and information was obtained, the application backlog often made it impossible to respond to events and opportunities quickly.

Using Client/Server computing, organizations can respond rapidly to varied market needs, industrial-design changes and product customization, and government or commercial events. However, integration of hardware, software, systems, and applications across an enterprise is necessary to realize the full potential of distributed Client/Server computing. Because most enterprise environments tend to be heterogeneous and multivendor, open systems and standards are an essential element of cost-effective integration. The complexity of distributed systems in heterogeneous, multivendor environments prevents them from being cost-effective to operate or manage without common user and programming interfaces, common network protocols, and common data-interchange/access formats.

An increasing number of companies and organizations worldwide have begun to move to open, distributed Client/Server systems, or to make plans and set dates and milestones for doing so. Many of these organizations need a body of literature, a methodology, or other users' experiences to aid them in their planning. Unfortunately, due to the newness of Client/Server systems and open systems, there is a scarcity of information and experience that can serve as guidance to the planners of these systems.

This book, *Distributed Open Systems Engineering: How to Plan and Develop Client/Server Systems*, is about planning open Client/Server systems in the commercial world. It was written to aid users, vendors, system integrators, and government agencies worldwide who wish to use heterogeneous multivendor computers in Client/Server environments, as well as any other kinds of distributed environments. The book's intended audience includes planners and facilitators of open Client/Server systems, as well as managers who are now (or in the future may be) responsible for costs, organizational benefits, or competitive leverage that can accrue from properly planned Client/Server systems.

The book is primarily based on both open systems and Client/Server planning work that the author's company, Emerging Technologies Group, has done with its clients.

Distributed Processing: The Old and the New

Distributed processing is not new. Geographically dispersed computers, which allow connected computers to share resources such as data, processing power, and printers, have existed since the 1970s. Bank networks, for example, allow people to go to one bank and deposit money, even though the person's account is at another bank. The information about the deposit is sent to the person's bank via a network. Networks also allow airline companies all over the world to process information whenever someone makes a flight reservation.

Traditionally, networked computers were connected either vertically, horizontally, or in some combination of these. Vertically networked computers are connected in a hierarchy of processors (Figure 1.1a). A *hierarchical network* is one that requires information to flow up and down a chain of command, maintaining master-slave relationships. IBM's Systems Network Architecture (SNA) in the 1980s is an example of a hierarchical network.

In contrast, *horizontally networked systems* are networks of systems in which all the distributed processors are of equal status or peers (Figure 1.1b). Since the processors are peers, such networks are referred to as *peer-to-peer networks*. Peer-to-peer networks allow anyone on the network to talk to any other network node, without having to go through higher-level control systems. The Arpanet, Internet, TCP/IP, and Digital Equipment Corp.'s DECnet are examples of peer-to-peer networks.

Throughout the 1970s and 1980s, computers and networks were mostly used to run an organization's day-to-day operations, or for decision support based on archived data. In the 1970s and 1980s, users of hierarchically or peer-to-peer networked computers typically accessed mainframes or minicomputers through termi-

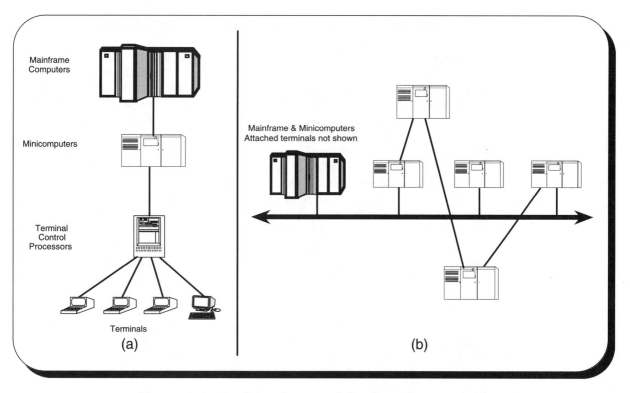

Figure 1.1 Traditional types of distributed processing systems.

nals. These users were extensively trained in the use of computers, and needed to know a lot about both mainframes and networks to access their systems.

If managers needed certain data because they foresaw a possible business opportunity or needed to respond to a particular event, they had to get the data through the MIS staff. This took time. Application development in the mainframe environment was difficult, and generally done only by the MIS group. User requests for new applications were put in a queue. Because there was just one queue, and mainframe application development took a lot of time, there tended to be a long application backlog. It was not unusual for a requested application to be completed after it was needed.

Software tool companies, government organizations, and internal developers have spent a good deal of time trying to solve the problems of the application backlog and timely data access. Their goal was to get data and other pertinent information to the people who need to analyze it and make rapid decisions based on it.

A solution is finally emerging now. It was partly the result of accidental circumstances.

Client/Server Computing: A Historical Perspective

It is not generally known that IBM, the dominant player in the proprietary mainframe environment, inadvertently instigated the move to open systems and Client/Server computing. The forces that would ultimately drive the open Client/Server market began in August 1981 when IBM introduced its first PC. This introduction followed, by one month, IBM's introduction of another computer—the Data Master.

IBM touted the Data Master as its desktop solution for the corporate environment. In contrast, based on the small size of its floppy disks (160 Kbytes in a pre-hard disk and pre-CD-ROM era), it was generally assumed that the first IBM PC was targeted at the educational and consumer markets.

The educational and consumer markets, dominated at the time by Apple Computer and Radio Shack, were not large. IBM, however, saw a market opportunity. Never a company to let an opportunity pass it by, but also a company that knew its bread was buttered in the large-scale corporate market, IBM designed its PC with an open hardware and software architecture. By so doing, IBM did not have to dilute its resources to support the PC. Instead, third-party hardware and software companies could supply a variety of add-in boards, add-on peripherals, and applications.

For several reasons, the Data Master never caught on, but the PC captured the world's imagination. Home-user hobbyists began to bring the IBM PC to their offices to perform productivity tasks and run applications. Between 1983 and 1985, PCs became widespread throughout the corporate world. The Apple Macintosh was introduced. Computer literacy and computer anxiety became the watchwords of the day.

In reality, users got educated about PCs pretty fast. Then they discovered how much time they were wasting rekeying data that already existed on mainframes and minicomputers into their PCs. Access to the mainframes and minis would eliminate this need to rekey data. Suddenly, large companies' communications ports on mainframes and front-end processors were continuously busy with users trying to access data. MIS people claimed that the PC users, with their interactive queries, were interfering with system overhead and performance.

PC users didn't understand why their accesses took so long. They also found that using the mainframe was very difficult. Why couldn't the MIS people give them instant data access in a friendlier manner that did not require them to know about mainframe operating systems, cryptic file names, and communications?

The situation became intolerable. Soon, LANs (local-area networks) eliminated some of the problems. Between 1985 and 1987, LANs began to become widespread. The LANs connected PC users so that they could share a departmental database on a server and a single gateway to corporate mainframes or minicomputers. With access to all this data, users quickly outgrew their PCs. Many bought larger PCs or workstations. Users on any PC or workstation wanted access to the corporate mainframes and minis to access data, and to other PCs and workstations to share resources. Furthermore, users wanted a Macintosh-like interface on all their computers to use for accessing workgroup and corporate data and applications, and users on interconnected computers.

Enterprisewide computing was born. The *de facto* multivendor environment also was born because organizations' diverse PCs, workstations, PC networks, backbone LANs, and mainframes were incompatible with each other. Users began demanding open systems in order to achieve interoperability among all their computer systems. The market for easy-to-use graphical user interfaces (GUIs) to access remote computers was born. These markets grew into Client/Server computing.

Early Client/Server systems were simple. They generally provided file and print sharing for PC productivity applications. Some early Client/Server applications also allowed client access to an SQL database.

Typically, early Client/Server systems were not mission critical. They supported only a small number of users who did not demand high performance. All of the application code for these early Client/Server applications ran on the client workstation, but the applications could access other files and data, and share resources.

Client/Server computing is now evolving toward higher-end, more complex applications. In many of these applications, the application code is distributed across client workstations and database servers. In other cases, the applications are distributed across client workstations, a database server, and an application server.

These emerging Client/Server applications typically support large numbers of users, and require higher performance and greater availability. Unlike early Client/Server systems, the new generation of applications is often much more critical to business needs. For example, Client/Server applications operating in production environments include accounting, contract tracking, customer service, electronic mail, human resources, computer-aided engineering, risk management, and transaction processing. These applications are in addition to traditional data access and file and resource sharing. Finally, tools are emerging to support this Client/Server evolution.

What Is Really Meant by Client/Server Computing

Client/Server computing means that work is split among two or more entities, called *clients* and *servers*, rather than being performed in a single monolithic application. Clients request data or ask for a job to be done. Servers do what the clients ask (Figure 1.2).

Controversy arises because people have different opinions as to what constitutes a Client/Server system. Most people agree that a system that allows users to interactively query a remote networked database is a Client/Server application. Many of these same people balk at the idea that accessing a file via NFS (Network File System) also constitutes a Client/Server application. Opinions vary as to how to classify X-terminal applications. Even fewer people know how to classify PCs using terminal emulation to access remote databases or applications, especially in cases where the terminal emulation runs in one PC window, and PC users can download and store files and also retain their PC capabilities (rather than only having the capabilities of a dumb terminal).

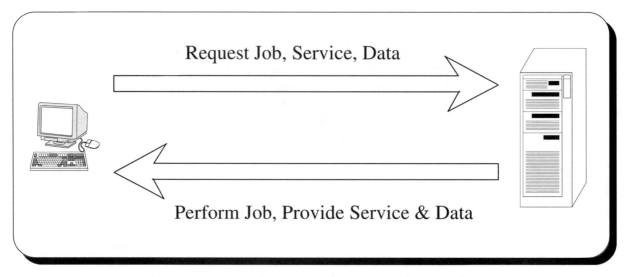

Figure 1.2 How Client/Server computing works.

This book will not address these controversial definitions because they make little difference to the benefits of Client/Server computing.

Client/Server Benefits

There are many advantages to Client/Server computing:

- Ease of use
- Timely accessibility of data, information, and applications
- The ability to maximize user productivity
- Individual control over environments
- Use of best-suited computer for a job
- Increased functionality
- Reduced costs

Ease-of-use is important because organizations are putting more and more data and information on line, allowing many more users to access this data and information—many of these are casual or unsophisticated users.

The result of the ease-of-use advantage is data accessibility. Authorized Client/Server users can use GUIs on PCs and workstations to access data, information, and applications located on a variety of types of computers, without going through MIS. Because that data is readily accessible, Client/Server computing can increase users' business and organizational productivity performance. Also, because the data accessed by the client can be analyzed, operated on, recalculated, and combined with other data and files without necessarily returning to the server, users can leverage the data to take advantage of new opportunities and rapidly respond to events and changes. Finally, because Client/Server application development is simpler than mainframe development, and is typically decentralized, users also have greater control over their business and computing environments and the use of data.

Another advantage to being able to distribute computing across multiple computers is the ability to perform different types of work within a single application on the kind of computer best suited to doing the job. For example, PCs are well suited to interactive, graphical interfaces. Mainframes, UNIX-based servers, and multiprocessing servers are well suited to managing and searching databases. Supercomputers are well suited to compute-intensive operations.

Still another advantage to Client/Server computing is increased functionality. Through Client/Server connections, users of any particular machine can access functionality much greater than their own machines can provide.

A final major advantage is cost. Most purchased software costs, as well as development costs, are lower for Client/Server systems than for proprietary mainframe computers. Also, the capital costs involved in Client/Server computing are lower than on traditional centralized machines because much of the computing is performed on relatively low-cost PCs. Types of computing that do not perform well on PCs can be performed on UNIX machines that also are lower priced than their predecessor proprietary mainframes and minicomputers.

Readers should carefully evaluate this last claim. It is the capital costs that are less. The life cycle costs may or may not be less. Logically, it would seem that they should be more because the environment is much more complex. Some organizations, however, that have carefully planned out and re-engineered their Client/Server environments claim that both their costs of the overall Client/Server environment and their system-management costs are less than they were in centralized proprietary environments. And the functionality is much greater and the machines are more flexible.

Client/Server costs will be covered separately in Chapter 12.

The Associated Need for Open Systems

Many planners of Client/Server systems are so busy defining their business requirements and getting their platforms and networks connected and running, that they miss the importance of planning and developing an open, integrated Client/Server environment.

By their nature, Client/Server environments are heterogeneous, and usually multivendor. Therefore, open systems, whether they consist of formal or *de facto* standards, are at the core of Client/Server environments.

Lack of planning for open systems in conjunction with the Client/Server planning process, can result in incompatible islands of Client/Server systems that are difficult and costly to integrate. Moreover, by not anticipating the means to connect all kinds of systems throughout the enterprise, and instead adding incompatible systems incrementally, the developer will produce a set of Client/Server systems that are a nightmare to maintain, manage, and administer. As a result, the Client/Server environment's flexibility will be reduced, while its cost will be greatly increased.

The importance of open systems to an enterprisewide Client/Server environment cannot be overestimated.

The Heterogeneous Multivendor Environment Trend

Most companies have not made an explicit decision to move to multivendor environments. If anything, they are trying to consolidate the number of vendors they deal with, preferring to reduce the complexity of their networked environments by dealing with a small number of vendors who work with them as strategic partners.

What companies want, however, is to connect their enterprises' PCs, workstations, and larger machines, commonly called *servers*. Servers generally contain the company's data and run its applications. The interconnection of an enterprise's various computer systems provides decision makers with access to the data they need when they need it. Decision makers will then be able to leverage this data and respond quickly to perceived business opportunities.

This enterprisewide networking trend, however, has created *de facto* multivendor environments because different departments and divisions within an enterprise have different needs and, over the years, favored different vendors. The various vendors' operating systems, database systems, networks, graphics, user interfaces, and so on are different. The applications that run on one computer brand are incompatible with those on another. The applications that run, and the data created by one vendor's software systems, are also incompatible with those created by another vendor.

The goal of open systems is to make it possible to cost effectively integrate heterogeneous multivendor computer platforms, networks, and software.

How Standards Help Businesses

Software standards (both formal and *de facto*) are very attractive to distributed heterogeneous computing because they help assure portability and interoperability. This allows increased automation, greater efficiency, and less training.

The use of standards also allows organizations to cut expenditures and streamline costs. Organizations can buy more computers yet reduce software costs because the users can purchase the right size platform for different departments and branches, but run the same applications on these heterogeneous computers (a capability known as *scalability*). In addition, the use of standards also can reduce software maintenance costs because it reduces the number and variety of programming interfaces.

Standards broaden the market for application developers. This helps ensure a greater supply of shrink-wrapped applications for the largest number of machines. Standards-based applications can be available at lower prices than those for proprietary systems because the broader standards-based market allows economies of scale.

It is important to realize that standards mean *interfaces*, not implementations. Interface standards define the services and characteristics that applications see. In theory, any software that provides required services can be implemented under the interface because applications see only the interface.

Why Now?

Open systems, portability, interoperability, and scalability were not problems in the past when the number of software systems was small. Most systems then were standalone systems purchased to do one type of job, such as accounting in a data center or CAD/CAM in an engineering department. Open systems were not needed in such environments. Furthermore, vendor research, followed by development of proprietary computer hardware and system software, was often the only way to meet a user's functional requirements.

Times have changed. Companies today have vast quantities of data on line. Large numbers of tasks within organizations are computerized. Users want to connect equipment in different departments so users throughout an enterprise can access data and applications in other departments.

The greatest cost of a computer system today is software and its maintenance. Very Large-Scale Integration (VLSI) and computer-hardware technology have advanced more rapidly than software technology. Consequently, it is not unusual for software systems to outlive hardware systems. When that happens, software must often be rewritten because of the inability to cost effectively reuse existing applications on different hardware. In addition, incompatibilities between platforms also require users to constantly rewrite interfaces to maintain interoperability.

Users can achieve interoperability and portability by buying from a single vendor, but so many tasks within an organization are computerized today that no one vendor can supply all of a user's needs. Even if a sole vendor could, users today have too much data on line, and are too dependent on computers, to want to put the heart of their business into a single vendor's hands.

Even if users were willing, the idea of depending on only a single vendor is no longer possible because of the trend toward enterprisewide computing. Having created *de facto* multivendor environments by hooking up different parts of their organizations, the organizations need a way to make the integration of their enterprise cost effective. Open systems and standards-based products can provide that method.

Why the Brouhaha? Standards Are Not a New Phenomenon

Standards are required in many industries, such as the audio, video tape, and facsimile industries. Few people, for example, would consider trashing all their compact disks (CDs) or video tapes because they won't work with a new CD player or VCR. But traditional computing environments were neither standardized, nor open. Until recently, almost everyone accepted the need to buy or write new software whenever a computer was replaced. Vendors who worry about standards restraining their ability to develop and penetrate markets forget that it is standards that are responsible for the development of the facsimile and other billion dollar markets.

When Will All This Wonderfulness Happen?

For several reasons, the move to open Client/Server systems will not happen overnight. First, all the standardized pieces of the environment do not yet exist, and some may never exist. Second, many of those that do exist are not yet mature. Replacing a company's proprietary computer system with a more open one may solve one problem, but create others. Third, the mere availability of standards is not enough to plan an open systems environment that provides a reasonable assurance of interoperability, portability, and scalability across heterogeneous, multivendor, Client/Server systems.

It is important to realize that standards will not always meet all of an organization's functional objectives. A standards-based system built for one department may not be adequate for another. Vendors generally must add some nonstandard functionality to their products to satisfy user requirements. Even so, in some cases, legacy systems may meet an organization's functional or financial objectives better than standardized systems. There should be a balance between too much and too little standardization.

Nevertheless, vendors and users are moving toward open systems. Users are motivated to move because of their heterogeneous Client/Server system plans. Vendors are motivated to move because most vendors have not been able to sell enough proprietary operating systems, proprietary networks, or other proprietary system software to bring in sufficient new business to expand their companies. Instead, for most vendors, the major buyers of proprietary networks and operating systems have been existing customers who need upgrades or want to expand their legacy systems.

At present, most vendors support two product lines—an open systems product line and a proprietary product lines. Ultimately, they must choose, because the cost of supporting two overlapping product lines will become prohibitive. It is likely that they will choose open systems because that market is much larger than that for proprietary systems.

Users must make certain that they are not left behind and stuck with obsolete products that do not support technologies they need for competitive leverage. At the same time, moving too soon can be very costly because the open systems field is not yet stable. It is important that users understand their proprietary and open system options so they can make their information systems choices proactively, rather than being dragged into open systems by their vendors. The distributed open systems environment engineering (DOSEE) methodology described in this book is a practical approach to achieving the interoperability, portability, and scalability needed for successful Client/Server computing.

What Users Must Do

In deciding whether and when to move to open distributed systems, each organization must evaluate its open system requirements against its functional needs, and then weigh the tradeoffs.

The question of what services to standardize, what standards to implement, and when, is key to developing a successful open systems environment. Which standards a user requires will vary with applications, departments, and changing business needs. To bring open systems technology into real-world production-oriented computing environments it is also necessary to address how the system fits into users' existing and future environments.

Open Client/Server System Requirements

To make open Client/Server systems a reality requires more than just networks and standards. It also requires that certain critical communications and other standards, with associated enabling technologies, be available in products. Furthermore, they must be available in a timely manner; reliable; simple to use; integrated with existing systems; and cost effective to maintain, manage, and integrate. If the distributed open systems cost too much to manage, are too difficult to use, or are not robust, they may not be viable. Figure 1.3 shows the major enabling technologies necessary for open systems to successfully achieve their goals.

Open Client/Server Systems' Functionality

Most software services that Client/Server applications need can be grouped into five major categories: human-computer interaction services, system services, information services, communications services, and cross-category services. These services encompass the following functional areas: operating system, networking and communications, data management and transaction processing, data exchange, command-level and graphical user interfaces, graphics, programming, software development tools, security, and system management (which includes the management of networks, platforms, devices, users, system software, and applications).

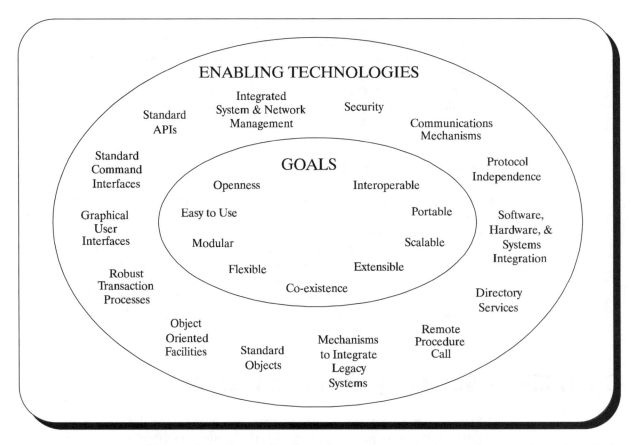

Figure 1.3 Open distributed system requirements. Source: Emerging Technologies Group.

Figure 1.4 shows a high-level view of the relationship between application software, the external environment, the types of services that applications and users need, and the interfaces among them. The major relationships shown in this table indicate that, in an open system, applications invoke the services they need through standardized interfaces. The interfaces between the services and the application are called application-programming interfaces (APIs). The interfaces between the services and the external environment are known as external environment interfaces (EEIs).

Cross-category services are those that are used by applications for multiple functional service categories. For example, internationalized facilities are needed by applications, user interfaces, and data-management services. Security and system-management services are used by every component of a Client/Server system. Distributed computing services (often part of what is called Client/Server *middleware*) can be considered cross-category services because they are used by applications,

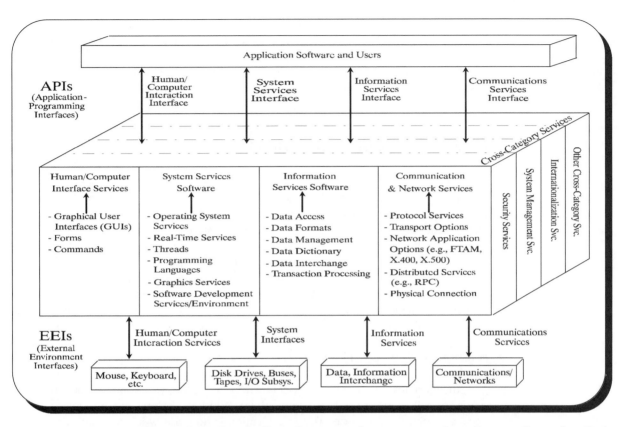

Figure 1.4 Open Client/Server environment services. *Source: Emerging Technologies Group. Based on a hybrid of IEEE P1003.0's, the US DoD's (Department of Defense), DISA's (Defense Information Systems Agency), and Emerging Technologies Group's Reference Models.*

and data-management and network services. Middleware, however, can also be considered to be part of network services and part of data-management services. The different types of middleware are discussed later in this book.

The cross-category services are shown at the right side of Figure 1.4. The broken lines across the top of the middle (large) box indicate that these services can be used by multiple service categories.

The actual software products that implement the various system, information, management, networking, human/computer, and cross category services are part of the application platform (which consists of particular vendors' hardware and software). These software products are proprietary, but the interfaces to them must be standardized in order to achieve multivendor heterogeneous system portability and interoperability.

Besides software standards in each of these areas, hardware standards, conformance test methods, and a way to ensure that standards in different areas don't conflict with each other, are needed for open systems success.

The concept of an open systems model and the relationships between its components, is covered in greater depth later in this book and in the appendices.

How to Fill Gaps in Standards

Software standards to accommodate all the services and interfaces needed are still emerging. Although hundreds of software standards have been defined to date by international and national standards groups, formal standards are not yet defined for all the functional areas needed for real-world systems.

To fill these standards gaps, several vendor consortia have defined specifications. Consortia specifications provide greater interoperability and portability than do proprietary products because they are based on a consensus of a group of vendors, many of which are major information system suppliers. Formal standards, however, provide the greatest compatibility because they represent a consensus of the widest diversity of users and vendors, and thus have the greatest acceptance.

A discussion of the types of standards and specifications, the most influential consortia, and understanding the status of standards is found in Appendices B, C, and D.

An alternative to consortia specifications is industry standards. Industry standards, best illustrated by TCP/IP and the X-Window System, are neutral specifications and/or software code. The specifications and code were generally developed by neutral bodies without vested vendor interests, such as academic institutions and government groups. Both the specifications and the code are usually available in the public domain, and are also supported by a wide variety of vendors.

If neither standards nor consortia specifications are available for particular functionalities, companies will have to standardize around a vendor's product. Some vendor products run on multiple vendors' platforms and have become *de facto* standards. Such products are a good choice for providing a large degree of integration and information sharing throughout an enterprise. For maximum interoperability and portability, users should, however, give strong preference to vendors whose products incorporate and conform to standards. Where this is not possible, users should require their vendors to indicate their strategy for moving to standards when they become available, and/or providing integration with other standards in the enterprise.

Microsoft's DOS and Windows, Novell's NetWare, and UNIX are good examples of vendor products that have become *de facto* standards. There are also some other products that vendors announce and market months to years ahead of delivery. In so doing, such high expectations are built up for these products that they are often considered *de facto* standards before they exist. Some of these products do eventually become such standards. Others fall by the wayside.

Achieving Practical, Standards-Based Open Systems

Even if the major required standards are available, open systems are not achieved by the use of any single, or even group of, *de jure* or *de facto* standards. Just choosing standards does not guarantee portability or interoperability, nor does it guarantee the ability to integrate heterogeneous, multivendor Client/Server systems.

Current thinking indicates that users planning open systems environments should begin by defining an open-systems profile, rather than just by specifying standards. As will be seen, *profiling* is a concept developed to make standards practical to deal with. One goal of this book is to help strategic planners, open-systems and Client/Server architects and facilitators, and program managers define open system profiles for their organizations' Client/Server projects and procurements.

Profiles Make Standards Practical

A *profile* is a collection of standards, along with selected options within these standards, and, possibly, additional defined functionalities required for the successful operation of an application area, platform, or organization. Profiles are becoming popular because they are more practical to deal with than traditional standards.

The problem with standards is that they tend to be large, generically defined, and confusing because they contain options to accommodate a variety of diverse application and platform needs, and there are many standards from which to choose. A particular application area or platform, such as office systems, manufacturing, logistics systems, supercomputing, or personal computers, uses only a subset of these standards and their options. The standards subsets required for different application areas and platforms often contain different functionality (Table 1.1).

Even if the same standards are used, different application areas and platforms may require options within a standard that are specific to their needs, and which are different from the options required by other applications or platforms. Each application area may also need some specialized, nonstandard capabilities to do its job.

For example, the ISO X.400 electronic mail protocol is a store-and-forward message system interface specification typically required by office-system applications. In contrast, robots, used in manufacturing applications, do not need a store-and-forward messaging system (the robots are usually in, and if they are elsewhere, their messages cannot be sent to another robot). Instead of X.400, plant floor applications may require the ISO Manufacturing Messaging System (MMS), a messaging protocol developed specifically for industrial environments.

Profiling Is Not New

The concept of profiling is not new. Users have traditionally developed profiles for their companies and organizations as part of their normal information systems

Table 1.1   Profiles Make Standards Practical

Standards	Profiles
Tend to be large	Tend to be smaller than standards and, therefore, less intimidating
Very detailed	More conceptually oriented, and therefore more usable by managers and planners
Generically defined	Specific and focused on a particular application area, platform, industry segment, or organization
Contains many options	Selects relevant options
Accommodates diverse application and platform needs	Oriented toward a targeted platform or application area
Specifies functionality, syntax, protocols, and data formats in detail	Reference specifies one or more standards, subsets of standards, options within standards, and other profiles
Each standard specifies a single type of functionality	A single profile (e.g., for an application area or a market segment) may specify many types of functionality
Consists only of formal standardized specifications and their options	Some profiles may reference *de jure* or *de facto* standards, consortia specifications, and/or specialized nonstandard functionality

Source: Emerging Technologies Group.

planning work. They have not generally called their work *profile work*, but simply organizational or MIS guidelines.

In the past, the profiles that users defined for their companies were based on a vendor's products, rather than on standards. The specification of brand-name products often makes the implementation of systems that conform to the profile nonportable and noninteroperable. Cost-effective Client/Server computing environments, however, require the use of as many standards as possible.

Standardized Profiles

To help clarify how various standards fit together, some standards groups, such as ISO and the IEEE, are defining profiles that specify the major services and standards needed for particular application domains, platforms, and networking. ISO has concentrated on profiles for transferring different types of data, files, and information across different types of networks. The IEEE's focus has been on defining profiles for various application domains and platforms. Examples are the IEEE profiles for supercomputing and real-time environments, and for multiprocessing platforms.

In addition, some industry groups, such as the petrochemical and power industries, are developing generic profiles for their industries. Most of these industry profiles consist of formal standards and their options, along with some industry standard specifications, and some industry-specific specifications.

More information on what makes applications incompatible, open systems, and standardized profiles are described in detail in Appendices E, F, and G.

Planning Real-World Open Client/Server System Profiles

Standardized profiles are a target to aim for, and a help in understanding what an organization planning open systems must do. Rarely, however, can a real-world production environment be built exclusively on a standardized profile's specifications, because standardized profiles represent the ideal case. Real-world companies have a number of considerations that may not be addressed in an ideal case.

For example, besides designing for portability and interoperability, real-world production-environment systems must contain sufficient functionality to be able to perform users' business tasks. The functionality that a particular organization needs may not yet have been addressed by standards groups, and, therefore, cannot be specified by a standardized profile. Performance also may be required for certain real-world applications. This is usually considered an implementation issue and is, therefore, not usually addressed in standardized profiles.

Because certain nonstandard functionality may be paramount in an organization, a profile developed for a particular organization's open systems environment will likely specify a combination of formal and *de facto* standards. In addition, in some cases, nonstandard extensions will be needed. In other cases, legacy systems will best meet an organization's objectives, especially if the legacy systems support some standards. Even if the legacy system does not support standards, it may be a working legacy system that users want to continue to use. Also, important applications may not be available for an open-systems platform that users would like to buy.

A good way to deal with these issues is with an organization-specific group of profiles for different application and platform areas. The profiles should be based on an architectural model that accommodates all interoperable and/or portable software, and the maximum amount of legacy or specialized software that the organization requires. Such an architectural model and set of profiles helps users to visualize and crystallize their plans for an interoperable, portable, Client/Server application environment that supports varying business requirements throughout an enterprise, and can grow to accommodate future technology. Development of such a model and set of profiles is a goal of *Distributed Open Systems Environment Engineering*.

Five Different Planning Views

A successful open Client/Server environment must reflect five different views:

- **The Business View.** This includes an organization's business goals, policies, procurement requirements, and information system objectives.
- **The Application View.** This includes activities performed by an organization's diverse departments, the applications used to perform those activities, the types of functions and services needed to support these applications and the connections and relationships between applications.
- **The Client/Server View.** This includes the Client/Server architecture(s) best suited to an organization's Client/Server applications; the local and remote parts of the application; the distribution of an application across client and server nodes; and Client/Server tools.
- **The Open Systems View.** This includes application processes, and systems within departments and across departments; applications that interact and are targets for interoperability; applications that run on heterogeneous systems and are portability targets, the information system infrastructure that provides interoperability and portability; and the availability of practical standards.
- **The Technology View.** This includes the technology trends, the types of networking, platform, system software, and application technologies required and anticipated for the future; the integration of these technologies on different platforms and networks, access to these technologies from other local and remote systems, and vendor capabilities.

The technology view overlaps all the other areas. It will, therefore, be covered throughout this book where appropriate. Planning the open Client/Server environment to reflect the remaining four views constitutes different phases of the distributed open systems environment methodology, and is covered in separate sections of this book.

The actual building of a real-world open Client/Server environment involves both top–down and bottom–up planning. It involves planning for application and process interoperability and portability through common application programming interfaces and communication protocols, and for user portability through common user interfaces. Most important, it also requires planning for data portability. Data is the lifeblood of companies today, yet it is often more difficult to achieve than application or user portability and interoperability.

Distributed open systems environment engineering also requires planning for physical, software, and human resources. The costs involved in designing, integrating these resources, and in training people to use and manage them, must be understood.

Finally, there are political and human issues involved in implementing an enterprisewide open distributed environment. These issues arise because an enterprise's distributed environment crosses many different departments. Individual department managers are responsible for pieces of the networked environment, yet a centralized authority may be dictating standards and network policies that a department manager feels are not in the department's best interest. Setting up a distributed enterprise, therefore, requires people with good interpersonal relationship skills.

An Overview of Distributed Open-Systems Engineering

Figure 1.5 shows a summary of the recommended steps for planning an open systems environment. As the figure shows, the planning process consists of eight separate and distinct phases. Each of the phases is the subject of a different chapter in this book.

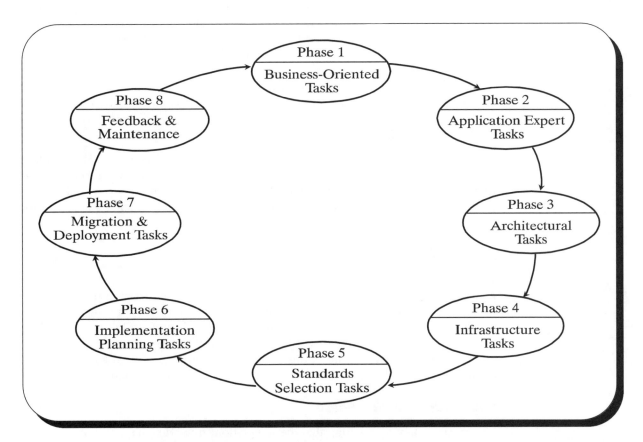

Figure 1.5 Distributed open systems environment engineering overview. *Source: Emerging Technologies Group.*

Business-Oriented Phase

The methodology begins by developing a vision of an organization's open Client/Server directions and getting some level of open systems commitment from management.

Once commitment has been obtained, planners identify the organization's business and technical goals, and consider the organization's business models, business units, departments, activities, and the relationships between departments, and so on. These goals and relationships influence the planners' open systems vision, and the organization's targeted areas for portability and interoperability.

Application-Expert Phase

This is an information-gathering phase in which users are interviewed in order to identify and analyze the activities performed, and the applications and resources in local and interconnected departments that users need to do their jobs. The aim of the interviews and analysis is the determination of the short- and long-term requirements and Client/Server architectures for these activities and applications.

Client/Server architectures and applications are examined and classified to help Client/Server planners decide how to structure their Client/Server environment, and to determine which applications are most suitable for Client/Server computing. The result of this phase is a picture of trends and strategy ideas, summarized in a series of tables that will form the basis for infrastructure determination tasks in future phases.

Architectural Phase

After studying business objectives, policies, user requirements, and technology trends, open Client/Server planners develop an abstract reference model around functions, platforms, and data. This model is used by planners to visualize their planning as it develops, and to communicate their ideas to other people in the organization.

Infrastructure Phase

The infrastructure phase is the heart of both open systems and a Client/Server planning process. In this phase, planners determine the targeted application areas for interoperability and portability using a set of interoperability and portability matrices. The applications are characterized by a number of attributes and attribute values, which are mapped to explicit service requirements for which standards might be needed. The output of this phase is the mapping of the identified service components onto the architecture defined in the architectural phase.

Standards-Selection Phase

This phase is key to ensuring that the integration, upgradeability, and use of a heterogeneous Client/Server environment is cost effective and not intimidating because of the need to learn multiple interfaces to different systems. The phase tasks include the identification of required standardized services, interfaces, protocols, and formats (e.g., communications, database, user interface) for the platforms and software for which portability and/or interoperability are desired.

Later in this phase, planners determine the practicality of the standards chosen, and develop miniprofiles for desirable application areas. The output of this phase is a prioritized list of standards and a group of miniprofiles.

Implementation-Planning Phase

In this phase, open Client/Server planners begin to move out of the conceptual world into the real-world information technology environment. In this world, planners concentrate on practical realities such as how to manage the open Client/Server systems, the cost of the systems, how to distribute the Client/Server applications, which Client/Server applications to implement first, and which applications to re-engineer.

Migration-and-Deployment Phase

This phase moves the paper plans into the real world of information systems. Among other things, this phase requires planning and/or choosing a migration strategy, and deciding what to do about mainframe legacy investments. The output of this phase is Client/Server systems as open as possible for real users and applications.

Feedback-and-Maintenance Phase

This phase occurs over the life of the open Client/Server systems. It reflects the need to continuously modify the open Client/Server environment based on what works well and what doesn't, as well as on changes in business directions and advances in technology.

DOSEE Details

Figure 1.6 summarizes many of the details of the distributed open systems environment engineering phases just discussed. The order in which these steps could be performed is approximated in the figure, but the order is not always critical.

Several organization's experiences have shown that moving to open Client/Server environments can save significant amounts of money (e.g., millions of dollars per year). These organizations all have devoted time to appropriate planning of the infrastructure and properly engineering their applications. Strategic open Client/Server planning, if done efficiently, costs little compared to the costs of uncoordinated, haphazard implementation of open Client/Server systems.

In fact, absence of a coordinated foundation for the open Client/Server environment is one of the reasons that many organizations moving to Client/Server systems bog down in unanticipated people costs. These people costs, frequently caused by the failure to plan for openness, enterprisewide integration, and manage-

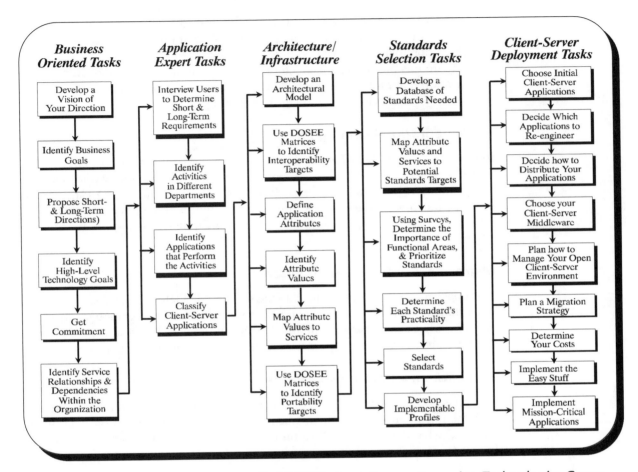

Figure 1.6 Detailed DOSEE steps. *Source: Emerging Technologies Group.*

ment of the Client/Server environment, are much more expensive than a methodical planning process would have been. Such planning, however, needs a fine-grained methodology, rather than a coarse-grained gut-feel methodology. The rest of this book presents a fine-grained methodology needed for successful open Client/Server planning.

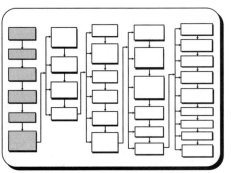

Chapter 2

Phase One: Business-Oriented Tasks

Introduction

If a company is building a one-of-a-kind system, it can buy a computer or software system just based on best-in-class technology. To bring open Client/Server systems technology into real-world production-computing environments, it is necessary to also be concerned with interoperability, portability, scalability, the systems' fit with the organization's existing and future business objectives, and enterprisewide environments.

It is not easy to determine this fit. To define an open Client/Server systems environment within a real-world organization, each organization first needs to understand its business goals and objectives. It must determine what it needs to meet its functional objectives. And, in making this determination, the organization must evaluate its Client/Server and open systems considerations against its functional needs.

This chapter describes the business tasks that must be addressed in planning an enterprisewide open Client/Server environment, and provides a framework and guidelines for addressing them. It also discusses the problem of justifying open Client/Server systems to senior management without hyping the systems, and summarizes some real-world case studies that users have employed as part of their business justification strategies.

The Business-Oriented Tasks

Phase One in planning open Client/Server systems concerns business-related tasks. Such tasks range from making a business case for management, and getting commitment from management, to analyzing the organization's business and technical goals and identifying the organization's structure (Figure 2.1).

Develop a vision for your organization that embodies your organization's goals at a very high level.

Identify your organization's business and technical goals, and business models that are used in determining how to reach these goals.

Understand the difference between where you are today and where you want to be five years from now.

Get management commitment.

Identify the business units, divisions, functional areas, and departments within your company (e.g., office automation, engineering, industrial processing, system development, operations management) because these may influence your targeted interoperability, portability, and Client/Server areas.

Define and establish a group of teams within the organization that will be responsible for the open systems planning, analysis, and deployment processes.

Figure 2.1   Phase One: Business-oriented tasks.

Getting Started

In open Client/Server systems, as in any other field that is new, different, and requires big steps to adopt, there are people who pioneer and people who copy. The process of adopting open Client/Server systems technology into an organization usually requires a pioneer—a person with some sort of gleam in his or her eye. That person might have heard that open Client/Server systems technology is the latest trend, but is also aware that it might do something for the organization.

Open Client/Server technology pioneers generally have read some of the literature on Client/Server systems, open systems, standards, networking, interoperability, portability, and scalability. This reading is not enough to tell them how to integrate open Client/Server systems into their everyday workplace. However, it should provide them with enough background knowledge so that what they have heard about how open Client/Server systems might solve certain problems in their organization makes sense to them. Therefore, they are willing to investigate the subject further.

Open Client/Server technology pioneers are most likely to turn up first in high-technology industries where there are a large number of people who are used to reading about and dealing with new technology. They also tend to turn up in large organizations because most large organizations have technology scouts that keep an eye out for new technologies.

The open Client/Server systems vision may originate from an organization's chief executive officer (CEO). Often, however, the vision originates from technology-oriented people at the vice presidential, middle management, or information processing levels, or technology-oriented people at autonomous sites.

Regardless of who first conceptualizes the vision, the first steps in planning open distributed systems are business-oriented rather than technical. And first and foremost among these steps is to crystallize that vision by understanding where you are today and where you want to be in the short- and long-term future. The second step is getting commitment from management.

Develop a Mission Statement

It is senior management's commitment to open distributed systems, often stated in the form of a vision, that guides the development of an open Client/Server systems plan to meet the organization's information and business requirements. A vision statement is a conceptualization of an organization's goals at a very high level.

When Alcoa began its open Client/Server systems migration planning, the Alcoa management vision was the motivation and guiding force behind the Alcoa MIS open systems mission statement. Alcoa's mission statement includes:

1. Providing corporate oversight for a worldwide open information architecture that will efficiently gather customer-required data at its origin
2. Establishing communication networks to allow efficient worldwide access and transfer of information between locations.
3. Presenting information to any Alcoan, any time, any place, in any form, as required to enable them to excel in performing their work.

Both the vision and the mission statements have been guiding Alcoa's architecture groups and MIS departments, first in their planning of open systems, and subsequently, in their implementation of Client/Server systems (Figure 2.2).

Identify Business Goals

After developing a vision and mission statement, the next open distributed systems planning steps are to identify the organization business goals, and understand the organization's business models. The organization's business goals and models are important because they must drive the open distributed systems planning process. The business goals must drive the Client/Server strategy and satisfy the business goals. This increases the chances of Client/Server success, and reduces the chances of developing a state-of-the-art environment that is "new, improved, and useless."

In 1991, Paul O'Neill, President of Alcoa, stated in his information technology vision that "Each person in Alcoa should have available the data or information they require, when they require it, to enable them to excel in performing their work. This objective will require a common language and a high degree of interconnected capability across the Company to enable communication and the sharing of knowledge."

"In Alcoa's current computing environment, which comprises non-networked, non-integrated heterogeneous systems, Alcoans at all levels are prevented from excelling in the performance of their work and in bringing their processes into control because the data and information required are not identified and/or available when needed."

To achieve Alcoa's information technology vision, O'Neill led the formation of Alcoa's new information policy. This policy recognizes that frequent and timely information sharing is needed to support Alcoa's values and to achieve its milestones. It also recognizes that not all beneficial uses or users may be anticipated, and sometimes pieces of information that seem unrelated can be combined to solve problems and identify new opportunities.

Alcoa's information policy is intended to foster an environment where the amount of information that is unshareable or inaccessible will be minimized, the proactive sharing of information will be increased, and information sharing will not be hindered by organization or geographical boundaries. Alcoa believes that the realization of this vision is a key enabler toward achieving business quantum leaps and major and continuous improvement milestones.

The subsequent coalition of Alcoa's largest business information technology managers, formed to make this vision a reality, has as its mission the development of an information systems architecture, with associated standards and strategies, which facilitates the achievement of Alcoa's information vision and information policy. The coalition team's charter is to achieve Alcoa's information vision through:

• Effective and efficient communications and information transfer between natural work groups and process owners, with appropriate data security and integrity.

• Accessibility to all systems that Alcoans need to do their jobs, through an easy-to-use interface which is common throughout the company.

• A flexible computing infrastructure which supports the re-engineering of the various business and manufacturing processes.

• The ability to protect technology investments and to quickly realize business opportunities offered by new technologies.

• Self-sufficiency of end users in accessing and manipulating data.

Figure 2.2   A vision from Alcoa's senior management. *Source: Alcoa.*

The development of business models, and the mapping of these business models to a complementary information system support model, is a vast subject and not suitable for this book. In-depth information about building and interpreting business models is available in many management-technology books and is also probably available from the planner's organization. Here it is only necessary to say that business models differ between companies. They are important because they identify the business capabilities and functionalities which an organization's information technology structure needs to support. Some information-systems modeling sources are cited at the end of this book.

Various business models take into account such elements as the parts of an organization (e.g., business units, divisions, branches, departments), and the purpose and description of these entities, their size, location, number of employees, assets, the functions and activities they perform, the importance to the overall business of these organizational entities, and examples of their critical success factors. Customer needs, distribution of products or services, special value that an organization or company can provide, pricing, and competition also are taken into account by business models.

Short-Term versus Long-Term Goals

In planning goals, and the strategies for reaching these goals, it is necessary to take into account, and justify, both short- and long-term goals (Table 2.1).

The shortest-term goals are generally the easiest to justify for two reasons. First, any goals that keep the business operating today are essential. Second, the trend among executives today is to worry about short-term goals, and let their successors worry about the long-term goals. Nevertheless, businesses, market conditions, and world affairs constantly change. Therefore, organizations that do not plan for the future might not have one.

Besides goals, the technologies and information systems, as well as the obstacles to, and cost involved in, reaching the organization's goals, must be considered.

Identify High-Level Technology Goals

It will take some time and detailed planning to determine exactly how to move to open Client/Server systems. Before beginning this planning process, it is necessary to

Table 2.1 Business Goals

	Short-Term	Long-Term
Easiest Cost Justification	Business Today (Must Have)	Betting the Company's Future (3–5 years)
More Difficult to Justify	Desirable, But Not Essential, Short-Term Goals (2–3 years)	Nice to Have (3–5 years)

have an idea of where you are now, and where you want to be in five years. One way to understand your present situation, and to begin to crystallize your organization's generic vision, is to identify the current types of hardware and software systems, networks, and information-handling methods in your organization, and how you might want these systems and information-handling methods to change.

Strategic planners and information systems architects should develop a generic inventory matrix for the organization's systems and information-handling methods. This matrix should show the current types of systems and information-handling methods, the near- and long-term goals for these systems and information handling methods, and the envisioned means for accomplishing these goals.

Such a matrix not only helps planners understand the organization's current situation, it helps high-level management, strategic planners, and information system architects to crystallize a vision of future information technology within the organization. The matrix also helps communicate that vision to department and operations managers.

Table 2.2 shows a sample generic information technology vision matrix. The information shown in the table represents only one set of short- and long-term goals and methods of reaching those goals. Others means of showing methods or goals are possible. Each organization will have its own goals and plan for attaining these goals. Also, organizations can add other rows and columns to the matrix depending on their business models and information technology requirements. Rows that organizations might consider adding include rows for financial resources, network management, system administration, and hardware.

Get Commitment

Having conceptualized a vision of information technology's future in your organization, and identified generic technology goals, the next step is to get commitment from management. Management may refer to corporate management of a large company. It also may refer to managers of autonomous sites of organizations, who are responsible for that autonomous site's technology or information technology strategy.

Commitment has different meanings depending on an organization's current phase of open-systems planning or migration. In the early decision stages, commitment might involve the willingness to spend a few thousand dollars to investigate the benefits and ramifications of open systems or Client/Server systems compared to alternatives. The pilot and implementation phases involve a much greater level of commitment. For example, a successful pilot requires management to commit both the dollars and the staff to get the pilot done. Moreover, open systems usually involves Client/Server computing and vice-versa. Consequently, a successful move to open systems or to Client/Server systems requires, from the beginning, the involvement and support of different groups within the organization.

Table 2.2 A Generic Information Technology Vision Matrix

	Current Situation	Near-Term Directions	Long-Term Directions	Methods of Reaching Goals
Setting IT Objectives	Mostly independent within each department or business unit	Cooperative & interdependent within parts of the organization	Cooperative & interdependent throughout most of the enterprise, & with some external customers/suppliers	Strategic IT plan, driven by business goals & policies
IT Processes	Functionally oriented	Functionally oriented, but also interoperability-oriented for some processes	Functionality-, interoperability-, & scalability-oriented across the enterprise	Business & application re-engineering plan to take advantage of enterprisewide computing
Networks	Hierarchical	Mixed hierarchical, peer-to-peer, & PC LANs with a small number of connection between LANs, PC LANs, & centralized systems	Flattened out, horizontal networked structure throughout the enterprise with interconnected PC LANs & other local networks	Organizational analysis; Client/Server analysis; Network management plan
Information Systems	Centralized; Stand-alone; Single vendor within each department	Interfaced and front-ended with gateways & GUIs	Integrated open Client/Server & co-operative processing systems	Backplane-like architecture to link diverse systems; Standards; Client/server tools; Migration strategy; System management plan
Data & Information	Specific to a vendor's OS & DBMS; Nonstandard; Accessible only by a few people	*De facto* standards, few formal standards, some data interoperability	Shared data, accessible from heterogeneous, multivendor systems; Timely access	Integrate systems & DBMSs; Data exchange standards; Some data ported to new standard systems; Gateways & GUIs to access legacy systems
Human Resources	Act independently & individually; Strong knowledge of systems	Some individual; Some cooperation; Learning some new systems & technologies	Mostly cooperative; Users empowered	Plan for change; Training programs; Realigned jobs; Incentive & reward system

Senior Management Commitment Is a Must

There are many reasons why open Client/Server systems may not be successful without top management's commitment, even if they have the full support of management information systems (MIS) people. First, MIS executives and middle managers do not have enough authority to make everybody in an organization conform to a standards-based procurement policy. Second, a large amount of funding and human resources is required for the full-scale planning and deployment stages of open systems.

Third, a move to open systems is normally accompanied by a move to Client/Server systems throughout many departments, divisions, branches, and business units. A common infrastructure needs to be planned for these Client/Server systems in order to link these diverse departments' and divisions' applications, databases, and office, industrial, engineering, network, and other systems. This infrastructure is important since the desire for this linkage is a major reason for most organizations moving to open systems in the first place.

Because the infrastructure developed affects all the parts of an organization, an open Client/Server systems strategy requires insight and input from senior management individuals who understand and have a perspective of the business as a whole. Also, perspective and input is needed from senior management because a move to open Client/Server systems is a strategic decision that affects corporate data and information. Corporate data and information is a vital corporate resource that affects productivity, profitability, and, therefore, strategic decisions.

Despite the natural potential for political problems in environments with open Client/Server systems, it is often easier to sell such systems to corporate management than it is to middle management. The reason for this is that corporate management's business is to be visionary. In contrast, middle management's business is keeping the existing environment (including applications, platforms, networks, and system solutions) available and running smoothly. Any engineer knows that if an environment which has been running smoothly starts to develop problems, the place to look for the cause of the problems is in the last place where a change was made. Consequently, middle management can justifiably be resistant to change.

Involve Management

To a large degree, the importation and diffusion of technology throughout an organization in the face of resistance to change and unforeseen technical obstacles, depends on planning for change. For example, an important variable in the process of successful importation of an emerging technology is who commits to, sponsors, and transfers the technology. In the best case, the initial people involved in the emerging technology are known for their flexibility and rationality. If this is the case, chances are that attitudes will be better, resistance to change will be minimized, and the technology diffusion time will be compressed.

Because Client/Server systems and open systems technology are both so new, technology importation is facilitated if the senior managers responsible for the new technology value and like to nurture innovation. Even after management commits to open systems, it is important that both senior and corporate management are involved in the projects they are managing or supporting. Open Client/Server systems planning, implementation, and payback are usually not short-term prospects. It takes dedication on the part of organizations to stick with the new and unfamiliar when only potential benefits (rather than products or services) will be produced for some time. Under these circumstances, the organization's managers should have something to back up their dedication. They are also entitled to know what they are getting for their money.

To keep managers involved, informal communications between open and Client/Server systems experts and management should be developed to communicate the progress of the new technology. In addition, open Client/Server systems architects must be prepared not only to give presentations on their projects, but, wherever possible, to provide demonstrations or even hands-on experience for managers, showing the benefits the system will be able to provide, even while the project is still under development.

Don't Hype Open Systems or Client/Server Systems

Some words of caution regarding open systems are necessary here. Although Client/Server systems and open systems can provide many technological and economic benefits, they are perceived by many as a high-risk proposition. It is most important to maintain such systems in a proper perspective by not allowing the hyping of any people's expectations for Client/Server or open systems (including yours). Keeping the right perspective is important because history shows that, after a buildup of expectations, several technologies have flopped on this score. A surefire way to be disappointed in open Client/Server systems is to expect more of them than they can deliver.

What Client/Server systems can currently deliver is an easy collaborative approach to business decisions. Open systems is at the core of Client/Server computing.

What open systems can currently deliver is a common core of standards that run on almost every machine in existence today. This makes interoperability, portability, and, by extension, scalability far more possible than was ever dreamed of five or ten years ago. And the open systems community is continuing to make progress toward interoperability, portability, and scalability at a reasonable rate.

On the other hand, perfect interoperability or portability do not exist now. Nor is it likely to be achieved because technology is dynamic, and business and organization needs continuously change. Time and the International Standards Organization (ISO) bring many divergent specifications into line. As business needs and technology change, however, users will want to take advantage of new technology developments, whether or not the new technologies are standardized. Consequently, there is no easy way to guarantee total interoperability or portability.

It is important to realize, however, that these variations will probably always exist. Only rarely can a system be built exclusively on standards. What is sufficient for one department will not be sufficient for another. What is adequate one year may not be adequate the next. Users' standards requirements varies with the users themselves, their departments, applications, and changing business needs. Vendors may need to add nonstandard extensions to meet customers' functional requirements. After all, what good is the most open system in the world if it doesn't do what the customer wants?

In some cases, legacy systems with some standards added will meet a company's open system objectives without the expenditure of large amounts of money. In other cases, users may have working legacy systems that they want to continue to use, regardless of these systems' standards support. Finally, even if standards are available for an open system platform that a user would like to buy, applications may not yet be ready.

The Problem with Minimal Commitment

The problems that can occur when a company tries to move to open Client/Server systems without full commitment from senior management are illustrated by a midwestern information provider company in the business of collecting and selling timely information about consumer goods. The company decided to do a pilot open system implementation demonstrating cooperative processing between its IBM MVS machine and UNIX systems across a TCP/IP network. To do this pilot, the company put together a highly qualified team. The team consisted of in-house people and new people hired from the outside. The company also brought in a consulting firm that specialized in cooperative processing.

The project was well funded. The company and its consultants investigated *de jure* and *de facto* standards, consensus specifications, and vendor suppliers. As part of the pilot, the deployment team moved various data entry tasks and some applications out onto the network. The pilot took 90 days, and was highly successful.

The effectiveness of the open Client/Server systems was demonstrated. The company's planning and deployment teams were delighted with their work.

This story has an unfortunate ending: When the pilot was completed, the company management fired the entire team. The firings occurred because the management was not really committed to open systems. They did the pilot only because the company's board of directors had read about the advantages of open distributed systems, and wanted the company's top operations personnel to investigate and implement an open systems pilot project. But management was more comfortable with IBM mainframes, and wanted to continue to buy them. So management did only what the board told them to do—investigate open distributed systems and implement a pilot. After demonstrating the pilot, management felt they had fulfilled their obligation to the board. So they went back to running their business the way they wanted, which meant buying IBM mainframes.

Justifying Open Distributed Systems to Management

To get management commitment to open distributed systems, management needs to be convinced that the new technology will benefit the organization in several ways, particularly financially. Most organizations' management is generally composed of nontechnical people who are trying to achieve a certain business result. It is up to the organization's pioneers to create the image and vision of what open distributed systems can do for an organization in the short and long term so that management will feel that the benefits are worth the risk.

Upper management generally regards the idea of employing any new technology as they regard any other business investment. Discussions with management reveal that they are pretty matter of fact about what facets of a new technology concern them most. One question is foremost in their minds: "What is my return going to be?" The answer to this question mostly determines whether they will want to make that investment.

The Spirit Is Willing, but Long-Term Funding Is Weak

The best way to make a business case to management for open systems or Client/ Server systems is to show figures comparing the fixed and recurring costs in a distributed open system environment and a traditional centralized proprietary environment. Presumably, these figures will show management how open systems and Client/Server can either save money or increase revenues for an organization.

Some real-world examples of cost savings are discussed in Chapter 12. Unfortunately, it is too early in most users' open Client/Server systems strategies to have obtained many such figures, and many companies that have obtained such figures will not release them. If the available cost-saving figures do not apply to your organization, qualitative logical justifications, such as those discussed in the next section, are necessary instead.

Qualitative justification figures also can be difficult to obtain because a migration to open Client/Server systems is an evolutionary move. Even if every standard, products implementing these standards, and Client/Server tool that an organization requires, as well as appropriate standards-based applications, were available now, companies would not instantly trash all their existing systems in order to buy the latest, greatest open or Client/Server systems. Most organizations moving to open Client/Server systems generally have a five-plus year migration plan. And most companies who have made the migration decision are only a short way into that migration.

Even if they were further along into their migration, calculating payoff would still be a problem for two reasons. For one, an open client-systems payoff is often an intangible quantity, calculated in terms like "improved utilization of assets," "improved delivery cycles to customers," and "improved information flow through the operations staff," rather than in concrete terms such as direct labor savings. Second, the payoff from open Client/Server systems is often far off, rather than short term.

Unfortunately, it is often difficult to obtain funding for open Client/Server systems because so many companies and organizations are filled with short-order executives, looking for concrete, short-term payoff results. In some cases, the executives are looking for improved financial statements. In others, the short-term nature of management positions in many modern organizations makes managers less willing to fund long-term projects that may increase their budgetary requirements and will, in the end, only make their successors look good.

The managers who finally negotiate and approve an organization's entry into the open distributed systems arena must perceive a relative advantage for open Client/ Server systems over the organization's present way of operating. Many factors—financial, training, experience—influence whether or not open Client/Server systems is the best path for a company. Most important, however, the perceived risk associated with adopting an open systems and/or Client/Server solution, to accomplish a particular task or to integrate an enterprise, must lie within acceptable limits.

An open Client/Server systems solution may have a very high perceived advantage, but the risk perceived may also be very great because both the open systems and Client/Server fields are still relatively uncharted. Present computing systems have problems, but they are known. It can be a tough decision to sign off on trading a system with known problems for one whose problems are unknown. If this decision does not work out, its ramifications may not be career enhancing.

Selected User Business Justification Experiences

In the absence of sufficient financial figures to convince management, users must rely on their own forecasts and projections and on other users' experiences and partial case studies as success stories, even if the information is qualitative, rather than quantitative. As an aid to developing a management justification for open systems and Client/Server systems, summaries of some user experiences, partial case studies, and business justification methods are included in Figures 2.3 through 2.6. Although these partial case studies describe the experiences of users in certain market segments and types of companies, the information contained in these case studies can be extrapolated to many other fields.

As will be seen, each type of organization has its own reasons for moving to open systems or Client/Server systems. What is shown in some of the case studies and business justification stories is the realization that a short-term cost-cutting focus

The use of open systems in planning for the long term, while getting short-term payback, is illustrated by two examples, one a large automotive manufacturing company, and one a large aerospace company/system integrator. The software cost savings discussed are possible only if the organization in question has a common environment to run its applications.

The manufacturing company in the example has standardized about 40 percent of its plants around HP-UX (Hewlett Packard's real-time UNIX system). Eventually, it plans to integrate its HP-UX-based manufacturing and engineering systems with Digital Equipment Corp.'s Digital UNIX and AIX (IBM's UNIX system). The aerospace company has a mix of IBM, Digital Equipment Corporation, and Sun Microsystems systems running both proprietary and UNIX-based systems (MVS, VMS, AIX, Ultrix, OSF/1, SunOS, and Solaris.) Its plans are to ultimately move (mostly) to POSIX/UNIX-based systems and integrate all these systems across the enterprise.

Leverage via Flexible Manufacturing

Both companies' plants produced most of their products using fixed automation machinery. *Fixed automation machinery* (common since Henry Ford's days) is dedicated to the production of a specific product. It requires changes in, and/or installation of, mechanical equipment to accommodate different product models or order types.

To modernize their manufacturing plants, the companies' planners proposed the purchase of flexible manufacturing systems. Flexible manufacturing systems allow a manufacturing facility to produce a variety of different and constantly changing products just by changes in programming.

With flexible manufacturing, companies can respond rapidly to varied market needs, design changes, and product customization. Flexible manufacturing systems, however, are more costly than fixed manufacturing machinery. A company's payback policies often makes it difficult to justify the cost of a flexible manufacturing system for a single project or department.

Short-Term Planning: Why Manufacturing Users Lose

Users lose with a short-term planning approach (fixed automation) because a few years after fixed equipment is bought, the products for which the equipment is purchased may change. For example, consumer preferences may change from small to large cars. Radiator shapes may be different.

When that happens, machinery to build the new size cars or the next radiator line goes out for bid. And again, the plant purchases fixed-automation equipment because it is less expensive.

Because the company must repeatedly purchase new, dedicated equipment, in five years the company will have paid out much more than if it had paid the higher initial costs for

Figure 2.3 Long-term planning with short-term payback in the manufacturing and aerospace industries. (Continued).

flexible manufacturing systems. Worse, it may have lost a competitive edge to another company that can respond more rapidly to customers' changing requirements.

Short-Term Planning: Why Aerospace System Integrators Lose

Aerospace system integrators/contractors lose with a short-term approach because they must bid a job at the lowest cost, even though the lowest cost equipment may not be best for the integrator in the long run. For example, for a single project, it is cheaper to bid with fixed automation machinery, even though that dedicated machinery may be good only for a few years.

Investing in the Future

If different departments of a company have a common environment to share resources and equipment, the departments can buy in quantity, gain cost savings through economies of scale, and share the initial costs. To achieve a common environment, the companies in this example have begun to migrate to open systems. To these companies, open systems means standardizing about 40 percent to 50 percent of their plants around HP-UX AIX, or DEC UNIX, with plans to move to POSIX and X/Open Spec. 1170. It also means standardizing on TCP/IP networks, SQL for database access, ODA/ODIF (Office Document Architecture/Office Document Interchange Format), and SGML (Standardized General Markup Language) for data document definition and interchange.

Realizing that they would have a common standards base across their various vendors' platforms, both companies established a factory of the future fund. The purpose of this fund was to subsidize initial projects by paying all or part of the difference between the dedicated and flexible machinery. Participation in the factory-of-the-future fund activities was voluntary.

In the manufacturing company, one manufacturing division successfully used this factory-of-the-future fund to get funding for automation equipment and open systems software and training. The company did not have to purchase new dedicated machinery for a single car model. And the cost of the flexible manufacturing machinery was spread over multiple divisions participating in the factory-of-the-future fund. The accounting department reports that in two years the automated division returned the money to the fund for use by other divisions.

Similarly, one system integrator group in the aerospace company calculated the return on investment of flexible manufacturing equipment and open systems by amortizing the cost across two projects in three plants. After the two years that it took to pay back its share of the equipment, it was able to successfully quote several jobs based on flexible manufacturing systems because the company could quote jobs at a price significantly less than its competitors.

Figure 2.3 Long-term planning with short-term payback in the manufacturing and aerospace industries (Continued).

Without fanfare, and with a minimum of publicity, some of the biggest, as well as the smallest, hotel chains are moving, or have moved, to open distributed systems. To the hotels, open distributed systems means they are now using standardized multivendor networks, such as TCP/IP, and that they have moved to a UNIX-based operating system, and that they are using standardized SQL for database access. Typically, these hotels run their operations on distributed UNIX-based minicomputers and PC workstations from Hewlett Packard and NCR (formerly AT&T Global Information Systems). They are using UNIX for the hotels' front-office and back-office work, their reservations systems, and for their restaurants and catering operations.

Among the hotel chains moving to open distributed systems are the Hyatt, Sheraton, Four Seasons Hotel, LaQuinta Inn, Quality Inn, Marriott, and Holiday Inn. For these hotels, moving to open distributed systems is not a thing of the future. At the beginning of 1992, the Marriott Corporation had already moved three of its four lodging divisions (the Courtyards, Fairfield Inns, and Residence Inns) to distributed UNIX-based open systems, and had begun moving its flagship Marriott Hotels and Resorts to UNIX. Also, as far back as 1992, the Hyatts had also moved almost all of their hotels to open distributed systems.

The hotels' rationale for moving to open distributed systems was based on the ability that open distributed systems provided both to cut costs and to optimize revenues. Here is the thinking as it was presented to management.

The hotel industry today is overbuilt in that there are often more rooms than there is demand for them. Furthermore, many people are cutting back on travel. Consequently, the hotel industry must find ways to cut expenditures and optimize revenues. The high cost of software applications for proprietary platforms, and the inability of proprietary platforms to easily communicate and interoperate with heterogeneous, multi-vendor machines, have forced the hospitality industry into the open systems arena.

Thus, the hotels are automating several new areas. One new class of applications results from the trend in the last few years to cut personnel costs by automating many hotel procedures that used to be done manually. Another new class of applications, called *yield management*, uses the reservation history of a location to figure out the best rate to charge for a room and the best way to sell different rooms.

These automation applications are usually available from third-party vendors. These vendors charge much higher prices (higher by four to ten times, according to users) for applications targeted at proprietary systems. The hotels maintain that these prices are out of line with the economy of the 1990s, and are not affordable.

Figure 2.4   The hotel industry's business case for open distributed systems (Continued).

Also, in an effort to optimize revenues by maximizing the number of rooms occupied, hotels are moving away from centralization and toward regionalization. According to several of the hotel chains, regionalization has become the only way to sell the largest number of rooms for the highest possible amount of money. In order to increase the number of occupied rooms and resulting revenues, the hotels need what they call a *single-image inventory* of rooms. This capability requires a multivendor network. The hotels have had neither a multivendor network nor a single-image inventory in the past.

Instead, in the past, every hotel had a local computer that was the final word on how many rooms were available. Individual hotels could decide how many rooms they would allow the national center to sell. If the hotels mistakenly anticipated a busy weekend and as a result allocated too few rooms to national center sales, the hotel could end up with 10 percent or more unoccupied rooms that could otherwise have been sold. The way around the problem is to have only one image per inventory of rooms for an entire hotel chain, regardless of how the rooms are sold.

Maintaining a single-image inventory and maximizing room sales between the hotel and national reservations center requires a network that easily handles multivendor, heterogeneous computer networking. Having only a single picture of a hotel's inventory makes it much easier to apply yield management principles and use yield-management applications.

None of the described regionalization, yield management, and increased automation at all the hotel properties could have been done cost effectively by distributing proprietary minicomputer or mainframe platforms and data to many different type and size hotels, restaurants, and catering establishments, and creating data centers in every region across the country or world. Heterogeneous, proprietary computers tend to have a difficult time talking to each other, much less to other vendors' systems.

UNIX and TCP/IP were chosen because they were *de facto* standards. UNIX-class machines come in every size. They all communicate fairly well, regardless of the manufacturer. And all the heterogeneous platforms can run the same applications. As a result, the hotel corporation could purchase the right size platform for an individual hotel and then easily modify the software to accommodate a particular region.

Figure 2.4   The hotel industry's open distributed business case (Continued).

Oil exploration is a complex, expensive undertaking in money, time, personnel, equipment, and materials. Oil companies typically drill large numbers of oil wells in scattered locations simultaneously. An offshore rig might cost an average of one hundred thousand dollars per day to operate, with a low of fifty thousand dollars per day for land rigs and one-half million dollars per day for offshore deep water drilling. The costs are primarily the costs of the rental of the rig itself (generally, these are rented pieces of equipment), associated operating costs for the machinery, and the cost of people on the rig. These costs are incurred 24 hours a day, seven days a week.

The cost of oil exploration turns out to be an enormous figure because a major oil company may be drilling as many as one hundred wells at the same time. Arithmetic calculations show that it costs a company drilling one hundred wells simultaneously, at fifty thousand dollars a day per rig, five million dollars a day just for the rigs. Worse, it is easy to spend five million dollars on a wildcat hole, and nine out of 10 times come up empty.

Before undertaking a drilling operation oil companies use state-of-the-art geological and information technology to increase their chances of finding a likely prospect for drilling exploration. Before drilling, for example, oil companies generally gather a variety of magnetics data, and information about wave propagation in seismic media for a particular geographic area. This data is used to gain information about the subsurface rocks, the rock characteristics (e.g., hardness and permeability), and rock formations in order to predict whether or not oil exists in a certain location. In general, the programs that handle, display, and help interpret this data are highly interactive, and they demand huge amounts of high-resolution graphics and a substantial amount of computer power (e.g., supercomputers and high-performance graphical workstations).

If the seismic data indicates the potential presence of an oil reservoir, test holes are drilled. Then the drilled rock pieces, mud, and other subsurface material that comes out of the drilled hole are examined and interpreted by experts to verify the accuracy of the original predictions, and to further resolve the location of the reservoir and gain information about the volume of oil under the surface, the production capacity of the individual well, and the best way to place wells that tap the same reservoir. Typically, raw data gathered from drilled test holes are sent over a network to the supercomputers for processing. Interpretations of the processed data are sent over the network for display, in a variety of different ways, on high-resolution graphics workstations.

To increase their chances of striking oil, oil companies typically spend millions of dollars (or francs or pounds) annually on information processing. Unfortunately, despite all the software tools and computing power there is no guarantee of being right.

The high cost of being wrong has caused the oil companies to come up with a unique method of sharing certain initial exploration costs through service company intermediaries. Rather than performing all the seismic and other predrilling studies themselves, the oil

Figure 2.5 Collaboration drives open systems in oil exploration firms (Continued).

companies hire a number of service companies to do the study. These service companies perform the seismic and other tests for an area. They generate tapes containing all their collected seismic information that are given to the oil company that requested the study.

The service companies may provide the same seismic data to multiple oil companies. Each company interprets this data using its own tools, processes, knowledge, and expertise in order to determine the most likely drilling prospects. Based on its interpretations, each company might arrive at different conclusions. But the high cost of initial seismic data gathering can be shared among the oil companies, just as real estate agents share a common database of properties. The difference is that instead of looking at the surface aspects of the properties, oil companies look at what's under the surface, which is oil or a gas.

Although each oil company processes the geological data differently, the actual data of interest is basically the same. The problem is that the data obtained by service companies cannot be used by the different oil companies' tools, applications, and databases, nor can they be transferred between sites, without the use of standards. Standards are important in oil exploration because they allow interoperability, electronic conferencing, and preservation of the investment in different vendors' software tools and applications for data gathering and interpretation. They also allow data to be taken from one program and put it into another, so there is a very strong need for tight integration and commonality. And it is standards (especially standard formats and data-access methods) that make possible the sharing of seismic data generated by service companies, and eliminate the time wasted in constantly reprocessing information to fit each vendor's data model.

The use of standards-based open systems, leveraged with communications networks, is what allows certain subsurface geological information to be freely exchanged between oil companies, to everyone's benefit. It allows geographically dispersed exploration and production groups in a single oil company to combine their skills to look at offshore resources in a new geographical area, without needing expensive retraining on accessing data on another division's different tools. This kind of geological data sharing and skills collaboration often constitutes the business case for success in oil exploration and production. The idea behind the data sharing and collaborative efforts is to allow geoscientists to spend more time working with data, while decreasing the time they spend looking for it.

The need for collaboration between oil companies, and the need to cost effectively use the data from the oil exploration service companies, are among the reasons that the Petrotechnical Open Software Corporation (POSC) was formed. Among other things, POSC was chartered to standardize on a common data model across the industry and an open systems-based profile for the oil industry.

Figure 2.5 Collaboration drives oil companies' open systems (Continued).

For telecommunications companies, open distributed systems mean new business because the telecommunications companies want to enable user organizations to share data that they (the telecommunications companies) can carry for them. For example, hospitals want to share X-Ray, CAT scan, sonogram, and MRI data with consulting doctors at other hospitals. Doctors want to be able to see test results in real time.

With today's increase in the amount and kind of shared data on line, the only cost effective way to compete in carrying the data is to make sure the data to be carried conforms to standards. The only cost-effective way for telecommunications companies to pick up and deliver users' data is to have standardized interfaces at the points that data is accepted for transmission and delivered after transmission.

Telecommunications companies can provide efficient data communications services to users because the telecom companies are concerned only with the lower three levels of the OSI model, which are standardized. Unfortunately, without upper-level communications and other types of standards, telecommunications companies will not be able to create a large enough market for new data communications services to users. One reason is that transferring data between user sites is of little benefit to the users at the receiving site if they cannot use the data because it is incompatible with their applications. Therefore, the users will not buy the new data sharing services. The second reason for standards is that the only way for the telecommunications companies to sell this data sharing concept to customers is to be able to work with the users and use their equipment (e.g., LANs, T1 lines, databases, operating systems). It would not be cost effective to provide data sharing services if every customer constituted a labor-intensive special case.

The only cost effective way to work with diverse systems in transmitting and using data is to have standardized interfaces so that programmers and system managers do not have to learn a different interface for every system.

Figure 2.6 New business drives open distributed systems in telecommunications companies.

can cost a company more in the long term, and, sometimes, even in the short term, whereas a well-planned open system focus or a re-engineered Client/Server system focus may not only cost less in the short term, but may be a key to increased revenues.

Iteratively Zero in on a Client/Server Strategy

Once top-level business and technology goals have been defined, and management commitment is obtained, Client/Server planning begins. Client/Server planning should be an iterative process, to obtain the most successful results. This means that, on the one hand, the business goals drive the open Client/Server planning process. But, as the Client/Server planning progresses and implementation begins, it is also important to align certain business goals, as well as employees, with the changing environment.

Such two-way alignment is necessary because the initial Client/Server design developed is essentially an idealized design based on current business goals, market conditions, and available technologies and tools. Business goals and market conditions, however, are constantly changing. In fact, one of the original goals of open systems environments, even before the advent of Client/Server computing, was to allow companies to constantly change their business goals in order to rapidly adapt to changing market conditions and take advantage of new opportunities. Several examples of this easy adaptiveness were given earlier in this chapter.

Client/Server technology is still evolving. New tools and ways of using the technology are emerging. Some obstacles in the initial Client/Server implementations will crop up. Some will be able to be fixed. In other cases, however, the obstacles may not be surmountable, and some of the initial, idealized implementation plans will have to be modified.

It is just as likely that users will discover some new Client/Server features and benefits as they become acquainted with the technology, or new ways of using Client/Server computing will occur to them as they actually use it. Client/Server systems should be designed to be sufficiently flexible and dynamic. Over time, they should be able to incorporate new technologies, and to be integrated with new systems from other vendors. This is one reason that open systems lies at the heart of Client/Server computing.

For all these reasons, Client/Server planning should be an iterative and dynamic process. This ensures adaptiveness and the greatest usage of the Client/Server environment. In addition, all business activity, tasks, and performance metrics, as well as employee evaluations, must be aligned with the changing environment and changing business goals. This alignment increases effectiveness and acceptance (Figure 2.7).

Identify Organizational Relationships

In planning for open Client/Server systems, Client/Server and open systems planners must take into account relationships among the organizational entities, business activities, critical success factors, and information technology activities. A preliminary step in planning for enterprisewide Client/Server systems or open systems is to identify the relationships between the different parts of the enterprise, as well as the relationships between the enterprise and external customers and/or suppliers.

The relationships among an enterprise's departments and divisions are important when planning Client/Server systems because many companies are using Client/Server systems to provide new services to users both inside and outside the organization. These same relationships are important in planning open Client/Server systems because a major reason for considering open systems is to facilitate enterprisewide

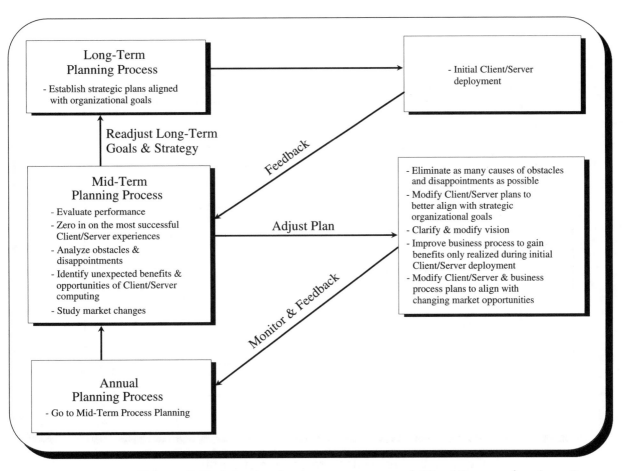

Figure 2.7 Iterative business process and Client/Server planning. *Source: Emerging Technologies Group.*

computing. The relationships between departments will, therefore, influence the targeted areas for interoperability, portability, and Client/Server systems.

For example, as Figure 2.8 shows, for a typical organization, the interface between corporate MIS and external suppliers suggests the need for either business electronic data interchange (EDI) systems and/or just in time (JIT) manufacturing systems. Multivendor interoperability will probably be required across platforms involved in EDI and JIT because industrial companies and their suppliers do not necessarily use the same computer systems. In addition, industrial-plant floor systems, which often operate in a real-time environment, must interoperate with engineering, transportation, field sales and support, and corporate MIS systems. To determine the functionality and standards needed for interoperability and portability across these

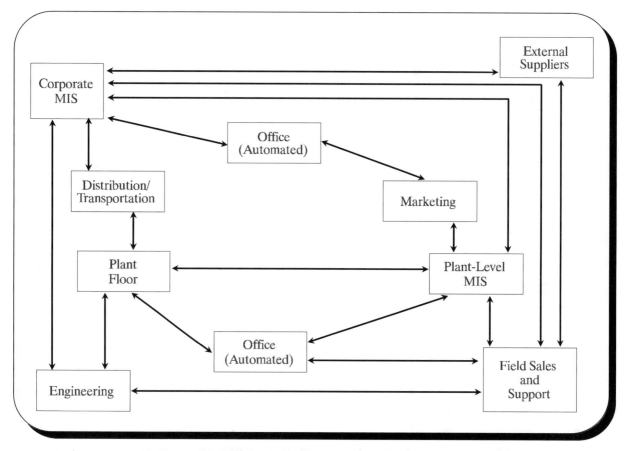

Figure 2.8 Typical departmental relationships.

departments, it is necessary to further examine the relationships between these departments' applications in greater detail. This is done in a later planning phase (discussed later in this book).

Define the Planning Teams

Before actual open Client/Server planning can occur, it is necessary to establish specific teams to do the planning. There is no one set way to establish teams. Different organizations establish different teams for different purposes.

There are some cases where one single team has attempted to take on the early planning stages (e.g., requirements definition, architecture). The best results, however, are usually seen when the planning teams have representatives from all parts of the organization.

In general, at least three types of teams (architecture/infrastructure, application oriented, and deployment) are needed to plan the importation of new technologies. More often, companies establish five types of planning teams. The following is one method (though not the only one) which is used by organizations for planning enterprisewide open distributed systems, from concept through deployment.

- One architecture team
- A series of application-expert teams
- One, two, or multiple infrastructure teams
- A series of deployment teams from different departments
- One steering or coordinating committee

The architecture team is the team that, in conjunction with business management, performs the initial analysis of the organization's business models and maps these business models into a complementary information-technology model. In later stages, the architecture team investigates and develops an enterprisewide open systems model and Client/Server architecture for the organization. Into this model and architecture, this team maps the organization's business and information technology requirements.

The application-expert teams consist of experts in specific application areas (e.g., statistical process control, office automation). These teams identify and specify their requirements. They also model their computing environment requirements in terms of where they are today and what they expect four to five years from now.

The infrastructure teams work with the architecture, deployment, and application-expert teams. In some cases, the architecture team becomes the infrastructure team. In other cases, the infrastructure team becomes a deployment team. It is the infrastructure teams, however, that come up with the actual design for an open systems environment for various parts of the organization, as well as the specific standards and specifications to implement. The infrastructure teams, in conjunction with deployment teams, decide when proprietary products are necessary. Infrastructure teams also determine the availability of desired standards, and make decisions such as exactly when to use native TCP/IP and/or OSI networks or X.400-based electronic mail, and when to use gateways.

The deployment teams handle deployment of the specified environment after the infrastructure and application expert teams have finished their work. These teams handle development, implementation, and testing of vendor products to see if they fulfill system parameters, running of pilot versions, and maintenance support.

The steering committee oversees and coordinates the work of all the teams, helps establish milestones, and communicates with senior management. The steering committee is sometimes formed from the original architecture team which performed the business analyses, leaving the development of the actual architecture to other, more technically oriented information system planners.

Architecture/Infrastructure Team Issues

In developing the enterprisewide architecture, the architecture team studies and models the external environment in terms of the underlying computing structure needed to support the local offices, departments, plants, branches, divisions, logical business units, and so on. This team defines logical and physical views of the environment and maps between them.

Different organizations use different modeling methods. If possible, a computerized tool should be used. Manual modeling methods are often too coarse grained to be used without extensive modification as planning and deployment proceeds. Unfortunately, modification during the later stages of open systems planning and deployment is expensive and may require other related modifications. Also, without computerized tools, there is often a tendency to look for shortcuts to avoid details which are too time-consuming to handle. In addition, there may be resistance to making modifications to manually prepared charts because of the effort involved.

One modeling method that has been used in distributed open system planning, modeling, and re-engineering, both by commercial companies and government agencies, is the IDEF documentation and process improvement methodology. IDEF, developed initially by the U.S. Air Force to support its Integrated Computer and Manufacturing (ICAM) program, consists of eight methods: IDEF0 through IDEF6 and IDEF1X. These various IDEF methods essentially consist of graphical notations to identify, describe, and model system activities and data. They are also used to analyze procedures to identify the logical relationships among information, including information across functional boundaries, and the problems caused by inadequate information management. The IDEF methods deal with the world of objects and simulation, as well as with relational databases.

IDEF has been used in the 1990s by both government agencies and commercial companies for planning distributed open environments and re-engineering existing information systems. IDEF0 is a graphical notation used to describe the activities of a system being modeled, the inputs, outputs, constraints, and data for each of these activities, and a set of analysis procedures for describing and understanding a system before it is implemented. IDEF0, along with two related modeling methods, IDEF 1X (used to design relational databases) and IDEF 4 (used for object-oriented data modeling), are currently being standardized by the National Institute of Standards and Technology as U.S. Government Federal Information Processing Standards (FIPS). IDEF0 has also been automated and is available in software, which makes it easier to use.

Other well-known software-engineering methodologies are used to model the enterprise and its software processes. In addition, CASE tools (computer-aided software engineering), as well as a number of Client/Server tools that help users plan and deploy two-tier and three-tier Client/Server computing environments, are available from a number of vendors. Many of these tools help define the enterprise in terms of places, things, activities, events, and rules, and help define the processing logic and data structures necessary to provide the applications that support the various elements of the enterprise.

One major difference between the Client/Server tools and IDEF0 is that the Client/Server tools include an applications generator that generates separate code for both clients and servers. Some of these Client/Server tools are specifically geared to transaction processing; others are geared to server-based data access from client-based applications.

Steering-Committee Issues

The steering committee's responsibilities cover the entire life cycle of the planning and deployment of open distributed systems technology. The guiding issues that the steering committee considers include defining the difference between where the organization is today and where it wants to be in four to five years, establishing procurement policies, investigating nontechnical issues, and developing metrics for measuring cost, productivity, and quality.

Remarks and Recommendations

It is very tempting to develop an open Client/Server plan by identifying functional Client/Server areas and selecting standards for those areas without a foundation analysis and architecture. It is also tempting to develop a Client/Server plan by buying groups of PC networks and connecting them to a UNIX database server purchased for this purpose.

Such nonanalytical planning can result in random islands of automation, rather than an integrated, distributed enterprise. Like building one's house upon the sand, uncoordinated planning will result in systems that sooner or later are likely to be in trouble and have to be rebuilt. In contrast, coordinated open-systems planning is more likely to provide an integrated enterprise, while not restricting the freedom of local developers or vendor choices. The technical foundation for this effort is the focus of the rest of this book.

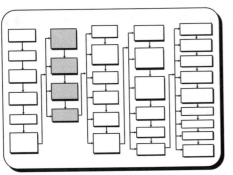

Phase Two:
Application Expert Tasks

Introduction

Phase Two is an information-gathering phase during which the open Client/Server environment is examined from the application viewpoint to determine application requirements. In this phase, the application and/or architecture/infrastructure teams interview personnel in various departments and functional areas throughout an organization. The planning teams translate the business goals into technology goals, and begin to develop a Client/Server application strategy that will form the basis for determining the open Client/Server infrastructure in future phases.

Phase Two Tasks

Phase Two of the DOSEE planning process involves surveying, and conducting interviews with, managerial and applications personnel in various departments and functional areas throughout an enterprise. The purpose of the interviews and questionnaires is to identify activities performed and applications used and planned, with the additional aim of determining the short- and long-term requirements and Client/Server architectures for these activities and applications (Figure 3.1).

The results of these interviews usually reflects the opinion of middle management. The format of the interview results can be structured in a tabular format that is easy to summarize and enter in a computer database. Some of the data-gathering interview results also are likely to be output in a free-form format, reflecting requirements details and individual manager's concerns and agendas that are not caught elsewhere.

The architecture and/or infrastructure teams analyze the findings of the interviews for trends and strategy ideas, and summarize the straightforward and structured requirements into a series of tables that will form the basis for other

1. Plan interviews and/or surveys to accomplish Phase 2 Steps 2, 3, and 4.
2. Identify the major activities that different functional areas perform to satisfy the organization's business goals (e.g., invoicing, shipping, funds management).
3. Identify the applications and/or systems that are used to perform these activities, and the services that are required by the applications.
4. Classify applications for Client/Server computing.
5. Choose a Client/Server architecture for planned applications.

Figure 3.1 Phase Two: DOSEE application identification tasks.

infrastructure determination tasks. The free-form information gathered should also be structured in some easy-to-retrieve database, such as a structured database with variable data or a text database with a comprehensive search program. The information should be linked to, or referenced by, the applicable activity and application information gathered. This free-form information will be referenced many times during the final decision making part of the Client/Server planning process.

The application data gathered will also be used in an application classification matrix to help identify the applications most suited for Client/Server computing.

The interview process itself varies with different organizations. As part of the Phase Two tasks, application, architectural, and infrastructure team planners will have to evaluate existing interview, survey, and other data-gathering processes, and decide on the interview process that they will use. The planners also will have to reconcile the free-form interview information gathered with the organization's current information systems and applications and with its planned information technology directions. Some ideas as to how this can be done are discussed in this chapter.

In the final Phase Two task, the planners will examine the various Client/Server architectures and make a preliminary determination of which Client/Server architecture might be suitable for particular applications. This choice will influence the type of interoperability, portability, and scalability needed for the planned environment, and the requirements for standards.

DOSEE methodology users should note that surveys will be used to determine information in future phases of this planning process. These future surveys are concerned with determining interoperability targets throughout an enterprise, determining portability/scalability targets, and determining familiarity with certain *de facto* and *de jure* standards. To avoid having to distribute multiple surveys and questionnaires, the interviews and questionnaires in Phase Two can be combined with surveys in the subsequent phases of the open Client/Server planning process.

A summary of the interview findings, and the initially planned information-technology directions based on a combination of these information-technology findings and on the architecture group's expertise, should be circulated to the managers interviewed and other cognizant personnel. It also is helpful if this information is presented in an open Client/Server computing workshop.

Phase Two Step 1: Plan Interviews

Although the DOSEE application expert phase can be performed solely through questionnaires, it is better if the architecture and infrastructure teams conduct face-to-face interviews—preferably before the interviewees have finished answering the questionnaires. Face-to-face interviews allow the architecture/infrastructure teams to present the rationale for the questionnaires in their own words, which are, presumably, less dry than text. At the same time, face-to-face interviews allow the planning teams to understand the agendas of the various department managers and increase the chances of agreement on the organization's information technology directions. The greater the agreement, the greater the chances of success of the open Client/Server systems.

A series of questions should be developed by the interviewers before the interviews. Many of these questions also may be included in the questionnaires.

The first interview question asks for the interviewee's name, position, and responsibilities. Other face-to-face questions include the interviewees' current and long-term priorities, what the interviewees consider to be the critical elements for success in their jobs, and their wish lists of technology improvements that can enhance their departments' performance and productivity.

Questions about existing systems, the current environment, the adequacy of this environment and systems in satisfying application requirements, and the skills of existing employees also are important because the existing environment helps shape requirements for new systems. New open Client/Server systems often must be integrated with existing systems, either in the short term or long term. If such integration is planned, then the interfaces to existing systems must be known. Also the data environment, data recoverability time and characteristics requirements, programming languages, data retrieval and manipulation languages (e.g., SQL, and which vendor's SQL is currently being used), and the skills level of existing information technology employees are important subjects for inquiry. All this information about existing systems and the requirements they satisfy will influence the requirements for the new open Client/Server systems being planned.

Figure 3.2 highlights some of the important interview and questionnaire areas.

Three points concerning this interview process and questionnaire are important. First, and most important, users of the DOSEE methodology should note that not all requirements need be determined by this questionnaire. Many application requirements will be specifically output from future stages of this methodology that deal with application attributes and application attribute values.

- Interviewee's name, position, responsibility
- Current and long-term priorities, the critical elements for success in the interviewees' jobs and/or departments, and their wish lists of technology improvements that can enhance their departments' work performance and productivity.
- Current infrastructure (including computers, networks, operating systems, database management systems, tools, programming languages, applications, and their manufacturers)
- Number of existing systems and applications
- Age of systems and of system designs
- How well current applications meet their functional and performance requirements
- Current and desired cross-platform support
- Stability of applications
- Consequences of lost functionality
- State and currency of the documentation
- Who supports and maintains the current systems
- Average length of time to respond to requests for new or modified capabilities
- Number of people-hours required to support and maintain present systems
- Skills level existing in the department
- Familiarity with Client/Server computing and open systems
- Familiarity with related emerging technologies such as object-oriented systems and multimedia
- Current usage of, or requirement for, TCP/IP and the Domain Naming Service (DNS)
- Current database management system(s), access and data manipulation languages, data dictionary, and transaction monitor
- Current data update environment, in terms of interactive updates, on-line transaction processing updates, batch processing updates
- Data currency and recoverability requirements (e.g., data must be recovered and guaranteed current as of 15 minutes before a machine failed, or data can be recovered and current as of one week ago)
- International requirements of applications
- Special requirements (e.g., supercomputing, multimedia, real time, parallel processing)
- Whether software will be purchased or developed in-house
- Cost to maintain particular applications
- Cost to re-engineer particular applications
- The need to run applications on differently sized machines (scalability)
- Desired types of platforms to run applications

Figure 3.2 Sample interview and questionnaire inquiry areas. *Source: Emerging Technologies Group.*

The second point concerns the strengths of face-to-face interviews and question-naires. The chief strength of questionnaires is the permanent record that it provides for future reference. On the other hand, face-to-face interview techniques surpass questionnaires in the ability to ask why, and to discuss the answers. Some inter-viewees, for example, may not need interoperability. These interviewees' applica-tions may not lend themselves to Client/Server computing. They may, therefore, not want to pay their share of the overhead burden imposed by an open Client/Server infrastructure or want to change from their present systems, which work well and which they know.

Interviewees also may have valid reservations about the ability of open systems to do the job. Their objections, however, may be due to a difference in their and the architecture team's definition of open systems. Interviewees, for example, may interpret open systems as meaning DOS or Windows running on all their computers, but they may believe, possibly mistakenly, that the open Client/System planners interpret open systems to mean only formal international standards.

Such miscommunications are generally best resolved by face-to-face communi-cations. Busy managers may not have time to write long, understandable opinions in a questionnaire. If they do, busy planners are just as likely not to have the time to respond with a lengthy justification, assuming they were able to zero in on the department manager's real objections, priorities, and agenda. Consequently, without face-to-face communications, many department managers may form biases that can delay (and possibly undermine) the Client/Server plan or reduce its effectiveness. It is necessary, as much as is possible, to preempt such biases before they happen.

In addition, a deeper understanding of the various managers' viewpoints and reasons (discovered through interviews) may steer the developing open Client/ Server plans in some different directions.

Of course, there are some points on which some department managers and the Client/Server planners just cannot agree. In these cases, the face-to-face interviews help the planning team members to anticipate underlying issues and objections, and how best to deal with them.

The third interview/questionnaire point concerns the questions about existing systems. Questions about current systems do not mean taking an information tech-nology equipment inventory. Taking such inventory is time-consuming and often inaccurate. Computers may be in the office, at home, or on the road. PC appli-cations may be temporarily removed to make room for a new, fatter PC applica-tion. People don't always know what software they have (they just use it), and may not know where all a department's hardware is at a given time. Worse, start-ing the open distributed planning process by taking inventory may send out the wrong messages to department and operations managers about life in a Client/ Server environment.

As opposed to the exacting inventory process, the questionnaire goal should be to collect sufficient data to characterize the environment. This will allow the architecture and infrastructure teams to understand how the existing environment will affect the planned open Client/Server environment.

Phase Two Step 2: Identify Functional Areas and Activities

Step 2 of Phase Two identifies the major activities in different functional areas that satisfy an organization's goals. A functional area is a major center of activity such as business planning, product planning, engineering, production planning, production, materials, marketing, sales, distribution, accounting, personnel, research, and so on. Functional areas were identified in Phase One of this planning process, as part of the identification of organizational and departmental relationships.

The activities information for these functional areas will be used to pinpoint present and future applications, platforms, networks, systems, and other functional components for which interoperability, portability/scalability, and Client/Server systems are needed. The activities information also will be used to determine the services that should be standardized in order to achieve the interoperability and portability/scalability needed in a Client/Server environment.

Information about activities in different functional areas is usually obtained, at least partly, from interviews with managers because this information is not well represented by formal business models. Interviews also help establish that no activities have been omitted. Table 3.1 lists typical functional areas and activities within a combination of four manufacturing and industrial companies.

Some organizations skip this identify-activities step. They begin their information gathering with Step 3, during which they question people in different departments in order to identify the applications or systems used in each functional area.

The problem with skipping the activity-identification step is the possibility of ending up with a Client/Server plan that accommodates interoperability and portability of current applications, but that will not port well into the future. I recommend starting at a higher level by first identifying the activities performed within each functional area identified in Phase One, which allows the open Client/Server systems plan to be driven by fundamental requirements for an organization's activities now and in the future, rather than by currently working applications which may change.

Another advantage to beginning open Client/Server systems planning by identifying the organization's activities is this approach's potential ability to involve higher-level management people from different departments, divisions, and business units. This stands in contrast to talking only to operations-oriented people who mostly identify current working applications and their technical requirements. Much of the input about a department's activities should come from interviews with senior managers.

The interviews to determine departmental activities should consider not only the organization's current activities, but how these activities might, or ought to, change in the future. Interviewers also should try to extract information about the various underlying agendas of the different managers interviewed, especially where this information could later polarize the company into factions for and against either open systems or Client/Server systems.

Table 3.1 Typical Functional Areas and Activities

Functional Areas	Activities		
Accounting	Accounts payable Accounts receivable Profit and loss analysis	Budget planning Cost accounting	Cash flow Payroll
Business Planning	Market analysis	Sales forecasting	Product range review
Finance	Financial planning Capital acquisition	Funds management	Capital cost control
Product Planning	Production design Product/component modeling System developer support Documentation production	Product specification Prototyping Maintenance	Product costing Product pricing Programming
Engineering	Computer-aided manufacturing Technical illustrating & publishing Environment management	Product information management	Computer-aided design Automated testing
Production Planning	Capacity planning	Plant scheduling	Workflow layout
Materials	Materials requirements Quality control	Purchasing Receiving	Inventory control
Production	Manufacturing planning Production control Job safety	Materials control Process support Utilities management	Machine operations Quality control
Office Automation	Electronic mail Electronic Data Interchange (EDI)	Corporate directory Decision support	Project management General support
Sales	Selling Customer relations	Sales administration	Territory management
Distribution	Finished stock control Order serving	Packing	Shipping
Personnel	Personnel planning Industrial relations	Employment Compensation policy	Employment Insurance
System Operations	Error management Device operation maintenance Communications & networking Software/hardware deployment Capacity planning/certification	Account billing Performance management Security administration User account management Facilities planning	Backup/Archive/Restore Configuration tracking Disaster recovery Job management

If the distributed open-systems planning interviewers are willing to submerge their own agendas and play a diplomatic role (not always an easy task when facing opinionated managers), then these interviews present an opportunity for the planners to discuss management's beliefs with them, as well as ways to accommodate these beliefs, although this is not always possible. Properly conducted interviews with managers can lead to extra support for the open Client/Server plan. These interviews also give planners the chance to minimize the number of enemies of the open Client/Server plan.

It is important to realize that anything that can be done to minimize the number of enemies of an open-systems based Client/Server plan should be considered of primary importance. It is always possible to find supporters of an emerging technology, but it is just as important, if not more so, not to make enemies. Therefore, any steps that might establish a rapport with potential opponents of a project are recommended.

Relationships Between Activities and Applications

The interconnections and relationships between applications, application processes, and systems within departments, and across departments, influence the targeted areas for portability and interoperability. In Phase Two Step 3, the application experts planning team maps these interconnections and relationships.

There are several ways to map the interconnections and relationships between applications and systems. The most commonly used method is a simple diagram showing applications, with arrows used to show connections and/or relationships between the applications (Figure 3.3).

The problem with this kind of diagram is that it is impractical for any but a small percentage of an organization's applications because of the number of relationships involved. The typical medium-to-large organization has about 30–35 diverse functional areas (e.g., accounting, business planning, product planning, engineering, production planning, production, materials, marketing, sales, distribution, information systems, personnel, research, and so on). Each functional area has about 10–30 or more types of applications that are specific to its business function, and perhaps another 10–20 that are common to multiple (but not necessarily all) functional areas.

Even if the number of combinations of these applications' connections could be diagrammed, the size and complexity of such a diagram would make it a maddening mess to visualize and understand. Moreover, such a diagram does not make it clear whether it is showing relationships between generic activities or specific applications.

Instead of drawing multiple complex diagrams, in Phase Two Step 3 the Client/Server planner should build a matrix to show the activities within each functional area (identified in Phase Two Step 2) (e.g., sales, product planning, personnel, engineering). These activities are mapped against the applications used to perform the activities (Figure 3.4). In future steps of this methodology, other matrices will use the

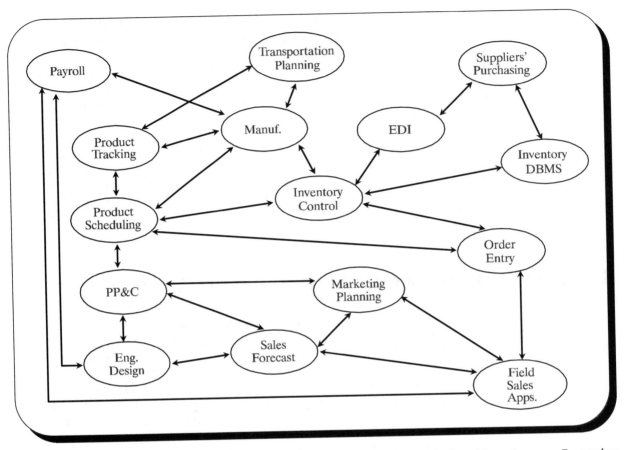

Figure 3.3 Typical application and activity relationships. *Source: Emerging Technologies Group.*

For each functional area (e.g., department, branch) (identified in Phase One and used in Phase Four Step 2) within an organization, generate a matrix showing the activities on the vertical axis and the functional components (or applications or systems) on the horizontal axis.

Check off the functional components that each activity uses.

Figure 3.4   Phase Two Step 3: Map activities versus applications.

information in the applications-versus-activities matrix to show explicit relationships between applications.

In generating the activities-versus-applications matrix, only active words, particularly verbs (rather than labels) should be used to describe activities. Separate matrices should be generated for each functional area because these matrices will be used later to define the areas where interoperability is needed between functional areas. Table 3.2 shows a typical applications matrix generated for the consulting department of a small, highly automated consulting company that has four functional areas: administration/accounting, sales, consulting/analysis, and computer-system operations.

The DOSEE planning teams should attempt to identify all of the activities and applications in their organization. They should not eliminate duplications from the list of activities and applications at this point because the duplicate activities may use different applications implemented in a incompatible way on various platforms.

Table 3.2 Activities Versus Functional Applications. *Source: Emerging Technologies Group.*

CONSULTING DEPT. ACTIVITIES & APPLICATIONS (Subset)

Activities / Functional Components / Applications	Word Processing	Electronic Mail	Database Mgmt.	User Data Query	Document Mgmt.	Spreadsheet	Presentation Graphics	Plain Paper Printing	Calendaring	Fax
Research/Gather Info.	✔	✔	—	—	✔	—	—	✔	✔	✔
Develop Reports	✔	✔	—	—	✔	✔	✔	✔	—	✔
Write Articles	✔	—	—	—	✔	—	✔	✔	—	✔
Produce Reports	✔	—	—	—	—	✔	✔	✔	—	—
Visit Clients	—	✔	✔	✔	—	—	—	✔	✔	✔
Manage Stds. Activities	✔	✔	—	—	—	—	✔	✔	✔	✔
Present Seminars	✔	✔	—	—	✔	✔	✔	✔	✔	✔
Interact With Analysts	✔	✔	✔	✔	—	✔	—	✔	✔	✔
Develop Contacts	—	✔	✔	✔	✔	—	—	✔	✔	—
Maintain Library	✔	—	✔	✔	✔	—	—	✔	—	—
Distribute Reports	✔	✔	✔	✔	—	—	—	—	—	✔

Key: ✔ = *Uses or Requires*   — = *Does not Use or Require*

Activities and applications should not be artificially combined to reduce their number because doing so will provide an inaccurate picture of the organization and its computerized applications. Separate matrices should be generated to show existing activities versus applications and activities versus applications planned for the future.

It is strongly suggested that the distributed open-systems planning process be computerized so that the distributed open-systems plan can be computer maintainable. Computer maintainability of the open-systems plan is necessary because of the many applications and services that need to be coordinated and harmonized in an organization. The distributed open-systems planning process typically involves manipulation of various applications and services during different stages of the planning process. Companies may have many activities, which use hundreds of applications. The applications may require hundreds of services. Hundreds of these services may need to interact with each other in various ways. It is difficult, if not impossible, to keep track of all these applications, services, and interactions without a computer-maintenance scheme. For this reason, several companies are using computer-aided software engineering (CASE) tools and a variety of types of databases for their planning.

Maintaining an Open Client/Server Planning Database

The information extracted from the activities and applications matrix should be stored in a database created for this purpose. The database should list the activity and the application, and any other pertinent data gleaned from the interviews and questionnaires. Interoperability and portability requirements, importance rankings for applications, prioritization of interoperability and portability targets, standards data, prioritization of standards, and surveyed Client/Server requirements will gradually be added to this database throughout the planning process.

A relational database, electronic spreadsheet, or a groupware product can be used to store the information. To facilitate the survey process and make it as easy as possible for the organization's survey participants to input their information and for the system planners to analyze the surveyed data and make good, timely decisions, it helps if the data is stored in a groupware database-type product.

Client/Server Application Domains

Three of the most critical success factors in Client/Server computing are the Client/Server applications'

- Selection,
- Usage, and
- Distribution.

The selection of appropriate applications for Client/Server computing affects their cost, tool availability, ease of use, ease of development, and manageability. The usage of Client/Server applications affects the way they are built and distributed. The way in which Client/Server applications are distributed affects their ease of development, efficiency, performance, sophistication, and manageability. Finally, the types of Client/Server applications selected, and the way in which they are distributed, affects the determination of the enterprisewide infrastructure (including hardware, software, and networks), subnetworks within the enterprise, and standards selected for Client/Server system implementation.

Table 3.3 shows a matrix that can be used to classify most types of applications. This matrix classifies applications as monolithic or Client/Server. Each of these application categories can further be classified as interactive and batch.

Some applications in Table 3.3's Client/Server column are Client/Server versions of existing monolithic types of applications. An example is front-end graphical user interfaces that provide easier access to nonrelational data and traditional applications. Other types of applications are newly developed, designed to take advantage of Client/Server computing. In most cases, organizations achieve their greatest

Table 3.3 Eminent Domains

	Monolithic	Client/Server
Interactive	• Nonrelational transaction processing • Some relational transaction processing • System administration of homogeneous, centralized, monolithic systems • Standalone autonomous processing	• Information/resource sharing • Interactive workflow & simple decision support • Relational operational data access • Nonrelational operational data access • Software development • Relational transaction processing • Electronic forums • Sophisticated decision support • Autonomous processing that affects other people in the enterprise • Monitoring • Distributed system management
Batch	• Relational & nonrelational data access • Bulk data transfer • Bulk file transfer	• Store-and-forward electronic mail/messaging • Noninteractive workflow • Networked backup • Distribution of services (e.g., news feeds) • Relational data access by applications

Source: Emerging Technologies Group.

leverage from the applications listed in the Client/Server column, that have been re-engineered to take advantage of Client/Server capabilities.

Many of the monolithic batch applications are candidates for open systems. Examples are bulk file transfer, bulk data transfer, and applications that run at scheduled times and use database data. Such batch applications need open systems, because to transfer or access files and data interoperability between computer applications is needed, and the files and data must be portable between computers.

In order to properly plan a Client/Server environment and an associated open system environment, it is necessary to understand a bit about the different kinds of Client/Server applications and architectures. Certain Client/Server applications are suited to particular Client/Server architectures, which in turn affect the kinds of interoperability that needs to be planned, and the functionality and standards selected.

Some Client/Server facts about the applications in Table 3.3 are described in the following sections. Because managers in different departments have strong opinions about many of these applications, it is a good idea to use some of this Client/ Server application information in the application requirements interview discussions (described earlier in this chapter), if not in the questionnaires themselves.

Information- and Resource-Sharing Applications

Information and resource sharing became common with the advent of PC networks. Often labeled *workgroup* computing, it represents such applications as file sharing and printer sharing. These applications are, perhaps, the simplest kinds of Client/ Server applications. Convenient though they are, they do not take full advantage of Client/Server capabilities.

Workflow Applications

Workflow applications—interactive and noninteractive—are a relatively new phenomena, developed for Client/Server computing. They grew out of the PC world, and extended the original workgroup-based information and resource-sharing applications. Workflow applications most often involve sharing and transferring of documents, spreadsheet data, and relational database data.

Workflow applications are becoming popular because they are easy to understand and develop. They also are inexpensive, since most workflow applications run on PCs, attached to PC networks. In large organizations, the PC networks are often connected to backbone enterprisewide TCP/IP networks. In addition, the PC networks and workflow applications are attached to remote users via wide-area networks or modems. In this way, Client/Server capabilities can serve remote users.

Electronic Mail

Electronic mail is one of the first applications chosen for implementation in Client/ Server and/or open system environments. Typically, electronic mail runs either on PC servers or on UNIX servers with PC clients.

Relational versus Nonrelational Data Access

Relational data access is one of the most widely implemented Client/Server applications. The relational database usually runs on a UNIX-based machine because UNIX supports several excellent databases, and most UNIX machines communicate easily. Relational data access is often tied to workflow applications.

Nonrelational database access is much more difficult. Nevertheless, many organizations are getting started in Client/Server computing by building front-end graphical user interfaces (GUIs) to their nonrelational legacy mainframe and minicomputer databases. This front-end GUI, which generally resides on a PC, allows users to more easily access data in the mainframe database, and it helps preserve the organization's investment in legacy mainframes and databases.

While this Client/Server solution provides some benefits, Client/Server planners should be aware that this solution also imposes high overhead, maintenance, software development, and upgrade burdens on the mainframe.

The problem with nonrelational data access in Client/Server environments is twofold. First, as mentioned, data access is difficult with nonrelational databases, and *ad hoc* data access (a major capability in Client/Server environments) is more difficult. Nonrelational data access requires the intervention of MIS data-processing programmers to write a program (e.g., about 350 Cobol lines) to perform even a simple retrieval or update operation.

The second Client/Server problem with nonrelational databases is difficulty of retrieval. Nonrelational database queries are lengthy procedural programs that require the ability to navigate the database to get a record, process it, get the next record, and so on. The need for such a series of procedures that operates on one data record at a time, and then starts the next one, makes remote data access difficult and impractical.

In contrast, relational databases have the ability to dynamically establish relationships between data. This makes it easy for nonprogrammers to issue *ad hoc* queries without having to write (or ask MIS programmers to write) a program. Furthermore, relational DBMSs use a query language that allows users to express a large volume of data very concisely. This facilitates the retrieval of data across a network.

Figure 3.5 shows some of the architectural differences between monolithic nonrelational, monolithic relational, and Client/Server relational systems. Because of the difference in difficulty between nonrelational and relational data access, particularly where remote database access is concerned, the type of DBMS used affects the Client/Server networking, application practicality, system management, and cost. Consequently, during the rest of the Client/Server planning process, the type of

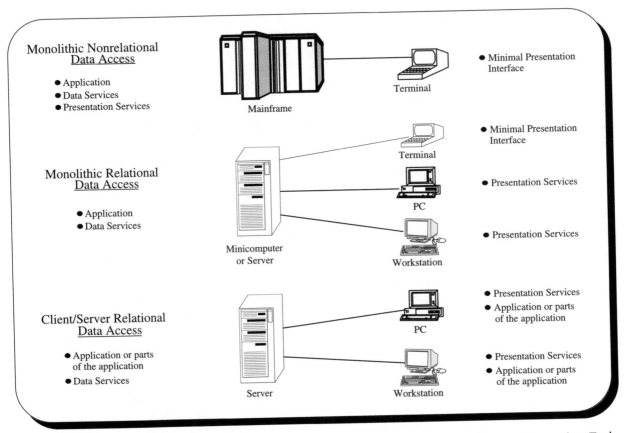

Figure 3.5   Relational and nonrelational data access. Source: Emerging Technologies Group.

DBMS must be considered in planning the infrastructure, selecting standards, planning how to manage the systems, and deciding how to distribute the applications.

Operational Processing versus Decision Support

Operational processing and decision support are two types of Client/Server applications, both of which lend themselves to Client/Server computing. The difference in the usage of operational processing and decision support applications affects not only Client/Server application development, but also the overhead, cost, infrastructure, and standards chosen for a Client/Server environment. Unfortunately, the difference between operational processing and decision support application usage is often poorly understood.

Operational processing affects day-to-day revenues and/or running of the organization. It includes applications like *ad hoc* data query, data updates, on-line transaction processing, and system management. Typical operational processing users are clerical workers who are trained to use a particular application, for example, bank tellers and insurance-claims processors.

Operational-processing applications typically operate on data whose accuracy is current at the moment of usage. Data integrity, reliability, and consistency are generally critical requirements for operational applications. If a system node fails, it must be restored as soon as possible to its state just before the system failure. Recovery difficulties in a networked environment and complexity are two of the reasons that many important operational applications (e.g., OLTP) have not become so widespread as Client/Server applications such as workflow and electronic mail.

Often, the task and process requirements for operational processing are well known and run repetitively. This repetition gives developers a chance to optimize applications for performance and throughput. Such applications also are often designed with a small number of processes in order to further conserve system resources.

Decision-support applications are applications that support decision makers such as upper and middle management, and high-level professionals like investment-banking traders. Decision-support applications include electronic spreadsheets, document and data access, high-powered modeling, simulation and analytics programs, and expert systems.

Decision support applications try to provide the most up-to-date data possible. Decision-support applications, however, operate on archival data. For example, investment traders use the latest updated data in their decision-support programs. This data is archival, however, compared to the data traders use at the moment they execute a trade. Investment traders cannot count on making money by purchasing stocks or bonds at an old price, even if it is just minutes old.

Since decision-support data is archival, it cannot be updated. Consequently, currency of archival data is not an issue.

Decision-support applications do not tend to be as business critical as are operational processing applications. Decision-support applications also do not require the level of synchronization between processors to ensure data reliability in the case of network or processor failure.

Decision-support requirements are not repetitive. In fact, from day to day, the frequency and type of decision support requested by users can be completely unknown. In general, decision support queries tend to be somewhat undisciplined and can be extraordinarily complex. A single user can often tie up a whole machine.

Because of the less critical requirements for decision support applications, simple decision-support applications such as the sharing of PC spreadsheets and other PC productivity tools, are Client/Server application leaders. Client/Server-based sophisticated decision support applications have been slow to emerge, partly because of the large amount of resources needed in a networked environment.

What Client/Server planners should note about the differences between operational and decision-support applications, besides the application development, infrastructure, and standards requirements, are the problems that can occur if these two types of processing are mixed. Because of the differences in requirements, mixing operational processing and decision-support applications can lead to significantly greater overhead and cost.

On-line transaction processing applications, for example, require high-overhead networking protocols that ensure data integrity. Decision-support applications have less critical requirements and do well with less expensive networking protection such as TCP/IP's sequenced datagram or byte-stream protocols. Although not perfectly reliable, these protocols are adequate for decision-support applications.

Organizations which mix OLTP and decision-support applications must be prepared to pay the high OLTP overhead for both OLTP and decision-support systems. In the past, some companies (particularly banking institutions) elected to pay the extra overhead for decision-support applications because running both the OLTP and decision-support systems with the same networking protocols ensured protocol software transparency for the traders, provided protocol software portability, and simplified the in-house development of software that accesses remote servers and applications.

Banks no longer want to pay this extra overhead. As they move to Client/Server computing, banks want an approach that allows the associated networking of OLTP and decision-support systems to remain distinct. One solution that some banks have chosen is object-oriented tools, which allow the banks to encapsulate OLTP applications with the high-overhead OLTP synchronization protocols that ensure data integrity. They use the object-oriented tools to encapsulate decision-support system with lower overhead, but less reliable but adequate networking protocols. As a result of this encapsulation, the different types of networking are transparent to the traders, while the overall networking overhead expense is reduced. The Client/Server planners, however, must design their environments with different types of interoperability in mind.

Architecting a Client/Server Environment

The Client/Server architecture used to structure an organization's Client/Server applications affects the kinds of networking and data interchange needed, as well as the system software, information systems infrastructure, and standards selected. There are a few major Client/Server architectures, each of which is suited to different types of Client/Server applications. To properly plan a Client/Server environment, and an associated open system environment, it is necessary to understand what these Client/Server architectures are.

The following sections briefly explain, at a high level, the different Client/Server architectures. Readers who already understand the differences between two-tier and three-tier Client/Server architectures can skip to the end of the chapter where guidelines for choosing different Client/Server architectures are presented.

Client/Server Application Components

All Client/Server applications depend on dividing an application into three basic components:

- Presentation logic (the human-computer interface)
- Application logic (encodes an organization's business logic)
- Data logic (stores, manages, retrieves, and updates data)

The component parts are distributed in different ways across different parts of the Client/Server system that cooperate to get the client's job done.

Such Client/Server partitioning and cooperation represent a major change in application architectural design compared to monolithic applications. For monolithic applications, the application logic, data, and presentation logic (user interface) are all combined into a single monolithic program that runs on a centralized computer.

There are several Client/Server architectures that represent how Client/Server applications can be distributed. It is important for Client/Server planners to identify the best Client/Server architecture for their applications because the application structure, design, and code, as well as the system services, protocols, and standards, are different for each. Once an application is written for one type of Client/Server architecture, it cannot easily be moved to a different environment.

The most important Client/Server application architecture and design issues include:

- Whether the data, application, or parts of the application are local or remote.
- How to distribute an application across client and server nodes.
- The kind of performance an application requires.
- Whether the application runs, or data is used, at heterogeneous nodes.

If the application runs or data is used at heterogeneous nodes, then open systems and standards become vitally important.

Whether the data, application, or parts of the application, are distributed on local or remote machines, the application users should not see the different machines. Instead, users should be able to view an integrated, coherent environment. Different machines and operating environments that are part of the Client/Server environment should be transparent to applications and to the users. Such transparency requires distributed computing services, such as directory services, common-naming services, and a new type of Client/Server service known as *middleware*. Middleware is a large group of services encompassing communications and remote database access in a distributed Client/Server environment.

Open-systems planning and practical standards selection for distributed Client/Server environments are covered in later chapters, as are the different types of middleware. Further strategic open Client/Server planning, however, is not possible without first having a knowledge of the different types of Client/Server environments. The next sections of this chapter, therefore, discuss different types of Client/Server environments, and the reasons for choosing a particular Client/Server architecture. These Client/Server architectural approaches constitute the fundamentals of Client/Server technology.

Client/Server Architectural Approaches

There are three major Client/Server architectural approaches, in addition to variants of all three architectures. The three major Client/Server architectural approaches are:

- **Two-Tier Client/Server Computing.** Distribute the basic application components across a server and interconnected clients.

- **Three-Tier Client/Server Computing.** Distribute the application components across two or more tiers of hierarchically arranged servers and a tier of interconnected clients.

- **Cooperative Processing.** Distribute the application logic for different applications across both servers and desktop computers so that parts of an application can be performed on the type of computer best suited to the particular types of processing required.

These three Client/Server approaches, contrasted with the traditional monolithic computing approach, are shown in Figure 3.6.

There is no single Client/Server architecture that is best for an organization. Which architecture is chosen depends on the Client/Server application being built.

The Current Legacy Situation: One-Tier

Most legacy applications are essentially one-tier and monolithic. This means that the application logic, data, and presentation logic (user interface) are all combined into a single monolithic program that runs on a centralized computer.

One-tier environments are simple environments in that they consist of one computer with attached terminals. The terminals are just I/O devices. Even interconnected PCs access the mainframe through terminal emulation and are just other I/O devices.

The problem with one-tier monolithic applications is the lack of modularity. To modify only one part of the application (such as the data logic, application logic, or user interface) it is necessary to upgrade the entire application. A change to any of these application components may ripple through the entire application, thus causing errors to creep into the application. This ripple effect results in a long debugging time for even a small application modification.

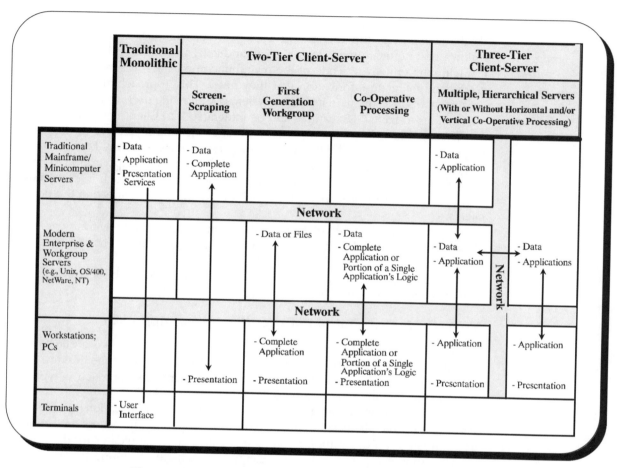

	Traditional Monolithic	Two-Tier Client-Server			Three-Tier Client-Server	
		Screen-Scraping	First Generation Workgroup	Co-Operative Processing	Multiple, Hierarchical Servers (With or Without Horizontal and/or Vertical Co-Operative Processing)	
Traditional Mainframe/ Minicomputer Servers	- Data - Application - Presentation Services	- Data - Complete Application			- Data - Application	
			Network			
Modern Enterprise & Workgroup Servers (e.g., Unix, OS/400, NetWare, NT)			- Data or Files	- Data - Complete Application or Portion of a Single Application's Logic	- Data - Application	- Data - Applications
			Network			
Workstations; PCs		- Presentation	- Complete Application - Presentation	- Complete Application or Portion of a Single Application's Logic - Presentation	- Application - Presentation	- Application - Presentation
Terminals	- User Interface					

Figure 3.6 Client/Server architectural approaches. *Source: Emerging Technologies Group.*

Simple Two-Tier Client/Server: A Front-End GUI

In the simplest Client/Server case, the presentation logic for an application is separated from the application and the data. The presentation logic is moved onto the desktop client (PC or workstation). The application and the data reside on the host server.

This GUI front-end kind of two-tier Client/Server approach, sometimes called *screen scraping*, is the easiest way for an organization to introduce itself to Client/Server computing. Some organizations implement this kind of two-tier architecture for their mainframe applications. They leverage the functionality of existing mainframe applications by developing a graphical, desktop-based interface using tools designed for this purpose.

The result is an interface that integrates existing mainframe applications and databases with desktop clients. The GUI provides friendlier access to the organization's host software than does a command-level interface, and does so without changing the underlying code of the mainframe application. Users can more easily access and integrate information that they need. This approach also preserves the organization's investment in its legacy systems by allowing users to recast mainframe applications to have GUI features and be integrated into Client/Server systems.

This approach is commonly used with large mainframe databases that service large numbers of users. The two-tier Client/Server approach allows better scaling of the parts of the application than does the one-tier monolithic application approach because of the former's modularity. For example, should the back end need more processing power or disk space, these can be added without affecting the desktop clients.

The two-tier Client/Server approach supports a networked environment, which allows data access and workflow to proceed across geographically dispersed locations.

The disadvantage of this Client/Server approach is that its ability to take advantage of other Client/Server benefits is limited.

More Highly Distributed Two-Tier Workgroup Approach

A more highly distributed, although still simple, two-tier approach is a Client/Server system built so that the application and presentation logic run on the desktop client, while the files or data reside on the back-end server. This approach is typical of many first-generation workgroup applications.

The problem with this approach is that almost all application processing is performed on the client PCs. Only certain functions (e.g., file access and printing) are distributed, yet other application parts are also good candidates for distribution.

This approach can also be inefficient. For example, if, during the application processing the application requests data from a server, the server processes and makes the entire file available to the application on the desktop machine. Yet a file server's computing resources are geared to compute-intensive operations, such as picking individual records.

The desktop computer's resources, on the other hand, are geared to running graphical interfaces. A significant portion of its resources must be used to run an application that reads every record of the file and selects the requested ones. In addition, if the server sends back a lot of files, it may overburden the communications lines.

Many organizations are beginning to solve this problem with a second generation Client/Server approach known as cooperative processing.

Cooperative Processing

In the most highly functional Client/Server processing, the application logic and/or data logic is split vertically between the client and the server, and/or horizontally between multiple servers. The partitioned application is then distributed across clients and servers so that each application part runs either on the most functional machine or the most local machine. All the partitioned application code running on these different platforms cooperate to accomplish the application's goals.

In such a Client/Server environment, if an application requests data from a server, the server processes the requested files or database locally and sends back only the desired records to the desktop application. This approach is commonly used for PC client applications that need particular data from a database. In such cases, the application developers embed SQL database operations requests, such as SELECT and UPDATE in the PC application. When the database server receives the PC's SQL request for data, it navigates the database, and finds and sends the requested data to the client. Besides being efficient, this cooperative approach reduces the network traffic so that more users can be attached to the server.

With cooperative processing, computing is not only distributed vertically but also horizontally. This means that portions of an application can run on different computers within a single tier, and data can also be located on one or more computers at one or more sites. Depending on the technical characteristics of the parts of an application and the different types of computers, the different platforms cooperate with each other to perform application functions.

For example, a single cooperative processing application might use a bottom-tier PC to initiate an application and run some business logic. Highly computer-intensive parts of the application might run on a mid-tier computer, multiprocessing machine or supercomputer, with transaction processing portions running on a mid-tier information server, and CAD/CAM parts on a bottom-tier technical workstation. Database searches would be performed on a UNIX database server, or even on a higher-tier mainframe.

Unfortunately, except for certain database-access applications, at present there are few good examples of such cooperative processing environments. One reason is that tools to provide such distributed application logic are just starting to emerge. In contrast, the market is filled with a myriad of tools for front-end development.

Cooperative processing architectures, however, in which database access and navigation logic are distributed across servers and desktop clients, and where entire applications each run on different clients and servers, are the heart of workflow applications. Typically, proprietary tools such as Microsoft's Visual Basic and Sybase's PowerBuilder are used for front-end GUI development. Home-grown procedures are usually used to develop and distribute the server parts of the applications.

Although two-tier Client/Server systems are well suited to certain types of applications, they have their flaws. For example, most two-tier Client/Server applications are built around PCs. PC-system management is difficult. There is little support for monitoring groups of PCs. Security is often ignored, as is performance tuning and capacity planning. The lack of problem-management software tools, such as exist for UNIX-based servers, tends to make PC problem management very labor intensive, and PC LANs very support intensive.

Because of the system-management difficulties and the nature of PCs, two-tier Client/Server systems don't easily scale up to enterprise systems. Many of these scalability and system management weaknesses can be overcome with three-tier

Client/Server architectures, which are also well suited for types of applications that two-tier architectures do not generally handle.

Three-Tier Approach: Multiple Mainframes Access

A more complex Client/Server approach is typically used in organizations with a large network, a large quantity of data relevant to many applications, and where many users in diverse locations must access data in multiple databases running on different mainframes. Called a three-tier Client/Server architecture, this approach refers to a logical division of computing platforms into a hierarchical organization. The computing resources in this hierarchy are distributed vertically in three tiers.

As is the case with the two-tier architecture, desktop machines are generally at the bottom tier in the hierarchy. The desktop machines consist of workstations and/or PCs. The PCs are often connected by PC networks, which usually have their own workgroup server.

The bottom tier machines are connected by LANs, which are connected to servers that are located in the middle tier of the hierarchy. The middle-tier servers may be PC workgroup servers (typically, Intel-based NetWare and NT machines), UNIX-based servers, or AS/400 midrange machines. Bottom-tier clients may talk directly to UNIX or AS/400 servers. Alternatively, bottom-tier PC clients may talk to a PC Workgroup server in a PC LAN. The PC Workgroup server talks to the middle-tier servers.

The middle-tier servers are usually networked to, and talk directly to, the organization's legacy mainframes/minicomputers. These computers are located at the top of the three-tier hierarchy. They are the source of corporate data.

In the three-tier approach, the presentation logic, application logic, and data logic are all separated from each other. The presentation logic is put on the desktop clients, which provides easy to use, intuitive access to UNIX- or mainframe-server information. Applications and data are implemented on middle-tier servers, which can be accessed by users throughout the enterprise.

The middle-tier machines also serve as a bridge to other types of servers. In this capacity, the middle-tier machines contain logic to determine which of multiple mainframes or other middle-tier servers contain the data that a desktop client requested. They also have the logic to transparently access the data, regardless of the mainframe on which the data resides.

The middle-tier server plays two roles. One is to be a server to the desktop computers. Its other role is to be a client to the mainframe. Both the middle-tier UNIX machines and top-tier mainframes provide the large memories and high performance needed by applications and database management systems.

From the viewpoint of the desktop users and desktop applications, the desktop clients can get data and information that may reside on multiple mainframes without having to worry about where the data is and how to get it. The desktop computer is a client to the middle-tier server. It does not have to know how to access multiple mainframes.

Three-tier architectures are not new. The concept originated with database companies. I contributed one of the early visions and pictures of a three-tier architecture in 1987 to the magazine *Mini-Micro Systems* ("True Distributed DBMSs Presage Big Dividends," May 1987, page 72) based on the inspiration and innovations of Unify Corporation, a UNIX database and database-tools company.

Which Client/Server Architecture Is Best?

Which Client/Server architecture is best, most efficient, and most cost-effective depends on the application in question. Table 3.4 provides some guidelines for choosing a two- or three-tier Client/Server architecture.

Very large applications, such as an airline-reservation system, are considered good candidates for a three-tier architecture because of the sheer size of the system. The airline, for example, might offload its central single-host data center by building LANs in each of its headquarters departments and connecting corresponding LAN servers to the host. At the same time, it might expand this architecture horizontally by adding mainframes to the top tier in its regional data centers, and adding WANs, LANs, and servers to the middle and bottom tiers. The smallest LANs, servers, and client platforms in this system would be located at the bottom tier, perhaps in travel agents' offices. The travel agents could use graphical user interfaces on these client platforms to access data on the midtier servers, which would, in turn, access the mainframe information.

For smaller systems, however, there might be little benefit to having a lot of extra nodes hanging around and having to go through two hubs instead of directly to a database. As a result, many organizations' position on two-tier versus three-tier architectures is to decide based on the application.

Typically, two-tier systems run at a single site rather than across the corporate backbone network. These systems are not highly integrated with multiple other systems or with existing mainframe systems.

In contrast, three-tier systems tend to be systems that are highly dependent on existing systems. These systems would not function without the underlying mainframe-based layered software base. These three-tier systems tend to replicate interfaces to multiple DBMSs, and export information used corporate-wide by multiple systems.

Some applications clearly benefit from a two-tier architecture, and others benefit from a three-tier architecture. But there are many applications whose design for, and position in, a two- versus three-tier architecture is not yet clear. More information and experimentation with these types of Client/Server systems is needed.

Integrating Applications across the Enterprise

This chapter was devoted to discussing the different types of Client/Server applications and their requirements, and developing an initial idea of the Client/Server architectural approaches suited to these different applications. How to develop an open

Table 3.4 Guidelines for Choosing a Two-Tier or Three-Tier Architecture

	Two-Tier Architecture	Three-Tier Architecture
Strengths	• Simpler • Costs less • More mature development tools. Application development requires less expertise than three-tier architectures • Provides easy way to introduce Client/Server computing into organizations • Well suited for departmental applications • Well suited for sharing PC productivity applications, groupware applications, executive-information systems, small simple business applications, and for UNIX database access • Often used to preserve an organization's investment in legacy systems by developing a desktop GUI to legacy mainframe applications • Often built around PCs	• Very flexible • Handles large, complex systems • Runs across corporate backbone LAN • Scales well to enterprise systems • Handles multiple computer types (PCs, workstations, UNIX servers, mainframes, supercomputers, etc.) • Often integrated with legacy systems and multiple DBMSs • Good for applications where users in diverse locations must access data in multiple databases on different mainframes and servers • Good for organizations with a large network and a large quantity of data relevant to many applications • Necessary for distributed transaction processing • More parallel processing possible because of multiple tiers & paths • Because of the presence of larger machines, automated-system management and greater security is possible
Weaknesses	• PC focus makes system management difficult • Minimal security, monitoring, fault management, performance, & capacity planning • PC focus makes applications very support and labor intensive • Doesn't easily scale up to enterprise systems due to system management difficulties	• Development is more complex than for two-tier applications • Few development tools available • Development tools are immature (Tools are first emerging now)

Source: Emerging Technologies Group.

enterprise architectural model to accommodate an organization's targeted Client/Server applications is the subject of Phase Three of the open Client/Server planning process, covered in Chapter 4. The targeted Client/Server architectures and desired Client/Server applications will also be used to determine application attributes and required system services in Phase Four, to determine applicable practical standards in Phase Five, and to develop implementable profiles in Phase Six.

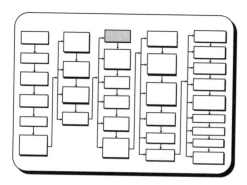

Chapter 4

Phase Three: Develop an Architectural Model

Introduction

The last chapters focused on determining business and technology requirements, and getting an idea of the Client/Server applications to be built for different Client/Server architectures. Now it is time to begin translating the requirements and application information into implementable technologies, standards, and products. Phase Three in planning open Client/Server systems begins this translation process by developing an architectural model for organization-specific open Client/Server environments.

In Phase Three, the architecture team develops an architecture, that concretely shows the organization's Client/Server directions and strategies. Then it develops an abstract model around functions, platforms, and data, which provides a visual idea of how to get to where it is going (Figure 4.1).

Establishing an Implementable Architecture

In planning for an open Client/Server environment, most people need to (or want to) start with a concrete idea of where they are going. A diagram showing every interconnected node in an organization is concrete, but impractical to draw and difficult to use to visualize common services except in a small organization. What is more practical is an integrated architecture diagram that shows, at an intermediate level, the common, interconnected server, client, platform, and network elements for an enterprise.

In Phase Three, Step 1, the architecture team develops an integrated architecture picture. The integrated architecture picture shows the types of servers, workstations, legacy computers, networks, operating systems, and certain major types of devices, along with a generically defined set of functional services, and possibly the major

- Develop a picture showing the open Client/Server architectural directions and strategies for an organization.
- Based on business objectives, policies, user requirements, and technology trends, develop an abstract open distributed systems model around functions, platforms, and data.
- To develop this model, decompose the environment of interest into applications, system services, platform elements, and data.
- Identify, generically, the interrelationships between elements in the environment (e.g., applications use system services for input/output, communications, computing, and accessing logical data views).

Figure 4.1   Phase Three: Architectural tasks.

method to be used to integrate the environment. This architecture can be shown for each location within an organization, or it can be shown as a generic architecture for the enterprise.

Figure 4.2 shows the enterprise computing architecture developed by Alcoa. As the figure shows, three types of platforms are targeted for the Alcoa environment—servers, desktop workstations, and information processors.

The servers are the mainstay of the Client/Server environment. They provide sharing of physical and data resources (e.g., disks, printers, modems, directories, files). The servers, along with LANs, connect people and groups across locations, thus providing infrastructure services (e.g., file sharing, data sharing, electronic mail) common to the different groups and locations.

Desktop computers are of two types—personal computers and workstations. Both are characterized by a huge growth in processing power and storage capacity, at the same time exhibiting the dramatic price reductions of systems that have become commodity products.

Personal computers (PCs), which initially provided personal productivity tools for a single user, now provide both personal and group productivity tools. Tied together in PC LANs, PCs allow device and file sharing among groups. Connected to backbone networks and large servers, PCs support data sharing and traditional application access. Finally, PCs support dumb-terminal emulation to access traditional information processors.

PCs are popular because they are inexpensive and because they provide easy-to-use graphical user interfaces to Client/Server applications, personal productivity tools, and to networks, data, and mainframe applications. PCs are dominated by proprietary operating systems (e.g., DOS, Windows, OS/2, MacOS, NT). PC operating systems, except for OS/2 and NT, are generally single tasking.

Because of the increases in processing power and disk-storage capacity, high-end PCs, running OS/2 or NT, are often used as servers. Most commonly, PC servers act either as workgroup servers on a workgroup LAN or run applications such as electronic mail and Lotus Notes for an enterprise. The larger enterprise application and data servers typically run UNIX. Having been designed for interactive graphical user interfaces, rather than fast database searches, PC-based servers have not made much of a dent in the UNIX server market.

UNIX-based workstations provide a multitasking operating system for scientific and engineering applications, and for software development. UNIX-based workstations differ from PC-based workstations in that they support advanced graphics (e.g., for computer-aided design), intensive computations, and high-volume multitasking networked applications (e.g., for the stock exchange, engineering graphics applications, and some airline reservations).

Information processors are the legacy information systems, such as those used for transaction processing and physical control in industrial and manufacturing plants. Information processors are typically proprietary and closed, difficult to use, difficult to network, and cannot be easily or quickly changed. On the other hand, they tend to have security and storage management capabilities that are unsurpassed (at least, not by present UNIX or high-end PC servers). Many vendors have been adding open operating system interfaces, SQL databases, and networking capabilities to their information processing mainframes, thus making them more open.

Information processors and their applications constitute several hundred million dollars of investments. They support massive databases, high-transaction processing volumes, hundreds of applications, and thousands of users. Information processors will probably not go away quickly. More likely they will be with us for a long time, but will be tied into Client/Server environments by various means. Information processors also will act as servers to mid-tier servers, workgroup servers, and to workstations, especially in three-tier Client/Server environments.

As Figure 4.2 shows, there are many types of servers, including file servers, data servers, electronic mail servers, communications servers, security servers, name servers, and application servers. Various servers, workstations, PCs, information processors, and control systems are manufactured by different vendors, run different operating systems (or different versions of the same operating system), and run on different networks. Nevertheless, it is Alcoa's aim (and the aim of most organizations moving to Client/Server environments) to integrate the different systems. OSF's Distributed Computing Environment (DCE), with its Remote Procedure Call (RPC), directory services, time services, security services, threads services, and distributed-file system, is one way. The aim of the entire class of software, known as *middleware* (of which DCE is part), is also to integrate heterogeneous systems. Middleware is covered in detail in Chapter 9.

An Enterprise-Computing Architectural Model

In Phase Three Step 2, the architecture team develops an abstract model around functions, platforms, and data. The architecture may or may not be based directly on standards or industry models (e.g., the IEEE P1003.0's Open System Environment

Workstations

Significant legacy & investment—requires change

- Individual, personal computing services
- Common point of access to server and information processor functions and data
- Fast response time for personal and local applications
- Graphical user interface technology

Servers

Small legacy & investment—adopt common, new technologies and build a new open environment

- Target environment for new Client/Server OLTP systems
- Network services - print and file sharing, mail, bulletin board, file transfer, directories, modems
- Interoperable, Shareable, common methods, data, and function
- Standards-based open systems
- Data/information source for Client/Server business support applications, including database servers for shareable information from IP's

Information Processors

Significant legacy & investment—maintain, migrate or replace

- Data capture computers for process control and transaction processing (real-time, OLTP, batch)
- Store, manage and process large volumes of data at the plant, business or corporate level via business specific applications
- Collect, summarize and aggregate data for information database servers
- Very high response time, security, integrity, availability (24x7), realiability (uptime), recoverability
- Generally, proprietary/closed environments with increasing connectivity to an open systems environment.

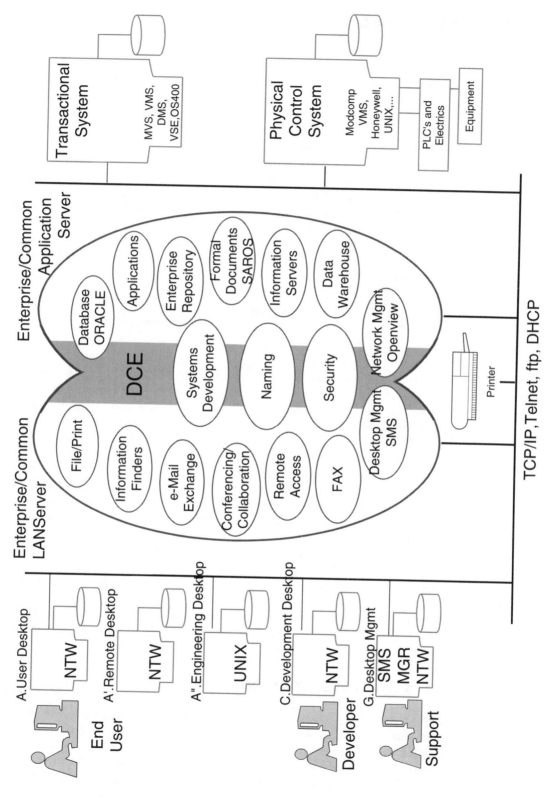

Figure 4.2 Alcoa's Client/Server architecture directions. *Source: Alcoa.*

[OSE] Reference Model described in Appendix D of this book). In all likelihood, an organization's architecture will be a superset or variant of any standardized models.

There is no single best approach to defining an organization-specific architectural model. Each organization defines an architecture that meets the needs of most of its application software, hardware, users, processes, and procurement rules.

There are two major purposes in defining a model. One is to visually understand what needs to be done, in what areas, to move to open Client/Server systems. In this sense, the model is a productivity tool. The second major purpose of a model is to use it to communicate with higher-level management, software developers, operations managers, and suppliers.

Two different models, developed by the General Motors (GM) and Alcoa architectural teams for different purposes, are shown and discussed in this chapter. They are good examples of what can be done in the real world.

GM's Open-Systems Model

Figures 4.3 and 4.4 show the simplest form of GM's initial abstract model, covering its computer, communications, CIM, and CAD (C4), office automation (OA), and plant system logical design. Both models were used primarily to communicate with management when GM formulated its plans for an open-systems strategy.

As GM got on with its planning, it decomposed the simple, abstract model in Figure 4.3 into a number of types of platform elements, system and application services, and functional application types. This decomposed model, shown in Figure 4.4, shows the major platform elements used by systems services, the systems services that are used by application services and tools, and several basic application services and tools that are common to many types of applications within GM.

During subsequent stages of the planning process, the boxes in the Figure 4.3 and 4.4 models were further decomposed to provide the details of required services, systems, networks, and data. GM also coupled its open-systems planning with an analysis of the organization's data. The resulting detailed models were used as the basis for the company's open systems planning.

These GM models are good examples of the very high-level abstract models that can be presented to management at the beginning of the planning process. To facilitate more thorough planning by the planning teams, the Alcoa model will be used in this book to develop greater details and specify individual components and standards.

Alcoa's Open-Systems Model

Figure 4.5 shows the abstract model that Alcoa developed to assist in its understanding and expression of standards-based distributed open systems. The model is compatible with, but more detailed than, the IEEE 1003.0 model.

Alcoa's open-systems model has three major parts: users, software, and hardware. Hardware (e.g., processors, memory, disk, network, devices, and peripherals),

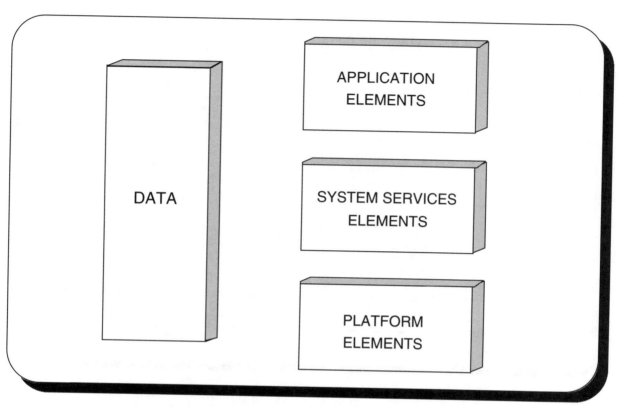

Figure 4.3 Major logical elements of General Motors' systems abstract model. *Source: General Motors.*

along with interfaces to the hardware (shown as EEIs, or external environment interfaces), comprise the bottom level of this model. As the model shows, the software runs above the hardware. The software implements input and output, and controls interfaces with the users.

Four levels of software are shown in the model: operating system and other system software, tools and utilities, application support and end-user tools, and applications. Application-programming interfaces (APIs) exist between each of these levels.

The API boundary between the operating system and other software is shown as a solid line because a privileged operating-system state (called *kernel mode*) must be entered to access-system resources. Broken lines are shown between other software levels because the boundary between these levels is fuzzy. For example, some software packages span two levels. Also, applications, tools, and utilities may talk directly to each other without going through the various layers. In addition, it may be necessary (for performance reasons or to take advantage of specialized or existing capabilities) for tools or applications to bypass the software interfaces at these levels and interface directly with the operating system.

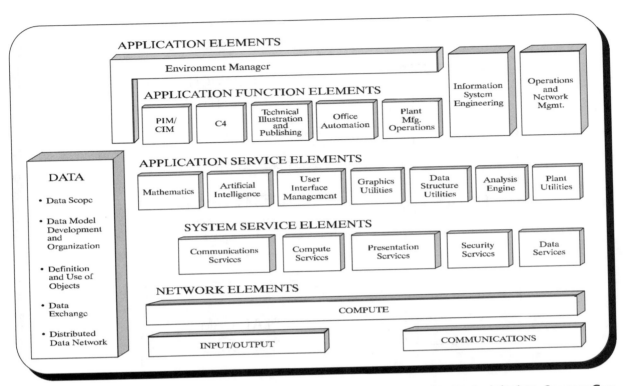

Figure 4.4   General Motors' C4/OA/plant systems logical design. *Source: General Motors.*

The tools and utilities category holds software that can be used both at run-time and during development. This category includes DBMSs, TP monitors, forms, graphics libraries, distributed or Client/Server file systems, windowing systems, multimedia I/O systems, page description languages (e.g., PostScript, SPDL), and others.

The application support and end-user tools category consists of tools that are largely needed by end users, rather than an organization's data-processing staff. Such tools include word-processing programs, electronic spreadsheets, graphics packages, electronic mail, data-access and text-retrieval tools, decision-support tools, CAD/CAM, modeling and simulation systems, and statistics packages. Many of these tools (e.g., word-processing programs and spreadsheets) are used across departments to solve a wide variety of business and functional problems.

Software tools used primarily for system or application development include CASE tools, language-sensitive editors, compilers, debuggers, and DBMS development aids. These tools, along with system-management tools, are placed at the sides of the model. For several reasons, they are partly separated from other tools and applications by a solid line. First, they can run (at least partially) on a separate computer. Second, separating these tools shows at a glance the tools which directly impact users. Third, software that does not have to be purchased multiple times (for

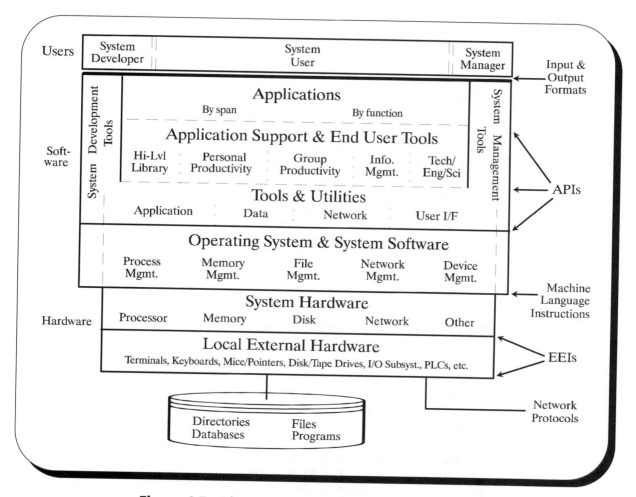

Figure 4.5 Alcoa computer reference model. *Source: Alcoa.*

a multiple-instance production environment) is clearly delineated. Fourth, the side location of these categories portrays the overhead or support nature of these tools.

End-user tools, such as word-processing programs and electronic spreadsheets, are sometimes considered applications. In the Alcoa model, however, applications are collections of software procedures, calculations, inputs, and outputs that are used for specific business purposes, and are closely linked with business processes.

Alcoa classifies applications by span and by function. *Span* refers to applications targeted either at all, or at a segment of, an enterprise, business unit, location, department, and personnel. *Function* refers to applications targeted at specific business functions. Examples are applications for marketing, sales, production, accounting, engineering, and so on.

Three primary classes of users are shown in the Alcoa computer reference model:

- General system users
- Application developers
- System managers and support people

The different user categories are located closest to the vertical segment of the model that represents their primary role. For example, system developers are placed on the left side of the model, on top of the system-development tools section. System managers are located on the right side, on top of system-management tools. General end users are located in the middle, on top of the business-oriented applications and end-user tools that directly support them. The user categories are separated by dotted lines, which indicate that the roles of the different users may overlap.

In subsequent open-systems planning phases, Alcoa refined this architecture and used it to determine and communicate its required functional components and standards. The refined model will be shown in subsequent chapters of this book.

The POSIX.0 and Alcoa Models Compared

Alcoa designed its model to be similar to the IEEE POSIX.0 Open Systems Environment (OSE) model, discussed in Appendix D. There are some differences between the Alcoa and POSIX.0 reference models, the major one being the level of detail.

The Alcoa model addresses a much greater level of detail than the POSIX.0 model, which is to be expected. No standards group could, or should, get into such details. Furthermore, details tend to be specific to an organization.

The Alcoa model does not conflict with the POSIX.0 model. It is a good example of a model that can be used to plan and communicate increasingly detailed enterprisewide interoperability, portability, and standards information. The Alcoa model will be used throughout the rest of the book as an example.

Using the Distributed OSE Architecture

The model shown in this chapter must now be populated with standards to support an organization's desired interoperability and portability areas. How these interoperability and portability areas are determined is the subject of Chapter 5. How to populate the architecture with the appropriate standards and how to prioritize the interoperability/portability areas and standards are covered in the chapters following.

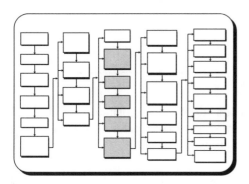

Phase Four: Infrastructure Planning Tasks

Introduction

All of the tasks described in this guide are used to plan the infrastructure for an open Client/Server system environment (DOSEE). The Phase Four tasks described in this chapter, however, differ from the earlier planning tasks in that they are directly concerned with defining the specific services for the organization's open Client/Server environment. The various business, application, and architectural tasks (discussed in the previous chapters) are preliminary to the Phase Four tasks.

Phase Four Tasks

DOSEE Phase Four involves four major open Client/Server environment preparatory planning tasks. This phase is the heart of any distributed open-systems environment engineering planning process. It is during this phase that an organization begins to determine how to move to an integrated, enterprisewide environment that supports interoperability, portability, and scalability across the heterogeneous, multivendor parts of the enterprise (Figure 5.1).

At the end of this phase, the architecture and planning teams will have explicitly defined many of the specific technology requirements for applications throughout the enterprise. They will further decompose the architectural model developed in Phase Three, and add more details showing many of the software services needed for open Client/Server systems.

1. Map the connections between functional components (such as applications, platforms, and systems) (identified in Phase Two) within each department, and also to different departments which interact with the department in question, in order to determine the targeted areas for interoperability.
2. Define or identify attributes and characteristics of the various application interoperations, and of the applications themselves.
3. Define attribute values for the application interoperation and the application attributes, because these application attributes will be used to determine functional service requirements for which standards might be needed.
4. Map the attribute values for application interoperations, and for the applications, to service requirements.
5. Identify the services which are common to applications within each department, and across other departments, to determine the targeted areas for application, user, and programmer portability and scalability.
6. Map all the required service requirements onto the architecture defined in Phase Three.

Figure 5.1   Phase Four: Infrastructure planning tasks.

Determine Targets of Interoperability

In Phase Four Step 1, DOSEE planners identify the interoperability targets. To determine the areas for which interoperability may be an issue, generate a set of interoperability matrices with the information described in the following paragraphs.

Each interoperability matrix should show the applications used by each department, division, or other functional area. The applications in the matrix should be the ones identified in the activities-versus-applications matrix in Phase Two. The same applications should be shown on each axis.

Applications in the interoperability matrices should be shown for the extended department. This means that each department's matrices should show applications owned by other departments, but used by the department generating the matrix, as well as applications owned and used only by the department in question (Figure 5.2).

Two separate matrices should be generated. One should show Applications versus applications on the X and Y axes for existing systems. The other matrix should indicate the same information for planned or desired systems.

Table 5.1 shows an interoperability matrix generated for the consulting and analysis department of the consulting company whose activities-versus-applications matrix was shown earlier (in Phase Two). Table 5.2 shows an interoperability matrix

Within each functional area (department), and across functional areas (departments, divisions, etc.), generate two sets of matrices showing the same applications (functional components, systems) on both the X axis and the Y axis. One set of matrices should show existing systems. The other set should show planned or desired systems.

Check off every cell in the matrix showing an interaction, interconnection, or other interoperability relationship between the applications or systems.

This filled-in matrix shows the areas for which interoperability may be desired.

Figure 5.2 Phase Four Step 1: Identifying interoperability targets.

Table 5.1 Interoperability Determination Matrix for a Consulting Company. *Source: Emerging Technologies Group.*

CONSULTING DEPT.: INTERACTIONS BETWEEN APPLICATIONS (Subset)

Applications	Electronic Mail	Word Processing	Data Mgmt.	Document Management	Spreadsheet	Presentation Graphics	Plain Paper Printing	Calendaring
Electronic Mail	✓	✓	—	—	✓	✓	—	✓
Word Processing	✓	—	✓	✓	✓	✓	✓	—
Data Management	—	✓	—	—	✓	—	✓	—
Document Management	—	✓	—	—	✓	✓	✓	—
Spreadsheet	✓	✓	✓	✓	—	✓	✓	—
Presentation Graphics	✓	✓	—	✓	✓	—	✓	—
Plain Paper Printing	—	✓	✓	✓	✓	✓	—	✓
Calendaring	✓	—	—	—	—	—	✓	—

Key: ✓ = *Interacts with*   — = *Does not interact with*

Table 5.2 Interoperability Matrix for a Manufacturing Company. *Source: Emerging Technologies Group.*

MANUFACTURING PLANT: INTERACTION BETWEEN APPLICATIONS (Subset)

Applications/Systems →

	Payroll	Production Tracking	Production Scheduling	PP&C	Engineering Design	Sales Forecasting	Field Sales	Marketing	Order Entry	Manufacturing	Transportation	Inventory Control	EDI
Payroll	—	—	—	—	✓	—	✓	✓	—	✓	—	—	—
Production Tracking	—	—	✓	—	—	—	—	—	—	✓	✓	✓	—
Production Scheduling	—	✓	—	✓	—	—	—	—	✓	✓	—	✓	—
PP&C	—	—	✓	—	✓	—	—	—	✓	✓	—	✓	—
Engineering Design	✓	—	—	✓	—	✓	—	✓	—	✓	—	—	—
Sales Forecasting	—	—	—	—	✓	—	✓	✓	—	—	—	—	—
Field Sales	✓	—	—	—	—	✓	—	✓	✓	—	—	—	—
Marketing	✓	—	—	—	✓	✓	✓	—	✓	—	—	—	—
Order Entry	—	—	✓	—	—	—	✓	✓	—	✓	—	✓	✓
Manufacturing	✓	✓	✓	✓	—	—	—	—	✓	—	✓	✓	—
Transportation	—	✓	—	—	—	—	—	—	—	✓	—	—	—
Inventory Control	—	✓	✓	✓	—	—	—	—	✓	✓	—	—	✓
EDI	—	—	—	—	—	—	—	—	✓	—	—	✓	—

Key: ✓ = Interacts with   — = Does not interact with

generated for the manufacturing company whose interoperability interrelationships were partially diagrammed earlier (in Phase Two).

Both matrices show only a subset of interoperability interactions within the respective organizations. The full set of interactions would consume far more room than is available here. The boxes are shaded below the main diagonal because the matrix is symmetrical about the main diagonal. Therefore, the entries below and to the left of the diagonal reflect the entries above and to the right of the diagonal.

The checkmarks show areas where interoperability may be an issue. Columns that contain many checkmarks indicates an application with which a large number of other applications interact. This may be justification for specifying standardized interoperability interfaces for this application area. On the other hand, for various reasons, an application that interacts with a lot of other applications may not be a high priority interoperability area. The importance and priorities of these different interoperability targets will be determined in a later step.

Note that the applications and interoperability interactions shown in the interoperability matrix for the consulting company are typical of applications in an automated office.

A different although somewhat similar matrix will be generated to determine areas for which portability/scalability is an issue. Examples of a portability matrix will be shown later in this chapter.

Services Are the Key to Functionality

Once the interoperability targets are determined, the next step is to identify the kinds of interoperability required, and the specific interoperability services needed.

To identify interoperability services (and, later in this chapter, portability services), it is necessary to understand what is meant by a service. Until now, the term *service* has been used in the intuitive sense of the word. Unfortunately, there is often a lot of confusion about the terms *service*, *interface*, and *standard*.

A *software service* is a high-level description or expression of a particular functionality that can be implemented in software in order to satisfy a specific application requirement. Examples of software services are the ability to search for particular records in a remote file, to size and move windows on a screen, to allocate memory in a system, and to start and stop the execution of a process or program.

An application accesses a service through an interface. If the interface to the same service on two systems is different, there can be no interoperability or portability except through a custom program. A standard is created to satisfy the requirements for a particular service through a common interface. The service, however, exists whether or not the interface is standardized.

Software services can be described at a high level and a detailed level. Examples of high-level descriptions are window management, data definition, and graphics-data interchange. Examples of detailed service descriptions are move and resize a window; attach to each window-related event a function that is automatically executed when the event is triggered (callback); get and set attributes (e.g., in a network or graphics application); and create, alter, or drop tables, views, records, fields, classes, objects, instances, attributes, and/or data.

Software developers need a detailed description of a service in order to write code that provides the service. Open Client/Server planners are concerned with a higher-level description. Overly high-level service descriptions, however, may not provide what the user wants. For example, just requiring a windowing system can provide windowing systems with services that differ in ways like the following:

- The windowing services run only on a standalone machine.
- The windowing services include a library of macros to perform different mid-level windowing functions.
- The windowing services include different interface languages to prewritten windowing objects.
- The windowing services may or may not provide interactive dialogue management.
- The windowing services work differently from the company's other windowing systems.

Users buying systems do not want to become involved in the details of low-level service definitions. On the other hand, they need to specify the services they want in enough detail (or have someone specify the desired services for them) so that what they buy satisfies their requirements.

Determine the Interoperability Services Needed

There are two methods to identify required interoperability (and, later, portability) services. One method, which is most commonly used, is the *group brainstorm* technique, which puts together various groups of knowledgeable people to focus on a particular domain or application area (e.g., networking, EDI, accounting, sales, manufacturing scheduling, process control, health care).

After many weeks or months of brainstorming sessions, the groups will presumably have read through and summarized many pages of requirements questionnaires, surveys, and interview results. The brainstormers will then use their knowledge of each domain or application area to come up with the software and/or hardware services that will satisfy the requirements in each application area. This method has been used by many organizations. In most cases, it has been the only method available.

The problem with the group-brainstorm method is its dependence on the collective expertise, ideas, and intuitions of the group members. It can be a big leap from hundreds of pages of requirements written by managers of diverse, possibly geographically separated, departments to lists of specific technical services and standards that satisfy all those requirements.

Often brainstorm groups go directly from requirements to selecting products. This worked well in the past for planning centralized, proprietary, monolithic environments. At that time, each department purchased or built its own systems, and those systems were not dependent on any other department.

Client/Server environment planning is a different story. By its nature, different departments' software and hardware systems depend on each other, and interact with one another. Planning for cost-effective Client/Server environments must be done on an enterprise-wide scale to ensure interoperability, scalability, and portability. Planning also must be done so the Client/Server systems are extendible into technologies that will emerge in the future. Inadvertently omitting services that must be added and integrated later can be costly and result in chaotic maintenance and system-management nightmares.

Compounding the problem is the need for common services, interfaces, and standards across departments, if not enterprisewide, because of the interactions and dependencies between department applications. This means that the brainstorming group must not only be experts in a particular domain, but must also be experts in standards. In a typical organization, it is not likely that a process-control or investment-trading expert and a standards expert are one and the same person.

All these problems indicate the need for a different technique to determine specific technology services. The technique used should allow domain experts to use their domain expertise where applicable, and allow architecture/infrastructure/standards experts to contribute their standards expertise where applicable. One such technique was developed by the European Workshop on Open Systems (EWOS) for developing commercial open systems environment (OSE) profiles. *Commercial* refers to businesses, government agencies, and any other type of institution with production environment requirements.

EWOS used its technique to develop profiles for the health-care industry. The method described in the following sections for defining interoperability, portability, and scalability service requirements and standards is based on the EWOS method.

Start with Applications, Interactions, or Business Scenarios

The EWOS methodology starts with business scenarios. The EWOS techniques can also be applied to applications and interactions between applications. Business scenarios, application requirements, and interactions all drive the specification of a profile first in terms of functional business requirements (which EWOS calls *attributes* and *attribute values*), then in terms of technology requirements (also called *service requirements*), and, finally, in terms of standards.

Figure 5.3 summarizes how the EWOS attribute-attribute values technique is used, regardless of whether the starting point is business scenarios, applications, or application interactions. The boxed area in the figure indicates the steps covered in Phase Four. The starting steps, application identification and developing an architectural model, were done in Phases Two and Three, respectively. Standards selection is the subject of Phase Five, and will be discussed in Chapter 6.

One important thing about the attribute-attribute values technique is that users (not technical people) define a business scenario or application in terms of policies, strategies, application goals, tasks to be performed, and functions to be accomplished. As will be seen, these same users then characterize the business scenario or application with specific functional requirements, using easy-to-understand multiple-choice templates.

A scenario is a description of real-world information processing requirements that may be characterized by a (mostly) unique set of attributes and attribute values. An example of a user scenario is the health care industry's need to send radiology images from an imaging machine in one hospital to an imaging machine in another. Another example is the preparation of multimedia presentations.

Attributes Characterize Applications, Interactions, Scenarios

The DOSEE methodology starts with applications and application interactions rather than with business scenarios because applications and application interactions are convenient to use when planning an open Client/Server environment. In Phase Four Step 2, the applications previously identified in the Phase Four interoperability

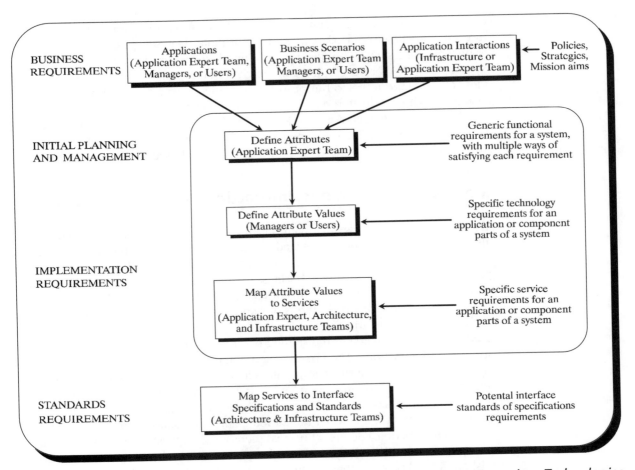

Figure 5.3 Determine required services. *Source: Emerging Technologies Group. Based on an EWOS Profile Development methodology.*

matrices are used to generate a set of generic attributes that characterize each application or scenario at the functional requirements level. Users who comprehend the business needs of the organization or application domain for which an open systems environment profile will be developed should define and understand these attributes.

Attributes are high-level task descriptors that describe, at the user's level (not at the technical detail level), the key conceptual features of the tasks that the user is trying to accomplish. Attributes may conceptually address such task descriptors as document content, format (e.g., of a document, graphic, or message), encoding method, size of a transmission, and design complexity.

Table 5.3 shows a set of nine attributes that EWOS has defined for information transfer in the health-care industry. As you will see, these information transfer attributes are also applicable to information transfer in other industries.

Table 5.3   Attributes for Health-Care Information Transfer

Attributes	Meaning and Possible Value
Content	What kind of information is transferred (text, images, graphics) and combinations of these.
Distance	Within a department, local or national/international (If the attribute value is international, it suggests the need for the specification of national and cultural dependencies, such as language and national cultural conventions as well as wide-area networks)
Priority	Low, medium, or high
Volume	The relative size of the information transfer
Connection	Between the communicating systems (permanent, intermittent)
Rendition	Is the data itself sufficient, or does it require information on how it is to be presented (e.g., if a report is transmitted for the purpose of printing, rather than for further processing, it must contain format information)
Distribution	Single or multiple recipient(s)
Information Flow	Send, receive, or query
Latency	Real time, interactive, or batch

Source: EWOS Technical Guide: EWOS Method for Defining Functional Profiles for Health Care.

Define Attribute Values to Tailor Attributes to Specific Needs

Attributes have values. An *attribute value* is one of a set of usually finite possibilities selected for a given attribute because it is most relevant to the original application function or user scenario function that the user wants to accomplish. For example, the attribute content may take the value text, graphics, or compound document (mixed text and graphics). The attribute that EWOS calls *distribution* can take such values as single recipient, multiple recipient, or broadcast.

Attribute values can be binary (such as present or not present); qualitative (such as high, medium, or low); and specific (such as monochrome, grey scale, or color). Attribute value examples are graphics, image, or compound documents (for the document content attribute); high priority (for the priority attribute), broadcast transmission (for the communications transport distribution attribute), and local or international (for the communications distance attribute). Phase Four Step 3 defines attribute values for the previously defined application or business scenario attributes.

To be defined and understood by application domain experts and managers, attributes should not be application or scenario descriptors with technical attribute values. Instead, they should be selected to be meaningful to non-specialists in information technology, and intuitive to apply.

For example, an application domain expert or manager might specify that the attribute data compression, with attribute values required or not required will have the attribute value required. The business user or domain expert will not be expected to state the type of data compression to be used in the scenario in question. This issue is left to the organization's technical staff.

Attributes and attribute values that are highly technical are not appropriate to a Client/Server planning methodology to be used by managers, users, and application domain experts. Sometimes, if there is no alternative, however, an attribute value might need to be highly technical.

The attribute values defined by application experts and managers may explicitly identify service requirements for an application area. For example, a user who needs to transfer instruction manuals containing large amounts of mixed text and graphical data will likely define required as the attribute value for the attribute data compression. Data compression is also a service requirement for this system.

In other cases, attribute values suggest application service requirements. For example, the attribute value international for an application's distance attribute suggests the need not only for wide-area network communications, but also suggests that the application needs internationalization facilities for converting currency, dates, or native language messages. The attribute value high for the attribute security level suggests that the application in question may need authentication and authorization facilities, or that it may need security facilities that conform to a B1 level security service (a U.S. Department of Defense specification for very high-level security).

It remains for a technically oriented member of the architecture/infrastructure team to map the attribute value to the final service requirement, such as the particular compression algorithm/system or the specific means of achieving the required security.

The definition of the proper and most useful attribute sets and attribute values for a set of applications or business tasks is a complex matter. Complicating matters is the fact that attributes and attribute values may overlap from one functional application area to another. Attributes are best understood by studying real-world examples.

Table 5.4 shows the attributes defined in Table 5.3, with possible values that EWOS has defined for transfer of a patient invoice in the health-care industry.

Table 5.5 shows the attributes and attribute values for a subset of the application interoperations shown in the interoperability matrix earlier in this chapter, to demonstrate interoperability targets for the consulting company. These applications use the same communications-oriented attributes and attribute values as those used for patient invoice transfer. Additional attributes and associated attribute values, oriented toward portability, scalability, and interoperability, are shown later in this chapter.

Identify Information Objects and Their Attributes

A patient invoice is an example of an information object. Besides patient invoices, health-care information objects include medical-history records, medical images,

Table 5.4   Typical Scenario with Attributes and Values

Information Object	Attribute	Value(s)
Patient Invoice	Content	Text
	Rendition	Representation or No Representation
	Volume	Medium
	Latency	Long
	Priority Required	No
	Connection	Networked or Direct
	Information Flow	Send
	Distribution	Single Recipient
	Distance	Local, Metropolitan, or National

Source: EWOS Technical Guide: EWOS Method for Defining Functional Profiles for Health Care.

medical graphics, and numerical results. Thus, application areas are concerned with contain many information objects.

Although each information object may have its own attributes and attribute values, many information objects are similar enough to use common attributes and attribute values without affecting a communications transmission or business function. This similarity narrows the number of attributes and attribute values that must be defined.

Identifying information objects is important because the information objects help to indicate attribute values, services, and, ultimately, standards. For example, if a user indicates that the information object to be transferred is X rays, the infrastructure team immediately knows that system requirements will include high-bandwidth communications, compression, and a choice of certain formats.

Determine Attributes and Values for Portability and Scalability

The nine EWOS attributes and associated attribute values are but a few of the attributes and attribute values possible for open Client/Server server applications. Table 5.6 shows a more complete list of possible attributes and associated attribute values that are applicable to many applications, application interoperations, business scenarios, and information objects.

Many of the Table 5.6 attributes and attribute values are applicable not only to communications, but also to interacting applications that reside on a single machine. Others are applicable to standalone applications for which portability and/or

Table 5.5 Basic Attributes and Attribute Values for Application Interoperations

Application Interactions	Attributes	Attribute Values
Spreadsheet—WP	Content	Text, Graphics, Numeric, Financial
	Rendition	Representation
	Volume	Medium
	Latency	Short
	Priority Required	Low
	Connection	Networked, Modem
	Information Flow	Send, Receive
	Distribution	Single recipient, Multiple recipients
	Distance	Local
Presentation Graphics—WP	Content	Graphics
	Rendition	Representation
	Volume	Small-to-Medium
	Latency	Short
	Priority Required	Low
	Connection	Networked, Modem
	Information Flow	Send, Receive
	Distribution	Single recipient
	Distance	Local
WP-Plain Paper Printing	Content	Text, Alphanumeric, Graphics, Image
	Rendition	Representation
	Volume	Small and Medium
	Latency	Fast
	Priority Required	Medium, High
	Connection	Networked
	Distribution	Single recipient
	Distance	Local, Enterprise
E-mail—Remote E-mail	Content	Text, Binary Data
	Rendition	Representation or No representation
	Volume	Small, Medium, and Large
	Latency	Doesn't matter
	Priority Required	No
	Connection	Networked and Modem
	Information Flow	Send and Receive
	Distribution	Single and Multiple recipient
	Distance	Intradepartment, Local, National, International
Document Management—WP	Content	Text, Graphics, Spreadsheet, Still Image, Video, Audio
	Rendition	Representation
	Volume	Small, Medium, and Large
	Latency	Medium-to-Fast
	Priority Required	Medium
	Connection	Networked and Modem
	Information Flow	Send and Receive
	Distribution	Single and Multiple recipient
	Distance	Intradepartment, Local, National, International

Source: Emerging Technologies Group.

Table 5.6 Attributes and Values for Portability, Scalability, and Interoperability

Attributes	Possible Attribute Values
Availability	Low, Medium, High, Fault Tolerant
Compression	Required, Not Required
Concurrency Management	File Locking, Version Control
Connection	Modem, Networked, None
Content	Text, Graphics, Image, Compound Documents, Structured Data, Maps
Determinism	Hard, Soft
Directory Location	Local, Distributed
Display	Bit-mapped, Character-Oriented
Distance	Workgroup, Local, Metropolitan, National, International, Interplanetary
Distribution	Single Recipient, Multiple Recipient, Broadcast
Encoding	Character, Binary, Graphical, ASN.1
Event Notification	Automatic, Polling
File Access Method	Sequential, Random, Indexed
File Size	Small, Medium, Large, Very Large
Fonts	Character, Graphics, Geometry, Glyph
Format	Text, Graphics, Image, Spreadsheet, Audio
Human Interface Type	Command-Level, Graphical, None
Image Color	Monochrome, Black and White, Gray Scale, Color
Information Flow	Receive, Send
Input	Keyboard, Mouse, Trackball, Eraser Tip Trackpoint, Joy Sticks, Touch Screen, Bar Code

(Continued)

scalability, rather than interoperability, are issues. In these cases, it may be desirable to run the same standalone application on multiple heterogeneous machines, often of different sizes and classes (e.g., a PC and a UNIX workstation, or a PC/Intel-based server and a large UNIX-based server). In both cases, to support portability, scalability, and compatibility between applications, a common set of interfaces, formats, and protocols are needed.

Table 5.6 Attributes and Values for Portability, Scalability, and Interoperability (Continued)

Attributes	Possible Attribute Values
Latency	Very Short, Short, Medium, Long, Deterministic, Doesn't Matter
Output	Screen, Printer, Typesetting Equipment
Peak Usage	Yes, No
Priority Required	Yes, No
Query Complexity	Low, Medium, High, Very High
Query Frequency	Low, Medium, High, Very High
Query Type	*Ad hoc*, Prestructured
Rendition	Representation, No Representation
Response Time	Less than 1 Microsecond, Low Microseconds, High Microseconds, 1–200 Milliseconds, 201–500 Milliseconds, 501 Milliseconds to 1 Second, Greater than 1 Second
Revisable/Updatable	Yes, No
Security Level	Low, Medium, High, Critical
Security Type	Password, Access Control Lists, Privilege (need to know), Audit, Authentication, Authorization, Callback, Firewall, Destroy before Reading
Software Complexity	Low, Medium, High, Very High
Software Obtained How?	Developed internally, Purchased, Contracted
Speed	Medium, Fast, Doesn't Matter

Source: Emerging Technologies Group.

To ensure portability, scalability, and compatibility, as part of Phase Four Steps 2 and 3, the infrastructure and application expert teams define a set of attributes and attribute values that characterize the applications at the functional requirements level. The applications for which these attributes and attribute values are defined should be the ones identified in the activities versus applications matrix in Phase Two, and in the interoperability matrices in Phase Four Step 1. If other attributes and/or attribute values are needed to properly characterize an application, application interoperation, or business scenario, they should be added to the list of predefined attributes and attribute values. The attributes and attribute values will be used later, in Phase Four Step 5, to determine the service requirements for the applications.

Table 5.7 shows the attributes and attribute values for a subset of the applications used by the consulting company's analyst department. Some of these applications'

Table 5.7 Typical Application Attributes and Attribute Values for an Office

Applications	Attributes	Attribute Values
Word Processing	Encoding	Character, Graphical, Binary
	Document Content	Text, Graphics, Mixed Text and Graphics, Still Image, Database Data, Spreadsheet
	Format	Text, Graphics, Image, Spreadsheet
	Fonts	Character Fonts, Graphic Fonts
	Type of Human Interface	Graphical, Command-Level
	Revisable/Updatable	Yes
	Security Level	Low-to-Medium
	File Size	Small, Medium, Large
	Display	Bit-mapped
	Input/Output	Keyboard, Trackball, Eraser Tip Track Point, Screen, Printer, Modem, Network
Presentation Graphics	Format	Graphics
	Fonts	Graphics, Character
	Type of Human Interface	Graphical
	File Size	Small-to-Medium
	Input/Output	Screen, Keyboard, Printer, Network, Mouse, Trackball
	Security Level	Low
Electronic Spreadsheet	Format	Spreadsheet, Character, Graphics
	Fonts	Character, Graphics
	Type of Human Interface	Graphical, Command Level
	Security Level	Medium
	File Size	Medium, Large
Document Management	Document Content	Text, Graphics, Mixed Text and Graphics, Still Image, Motion Video, Audio, Hypertext, Spreadsheet
	Encoding	Character, Graphics
	Format	Text, Graphics, Still Image, Motion Video, Spreadsheet
	Fonts	Character, Graphics
	Image Color	Color, Black and White
	Type of Human Interface	Graphical, Command Level
	Revisable/Updatable	Yes
	Security Level	Low
	File Size	Large
	Display	Bit-Mapped
	Compression	Required
	How Software Obtained	Purchased

Source: Emerging Technologies Group.

(Continued)

Table 5.7 Typical Application Attributes and Attribute Values for an Office (Continued)

Applications	Attributes	Attribute Values
Data Query	Query Complexity	Low
	Query Type	*Ad Hoc*, Prestructured
	Query Frequency	Low
	Peak usage	No
	Rendition	Representation, No Representation
	Encoding	Character
	Revisable/Updatable	No
	Security Level	High
	Directory Location	Local, Distributed
Electronic Mail	Document Content	Text, Graphics, Mixed Text and Graphics, Still Image
	Rendition	Representation
	Volume	Short-to-medium
	Latency	Long
	Priority Required	No
	Connection	Modem, Networked
	Information Flow	Send, Receive
	Distribution	Single Recipient
	Distance	Local (Workgroup), National, International
	Revisable	Yes
	Security Level	Medium-to-High
	Security Type	Password, Authentication, Authorization, Access Control Lists, Labeling
	Compression	Required
Plain Paper Printing	Document Content	Text, Graphics, Mixed Text and Graphics, Still Image
	Speed	Medium-to-Medium High

Source: Emerging Technologies Group.

attributes and attribute values, specific to communications, were shown in Table 5.4. To fully characterize these applications in order to determine service requirements that accommodate portability and scalability, as well as interoperability, it is necessary to determine the attribute values for the attributes as shown in Table 5.7, as well as the communications-oriented attributes shown earlier in Table 5.5.

Map Attributes and Values to Implementable Services

So far, so good. Using the methodology described, the domain expert rather than the technically oriented computing professional, can define business and application scenarios. Domain experts also can define functional requirements for applications, application interoperations, or scenarios in terms of attributes and attribute values.

The next step, in Phase Four Step 4, is to map the attributes and attribute values to implementable services. The infrastructure team performs this mapping. The services which require standards are then determined. In Phase Five of the DOSEE methodology, these services will be mapped to standards that provide the openness so disparate systems can interoperate, port, and scale.

Mapping from attributes and attribute values to services and standards generally requires varying degrees of standards knowledge, and/or access to a database of standards. As will be seen in Chapter 6 on standards, databases of standards are available from different organizations on CD-ROM or via commercial on-line services. Searches of such databases, however, can be lengthy and expensive.

To narrow the search fields, rather than map from attributes and attribute values to standards, a two-step (at least) mapping process is recommended. With this process, the attributes and attribute values are first mapped to general service areas (described in the next section). The general service areas are then decomposed into implementable base services (also described shortly), for which standards and specifications can be defined. The base services are then mapped to *de jure* or *de facto* standards.

If open Client/Server planners or application experts have sufficient knowledge of the service areas that can be used to search for applicable standards, they can directly identify their service requirements. Alternatively, a series of questions can be developed to eliminate some service areas and identify others as relevant to an organization's application and interoperability needs. For example, a question that asks whether an application is a standalone one or is intended to exchange data with remote machines may either determine or eliminate the need to consider networking standards. Similarly, a question asking if an organization's applications need to exchange documents containing graphics or images may determine the need for graphics exchange or image exchange standards.

Chapter 7 contains further information about developing questions to help identify service requirements, along with examples of such questions. The DOSEE software tool accompanying this book shows how services requirements can be identified both directly (including by selecting service requirements from a predefined list of service areas) and through a series of questions defined for this purpose. A comprehensive series of questions to identify general service areas and specific base-level service requirements in the general service area of data interchange is also included.

Map Attribute Values to General Service Areas

In the first step for mapping from attributes and attribute values to implementable service areas, the infrastructure team maps the attributes and attribute values to general service areas. General service areas are top-level functionality areas. Examples are communications/networking, data interchange, data management, distributed computing, graphics, human–computer interfaces, operating system services, system management, security, and software development.

The number and definition of the proper and most useful general service areas is an open question. Common sense is the best guide to deciding the general service areas, along with an estimation of where, and under what subject headings, *de facto* or *de jure* standards information about these service areas is normally found.

Map General Service Areas to Base Service Areas

In the next step for mapping from attributes and attribute values to implementable service requirements, open Client/Server planners further map the identified attributes and attribute values into subareas of the general service areas (called *base services*). Unlike broad-based general service areas, base services tend to explicitly state a service requirement. Base services often form the scope for standards work, and sometimes are equivalent to the name of a standard.

Interactive text retrieval, character sets, font information exchange, and still-image compression are some examples of base services that fall under the general service area of data interchange. Remote procedure call (RPC), local and distributed directory services, local network protocols, and data dictionary are examples of base service areas that fall under the general service areas of distributed computing, networking, and data management.

As was the case with the general service areas, the best guide to deciding which base service areas to use is common sense, and an estimation of what the right name or key word is to search to obtain information on specific base services and associated standards. Base service areas should be defined so they can be used as an index into an on-line database to obtain the most useful information in the least expensive manner.

Sometimes, Define a Mid-Level Service Area, Too

Sometimes a general service area is so broad that further subdividing the general service area into mid-level service areas makes it easier to think about service requirements. A *mid-level service area* is simply a classification of a service requirement area that is less generic than a general service area but more generic than a base service area.

Figure 5.4 shows one way to classify the general service area of communications/networking into mid-level service areas. Communications and networking services can be broadly classified into low-level communications services, high-level network protocols, networking applications, networking APIs, and distributed computing services (also known as *middleware*). Distributed computing services can also be considered a general service area.

The services described within each mid-level category described in Figure 5.4, such as media access, data link services, file transfer, virtual terminal, transparent distributed file access, and message queuing services are base services.

Low-Level Interoperability

Low-level interoperability services control the network hardware, the media access method, and the low-level routing, error correction, and addressing services and protocols for local- and wide-area networks. Low-level protocols include the protocols for OSI Model Layers 1 through 4. Examples are 802.3, 802.4, 802.5, X.25, FDDI, the OSI Data Link and Network services, and OSI and TCP/IP Network and Transport services. Other examples of low-level interoperability services are ISDN, Broadband ISDN, and T1 networking.

High-Level Networking Protocols

High-level protocols include the services and protocols for layers 5 through 7 of the OSI Model (i.e., Session, Presentation, and Application layer protocols such as the Association Control Service Element (ACSE), and Remote Operations Service Element (ROSE)).

Network Applications

Network applications include network services and protocols that use ACSE and ROSE services. Such services and protocols include file transfer (e.g., FTP and FTAM), virtual terminal (Telnet and VT), network management, message handling, ISO Commitment, Concurrency and Recovery (CCR) (2-Phase commit), security and the distributed transaction processing protocol.

Networking APIs

Although APIs to the various networking services are commonly thought of as promoting portability, rather than interoperability, API implementation details can affect interoperability. If it is desired to include APIs (e.g., to FTAM, X.400 Message Handling, X.500 Directory Services) among an organization's identified interoperability service requirements, these APIs should be included either among the high-level interoperability or middleware services.

Figure 5.4 Mid-level service areas for communications/networking. (Continued)

The major differences between the diverse networking and communications areas would make the process of searching for service requirements and standards information time consuming and expensive unless the general service area of networking and communications is subdivided into smaller areas. The same principle also holds true for many other general service areas.

Mid-level service areas for data management might include basic data management services, data dictionary, and transaction processing. Mid-level service areas for human–computer interfaces might include keyboard services, low-level windowing services, a window management API, and a user interface's look and feel.

Distributing Computing Services (Middleware)

Middleware is a new class of software that enables or facilitates networked client-server connections. Middleware is most often concerned with either transparent application-to-application communications or application-to-remote database access and update. Middleware is one of the cornerstones of distributed client-server computing and needs to be planned for in the same manner as low- and high-level networking.

Middleware encompasses a variety of functions and technologies needed to successfully implement and use open distributed systems. Middleware services include:

- Transparent Distributed File Access;
- Remote Procedure Call (RPC);
- Message Queuing Services;
- Directory Services;
- Global Naming Services;
- SQL (Structured Query Language) for Relational Database Systems;
- Data Translation Software (to translate between different data representations, and/or to convert source SQL into a target data-manipulation language);
- Remote Data Access Services;
- Distributed Transaction Manager;
- Object Management Services;
- Standardized APIs to be used by applications to access the middleware software.

Middleware resides between the networking software and application or database software (hence, the name middleware). If it did not exist, application developers would need to write their applications and Client/Server functions directly to network protocol primitives. This is a difficult, tedious, error-prone job that requires a large amount of expertise in networking and communications. Consequently, a lack of middleware, and middleware tools to facilitate the use of middleware, would greatly hinder the use of Client/Server computing.

Example of middleware standards and specifications are OSF's DCE (Distributed Computing Environment), the SQL Access Group's and X/Open's Remote Data Access (RDA) and Call Level Interface (CLI), the Object Management Group's (OMG's) Common Object Request Broker Architecture (CORBA), X/Open's XA, XA+, and TX Transaction Processing Interfaces; Transarc's Encina Transaction Manager, Microsoft's Open Database Connectivity (ODBC) Specification, and IEEE P1326 Common Object Services for X.400 and X.500: C Binding.

Figure 5.4   Mid-level service areas for communications/networking (Continued).

Generate an Interoperability Services Matrix

In determining interoperability and application-portability services, the infrastructure team should generate, for different departments, two sets of matrices similar to the interoperability matrices described earlier in this chapter. One set of matrices should show application-interoperations versus interoperability-service requirements. The other set should show the applications themselves versus their service requirements. In both sets of matrices, the service requirements means the specific base service.

The application-interoperation versus interoperability-services matrices should list application interoperations on the vertical axis of the matrix, and the interoperability service requirements on the horizontal axis. The application interoperations listed should be those previously identified in the interoperability matrices, and for which attributes and attribute values were subsequently defined.

Table 5.8 shows an application-interoperations versus interoperability-services matrix generated for the consulting company whose application-interaction attributes and values were shown earlier. The matrix shows only a subset of the company's application interoperations, and a subset of the services the interoperations require.

Table 5.8   Phase Four: Infrastructure Planning Tasks

CONSULTING DEPT. APPLICATION INTEROPERATIONS & SERVICES (Subset)

Application Interoperations	Network Transport	Message Handling	Dist. File Access	Data Access Language	Remote Data Access	Spreadsheet Exchange	Graphics Exchange	Page Description Language	Printer Queuing	Global Directory Services	Global Naming Services	Remote Procedure Call	Character Set Exchange	Security: Authentication	Internationalization	Object Linking	Modem Svc.	Time Svc.
WP--Spreadsheet	✓	—	✓	—	—	✓	✓	✓	—	✓	—	—	✓	✓	✓	✓	✓	—
Presentation Graphics--WP	✓	—	✓	—	—	✓	✓	✓	—	✓	—	—	✓	✓	✓	✓	✓	—
Data Mgmt.--WP	✓	✓	✓	✓	✓	✓	—	—	—	✓	✓	✓	✓	✓	✓	—	✓	✓
WP--Plain Paper Printing	✓	—	—	—	—	—	—	✓	✓	✓	✓	—	—	—	—	—	—	—
Document Mgt.--WP	—	—	✓	—	—	✓	✓	✓	—	✓	—	✓	✓	✓	✓	—	✓	✓
Email--Remote Email	✓	✓	—	—	—	✓	✓	✓	—	—	—	—	—	✓	✓	—	✓	✓

Key: ✓ = Uses or Requires

There are many more interoperability services than are shown in this matrix. Security alone encompasses numerous services, for example, password checking, authentication, authorization, access control lists, auditing services, and more. There also are numerous types of internationalization services, graphics exchange services (e.g., for 2-D graphics, 3-D graphics), and more. In addition, compression services are needed for the transport of large high-volume files, and numerous network and system management services are needed to keep a network and its attached nodes up and running. These are not included here.

The second set of matrices generated—the applications versus services matrices—is used not only to visualize and present the identified service requirements, but is also used to determine which services are common to multiple applications, and which services are required by applications that run on multiple size and class platforms. In this way, portability and scalability targets will be determined.

While determining service requirements, open Client/Server planners should reexamine the prose sheets and questionnaires generated during the Phase Three interviews and surveys. If the planners discover any service requirements mentioned in these interview summaries and questionnaires that are omitted from the attributes-attribute values tables, these service requirements should be added to other implementable service requirements. The infrastructure team should then define an attribute and set of possible attribute values to characterize this requirement so that it is not omitted in the future.

Determine Portability Targets

In Phase Four Step 5, the infrastructure team determines the areas for which portability and/or scalability might be issues. Scalability is actually portability across differently scaled or sized computers. To determine the portability/scalability targets, generate a portability/scalability matrix. A portability/scalability matrix is an applications versus service requirements matrix used to show areas where portability is important (Figure 5.5).

Generate a Portability/Scalability Services Matrix

A portability matrix shows the applications used in each department versus the services required by these applications. The applications, shown on the vertical axis of the matrix, should be the ones identified earlier in the interoperability matrices and the Phase Two activities versus applications matrix, and shown in the application attribute and attribute values tables. The services shown on the horizontal axis of the matrix should be the ones determined by mapping attributes and attribute values to services. As was the case with the interoperability services matrices, the service requirements in the portability matrices refers to specific base-level services. Separate sets of matrices should be generated to show applications versus services for existing and for planned or desired systems.

For each functional area (e.g., department, division) in an organization, identify the services that are common to the applications used within the functional area. These are the services for which portability and/or scalability may be desired.

Generate two sets of matrices showing applications (or systems or other functional components) on the vertical axis and the services required by these applications, etc. on the horizontal axis. One set of matrices should represent existing systems. The other set should represent planned or desired systems.

Make a check in every box indicating a service required by a functional component.

Count, or otherwise note, the areas where services are common to multiple applications and departments.

Figure 5.5   Phase Four Step 5: Determining portability and scalability targets.

Table 5.9 shows an applications versus service requirements portability/scalability matrix generated for the example consulting and analysis department of the consulting company. The matrix shows only a subset of applications used by the consulting department and a subset of the services they require.

The checkmarks in the table represent services required by the applications. For example, electronic mail requires a message-handling service. Data management requires a data access/manipulation language (a 4GL), forms-handling services, and network services. Word processing and document management both require services and formats to handle graphics and spreadsheet exchange. Additionally, document management requires a specialized interactive text search-and-retrieval language.

Columns that contain many checks indicate a software service used by many applications. A count of the number of services common to various applications within multiple functional areas provides some quantitative idea of the need for common services.

Intuitively, a service area with a high checkmark count is a potential target for portability, but this is not the only criterion for choosing portability targets. For example, what if many applications require a particular service, but all of them are games? Even if multiple legitimate business applications require a particular service, portability of these applications may not be critical. On the other hand, a service may be used by only a few applications, but those applications may be critical to the organization.

The portability/scalability matrix shows the various functionality services needed so that applications are portable across similar systems from different vendors (e.g., IBM's AIX and HP's HP-UX. systems). The matrix also indicates scalability targets.

Table 5.9   Determining Portability/Scalability Targets
Source: Emerging Technologies Group.

CONSULTING DEPT. APPLICATIONS & SERVICES (Subset)

Applications ↓   Services →

Applications	Character Sets	Document Interchange	2-D Graphics	Graphics Import/Exch.	Text Search/Retrieval	Hypertext Data Exchange	Spreadsheet Exch.	Image Interchange	Database Access Language.	Forms Handling	Page Desc. Language	Still Image Compression	Video Compression	Printer Queuing	Operating System	Authentication	GUI API
Word Processing	✓	✓	✓	✓	✓	✓				✓	✓	✓		✓	✓	✓	✓
E-Mail										✓	✓	✓		✓	✓	✓	✓
Database Mgmt.	✓				✓		✓	✓				✓		✓	✓	✓	✓
Data Query	✓							✓	✓			✓		✓	✓	✓	✓
Document Mgmt.	✓	✓	✓	✓	✓	✓	✓	✓		✓	✓	✓		✓	✓	✓	✓
Spreadsheet	✓		✓	✓			✓				✓	✓		✓	✓	✓	✓
Presentation Graphics	✓		✓	✓			✓				✓	✓		✓	✓	✓	✓
Plain Paper Printing											✓			✓	✓		✓
Calendaring														✓	✓	✓	✓

Key: ✓ = Uses or Requires

Scalability targets refer to the various functional services needed by a single application that needs to run on different size and class platforms (e.g., desktop workstations and workgroup servers in a remote site, a mid-size server in another department, and a large minicomputer or multiprocessor at headquarters). The goal of making the application's services portable to different size platforms is to help ensure that the application itself is portable to such differently scaled platforms. In open systems parlance, the ability to port an application to different size and class platforms is known as *scalability*. Scalability is important because if the same application runs on platforms ranging from PCs to workstations, servers, minicomputers, and so on, users and programmers need learn just one version of the application.

Users who claim not to care about portability because they are committed to buying from only one vendor should realize that the importance of portability applies to single vendor environments. Portability is important to scalability. There are many instances whereby users not only had heterogeneous size and class computers from the same vendors at different sites, but had three terminals on their desk, each attached to three different computers—all three from the same vendor. Planners should consider scalability when quantitatively or qualitatively determining the need for, and importance of, portable services.

Programmer portability is also an important portability service consideration. It may be necessary to modify applications frequently. If the services required by these applications are not standardized, not only must the application be reprogrammed for different machines, but some of the changes made will ripple throughout other systems in the organization, thereby necessitating changes to still other platforms.

If a few applications that run on multiple platforms must be modified frequently, the software services required by these applications might be a higher priority portability target than a service which is casually used by many highly stable applications that rarely change, run on the same platform, and rarely need reporting.

In some cases, there may be no standards available or in progress for a service. Therefore, portability for this particular service is a moot point.

The priorities of different services to departments in an organization is usually determined by surveys. Priority determination surveys are part of the Phase Five planning steps. Meanwhile, counting the number of different applications that require a particular service adds a quantitative criterion to the subjective ones. This count can be a help in justifying decisions.

In developing the portability matrices, beware of a tendency to fill in almost every box with checkmarks just because applications are related to services in many ways. For example, many users use their electronic-mail systems and networks to transmit database data, text, graphics, and spreadsheets. The users' electronic-mail system and networks need to be able to handle these documents. However, database-management systems, word-processing programs, graphics packages, and spreadsheets do not need electronic mail or distributed-file access in order to operate. Therefore, electronic mail is not a required portable service for a word processing or spreadsheet application.

The ability of electronic mail and distributed-file access programs to transmit various kinds of computerized data and information is determined in the interoperability matrix. Thus, interoperability relationships should not be checked in a portability matrix, the purpose of which is to identify portability targets.

Terminology can be a problem in developing the portability matrices. For example, many people assume that a fourth-generation language (4GL) is a high-level Englishlike programming language specialized for database applications. But there are other ideas on this subject. For example, are the languages specialized for writing spreadsheets and word-processing macros examples of 4GLs? Some people think they are. Similarly, some users claim that the Sendmail language used to configure UNIX-based UUCP electronic mail systems is a 4GL. Clearly, it is important for the matrix to be specific (e.g., database 4GL, other 4GLs).

Still another problem in arriving at a single set of rules for developing a portability matrix occurs, for example, because some word-processing, spreadsheet, and graphics folks insist that backup and restore are essential capabilities that must be checked off in the portability matrix, while other such users treat backup very casually. Those users who have previously run into a problem with incompatible backup systems would not consider any hardware or software system that did not provide backup, restore, and archiving capabilities in a portable manner.

The point is that it is not always clear what a required service is. Services that one company requires for certain applications may be considered irrelevant to the same application in another organization. If users in a company consider a particular service to be an important consideration, it should be included. Modifications can always be made later.

Updating the Portability/Interoperability Database

The services and application interaction information extracted from the portability and interoperability matrices should be added to the open Client/Server planning database created in Phase Two of the planning process. When the Phase Four information is added, the database should now list the application, the services required for that application, the interactions between the application in question and other applications, and the interoperability services required for such interactions.

The attributes and attribute values can also be stored for reference purposes in case of future questions concerning the definition of certain services. Counts of the commonality of services for different applications, as well as counts of the number of interactions between each application and others, can also be included in the database.

Table 5.10 shows a sample subset of a database of application, services, and interaction information gathered during the open Client/Server planning process. Some of the applications and services were listed in the consulting company's portability and interoperability matrices shown earlier. Others (e.g., authentication, authorization, and RPC services, and a mathematics application) were not listed because of space limitations. These are real applications and services, however, used in the consulting environment that is the source for the activities, applications, portability, and interoperability matrices, and the attribute and attribute tables, shown in this chapter and in earlier planning process phases.

Mapping Service Requirements onto an Architecture

The last step in identifying portability and interoperability service components is to map the service components identified onto the architecture previously defined for the organization. Figure 5.6 shows Alcoa's mapping of its portability and interoperability components onto its architectural framework.

Note that this architectural framework is only a subset of Alcoa's open systems architecture. The actual architecture consists of a declaration of the principles and the delineation of the major components of information systems, the relationships

Table 5.10   Preliminary Portability/Interoperability Database (Subset)

Application	Portability/ Scalability Services	# of Applications Requiring the Service	Interactions	Interoperability Services	# of Applications Using this Service
Word Processing	Character Sets	6	Data Mgmt.	Transport	5
	Document Interchange	2	Document Mgmt.	MHS	2
	2-D Graphics	4	Spreadsheet	Dist. File Access	4
	Graphics Import/ Exchange	4	Presentation Graphics	Graphics Exchange Spreadsheet Exchange	4 5
	Spreadsheet Exchange	5		Page Description	5
	Image Exchange	2		Language	
	Page Description	6		Global Directory Service	5
	Language			Authentication	5
	Still Image	3		Internationalization	5
	Compression			Object Linking	2
	Video Compress.	2		Modem Services	5
	Operating System	9		Time Services	3
	Authentication	8			
	GUI API	9			
E-Mail	Page Description	6	Word Processing	Transport	5
	Language		Presentation	MHS	2
	Still Image	3	Graphics	Graphics Exchange	4
	Compression		Mathematics	Spreadsheet Exchange	5
	Video Compression	2	Calendaring	Equation Format	1
	Operating System	9	Remote E-Mail	Math Symbols	1
	Authentication	8		Authentication	5
	GUI API	9		Internationalization	5
				Modem Services	5
				Time Service	3
Data Query	Character Sets	6	Word Processing	Transport	5
	Database Access	2	Spreadsheet	Message Handling	2
	Language		Printing	Dist. File Access	4
	Forms Handling	2		RPC	2
	Printer Queuing	8		Data Access Language	1
	Operating System	9		Remote Data Access	1
	Authentication	8		Spreadsheet Exchange	5
	GUI API	9		Global Directory Service	5
				Global Naming Service	2
				Authentication	5
				Internationalization	4
				Modem Services	5
				Time Services	3

Source: Emerging Technologies Group.

Functional Components

System Developer   System User   System Manager

Areas where standards are most important to INTEROPERABILITY are boxed

Dotted Outlines denote possible Future Issues

Areas where standards are most important to PORTABILITY are ovaled

4. Sys. Dev

4.1. Upper Case tools (Modelers)
4.2. Lower Case Tools (Code Generators & Analyzers)
4.3. Code and Specification Libraries (Repositories)
4.3.1. General Models (Business, organization, process)
4.3.2. Specifications/ Documentation
4.3.3. Source Code
4.3.4. Intermediate Code
4.3.5. Target (Object) Code
4.3.6. Dictionary and Directory
4.4. Editors
4.5. String manipulators (grep)
4.6. Compiler compilers
4.7. Compilers, Languages, Linkers/Loaders
4.7.1. For System & Util. SW
4.7.2. For Bsns SW
4.7.3. For Scient & Eng. SW
4.8. Conversion Tools, Reverse Engineering
4.9. Debuggers, Testers
4.9.1. Test Data Generators
4.9.2. Resource & Performance measurement
4.9.3. Code monitors, halt, patch, etc
4.10. DBMS development aids: DDL and DML
4.10.1. Graphic Data Structure support
4.10.2. Automatic Process Generation (Lower Case option)
4.11. Object Oriented Prog.
4.12. RPC PreCompiler
4.13. Sys Mgmt Precompiler
4.14. GUI PreCompiler

Hi-Lvl Library

5.1.1. Language Run Time
5.1.2. OS Access Libraries
5.1.3. Application libraries/EDI
5.1.4. Command Languages and Shells
5.1.5. Security tools (User invoked)
5.1.5.1. Protect (access control) commands
5.1.5.2. Encrypt decrypt tools,
5.1.5.3. Client/Server "key" exchange tools
5.1.6. PCS Tools (e.g. SETCON)
5.1.7. Artificial Intelligence Tools
5.1.7.1. Rules Evaluation Based
5.1.7.2. Frames and Rules
5.1.7.3. Neural Networks
5.1.7.4. Other AI
5.1.8. Graphics Libraries

8. Applications

5. Tools & Utilities

Application

Data
5.2.1. DBMS
5.2.2. TP Monitor
5.2.3. Data Conversion
5.2.3.1. Character Code
5.2.3.2. Bitmap to text
5.2.3.3. Graphics
5.2.4. Sorting
5.2.5. File Archival
5.2.6. Record Systems
5.2.7. SQL I'face Tools (DM Middleware)

Network
5.3.1. Distributed TP
5.3.2. Network File Transfer
5.3.3. Network File Access
5.3.4. PC File Access
5.3.5. Store & Forward (MTA)
5.3.6. Global Directory
5.3.7. Name Service/Dir.
5.3.8. Virtual Terminal
5.3.9. Client server GUI
5.3.10. PCS/PLC and Robotics
5.3.11. Other OSI
5.3.12. General Client server tools
5.3.13. Time Services
5.3.14. Dial up tools
5.3.15. Terminal Management
5.3.16. Terminal Emulation
5.3.17. Remote Procedure Calls
5.3.18. Other non-OSI
5.3.18.1 Legacy E-Mail Gateway
5.3.19. FAX Service

6. Application Support & End User Tools

Personal Productivity
6.2.1. Integrated Office
6.2.2. Word Processing
6.2.3. OfficeGraphics
6.2.4. Spread sheets
6.2.5. Personal File/Database
6.2.6. Presentation
6.2.7. Desktop Publishing

Group Productivity
6.3.1. E-Mail (UA)
6.3.2. Electronic Meeting
6.3.3. Conferencing
6.3.4. Bulletin Board Systems
6.3.5. Calendaring Systems
6.3.6. Departmental Database
6.3.7. Group Visualization
6.3.8. Concurrent Co-Authoring Packages
6.3.9. Workflow Routing and Tracking (via forms)

Info Mgmt
6.4.1. SQL Access Utilities
6.4.2.4 GL's & Query Languages
6.4.3. Decision Support
6.4.4. Document Management
6.4.5. Document Management with full text retrieval
6.4.6. Document Management with imaging
6.4.7. Easy Info Finders
6.4.7.1. Pub/Sub
6.4.8. Hypertext

Tech/ Eng/Sci
6.5.1. Project Management
6.5.2. CAD/CAM
6.5.2.1. 2-D modelers
6.5.2.2. 3-D modelers
6.5.2.3. Solid Modelers
6.5.3. Formula Processors
6.5.4. Statistics
6.5.5. Modeling & Simulation

User I/F
5.4.1. Screen/Forms Systems
5.4.2. High Level GUI libraries
5.4.3. Low Level GUI libraries
5.4.4. Menu Systems
5.4.5. Multimedia I/O Libraries
5.4.6. Print Management Spooling, distribution
5.4.7. Print Forms manager

7. Sys. Mgt

7.1. Operator Interface
7.2. Performance Management
7.2.1. Hardware error monitoring
7.2.2. Network monitoring
7.2.3. Current resource use by task/user
7.2.4. System tuning controls
7.3. Peripheral management
7.3.1. Disk Resource Management
7.3.1.1. Utilization reporting
7.3.1.2. Space recovery mechanism
7.3.1.3. File system reorg (Defrag)
7.3.1.4. Backup/Restore
7.3.1.5. File/Disk patching
7.3.1.6. File System Maintenance (e.g. Norton, defrag)
7.3.2. Tape Management
7.4. Database Operations
7.4.1. Key rebuilds and other physical restructure
7.4.2. Database backup/restore
7.4.3. Database patching
7.4.4. DBMS performance management
7.5. Network Management
7.6. Problem Tracking and Management
7.7. Capacity Planning
7.7.1. Workload Simulator
7.8. Software Installation and Distribution
7.8.1. for System software
7.8.2. for Utility software
7.8.3. for Applications
7.9. Accounting and Billing
7.10. Security and Access Control (Also see Tools for security) modules
7.10.1. Security administration modules
7.10.2. User Security tools support
7.10.3. Security Monitoring
7.11. Configuration Management
7.12. Print Management
7.13. Startup/Bootup

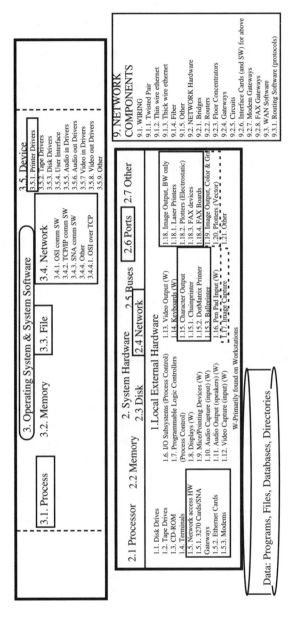

Figure 5.6 Alcoa computer reference model functional components. Source: Alcoa.

111

between them, and the standards and guidelines for their selection, integration, and application.

The numbers in the functional components diagram are Alcoa's reference numbers for various functional components beginning with local basic hardware and local basic software, and proceeding upward in numbers through tools and network components.

The reference numbers begin with 1.X for local external hardware. They proceed through a set of 2.X numbers, which represent system hardware such as processors, memory, disks, network hardware, system busses, and ports.

The reference numbers 3.X, 5.X, and 6.X indicate the operating system, system software such as database systems, communications and networking software, tools and utilities, application support, and tools that are used directly by end users. The 4.X and 7.X reference numbers indicate system-development and system-management tools that are used by specialized system developers and managers and may reside on different platforms. Finally, the 9.X numbers indicate networking hardware.

The boxes around certain functional components indicate functional areas where the standards needed are most important to interoperability. The ovals surrounding certain functional components indicate functional areas where the standards needed are most important to portability. Note that, in many cases, the functional components and standards important to interoperability and to portability overlap.

Making the Infrastructure Open

In this chapter, we determined application interoperability and portability functional requirements, and mapped these requirements to implementable services. How to map these services to standards and ensure that these services are implemented in the most open, practical manner possible, while also providing the required functionality, are covered in the following chapters.

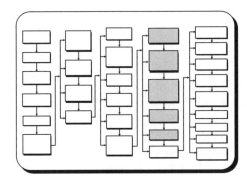

Chapter 6

Phase Five: Standards Selection and Prioritization

Introduction

Now that we have determined the functional components required for our open-systems environment, it's time to determine the importance of the functional components (often called *services*), identify standards that support these services, and then determine the importance, completeness, and practicality of the standards.

Overview of the Standards Selection Process

The determination of the services (functional components) and of the number of applications that need these services for interoperability or portability was done using the interoperability and portability matrices described in the last chapter. But the number of applications that require particular interoperability or portability services is only one measure of a service's importance. This metric is not always valid, since an application may require certain interoperability or portability services, but the application may not be very important to the organization. To determine the real importance of services and applications, it is necessary to ask the managers of departments using the applications, normally done through surveys.

Determination of service requirements is necessary, but not sufficient, to achieve interoperability, portability, and scalability in a heterogenous, multivendor environment. To implement heterogeneous, multivendor interoperability, portability, and scalability, the services must be available in a standardized manner. Therefore, standards—both formal and *de facto*—must be identified. The initial identification of standards for the services indicated by the portability and interoperability matrices is usually done by the architecture/infrastructure groups.

Once the applicable standards are identified, which of them to choose may not be a straightforward matter. In some cases, multiple standards may provide interoperability (e.g., OSI and TCP/IP) or portability (e.g., ISO RDA or X/Open RDA for Remote Data Access). Some choices may be more important to an organization's interoperability and/or portability than another. Some standards may be more functional or more accepted by vendors and/or users than others. Some may have gaps and deficiencies that render the standards useless for portability or interoperability until the gaps are filled. In other cases, there may be simple workarounds to fill the gaps or overcome the deficiencies.

Determining which standards are most important to various applications' interoperability and portability and which applications are most important to an organization is generally done by asking the managers of departments that use the applications. As is the case in determining the importance of functional services, determining the importance of standards is also done through surveys. Subsequent standards selection tasks, like determining which of the standards rated highly by users are most practical to use, should be done by the architecture/infrastructure groups, generally the staff with the greatest knowledge of standards.

Because the standards selected for implementation must be available in products and also must fit with the organization's Client/Server strategy, inclusion of the organization's deployment groups in the standards selection process can save time and avoid problems during the deployment stages of the open Client/Server environment. This will contribute to the open distributed environment's success.

The overall method for determining the usage, importance, and practicality of services and standards is shown in the flowchart in Figure 6.1. The flowchart begins with the interoperability and portability services identified in the interoperability and portability matrices, and goes through the identification of applicable standards. The flowchart also shows the determination of the most important services and standards through surveys of department managers/users. Finally, it shows the identification of the most practical standards that are available in products, or will be available in the short term.

The "S" numbers (e.g., S1, S12) represent the different steps in the standards selection process. Twenty-one steps are shown in this diagram, but many could be divided into substeps, or combined.

The shaded circles represent dead ends because of unsuitable standards or services. They may not, however, be the only dead ends. The process for determining whether a particular standard should be required could come to a halt at any step if the infrastructure group determines that a particular standard is not practical.

The standards that make it through the flowchart to Step 21 are those that should be considered as potential procurement requirements. Bear in mind, however, that even if a standard reaches Step 21, there will likely be some intraorganization disagreements about the standards' importance. Standards may be practical in some ways, but not in others. More likely, they will be almost, but not quite, sufficiently functional without some vendor-added capabilities.

The chances of making a wise and more objective decision can be enhanced by assigning numerical importance and practicality values to each step. At some point,

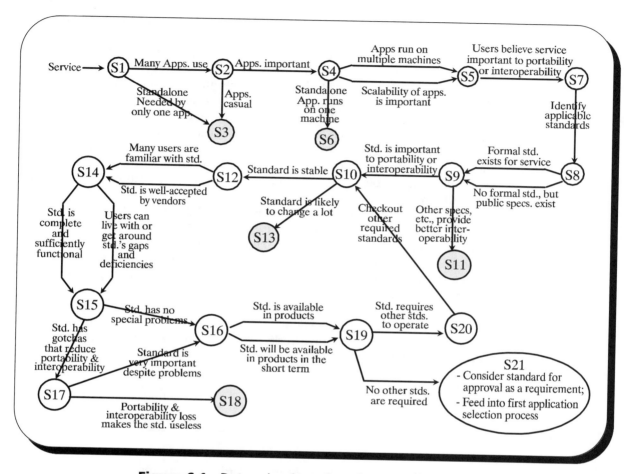

Figure 6.1 Determination of applicable standards. *Source: Emerging Technologies Group.*

however, standards decisions will be influenced by subjective criteria, which will include nontechnical as well as technical factors. Examples of technical decision-making criteria are the applicability of standards to planned Client/Server applications and the availability of tools that work with the standards. Nontechnical decision-making factors include cost, training, and vendor preferences (not all standards will be available and/or sufficiently functional, from all vendors).

Identifying Standards

In Phase Four, attribute-attribute value tables and interoperability and portability matrices were used to determine the services required by applications and the targeted areas for interoperability and portability. In Phase Five Step 1, standards that might provide the required interoperability and portability are identified (Figure 6.2).

Lists of standards are available from standards organizations. In the United States, ISO standards can be obtained from ISO (in Geneva, Switzerland), ANSI, which is the U.S. representative to ISO, the National Institute of Standards and Technology (NIST), and various Department of Defense (DOD) publications. The *IEEE P1003.0 Guide to a POSIX Open System Environment* includes a list of the most important standards in the major functional areas. Professional publications, such as the ACM Special Interest Group Publications, also are a standards reference source. In addition, various vendors and consultants who track standards have up-to-date lists of standards and profiles. See Appendix B for further information about the major standards groups.

Many of the standards organizations (e.g., ANSI, IEEE, NIST, X/Open) have made abstracts and the full text of their standards available on CD-ROM and/or in commercial on-line databases. To be useful, and not overwhelming, these standards databases must be used with a good text-search program. Such a program must facilitate searching, cross-referencing, indexing, abstracting, and retrieving to build suitable databases for an organization's use.

It is helpful for an organization to establish and maintain its own database of standards, which can be updated and used for reference. It also can be used in future open Client/Server planning work; for example, in determining implementation priorities for different standards.

Determine the formal, consortia, industry, and *de facto* standards that exist for a particular service that has been deemed of interest.

Establish a company database of standards that can be used for reference and for other open Client/Server planning work.

Choose standards according to a preference hierarchy, where international or other formal standards get first priority, public-domain specifications (e.g., industry and consortia specifications) maintained by a consensus process are selected only if no formal standards are available, and vendor products are chosen only as a last resort.

Map standards onto the architecture developed earlier, in the Phase Three architectural tasks.

Figure 6.2 Phase Five Step 1: Identify the standards and specifications needed.

Identifying Standards Using a Standards Database

If Client/Server planners use a well-organized and documented on-line standards database, the process of mapping from attributes and attribute values to services, and from services to standards can be partly, or mostly, automated. One example of a well-organized and documented standards database is the Information Technology Standards Guidance (ITSG) database from the U.S. Defense Information Systems Agency (DISA). The ITSG provides guidance for a large number of formal standards and some consortia specifications (e.g., X/Open's) required for U.S. Government procurements.

To provide standards guidance, the ITSG is organized into sections and tables identifying the standards, sponsor, reference, and status in each functional area. Other explanatory ITSG text lists and discusses related standards, gaps, deficiencies, interoperability and portability caveats, and so on, and provides the rationale for its included information.

Figure 6.3 is a partial extract from the ITSG's data-management standards section and illustrates how the DISA ITSG provides standards guidance. The entire ITSG is part of a much larger DISA open-systems–planning document called the Technical Architecture Framework for Information Management (TAFIM).

Another comparably organized and documented standards database is the Distributed Open Systems Environment Engineering (DOSEE) standards databases from Emerging Technologies Group (Dix Hills, NY). The DOSEE standards databases is designed for commercial as well as government requirements. It takes into account *de facto* and commercial standards, in addition to formal standards and consortia specifications. The data-interchange section from the DOSEE standards database is provided in the software accompanying this book, along with a demonstration application module that shows how to use the database to help automate the standards-mapping process. Further information on using and/or automating the open Client/Server planning process and using the standards database is provided in Chapter 7.

Both the ITSG and the DOSEE standards databases are divided in several parts, each representing a major service area such as data management, data interchange, user interface, graphics, networking, software development, security, operating system services, system management, and distributed computing. A series of questions can be used to eliminate the need to examine any of the standards in some of these sections.

Consider, for example, the question, "Does the application require the creation or manipulation (not display) of drawings or pictures?" If the answer is no, it indicates that graphics capabilities are not needed, and the section on graphics can be ignored. Similarly, a "no" answer to the question, "Do you plan to develop your own applications (rather than purchase them)?" indicates that the section on software-development standards can be ignored. On the other hand, if the answer is "yes" to the question, "Do any of your applications require the long-term storage of structured data (i.e., database data) rather than having all information processed and passed on?" it indicates that the section on data-management standards is rele-

4.0 Data Management Services

Data management service standards provide (1) database management services for accessing and modifying structured data, (2) data dictionary services for accessing/modifying data about data (i.e., metadata), and (3) distributed data services for accessing/modifying data from a remote database.

4.1 Data Definition, Manipulation, and Query

Data definition includes create, alter, and delete tables, views, records, fields, classes, objects, instances, attributes, and data. Data manipulation includes insert, select, update, and delete tables, views, records, fields, classes, objects, instances, attributes, and data. Data query allows the specification of search conditions containing combinations of select lists, predicates, and comparison operators.

4.1.1 Standards

Table 7.4-1 presents standards for data definition, manipulation and query services.

Table 4-1
Data Definition, Manipulation, and Query

Std. Type	Standard	Sponsor	Std. Reference	Status
Formal	SQL-2 (Replaces SQL:1989)	ISO	9075.2	IS
Formal	Database Language SQL (Same as ANSI X3.135-1989)	ISO	9075:1989	IS
Formal	NDL (Network Data Language)	ISO ANSI	8907:1987 X3.133-1986	IS Std.
Gov't	SQL-2-Based FIPS	NIST	FIPS 127-2	Mandatory late '93
Gov't	Database Language SQL (ANSI X3.135-1989 & X3.168-1989)	NIST	FIPS 127-1	FIPS: 1990
Emerging	SQL-3	ISO	9075.3	CD (IS: 199x)
Emerging	SQL 3-Based FIPS	NIST	FIPS 127-3	Planned

Figure 6.3 DISA ITSG standards evaluation. *Source: DISA ITSG.*

4.1.2 Alternative Specifications

- Open Data Base Connectivity (ODBC) specification, published by Microsoft.
- Integrated Database Application Programming Interface (IDAPI), a draft specification, published by Borland, IBM, and Novell, to allow DOS, OS/2, Windows, & NT applications to access a variety of SQL and non-SQL databases.

4.1.3 Standards Deficiencies

- ISO/ANSI SQL:1989 and 1992 and NIST FIPS 127-1 and 127-2 are designed for stand-alone, single environment databases.
- Interactive SQL is specified by FIPS 127-1, but not by ISO/ANSI SQL:1989.
- There is no standardized way to specify logical database access control, which is important to database security.
- Hashing methods to access data is not currently standardized or in progress.

4.1.4 Portability and Interoperability Caveats

- The 1989 versions of ISO, ANSI, and FIPS SQL specify state exception code values (called SQLSTATE parameters) as "0" for successful execution, "100" for non-existent data, and "implementation-defined" for particular exception conditions. Different SQL-conformant products all have different SQLCODE values for exception conditions.
- The set of SQL character values for character data types and collating sequence of characters is defined by the implementor and, therefore, nonstandard in products.
- FIPS 127 specifies a number of sizing constraints for database constructs. Since these are implementation-defined in ISO/ANSI SQL, they differ in conforming ISO SQL products.
- ISO/ANSI Level 1 SQL is minimal, not testable, and disallowed by FIPS 127-1.
- SQL 2's segmentation into multiple levels increases the likelihood of incompatibility between different vendors' SQLs because different vendors will implement entry level SQL 2 and then choose options from other levels.

4.1.5 Related Standards

a. ISO International Standard (IS) 9579: Remote Database Access (Generic RDA) (supports remote database access in client-server environments)
b. ISO 9579-2 (SQL Specialization)
c. X/Open Remote Data Access (RDA) Preliminary Specification (Identical to the SQL Access Group's RDA Specification)
d. SQL Access Group's Call Level Interface (CLI) (Published as an X/Open specification)

Figure 6.3 DISA ITSG standards evaluation (Continued).

4.1.6 Recommendations

- SQL-conformant and FIPS 127-1-compliant products all contain non-standard, incompatible options. To ensure portability, both commercial and government organizations should specify and use the FIPS 127-1 optional flagger to flag the non-standard options so developers can write conforming code. The flagger option is not part of the ISO/ANSI SQL standard.
- Specify SQL 2 (and later SQL 3) as soon as possible because SQL2/3 contains greater standardized functionality than the 1989 SQL standard. This will reduce the use of non-standard extensions. SQL 2 also standardizes more than 60 SQLCODE exception condition values to indicate specific reasons that a database program failed, instead of just "0" to indicate an error occurred. These highly-specific SQLSTATE value allow databases and application programs running on different platforms to interoperate more reliably.
- Both commercial companies, as well as government organizations, worldwide should specify the NIST's Transition Level SQL 2 and the SQL Access Group's (SAG) RDA and CLI interfaces and protocols for the following reasons. Most DBMS vendors will not conform to the Full Level SQL 2 because the Full Level SQL 2 is very large and complex. As a result, the time it will take to add the necessary features will likely exceed the time before the SQL 3 standard is completed. To ensure portability and interoperability, as well as functionality, it is recommended that users include the following two specifications in their procurements:
  - NIST's Transition Level SQL 2 (specified in FIPS 127-2) because it is a hybrid of Entry Level and higher levels of SQL 2.
  - SAG's Call Level Interface (CLI) and Remote Data Access (RDA) standards. The SAG specifi-cations are not segmented into levels like SQL 2 and they offer a balance between Full Level SQL 2 features and what users need now. SAG specifications include connection management capabilities (which are part of SQL 2's Full Level), schema manipulation and the CHARACTER VARYING data type (both are in SQL 2's Intermediate Level), and features not included in any SQL 2 level, such as the CREATE INDEX and DROP INDEX statements. SAG's specifications are published jointly with X/Open as X/Open specifications.
- Avoid NDL, if possible, because it is little used and will not be upgraded. Proprietary languages dominate network database products.
- Explicitly check and/or specify all sizing constraints to meet functionality requirements and avoid portability and interoperability problems because these are not specified in the ISO standard. The NIST's FIPS 127-2 sizing specifications are reasonable, but are fairly minimal.
- Wherever possible, require the use of conformance tests and/or services to validate conformance to the SQL standard for both required and optional SQL 2 features. Testing applies only to a specific platform, so call for conformance tests for each platform of interest. Use the NIST-published quarterly list of FIPS-validated processors to help evaluate bids.

Figure 6.3 DISA ITSG standards evaluation (Continued).

vant to your organization and must be examined with a view to choosing the most applicable and practical standards.

Having determined that the data-management section of the standards database is relevant to your organization, the next step in selecting standards is to examine the various base service areas within the data-management section. It is not necessary to wade through standards in all of the many base-service areas subsections. Numerous base-service areas can be eliminated through questioning.

For example, a "yes" to the question, "Will you need to define, store, and modify data so that it can be searched (queried) and viewed in different ways?" indicates the need to examine, and select standards from, the base-service area "Data Definition, Manipulation, and Query." In contrast, suppose the open Client/System planner answered "no" to the questions, "Will the application perform operations on database data and/or transaction data across multiple sites concurrently, with the consequent need to ensure data integrity and consistency across all sites in the event of a network or computer failure?" and "Will the database require the storage of complex, nontraditional data, such as images, motion video, audio, and combinations of these data types?" This indicates that the organization is not, currently, planning a distributed database, distributed-transaction system, object-oriented database, or state-of-the-art repository system. Thus, these base-service areas can be eliminated from consideration.

A Preference Hierarchy for Selecting Standards

Both the ITSG and the DOSEE Standards Database include tables of standards applicable to the different base-service areas. For each standard, the tables include the type of standard (e.g., formal, government, emerging, consortia, *de facto* standards), the name of the standard, the sponsoring organization that approved the standard, the reference designation for the standard, and the standard's status.

To maximize multivendor interoperability and portability, organizations should give precedence to types of standards in the order shown in Figure 6.4, from most to least important. In Figure 6.4, Number 1 is the most important; Number 11 is the least.

The preference hierarchy says that, except for government agencies, which may have special considerations, any specification that exists as an international standard is preferred. If no such specification exists, the second choice will be any standard whose specification by an international standards body is in progress and nearing completion.

If no international standard exists or is in progress, the next choice is any specification that exists as a regional or national standard, or is in progress and nearing completion.

If no international or national standard exists or is in progress, the next precedence should be given to formal standards that feed into international and national standards groups, such as the IEEE, EIA, and ISA standards.

1. US Federal Government agencies only: U.S. Government Federal Information Processing Standards (FIPS), DoD standards, or other applicable mandated standards.
2. Approved international standards (e.g., ISO, CCITT)
3. International standards in progress
4. Regional standards (e.g., CEN/CENELEC in Europe) approved or in progress
5. Approved national formal standards (e.g., ANSI, X3)
6. National formal standards in progress
7. Professional group formal standards (e.g., IEEE) or trade association standards (e.g., EIA, ISA) that have a close relationship with international and/or national standards bodies.
8. Consortia specifications, which are determined by consensus (e.g., X/Open, OSF), and preferably specifications that have conformance tests
9. Industry standards, which are not determined by consensus but which are in the public domain (e.g., MIT X Windows, TCP/IP)
10. *De facto* standards, which are owned by a vendor, but are available on many vendors' platforms (e.g., DOS, UNIX, CICS, MS Windows)
11. Proprietary products

Figure 6.4 A preference hierarchy for selecting standards.

If no formal standards exist, to achieve portability and interoperability companies and organizations should consider consortia, industry, and *de facto* standards that have publicly available specifications and multiple implementation sources. Examples of publicly available specifications include OSF's Distributed Computing Environment (DCE), the Internet Protocol Suite (e.g., TCP/IP, FTP, SNMP), and MIT's X Window System. Where possible, specifications that are defined by a consensus process, and especially those which provide conformance tests (such as certain consortia specifications), should be given preference.

If no other choice is possible, any *de facto* standard may be a candidate specification. Finally, if all else fails, it may be necessary to choose a vendor's product, regardless of whether the product is proprietary.

Governments have some special considerations. These considerations, for example, could cause the U.S. Federal Information Processing Standards (FIPS) to take precedence over ISO or ANSI standards. The FIPS would then be followed by international standards and so on, in the order shown in the standards preference hierarchy.

There rarely is a conflict between ISO, ANSI, IEEE, and FIPS. Many ISO, ANSI, and IEEE standards are word-for-word identical. The few differences in the FIPS are usually due to the NIST choosing from among diverse options offered by the standards, and clarifying certain ambiguous areas in the standards.

For the U.S. Department of Defense (DoD), DoD standards take precedence over the ISO standards because the DoD standards and regulations are designed specifically for DoD needs. Because of DoD's nature, DoD standards and regulations must be designed for the worst case, which is wartime.

Filling Gaps with Nonstandard Specifications

When the standards identified are mapped to the service requirements determined in the Phase Four DOSEE planning steps, gaps in the standards will become visible. Decisions must be made about how to fill these gaps. In some cases, a gap can be filled by a consortia specification. If none are available, then a *de facto* standard, with implementations available for multiple platforms, might fill the gap and still provide varying degrees of interoperability and portability.

If functionality is needed in a area for which no standards or specifications exist, then the only way to fill the gap may be through a proprietary product. In such cases, users should require vendors to outline their standards directions for the area in question, and their (the vendors') migration plans to achieve standards conformance.

Regardless of whether standards or products are chosen, there is a responsibility that rests with the user. If users wish to have an interoperable, portable environment, they must design their applications with interoperability and portability in mind. A poor programmer can make anything nonportable.

Determine Standards' Practicality

As a result of determining the organization-specific areas most important to portability and interoperability, and having various departments prioritize the standards they need, an organization's solution space of applicable interoperability and portability standards has been narrowed considerably. But even survey results showing both the use and importance of services and standards do not provide sufficient data to serve as criteria for planning a migration to standards.

For example, for a variety of reasons, many standards that are conceptually important to interoperability and portability may not be practical to implement. Among other reasons, the standards may not provide sufficient functionality to satisfy an organization's requirements. Or, they may include certain features (*gotchas*) that, if used, can reduce portability and/or interoperability. Finally, even if the standard in question seems to be practical, it may require other standards to operate, and those other standards may not be practical.

To further determine standards' priorities for implementation, the practicality of the standards in question must be determined. The practicality of standards is determined in Phase Five Step 3 of the DOSEE planning process (Figure 6.5).

Determine other standards that are required by the selected standards, and identify still other standards that are related to the chosen standards. These standards enlarge the list of standards that might be needed, and also might constrain the use of some standards.

Determine whether the standards chosen, and the standards required by the standards chosen, are available in products, whether the standards are mature, and whether the products implementing the standards are mature. Version 1.0 of anything (hardware or software) is never as robust or debugged as Version 2.X or 3.X.

Determine the deficiencies within the standards, and figure out how to get around these deficiencies.

Determine the "gotchas" in the standards that will cause interoperability and/or portability incompatibilities, and figure out how to get around these gotchas.

Determine the maturity of the standard because the maturity will generally determine the stability of the standard.

Determine whether conformance tests exist for the standard.

Figure 6.5   Phase Five Step 3: Determine standards' practicality.

There is no easy way to obtain practicality information about standards. Consultants who track standards in various areas are one source. As was shown in Figure 6.3 and in the software accompanying this book, the ITSG and the DOSEE Standards Database contain standards practicality information, including deficiencies in the various standards, portability and interoperability caveats, related standards and their deficiencies and caveats, alternative specifications, and recommendations.

The NIST also has practicality information about the standards specified by its Application Portability Profile (APP). The APP includes a standards evaluation table for each standard it specifies. This table contains information about the standard's level of consensus, product availability, maturity, and so forth.

Table 6.1 shows an example of one of the NIST's standards evaluation tables. The accompanying text explains these evaluations.

The Related Standards Issue

It is not sufficient to specify only the standards determined by users' requirements. Those standards may require other standards in order to operate.

For example, the ISO Common Management Information Protocol (CMIP) network management protocol requires the ISO Remote Operations Service Element

Table 6.1 Example NIST Standards Evaluation Table

SPECIFICATION	LOC	PAV	CMP	MAT	STB	DFU	PRL
FIPS PUB 151-2 POSIX	●	●	●	●	●	●	●
POSIX SHELL IEEE 1003.2-1992	○	●	●	●	●	●	●
REAL-TIME IEEE P1003.4	○		○	●	○		
SECURITY IEEE P1003.6				○			

Legend: ● High evaluation   ○ Average evaluation   Blank Low evaluation

LOC—Level of consensus   STB—Stability
PAV—Product availability   DFU—*De facto* usage
CMP—Completeness   PRL—Problems/limitations
MAT—Maturity

(ROSE) to operate. CMIP provides capabilities that are just not available in any other network-management standard. On this basis, CMIP has achieved theoretical acceptance from consortia, industry groups, and vendors. But few CMIP-compliant products exist. ROSE is a newer standard. Although ISO approved, ROSE is less known among some standards groups, many industry groups, many vendors, and most users.

Some ROSE services are implemented as part of some vendors' CMIP specifications. But not until the approval of the International Standardized Profiles (ISP) 11183-1, -2, and -3 for Network Management, could users be assured of obtaining the same ROSE services with CMIP from different vendors to ensure interoperability.

If an organization wants to specify CMIP, it must also look at ROSE, and ROSE's acceptance, product availability, deficiencies, and so on, before deciding whether CMIP is a good standard to implement in the short term, or whether it is it better to wait.

Standards Deficiencies

Each of the desired standards on the final selected standards list must also be investigated for deficiencies within the standard, gotchas that will cause interoperability and/or portability problems, and for product availability.

For example, SQL is a widely accepted standard with a high level of acceptance. Unfortunately, SQL has been so minimal that vendors have had to enhance the standard to make it sufficiently functional to use. As a result, almost no two SQL-conformant products are compatible. SQL 2 (ISO 9075:1992) adds more functionality. But it will be some time before the full-level or even the intermediate-level SQL 2 is available in products. Meanwhile, the emerging entry-level SQL 2 products, as well as the SQL 2 standard, have many deficiencies. For example, none of the SQL 2 levels specify features such as CREATE INDEX or DROP INDEX. Object management will not be included in SQL until SQL 3. Most importantly, SQL 2 does not support connection management until the full-level SQL 2 becomes available.

Users must decide what to do about the SQL 2 deficiencies, and whether they can live with the incompatibilities between SQLs that currently exist.

To overcome SQL 2's connection management lack, ISO has approved a standard for remote data access (RDA) in Client/Server environments. Unfortunately, ISO RDA only specifies a service and protocol for remote data access between a single client and server. It does not consider multiple connections and does not specify distributed database access. ISO RDA also does not specify any APIs or formats. These deficiencies led to the formation of a vendor consortia called the SQL Access Group (SAG), which was chartered to add more distributed functionality to RDA.

The X/Open RDA specification (developed by SAG and published by X/Open) is a superset of the ISO RDA standard. For example, the X/Open API specifications include an API and formats, in addition to a remote data access protocol.

The X/Open API specification is known as the *Call Level Interface* (CLI) specification. It allows an application program to directly call an SQL program, without having to embed the SQL program in a third-generation language, and without requiring a preprocessor for each language in which SQL is embedded. Although not formal standards, SAG and X/Open's RDA and CLI are the better choice for remote data access in most Client/Server environments because the SAG RDA and CLI comply with ISO RDA, and also fill many of ISO RDA's gaps.

Another case concerning standards deficiencies is network management. The Simple Network Management Protocol (SNMP) is a widely accepted *de facto* standard. The author has had the experience of asking groups of users which protocol they want to use for network management. In industry, the answer is overwhelmingly SNMP. When these same users are asked about their network-management requirements, they are almost invariably surprised to discover that there is no match with SNMP. SNMP just doesn't do the things that users claim they must have. It is deficient in certain user-required functionality. To get those capabilities, users must migrate to CMIS/CMIP.

Gotchas Within the Standards

An example of gotchas in a standard is the ioctl system call, which is under consideration by the IEEE P1003.4b Group specifying a revision to the real-time extensions to POSIX. The ioctl call performs terminal and device management. Unfortunately, the ioctl call is a very old call. Most vendors' ioctl calls are incompatible. So many existing applications and devices are dependent on old ioctl versions that it is doubtful whether vendors would accept a new version, and how much compatibility a new version could provide.

Maturity of the Standards

Immature standards tend to be unstable and likely to be changed in order to fix software problems that are discovered as companies and their people study and implement the standard. Adoption of an immature standard means that as the standard changes, products implementing the standard will change. Whenever the products implementing the standard change, application developers and software maintenance professionals will have to modify their applications and the interfaces to other software systems.

Conformance Tests

A *conformance test* is software that measures an implementation's software functions' conformance to a particular standard. Conformance tests are important because of the potential for ambiguities to creep into a standard as vendors interpret pieces of a standard differently. This can reduce interoperability or portability.

Conformance tests help solve this interoperability/portability problem because they provide reasonable assurance that software works as it is supposed to, and that users can mix and match systems and software, interchange their data, and preserve their investments in their applications and training. Also, conformance tests provide reasonable assurance to third-party vendors that the software, and data created by their software, will be interoperable with, and portable across, other vendors' software.

Various types of conformance-testing specifications and software are defined by standards groups, government standards organizations, consortia, and private companies. For example, standards groups, government standards organizations, and consortia typically define test methods, abstract-test suites, and test assertions. Test assertions, test methods, and abstract-test suites are important because they are the basis for vendors, consortia, and NIST-referenced conformance tests. They also are the basis for emerging automated conformance test tools. Neither ISO nor the NIST develop test suites. Private companies define the software-based test suites that are used to measure a software product's conformance to a standard.

IEEE POSIX working groups and X/Open are groups that develop test assertions. Test assertions do not define how to test, but what to test. More specifically, test assertions are statements of the specification to be tested. The statements are written in a form that actually defines a test that should be written to check a particular functionality for conformance to a particular standard.

ISO standards bodies develop test methods, abstract-test suites, and protocol implementation conformance statements (PICS). The ISO test methods and abstract-test suites include general rules for developing test assertions and test methods to evaluate the conformance of implementations to a standard. The PICS specifies the capabilities and options which have been implemented, and features which have been omitted, so that implementations can be tested for conformance against requirements.

The NIST identifies and references abstract-test suites, which are based on the ISO methods for testing conformance to individual standards. The NIST also validates vendors and consortia who implement conformance-test suites for various ISO standards in accordance with the ISO conformance-test methods. Both the NIST and X/Open validate vendors who actually perform the conformance testing. Companies that have been validated to implement and conduct conformance tests for specific standards include large and small computer, database, and specialized conformance testing companies. Such companies range from IBM and Unisys to Oracle and Mindcraft, and many more.

Implementations of Standards

Only one thing needs to be said about the need for the availability of products that implement the standards. The greatest, most desirable standards in the world are of little use without sufficiently functional, reliable products that implement the standards.

The Direction Must Come from the Users

An important part of the open-systems–environment planning process is the determination of standards implementation priorities. Since a move to standards-based systems will affect every functional area in the organization, determining priorities requires input from each of these functional areas. Attempts to determine standards and their priorities without such input is likely to result in the publication of open systems guidelines that are ignored.

Surveying Users to Prioritize Standards

Phase Five Step 2 of the DOSEE planning process is the phase where interoperability and portability services, standards, and other specifications are prioritized for implementation. The input from different functional areas in an organization, concerning priorities, is usually obtained through surveys (Figure 6.6).

The lists of services and standards should be categorized according to functionality (e.g., data exchange, graphics, communications, data management, user interfaces), and, depending on the organization, may include hardware and software standards.

The purpose of the services and standards survey is to determine the criticality of individual services and the standards relevant to those services to an organization's or department's functions and goals.

Survey participants should be asked to rank the importance of the software service, and the criticality of the applications which require the service. The infrastructure and application expert teams will use this criticality information in determining implementation priorities. For example, services that are crucial to the organization's most critical applications are probably not good candidates for early standardization.

The standards list should include the standard's sponsor (e.g., ISO, IEEE, OSF, X/Open), the standard's common name (e.g., SQL 2), the standard's designation

Develop a survey to obtain input from all functional areas in the organization to help prioritize the standards to be implemented.

In the survey, determine the importance of each software service to portability and interoperability in the organization's different functional areas (departments, divisions, groups, etc.).

Determine each department's familiarity with the various standards possibly suitable for each important software service.

Determine the importance of each individual standard (with which the departments are familiar) for the short, medium, and long term.

Figure 6.6 Phase 5 Step 2: Determine standards priorities through surveys.

(e.g., ISO 9075), the status of the standard (e.g., International Standard, X/Open CAE Specification), and the type of standard (e.g., formal, consortia, *de facto*, vendor). It also is helpful to provide standards practicality information indicating the maturity of the standard, whether it has achieved a high consensus among standards specifiers and a high acceptance among vendors and/or users, whether conformance tests exist for the standard, and whether products that implement the standard are available.

Participants in the survey should, at least, be required to rank their familiarity with each of the standards, and the importance of each of the standards to interoperability and to portability both now and in the future (e.g., short, medium, and long term). The rankings should use a scale such as high, medium, and low, or a scale of 1–10 (or 1–5). Where possible, especially if the rankings are extreme (e.g., very important or not important), participants should be asked to provide a rationale for their ranking. Participants who rank a standard very low should be asked to suggest alternatives that they believe can provide interoperability and/or portability.

Table 6.2 shows a small subset of a sample survey for prioritizing standards. This sample survey merges the surveyed rankings of services with the surveyed rankings of standards. As the survey headings across the top row indicates, the survey supplies the name of the standard and sponsor, the standards type (formal, consortia, etc.), and the status of the standard. Where a standard is still in progress, but there is an expected date for approval, that date is given in the status column.

The blank survey table is filled out by the survey participants. The Table 6.2 survey shows the filled-in entries for one particular company. These entries may differ from those that would be filled in by your company, and you may take exception to the way the survey was completed.

Table 6.2 Sample Survey for Prioritizing Standards

Service Area	Service	Importance to Application (1–10)	Importance of App. to Organization (1–10)	Platform to Support Service	Relevant Standards Available	Standard Type	Status
Data Interchange	Document Exchange	8	7	PC, WS, Server	ISO ODA/ODIF	Formal	IS
					ISO SGML	Formal	IS
					IBM DIA/DCA	Product	Avail.
					DEC CDA	Product	Avail.
Data Interchange	Graphics Exchange	8	8	PC, WS	ISO CGM	Formal	IS
Graphics	2-D Graphics	7	6	PC, WS	ISO GKS	Formal	IS
Networking	Message Handling	9	10	PC, WS, Server, Mainframe	CCITT X.400	Formal	Recom.
					SMTP	Defacto	RFC
	File Transfer	10	10	Server, WS, Mainframe	ISO FTAM	Formal	IS
					FTP	Defacto	RFC
	Distributed File Access				IEEE TFA	Formal	1996
					NFS (RFC 1094)	Defacto	RFC/ Product

Familiarity with Standard (H/M/L)	Standard Now in Use?	Importance of Standard to Interoperability (1–10)	Rationale	Importance of Standard to Portability/ Scalability (1–10)	Rationale	Suggested Alternatives
L	No	4	Not widespread commercially	3	Not commercially widespread	Filters
M	No	6	Widely used on the Internet	6	Becoming commercially widespread	
L	No	2	Single vendor	1	Does not scale well	
M	Yes	3	Single vendor	1	Single vendor	
H	Yes	8	Standard carries so much information that files may grow too large for PCs	4	Standard carries so much information that files may grow too large for PCs	Filters
H	Yes	—	Minimal functionality	7	Minimal functionality WS graphics is often vendor specific	SGI
H	No	10	Used worldwide	8	Many X.400 gateways exist	
H	Yes	7	X.400 more functional	6	Needs API	X.400
H	No	5	Overkill	2	Too big for most PCs	NFS
H	Yes	7		2	Deos not scale well to PCs Needs API	NFS
L	No	2	Incomplete	2	Incomplete	NFS
H	Yes	10	Ubiquitous	9	Available for PCs (PC/NFS) and for big machines	

Adding Survey Information to the Database

The survey information collected should be combined in a single database with the counts of commonality of standards and services obtained from the portability and interoperability matrices, and with general information concerning the targeted standards and their status and maturity. Future reference to the survey and general standards information can be made very convenient if the survey information ranking standards is directly incorporated in the organization's database of standards created for its portability and interoperability targets.

This combination of targeted portability and interoperability areas, general standards information for these areas, and organization-specific standards preference data also provides a better calibration of what needs to be standardized than does either a survey or a portability or interoperability matrix alone. Among other things, the procedure makes it clear that not every service needs to be standardized, even if it is commonly used. For example, it turns out that the mathematics programs at one organization surveyed only interact with identical mathematics programs. Therefore, in this case, the standardization of mathematical symbols and formats is not necessary.

To store all this information together, either a relational database or an electronic spreadsheet can be used. It is helpful if the information is accessible electronically by open-system planners located in different areas of the organization.

Table 6.3 shows a subset of an evolving interoperability/portability/scalability database. The database contains applications and their interactions with other applications (information from the portability and interoperability matrices in Chapter 5). It also contains a listing of portability and interoperability services and standards, determined by the open Client/Server planning infrastructure team. Finally, the table shows some of the survey data ranking the importance of services and standards to applications, to the organization, and to interoperability, portability, and scalability. The complete set of fields is not shown in Table 6.3, due to space limitations.

Ultimately, the importance-ranking numbers collected in the surveys should be combined with numbers showing standards' practicality and availability. The result will be a narrower solution space rather than an overwhelming large list of standards and services to be considered. The standards and services finalists will support the organization's specific interoperability and portability requirements, and also be acceptable to application users.

Both the standards survey and the standards database shown in this book contain *de facto* product standards. How much to emphasize *de facto* product standards is up to the organizations generating the surveys. It is expected that government agencies will emphasize formal standards, along with some consortia specifications, because of their procurement rules. Commercial companies, however, may standardize around certain *de facto* standards (e.g., Windows, NT, NetWare).

Table 6.3 Evolving Standards & Survey Database (Subset)

Applications	Interactions	Portability/ Scalability Services	Interoperability Services	Standards	Importance to Portability/ Interoperability
Word Processing	E-Mail; File Sharing; Presentation Graphics; Printing; Mathematics	Compound document architectures & formats	Compound document exchange	Formal: ISO IS ODA/ODIF	4
				Formal: ISO SGML	6
				Product. IBM DIA/DCA	2
				Product: DEC CDA	3
		2-D Graphics		Formal: ISO GKS	8
		Printing commands	Page description language	Formal: ISO SPDL (Standardized Page Description Language);	7
				Defacto: Adobe Postscript	9
			Distributed File Access	Emerging: IEEE P1003.8 TFA (Transparent File Access) (1996)	2
					2
				Defacto: RFC 1094;	10
				Product: Sun NFS (= RFC 1094);	10
				Consortia: X/Open NFS	?
			File Transfer	Formal ISO FTAM;	5
				Defacto: TCP/IP FTP	7
		Mathematics	Equation format;	None	1
			Math symbols format	None	1
			LAN	Defacto: Ethernet	10
				Product: Novell IPX	10
Presentation Graphics	Other Presentation Graphics; Word Processing; Printing	Graphics import/export format	Graphics exchange	Formal: CGM	5
				Product: Windows Metafile	8
		Printing commands	Page description language	Formal: ISO SPDL (Standardized Page Description Language);	3
				Defacto: Adobe Postscript	8
E-Mail	Word Processing; Presentation Graphics; Mathematics	MHS format	MHS	Formal: CCITT X.400;	9
				Formal: IEEE P1327.1 X.400 API;	3
				Consortia: X/Open & APIA X.400 API	3
				Defacto: SMTP	7
			Security: Authentication	OSF DCE Kerberos	7

Standards

Areas where standards are most important to INTEROPERABILITY are boxed

Areas where standards are most important to PORTABILITY are ovaled

Dotted outlines denote likely future issues

* Few Products exist for this std.
** Few products & other problems

System Developer	System User	System Manager

Sys.Dev

By Span

Hi-Lvl Library

4.1.CDIF*, PCTE+*, STL*
4.2.CDIF*, PCTE+*, STL*
4.3.ISEE+RDS*, SCCS
4.4.
4.5.
4.6.
4.7.Basic, C, C++, Cobol, Fortran 77(Posix.9) & 90(Posix.19), ANDF*
4.8.
4.9.Posix.3*
4.10.
4.11.OMG*
4.12DCE IDL*, ISO RPC+*
4.13OMGCORBA IDL*
4.14MOTIF UIL

Applications By Function

Application Support & End User Tools

Personal Productivity

6.2.1.ODA/ODIF*, SGML*,
6.2.2RTF*
6.2.3.CGM,IGESLotus PIC, McDraw PICT, PICT2, Grp 3/4
6.2.4DIF,CSV,WK1
6.2.5.SQL,Dbase
6.2.6.
6.2.7.

Group Productivity

6.3.1.X.400, X.500*
6.3.2.
6.3.3.
6.3.4.
6.3.5.
6.3.6.SQL,SQL Access
6.3.7.
6.3.8.
6.3.9.FIMS**

Info Mgmt

6.4.1.SQL,SQL Access
6.4.2.
6.4.3.
6.4.4.Z39.50*, Z39.58*, ODA
6.4.5.Z39.50*, Z39.58*, ODA
6.4.6.JPEG*, TIFF
6.4.7.
6.4.8. Hytime*

By Industry

Tech/Eng/Sci

6.5.1.
6.5.2.PDES/STEP
6.5.3.
6.5.4.
6.5.5.

Sys.Mgt

DME*, Posix.7*

7.1.
7.2.
7.3.
7.4.
7.5.SNMP,DME*CMIP/CMIS*
7.6.
7.7.
7.8.Posix.7.2**
7.9.Posix.7.3**
7.10Posix.7.3**
Kerberos*, OSF,Posix.6**
7.11.
7.12Postscript, Posix.7.1+** SPDL**
7.13BOOTP

Tools & Utilities

Application

5.1.1.
5.1.2Posix.9**(Fortran), Posix.1(C), No Cobol!!
5.1.3Edifact, X12
5.1.4Posix.282a**TM*
5.1.5OSF Kerberos*, OSI 7498-2**
5.1.6.
5.1.7
5.1.8STEP* GKS, GKS-3D*PEX* CORE, PHIGS, PHIGS+*, CGM/I**, IGES, NAPLPS*

Data

5.2.1.SQL,NDL*RDA* SQL2* SQL Access, IRDS*
5.2.2.DTP*, CCR* XA*,STDL*, Posix.11* CICS, ACMS, Tuxedo
5.2.3.X/Open XDR*, SVID XDR, IEEE, XDR*,OSF XDR*
5.2.4.
5.2.5
5.2.6.C-ISAM,SFS, RMS
5.2.7.SQL, SQL Access, ODBC

Network

5.3.1.DTP*, CCR* XA*, STDL*, Posix.11*'Encina
5.3.2.FTP,FTAM*
5.3.3.NFS,FTAM* DFS*, AFS, TFA*'RFS
5.3.4.PC-NFS, PCI*SMB
5.3.5.X.400SMTP,X.435
5.3.6.X.500*Name Svc Softswitch & ccMail dir
5.3.7.DNS
5.3.8.Telnet,VT+*
5.3.9.X
5.3.10.MMS*
5.3.11.Sockets,TLI*, XTI*, 1003.12**
5.3.12.ROSE*
5.3.13. OSF Time Svc
5.3.14. V.32, V.42MNP, X-Modem, Kermit
5.3.15.
5.3.16. Term. protocols
5.3.17.DCE RPC*,ISO RPC*, NCS RPC
5.3.18. OSF Name Svc RFC 1006

User I/F

5.4.1. XVT, Plus, ...
5.4.2. Motif, 1201,1&2* Open Look, XVT, Pres Mgr, NeXt Step, MS-Windows?
5.4.3. X prot, Xlib, Xt, X11*, Xview*, PM, ICCCM*
5.4.4.
5.4.5.
5.4.6. Posix.7.1+** SPDL** Postscript
5.4.7.

System Developer	System User	System Manager

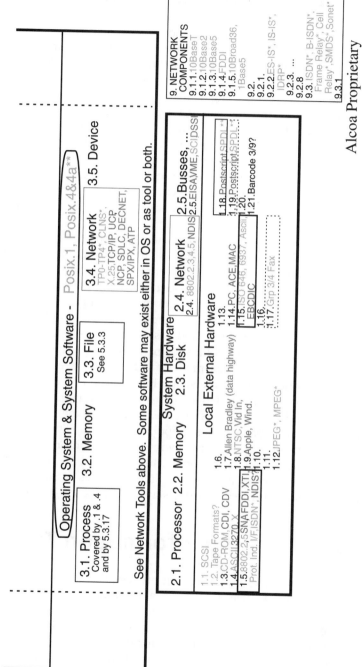

Figure 6.7 Alcoa computer reference model standards. *Source: Alcoa.*

135

Mapping the Standards Selected onto an Architecture

When the selected set of *de jure* and *de facto* standards is mapped onto the open systems architecture created in Phase Three of this distributed-OSEE process, the result is a standards-based draft version of an open-systems environment model, geared to a specific enterprise. Although generic, this model is sufficiently detailed to be usable by DOSEE planning teams for further planning work, for communications with management, and, ultimately, for planning procurements and implementations.

It is important to note that the model developed as a result of the DOSEE Phase Five planning step is only a draft model. Before it can be used for actual implementations or procurements, further DOSEE planning work is necessary to refine the model, determine priorities of different standards to different applications and departments, and ensure the practicality and functionality of these standards. These issues will be discussed in Phases Six and Seven of the DOSEE planning process.

Figure 6.7 shows the Alcoa Computer Reference Model with the initial standards proposed by Alcoa to accommodate the functional components shown in Chapter 5 in Figure 5.6. Such a model, with superimposed standards, is really a generic model geared to an organization. It is not intended that all the standards shown in this model be used at once (or at all), unless an organization plans to scrap all its information technology systems and begin again from scratch—an unlikely prospect.

Instead, such a generic model should be used as a basis for developing organization-specific miniprofiles for particular application domains and platforms. Alcoa, for example, used its model to identify subsets of standards and develop profiles for workstations, servers, and information processors.

In the Alcoa model shown in Figure 6.7, the squares surrounding certain groups of standards indicate standards that are most important to interoperability. The ovals indicate standards that are most important to portability. The use of color, if available, is also helpful in depicting various types of information and relationships in a generic computer reference model. In its internal documents, for example, Alcoa used different colors to indicate the different types of standards and specifications (e.g., formal standards with products available, consortia standards, and products).

Putting the OSEE Planning Information Together

At this point in the DOSEE planning process, the organization's targeted portability and interoperability areas are known, and standards appropriate to those areas have been identified and prioritized. It is rare, however, to migrate an entire enterprise to Client/Server computing at one time. Usually, organizations target certain functional areas, applications, and/or platforms for their initial open Client/Server computing implementations, and decide how to migrate these functional areas and applications. In Phase Six, we will use the Client/Server application and open-systems information gathered so far to plan implementable profiles for open Client/Server environments.

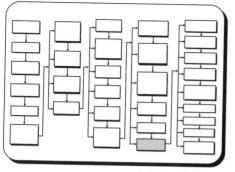

Phase Six: Develop Implementable Profiles

Good Things Come in Small Packages

Having developed a good idea of potential Client/Server applications and architectures to target, and then determined the related application and interoperability requirements and standards, open Client/Systems planners should develop profiles for these applications. Each profile will contain a subset of the services and standards defined for the enterprise in Phases Three through Five. The profiles also may contain other profiles developed either by standards groups or developed for other parts of the organization.

Profiles are developed during DOSEE planning Phase Six because profiles are easier and more practical to deal with than standards (as discussed in Chapter 1). Even within an enterprise, profiles are more practical to deal with than the enterprise superset of standards determined earlier in the planning process because each profile developed is geared to the requirements of a specific application area. Finally, profiles are a good way to communicate the requirements of each application area to management and others.

If profile development was a goal of this planning methodology, why was enterprise planning done first? The answer is that the enterprise planning is needed to ensure that the profiles developed and implemented for individual application areas can cost effectively and practically be integrated together.

There are many organizations that informally develop and implement individual profiles for particular Client/Server application areas rather than first planning a common enterprisewide infrastructure. Although this technique works for the application in question, it unfortunately can create islands of incompatible Client/Server systems within an organization, which are difficult and costly to integrate and a nightmare to maintain, manage, and administer.

Theoretically, incompatibility problems should not happen if each profile developed is based on standards. But few real-world systems can be built exclusively on standards. Also, there are differences in the vendors' standards-based products. If a profile developed is to be extendible to an enterprise, there is a need for enterprise planning.

As a worst-case example of what could happen without enterprise planning, suppose one department standardized on NetWare and SQL-based R:Base and DB2, while another department standardized on Windows '95, MS-Network, and Microsoft Access, and a third department standardized on UNIX and Sybase. There are similarities between these diverse products, but the similarities are superficial. Without having planned a common networking infrastructure (e.g., TCP/IP that talks to all the networks) and a common database, the organization will have to spend much money and time constantly installing, customizing, developing, and upgrading software for network, operating system, and database integration, and system management.

Develop Profiles to Implement

The profiles developed should identify the functionalities and services in the immediate and extended environment that the application areas to be profiled need to do their job. They should also show the relationships between the profile components. The following sections of this chapter discuss profile development using the Client/Server planning database. This chapter also discusses development from basic principles for cases where no prior interoperability, portability, or other work has been done.

Defining Profiles Using the Client/Server Planning Database

If the enterprise planning was done earlier and the results stored in a database, profiles should not be difficult to develop. Many of the profile-development steps are similar to, or based on, the steps used to define interoperability and portability targets, service requirements, and standards for the enterprise. This work need not be repeated. The portability and interoperability targets, interoperability and application attributes and attribute values, required services, and a prioritized list of standards that provide the required services should be contained in the open Client/Server planning database that has been built by the planning teams in Phases Three through Five. If the database is kept up to date, it should only be necessary to identify the application area to be profiled, and retrieve and tailor the stored lists of applicable attributes, attribute values, services and standards to form a focused profile tailored for particular needs (Figure 7.1). This profile work can be done by one or more users or managers who are authorized to access the open Client/Server database.

A review of Phase Four (in Chapter 5 of this book) would be helpful at this point to recap the definitions of attributes, attribute values, and services. The recap would also help reassess the current credibility of the data in the open Client/Server

1. Identify the targeted application area for the profile and the applications involved.
2. From your previously defined and stored attributes, chose the attribute sets applicable to your application area.
3. From the previously defined and stored allowable attribute values, choose the attribute values that meet the interoperability, portability, and functionality needs of your targeted application profile area.
4. Examine, study, discuss, or choose from the lists of previously defined and stored services and standards associated with the different attributes and attribute values.
5. Combine the services and standards into a profile.
6. Present the profile to others in your organization.

Figure 7.1   Phase Six: Defining an implementable profile.

database, and help you understand why you are using that data in the manner suggested in this chapter.

To extract the applicable information from the open Client/Server database and define an actual profile, profile developers first identify the application area for the targeted profile and the types of applications that will be involved in performing functions in the targeted profile area.

From the list of previously defined and stored attributes in the open Client/Server planning database, choose the attribute sets applicable to your profile application area. For example, you or your organization's infrastructure or application experts team might have previously defined attribute sets for electronic mail, transaction processing, document processing, or spreadsheet processing. Each attribute set is associated with a previously defined and stored group of allowable attribute values.

From the allowable attribute values, also stored in the open Client/Server planning database, choose the attribute values that meets the interoperability, portability, and functionality needs of your targeted application profile area. For example, transport attributes would require the users/managers defining the profile to choose attribute values like local or international for the transport attribute, networked or dial-up for the connection attribute, spreadsheet for the format attribute, or whether a file size or a volume of data to be transferred is small or so large that compression will be needed. If an attribute value needed to meet your requirements is not in the list of allowable attribute values, use that attribute value for your profile anyway, but inform the keeper of the database so it can be added to the list.

Note that with this profile-development technique, technical details are minimized in the profile-planning stage. Managers or users who know the targeted application are the most qualified persons to identify their attribute values.

The attributes selected constitute an index into a large space of generic profiles. These profiles are referred to as *generic* because each attribute, although applicable to a profile, may have more than one allowable attribute value. Some of those allowable attribute values may not be suitable for your particular requirements. For example, different profiles might be defined for local and international electronic mail. The local electronic mail profile might specify TCP/IP and/or a *de facto* PC network standard. The international electronic-mail profile would contain X.25 connections, along with standardized internationalization cultural conventions (e.g., for monetary symbols, local time, character sets, and native-language messages).

The attribute values defined are used to tailor a generic profile to an application's specific needs. The selection, for example, of the attribute value local for a distance attribute connotes the local electronic-mail profile. The selection of the international attribute value for the distance attribute implies wide-area network connections and internationalization facilities.

The attribute values act as a search criterion into the previously identified and stored services and specified standards, also stored in the open Client/Server database. The selection of a particular attribute value for an attribute should indicate the associated service requirements, as well as applicable practical standards. The selection of the services and standards based on attributes and attribute values can be automated.

Because of the infrastructure team's earlier elimination of many standards based on their practicality, the Client/Server planning database should show either one or a small number of *de jure* or *de facto* standards based on the attributes and attribute values selected. Any gaps or deficiencies in the standards, portability or interoperability caveats, workaround suggestions, and recommendations that were stored in the open Client/Server database during the infrastructure definition phase can also be displayed.

The last step of defining the actual profile is to meet with the concerned technical and nontechnical people in your organization to discuss the ramifications of the applicable *de jure* and *de facto* standards.

Since the profile being developed is to be implementable, and what doesn't exist can't be implemented, practicality dictates that during this profile development process the Client/Server planners determine which standards and specifications have products available. If such information was entered in the open Client/Server planning database more than a few months ago, it is not likely to be valid because product data changes too fast. Vendors should be surveyed for their current offerings.

Ask the vendors about their conformance with standards, where divergences and incompatibilities exist, where product capabilities are supersets of standards, and what kind of performance the standards-based capabilities can deliver. If products are desired that do not support standards, require the vendors to explain their standards directions and to outline a detailed migration plan to standards that will not leave you, the user, stuck at a later time. Where possible, give preference to vendors that truly conform to standards, or have a competent migration plan.

Also, discuss with your application developers and/or with the open Client/Server planning teams, how you might overcome some of the products' incompatibility problems by designing applications for portability and interoperability.

Finally, choose from the standards and specifications contained in the planning database those that best meet your organization's and application area's requirements. Many standards in the standards database can be eliminated from consideration by the process of defining and asking simple questions. The simplest of questions might be whether your organization is a government agency or an organization that deals with government agencies. A no answer eliminates from every standards section the entire class of government standards. Other standards might be chosen or eliminated based on questions about the organization's present environment and the need for compatibility with that environment.

The output of this process is a profile—an implementable collection of specifications and standards geared to a specific application area. The profile developed must now be checked to make sure that it indeed contains either all the interface standards required for your particular application area. If no standards exist for a particular interface area, then the profile must specify a way to fill the gap. It should be noted that this profile-development method constitutes one possible approach that could be taken, but it is not the only one.

This profile-development method is possible because most attributes and allowable attribute values, as well as many service requirements and standards, are reusable across many application areas. It is expected, therefore, that the profiles being developed will mostly use components and standards from the organization-specific architecture, developed, populated, and refined, and stored in the open Client/Server planning database, in Phases Three, Four, and Five. Looking in depth at a particular application, its functional requirements, and the service/functional components and standards it needs, may turn up some services and standards that were overlooked in developing the architectural models and infrastructure in Phases Four and Five. If such components and standards are identified, they should be added to the existing architectural model for the enterprise.

In some cases, it may be necessary to define some new attributes and/or attribute values to accommodate a new application or additional requirements. These attributes and attribute values should be added to the existing set of attributes and attribute values and mapped to new services.

Remember that profiles may specify not only standards and specifications, but other profiles. To quote an extreme example, profile developers may develop an office-automation profile. The office-automation profile may not directly specify any standards at all. Instead, it may specify a document-management profile, a spreadsheet profile, a presentation-graphics profile, an electronic-mail profile, and a workflow profile.

Defining Profiles from Basic Principles

Some organizations may not have performed the Phase Four enterprise infrastructure planning steps. They may wish to just define individual profiles for particular application areas or departments without first planning an infrastructure for an enterprise.

If your organization's choice is to develop separate profiles on an as-needed basis, you will not have developed a planning database of preidentified service requirements and standards applicable to different departments and applications in your enterprise. In that case, the interoperability and portability services needed for your profile, and the standards that provide those services, would have to be determined now. There are two ways to determine the required services and standards needed for a profile. Both methods will arrive at the same profile.

The first method is the group brainstorm technique, the traditional method of determining the required services. With this technique, the application experts and the infrastructure teams meet, pool their respective knowledge, and brainstorm until they come up with a list of services needed.

The second method of determining the required interoperability and portability services uses a more systematic approach. With this method, the application experts team and infrastructure team determine the profile's targeted interoperability and portability areas, and characterize the applications to be profiled by defining a number of application attributes. The application users or managers in the departments that use the applications then define attribute values for each of the attributes. With the aid of focused questions, the attributes and attribute values are ultimately mapped to services requirements, which in turn are mapped to standards.

The methods for determining interoperability targets and service requirements, application functionality and portability requirements; the definitions of attributes, attribute values, and services; and the procedures for mapping all these attributes, attribute values, and service requirements to standards; were covered in detail in Chapters 5 and 6. This information will not be repeated here. The software that accompanies this book also guides the reader to choosing attributes, attribute values, services, and standards.

Figure 7.2 shows a summary of the steps in defining a profile from fundamentals, based on the attribute-attribute value methods explained in Chapter 5.

Profile Development Example

How to identify and select the components for a profile was discussed in Chapter 5 on infrastructure planning tasks, Chapter 6 on standards selection, and in Chapter 7 on developing implementable profiles. The best way to understand how to develop a profile, however, is to build one. In this section, we, therefore, concentrate on actually building an open Client/Server profile for the area of document management.

Document management involves the creation of various kinds of documents, searching and retrieving all or parts of documents, revising the documents, and sending them to colleagues for information, comment, and further revision. The documents may incorporate text, graphics, image, voice annotations, hypertext, and other capabilities. Document management also requires the ability to generate and use tables of contents, style guides, forms, and templates. Generally, document-

1. Identify the application area for the targeted profile, and the types of functions or applications that will be required in this profile area.

2. Map the connections between the applications to be profiled, within departments using the applications, and also to applications in different departments that interact with the application in question, in order to determine the targeted areas for interoperability. Use the interoperability matrices discussed in Phase Four as an aid.

3. Define or identify attributes and characteristics of the various application interactions (See Chapter 5).

4. Determine values of the application interaction attributes, because these attributes will be used to determine explicit service requirements for which standards might be needed. Use the application interaction attributes and values tables developed in Phase Four as an aid (Chapter 5).

5. Map the attribute values to interoperability-service requirements. Use the application interactions versus services matrix developed in Phase Four (Chapter 5) and set of questions similar to those discussed in Chapter 6 for identifying standards as an aid.

6. Define attributes and determine attribute values for applications within each department to determine required functional services for the different applications. Use the attributes and attribute values tables developed in Phase Four as an aid (Chapter 5).

7. Map the relationships between applications and services within each department, and across other departments that use the same services to determine the targeted areas for scalability and application, user, and programmer portability.

8. Identify the standards and specifications needed to provide these services. These standards and specifications can be extracted from a predefined, appropriately organized standards database, such as the U.S. DoD DISA's ITSG (Information Technology Standards Guidance) (segment shown in Chapter 6) or the DOSEE Standards Database (shown in the software accompanying this book). A series of questions, as discussed in Chapter 6, helps select and eliminate standards.

9. Determine which standards and specifications have products available.

10. Decide how to fill the gaps in cases where no standards or specifications exist.

11. Interview vendors. Ask about their conformance with standards, where incompatibilities might exist, where product capabilities are supersets of standards, and what kind of performance the standards-based capabilities can deliver. If the products you want do not support standards, require the vendors to explain their standards directions and to outline a detailed migration plan to standards that will not leave you, the user, stuck in the future. Where possible, give preference to vendors that truly conform to standards, or have a competent migration plan.

12. Discuss with the planning teams how you might overcome some of the products' incompatibility problems by designing applications for portability and interoperability.

Figure 7.2 Procedure for developing a profile from basic principles.

management systems also need a graphical user interface (GUI) to facilitate use of the system, and security to protect sensitive information in the documents. Finally, document-management systems often require support for image scanning.

Determine Applications and Scenarios

Step 1 in developing a profile is to identify the types of applications to be used and the scenarios for the profile. The types of applications or scenarios defined for a profile are normally very general ones. Table 7.1 shows one organization's scenarios identified for document management applications.

In the past, it was common for an organization to define such scenarios, then search for the vendor with the applications that supported these scenarios. In a Client/Server environment, it is also necessary to ensure that the applications can interoperate and exchange data with certain other applications.

Determine Interoperations

Clearly, there are many possible applications and application interoperations, that support various scenarios depending on the organization and on the types of documents involved. To build this demonstration system, only a small number of the most common document-management applications and their interoperations are shown, using the kind of interoperability matrix shown in Chapter 5 (Table 7.2).

Determine Attributes and Attribute Values

To develop a profile tailored for your particular needs, it is necessary to characterize the application and application interoperations. It is not enough to say that an application must communicate captured document information or that a profile uses electronic mail. The applications, and hence the profile, have different service requirements depending on the document content, document size, whether the

Table 7.1 Document Management Scenarios

Functional Requirements for Document Management Applications
Document processing
Document access and search
Graphics art design
Image capture
Optical character recognition (OCR)
Communications of captured document information
World Wide Web access
Software development (maybe)

Table 7.2 Document Management Application Interoperations

DOCUMENT MGT: INTERACTIONS BETWEEN APPLICATIONS (Subset)

Applications	Word Processing	Document Search & Retrieval	Spreadsheet	Presentation Graphics	Image Capture	OCR	Printing	E-mail	Web Access
Word Processing	✓	✓	✓	✓	✓	✓	✓	✓	—
Document Search & Retrieval	✓	✓	✓	✓	✓	✓	✓	✓	✓
Spreadsheet	✓	✓	✓	✓	—	—	✓	✓	—
Presentation Graphics	✓	✓	✓	✓	✓	—	✓	✓	—
Image Capture	✓	✓	—	✓	✓	✓	—	—	✓
OCR	✓	✓	—	—	✓	✓	—	—	✓
Printing	✓	✓	✓	✓	—	—	✓	✓	✓
E-mail	✓	✓	✓	✓	—	—	✓	✓	✓
World Wide Web Access	—	✓	—	—	✓	✓	✓	✓	✓

Key: ✓ = *Interacts with* — = *Does not interact with*

communications is local or international, and so on. Based on these characterizations, for example, a real-world profile might need graphics- or image-exchange capabilities, graphics- or image-compression, different character sets, or local- or wide-area networking protocols and services.

Attributes and attribute values are high-level task descriptors that describe, at the user's level (rather than at the technical detail level), the key conceptual features of the tasks that the user is trying to accomplish. The document management profile, for example, might have attributes of document content, document size, and distance. Attribute values for content might be text, graphics, mixed text and graphics, image, and hypertext. Attribute values for document size might be small and large. Attribute values for distance might be local and international.

Many predefined attributes and possible associated attribute values are shown in several tables in Chapter 5. A fuller set of possible attributes and attribute values is contained in the software that accompanies this book. Table 7.3 shows a subset of attributes and attribute values defined for one document management profile.

Map Attributes and Attribute Values to Service Requirements

To map the attributes and attribute values defined for applications and scenarios to standards requires a person with sufficient knowledge to understand the general-service area category to use to search for applicable standards. A good

Table 7.3   Document Management Profile Attributes and Attribute Values

Application/Functions	Attribute	Attribute Value
Document search & retrieval and Document search & retrieval interoperations with word processing, spreadsheet, presentation graphics, image capture, OCR, printing, electronic mail, and World Wide Web access applications	Content	Text, Graphics, Mixed Text and Graphics, Image, Tables, Hypertext
	Human Interface Type	Graphical, Command-level
	Distance	Local (workgroup & enterprise), International
	Connection	Networked, Modem
	Document size	Small, Medium, Large
	Compression	Graphics, Image
Document Processing and Document processing interoperations with other applications as shown in Table 7.2	Content	Text, Graphics, Mixed Text & Graphics, Image, Hypertext
	Encoding	Character, Graphics
	Fonts	Character, Geometry
	Format	Text, Graphics, Image, Spreadsheet
Image Capture and Image capture interoperations shown in Table 7.2	Format	Image
	Image Color	Color, Black and White
Communications of captured document information and Interoperations between communicating applications sending or receiving the captured document information	Compression	Text, Graphics, Image
	Revisable/Updatable	Yes
	Security Level	High
	Connection	Networked, Modem
	Distance	Local, International
	Distribution	Single Recipient, Multiple Recipients
	Directory Location	Distributed
Software Development	Software Obtained How?	Purchased

set of general-service areas that are accepted by many standards organizations and the U.S. Defense Information Systems Agency (DISA) include user interfaces, data management, data interchange, graphics, networking/communications, distributed computing, operating system services, security, system management, and software development.

This is one of several possible classification schemes. Organizations may want to add other categories to the general services. The classification scheme provided here, however, was defined with the goal of identifying a set of general categories that allows users to use to look up every formal and *de facto* software standard in existence. How this is done will be shown shortly.

It is not difficult to map most of the emerging document-management profile attributes and attribute values to the general-service areas just mentioned. Clearly, attributes like connection, with attribute values of networked and modem, belong to the general-service area of networking/communications. The attribute human interface type, with attribute values of graphical and command level, belong to the general-service area of user interfaces. Attributes and attribute values related to directory services generally are considered distributed computing, although directory services used to be part of the networking services before distributed computing came on the scene. Software-development attributes and attribute values are most likely to be found under the general-service area of software development.

All the attributes related to the exchange of different types of documents (e.g., text, graphics, image), fonts, encoding, format, and compression belong to the general-service area of data interchange. Users would therefore search for standards applicable to any of these areas (document exchange, format, compression, etc.), in a standards database under the category data interchange. As Table 7.2 shows, many document management attributes and attribute values are related to data interchange.

The mapping of some attributes and attribute values to general-service areas may not be as straightforward as others. For example, there is no service area directly related to whether captured document information is revisable or updatable. However, if the Client/Server planners know that the captured document information includes graphics that must be revised, then the profile must include graphics capabilities (e.g., 2-D, 3-D, raster graphics, vector graphics). Such information is found in the general-service area of graphics. If the captured document information is database data then the place to look for services and standards is in the data management general-service area.

Some attributes and attribute values can be used to eliminate certain general-service areas from consideration. For example, the software obtained how? attribute in Table 7.2 has an attribute value of purchased. If the software will be purchased rather than developed internally, then there is no need to consider standards for programming-language compilers, software version control systems, and so on.

With the aid of a well-organized and documented standards database, on line or otherwise, the process of mapping from attributes, attribute values, and general-service areas to standards can be partly, or mostly, automated. One example of a well-organized and documented standards database discussed in Chapter 6 is the Information Technology Standards Guidance (ITSG) database from the U.S. Defense Information Systems Agency (DISA). A segment from the data-management section of the ITSG was also shown in Chapter 6. Another example of a comparably organized and documented standards database is the distributed open systems environment engineering (DOSEE) standards databases from Emerging Technologies Group, created for use with the DOSEE open Client/Server planning methodology.

The data-interchange section from the DOSEE standards database is provided in the software that accompanies this book. The data interchange section of the DOSEE standards database will be used to show how a standards database can be used to help define identify applicable base service areas and associated standards.

Table 7.4 is a table of contents to the data interchange general-service area in the DOSEE standards database. Like other sections in the DOSEE standards database,

Table 7.4 DOSEE Data Interchange Midlevel and Base-Level Service Areas

2. Data Interchange Services
   2.1 Text Exchange
      2.1.1 Character Sets
      2.1.2 Font Information Exchange
      2.1.3 External Data Representation
   2.2 Data Exchange Formats and Protocols
      2.2.1 Document Exchange
      2.2.2 Text Search and Retrieval
   2.3 Graphics and Multimedia Exchange Formats and Protocols
      2.3.1 Graphics Exchange
      2.3.2 Product Data Exchange
      2.3.3 Image Exchange
      2.3.4 Audio Exchange
      2.3.5 Hypertext Data Exchange
      2.3.6 Map Graphics Exchange Standards
   2.4 Business Data Interchange
      2.4.1 Electronic Data Interchange (EDI)
      2.4.2 Forms Transfer Standards
      2.4.3 Spreadsheet Data Exchange
   2.5 Software and Hardware Design Data Interchange
      2.5.1 CASE Tool Data Exchange
      2.5.2 Hardware Design Data Exchange Standards
   2.6 Printing
      2.6.1 Printer Data Exchange
   2.7 Bar Coding
      2.7.1 Bar Coding
   2.8 Data Compression
      2.8.1 Text Data Compression
      2.8.2 Graphics Compression
      2.8.3 Still Image Compression
      2.8.4 Motion Image Compression
      2.8.5 Audio Compression

the data interchange section is organized into subsections, called *mid-level service areas*, each concerning a different data interchange area. The mid-level service areas are further subdivided into subsubsections called *base-level service areas*. Each base-level service area describes a particular service needed to satisfy requirements in a particular application area. Each base-level service area is associated with one or more standards that provide these services in a standardized manner. The headings in the DOSEE data interchange table of contents that start with two-digit numbers represent mid-level service areas. The headings that begin with three-digit numbers represent base-level services areas.

The purpose of this mid-level and base-level service-area organization is to allow the elimination of standards areas from consideration, and to narrow the solution space of base-level service areas and standards that must be considered for inclusion in a profile. This process of eliminating some base standards areas and pinpointing others as applicable to a targeted profile is done through the use of two series of questions, developed for this purpose. The initial questions asked are each aimed at a different mid-level service area. The questions in the second series are each aimed at a different base-level service area.

The questions are all Boolean in nature, meaning the answers can be either *yes* or *no*. No other answers are acceptable. The Boolean nature of the answers allows the automation of the choice of applicable base-level service areas for which standards must be chosen.

Automation is possible because the questions are set up so that a *no* answer to a question about a mid-level service area means that the mid-level service area in question is not applicable to the profile, and the base services and standards associated with that mid-level service area can be ignored. A *yes* answer to the question means that the mid-level service area is applicable to the profile and the user must delve further down into the base-service area to find the applicable services and standards. The applicable base services are determined using the second set of questions designed to pinpoint or eliminate base-level service areas.

If the questions are asked on line, then a *yes* answer to a mid-level question causes the computer program to automatically ask the questions for the associated base-level area. A *no* answer to the mid-level questions causes the computer program to jump to the question about the next mid-level service area.

Figure 7.3 shows a sampling of the kinds of mid-level and base-level questions used to determine applicable mid-level service areas and base-level service requirements. The question numbers in Figure 7.3 correspond to the numbers in the data interchange table of contents shown in Table 7.4.

Identify Standards to Provide the Required Services

Generally, there are many possible standards for each service area, including formal, government, consortia, and *de facto* standards. The different formal standards usually provide services for different aspects of a base-level service area. For example, different standards for a base-level service area might specify a format, a protocol,

2. Data interchange: Does the application require sending data to, or receiving data from, remote computers or applications, or importing or exporting data to or from applications on a single machine?

    If yes, go to Question 2.1   If no, go to Question 3

    ANSWER: YES

    ↓

2.1 Text Exchange: Does the application require the display or printing of textual information?

    If yes, go to Question 2.1.1   If no, go to Question 2.2

    ANSWER: YES

    ↓

2.1.1 Character sets: Will the application require special display characters or international alphabets?

    If yes:

    - Select the most suitable character set standard   If no, go to Question 2.1.2 (on Font
      from Table 2.1 on character set standards   information exchange)
    - Go to Question 2.1.2

    ANSWER: YES

    ↓

2.1.2 Font information exchange: Will the application require multiple typefaces, sizes, etc. for attractive display and/or printing, rather than a default font?

                           ⋮

2.3 Graphics and multimedia exchange formats and protocols: Do the applications require the exchange of documents with multiple types of data, such as graphics, images, facsimile, voice, video, hypertext, etc.?

    If yes, go to Question 2.3.1   If no, go to Question 2.4

    ANSWER: YES

    ↓

2.3.1 Graphics exchange: Do the applications require the exchange of drawings and pictures that require editing?

    If yes:

    - Select the most suitable graphics exchange   If no, go to Question 2.3.2 (on product
      standard from Table 2.6: graphics data   data exchange)
      interchange standards.
    - Go to Question 2.3.2

    ANSWER: YES

                             ⋮

2.8 Data Compression: Will your application require the exchange or storage of large amounts of data or large size text documents in a short time or using capacity-limited storage media?

    If yes, go to Question 2.8.1   If no, go to Question 3

Figure 7.3 Sample questions to determine applicable service requirements.
Source: Emerging Technologies Group.

an application programming interface (API), and so on. However, there are often multiple overlapping *de facto* standards that are defined by a vendor or a small group of vendors.

Sometimes, the choice of a standard is very straightforward. Government users are often bound to choose government standards first, because government standards are geared to special needs of government agencies. Second, government users must choose formal standards to comply with government procurement rules.

In the commercial arena, it is a different story. Commercial user organizations are not bound to special procurement rules. Companies might, therefore, choose a particular standard because it provides the best compatibility with existing systems, even if it is not a formal standard. Other companies might choose a standard because it is promoted by Microsoft or Novell, or because it is *not* promoted by Microsoft or Novell. Some companies choose a standard because it is in widespread use, even though it may not provide the best functionality, it is still emerging, or its implementation is not as robust as some other standards. Numerous other companies, however, that are linking many diverse types of heterogeneous environments within their enterprise, or that are concerned with international business, must have the most interoperable, portable, scalable standards, as long as they have some assurance that the products implementing these standards are sufficiently functional and robust.

To provide standards guidance, the DOSEE Standards Database contains more than just the names, sponsoring organization, reference designation, and status of standards for each base-service area. It discusses standards gaps, deficiencies, interoperability and portability caveats, alternative specifications, and so on, and provides the rationale for its information. Moreover, this information is provided for *de facto* as well as formal standards.

Figure 7.4 shows an abridged version of the base-service area on still image compression from the DOSEE standards database. Formal standards groups have rules and policies that generally prevent them from developing standards in the same space as another standards group, on the grounds that multiple standards for one service defeat the purpose of the standard, that is, interoperability and portability. Vendors have no such policy. Every vendor believes it has a better way to provide a service than any other. The vendors, therefore, each publish the specifications for their product and call it a standard. The result is often a huge number of standards for each service equal to the number of vendors in the business—a situation equivalent to no standards. Figure 7.4 shows some of the multiple overlapping *de facto* vendor standards, as well as standards targeted at different aspects of the base service.

As new fields emerge or go through transitions, increasing numbers of *de facto* standards tend to be developed. Data interchange currently is an emerging field, driven by advances in computer technology, user needs in the international economy, and also by information available on the Internet.

Over time, the market decides which of these standards becomes dominant. The overlapping standards either evanesce, or coalesce into a small number of standards for a single base area (as is the case for relational-database access standards). The *de*

Figure 7.4 Abridged image and video exchange section from DOSEE.

Image Exchange

Image-exchange standards encompass the exchange of various kinds of images, transmitted and/or displayed in a variety of ways. Examples are still images, video images, color and grayscale images, transmitted via facsimile lines or networks, and displayed as hardcopy faxes, on computer screens, or on televisions consoles.

Standards

The table below contains standards for still image and motion video exchange formats and protocols.

Standard Type	Standard	Sponsor	Standard Reference	Status
Formal	JPEG/JIFF File Exchange for still images/digital video (Multicomponent and digital video data types)	ISO/IEC & JPEG	ISO/IEC 10198-1	IS
Formal	Coding of Moving Pictures and Associated Audio for Digital Storage Media up to about 1.5 MBit/sec (MPEG-I) (Digital video data type) Part 1: Systems Part 2: Video	ISO/IEC & MPEG	11172-1:1993 11172-2:1993	IS IS
Formal	Image Processing & Interchange IPI Functional Specification Part 1: Common Architecture; Part 2: Programmers Imaging Kernel System API; Part 3: Image Interchange Facility	ISO/IEC ISO/IEC ISO/IEC	12087-1 12087-2 12087-3	IS IS IS
Formal	Image Processing and Interchange (IPI): API Language Bindings Part 4: C	ISO/IEC	12088-4	IS
Formal	Facsimile Groups 3 and 4 for still images (Bitonal data type)	CCITT	CCITT (1988) T.4 and T.6	Recomm.
Formal	File Format for Storage and Exchange of Bilevel Images, Bilevel Image File Format: AIIM Level 1.1 (Covers CCITT Recommendations T.4 and T.6, and images having no compression)	ANSI/ AIIM	MS53-1993	Std.
Formal	Document Application Profile for the Interchange of Group 4 Facsimile documents	ITU-T	T.503	Recomm.
Formal	Release of Programmes in a Multimedia Environment (Exchange of Recorded Television Prog.)	ITU-R	785	Recomm.

Standard Type	Standard	Sponsor	Standard Reference	Status
Gov't	Facsimile Coding Schemes and Coding Control Functions for Group 4 Facsimile Apparatus (Equivalent to EIA 538-1988)	NIST	FIPS 150:1988	FIPS
Gov't	Video Teleconferencing Services at 56 to 1, 920 KB/s (equivalent to CCITT H.221, H.230, H.242, H.261, and H.320)	NIST	FIPS 178:1992	FIPS
Gov't	Raster Scanned Images (Engineering Drawings, TM Illustrations): GRP 4 Raster Scanned Images Representation in Binary Format	DoD	MIL-R-28002 MIL-R-28002B	DoD Std. (CALS Std.)
Gov't	National Imagery Transmission Format Standards (NITFS)	DoD	MIL-HDBK-1300A (NITFS)	MIL Std.
Gov't	Analogue Video Standard for Aircraft System Applications	NATO	STANNAG 3350	Std.
Emerging	Generic Coding of Moving Pictures and Associated Audio Information (MPEG 2), Part 1: Systems Part 2: Video	ISO/IEC and MPEG	13818-1 13818-2	DIS DIS
Consortia	Coding of Moving Pictures and Associated Audio for Digital Storage Media up to about 1.5 MBit/sec (Digital video data type) Part 1: Systems, Part 2: Video	MPEG	MPEG	Spec.
Consortia	JPEG/JIFF File Exchange for still images/digital video (Multicomponent and digital video data types)	(JPEG)	JPEG-8-R8	Spec.
Consortia	Multipurpose Internet Mail Extensions (MIME) (for sending formatted text, graphics, spreadsheets, audio, or video over the Internet or TCP/IP networks using SMTP)	IETF	MIME	Available, but not yet an IETF RFC
Consortia	UNIPACK (Format interface for interchange)	Apple/ SMPTE/ HDTV Group	P18.01-DO.141	Published

Figure 7.4 Abridged image and video exchange section from DOSEE (Continued).

Standard Type	Standard	Sponsor	Standard Reference	Status
De facto	Tagged Image File Format (TIFF) for still images & scanner data exchange (Multicomponent data type)	Aldus	Version 6.0	Published 6/92
De facto	WIN16-BMP/WMF for still images (Multicomponent data type)	Microsoft	Win 3.2-SDK	Published
De facto	PCX for still images (Multicomponent data type)	Z-Soft	Z-Soft Tech. Manuals	Published
De facto	Postscript for still images (Multicomponent data type)	Adobe	Postscript Level 2	Published
De facto	Photo CD for still images (Multicomponent data types)	Kodak & Philips	Kodak Tech. Manuals	Published
De facto	CCIR 601-2 Digital Video for digital video (Digital video data type)	CCIR	Version 1.0	Published
De facto	Targa-16, Targa-24 for digital video (Digital video data type)	Truvision	Targa-16 Targa-24	Available
De facto	Video 1, RLE & Indeo; RIFF -.AVI Files for digital video (Digital video data type)	Microsoft	RLE & Indeo	Published
De facto	DVI for digital video (Digital video data type)	Intel/IBM	Technical Manuals	Published
De facto	Video Disc (Analog data type)	Pioneer	Technical Manuals	Published
De facto	NTSC for television (Analog data type)	NTSC	1950 Standard	Published
De facto	OMF (Open Media Framework) (Format interface for interchange, and container for holding multimedia objects)	Avid	OMF	Published Submitted to IMA

Figure 7.4 Abridged image and video exchange section from DOSEE (Continued).

Alternative Specifications

Photo CD has five variations of CD Formats, including one to service the medical industry.

Standards Deficiencies

Not all standards can handle the exchange of calibrated color information. Notably, RGB formats are usually unreferenced as to colormetrically what pure red is.

Exchanging JPEG coded images across different JPEG implementations can lead to slightly inconsistent images when compared one for one with the original. Round-off errors in internal arithmetic are not all the same.

PostScript Level II was specifically targeted to address color images.

Portability Caveats

No standard algorithm exists for the reduction of color spaces from 24 to 16 to 8 to 4 bits. Each platform and output device uses generally different methods.

Even if calibrated color is included with the image, not all platforms are prepared to handle the specifications. Some low-end prepress systems are becoming color literate. The Photo CD does handle calibrated color information.

Related Standards

- ISO/IEC DIS 13818-4: Generic Coding of Moving Pictures and Associated Audio Information—Part 4: Compliance Testing
- ODA Document Standards
- CIE Colormetric Standards
- Bento
- ISO/IEC IS 9660 (High Sierra) (File interface for interchange). ISO 9660 covers the logical format that makes a compact disc readable. ISO-9660 is being revisited due to the introduction of CD-WO (Write-once appendable) discs and the desire to use CDs for multimedia in a UNIX environment with long names (known as the Rock Ridge proposal).

Recommendations

Select aspect ratios and resolutions equal to or greater than those available on target platforms, to protect against new display sizes and resolutions.

Keep source images if possible.

Figure 7.4 Abridged image and video exchange section from DOSEE (Continued).

facto standards are often submitted to consortia for consensus-based standardization and later to formal standards groups (e.g., ISO, ANSI, IEEE). The formal standards groups generally resolve the remaining differences between the multiple standards. Meanwhile, profile developers must make themselves aware of existing standards of all types, and choose their standards for each required base-service area as wisely as possible. Knowledge of information concerning standards deficiencies, and portability and interoperability caveats helps profile developers make wise decisions.

More additions must be made to an organization-specific profile before a profile is implementable. Procedures must be put in place to determine how to fill gaps and ensure interoperability in cases where no standards or specifications exist. Organizations must gather information concerning how different formal and *de facto* standards accommodate their performance, price, and cost-of-ownership requirements, and how to integrate new technologies and standards with the existing organization. Finally, it is necessary to determine which standards and specifications have products available. These are business and organizational matters, and are not covered in this book.

Presenting the Profile

Once the profile has been defined, a clear, coherent method is needed to present and communicate information about the profile to other people in the organization. One presentation method is to use diagrams similar to the Alcoa architectural diagrams shown in Chapters 5 and 6, populated with your organization's required services and standards. This is an attractive presentation, but it requires a lot of work to generate such a diagram. Another method is to use tables similar to those used in the DOSEE standards database, to list the standards, sponsoring organization, reference designation, and status for all standards chosen for a profile. Such tables are easy to generate, and may have already been generated by the process of defining the profile. The flaw in this latter method is that it sometimes communicates very little information.

A third way to present, and communicate information about, profile components to management and others uses a matrix based on one developed by the European Workshop on Open Systems (EWOS). As a bonus, this profile-components matrix can be also used to check the profile for completeness because it is set up to jog the memory and help ensure that interfaces and standards have not been missed. This profile-components matrix lists the standards in separate interface columns, each containing a label for a different type of interface. As will be shown shortly in examples, the interface columns are look and feel, APIs, formats, protocols, and other (miscellaneous) types of interfaces. The problem with this approach is that it is often difficult to differentiate between formats and protocols, or formats and APIs, and so on. Many standards have specifications for more than one type of interface.

Despite this flaw, several organizations have found this profile-components matrix helpful in presenting and communicating profiles. The next sections will, therefore, explain how to generate a profile-components matrix, and will show examples of defined profiles using this matrix.

The Profile-Components Identification Matrix

The EWOS matrix lists in its lefthand column the types of activity or scenario for which a profile is to be defined. The activities are defined in user terminology (e.g., text processing for the personal-workstation environment). The other columns list the various interfaces that must be addressed by an open-systems profile (Table 7.5).

Four types of interfaces are specified as column headings in the EWOS Matrix:

- Look and Feel (For portability of people)
- APIs (Application Programming Interfaces) (For portability of programs)
- Formats (For portability of data)
- Communication Protocols (For interoperability).

The identification of the best interface types for tasks and services in a profile is a complex matter, the technique for which is not yet universally agreed upon. It is, therefore, suggested that users add a fifth column, labeled *Other* as a placeholder for other types of interfaces that will be recognized over time.

Table 7.5 OSE Profile Components Matrix

Application/ Scenario	Look and Feel	APIs	Formats	Protocols	Other
Text Processing	N.A.	User I/F API System Svc. API Info. Svc. API Comm. API Cross-Category API	Info. Format Comm. Format . . .	CC (Mgt.) Protocol . . .	(. . .)
Data Access	Mgmt. L&F User I/F L&F Info. Svc. L&F	User I/F API System Svc. API Info. Svc. API 1 Info. Svc. API 2 Comm. API 1 Comm. API 2 Cross-Category API	Info. Format Data Format Comm. Format . . .	CC (Mgt.) Protocol 1 CC: (Mgt.) Protocol 2 Data Exchange Protocol . . .	(. . .)
Other Activities	(. . .)	(. . .)	(. . .)	(. . .)	(. . .)

Source: EWOS Guide to Profiles for the Open Environment, Issue 1 Draft 5. Contributed to ISO/IEC JTC1 SGFS.
Key:

API = Application Programming Interface	L&F = Look and Feel	Info. = Information	I/F = Interface
Comm. = Communication	Mgt. = Management	Svc. = Service	CC := Cross Category

Standards are entered in each of the interface columns of the matrix. These standards specify interfaces for the information-processing activities listed in the left-hand column. For each type of interface, standards are entered in the matrix for services that correspond to the "Functionality of Interfaces" (defined in Chapter 1).

- User interface services
- System services
- Information-processing services
- Communication services
- Cross-category services

Use of the Profile-Components Matrix

To generate a profile-components identification matrix, first identify the application area or scenario (e.g., transaction processing, data access, patient-invoice transfer) for which the profile has been defined.

Step 2 is to create the matrix. To do this, list the types of activity, using user terminology, in the matrix's lefthand column. List the types of interfaces (Look and Feel, APIs, Formats, Protocols, and Other (or Miscellaneous) in the topmost row as labels for the other columns).

The third step is to identify for each profile, all the types of interfaces required, and the services or functionality these interfaces must provide. The interfaces to identify include Look and Feel, API, Format, and Protocols. The services or functionality to identify should correspond to the major interface functionalities defined earlier in this book (e.g., user interface, system services, information processing, communications services, and cross-category services). Enter the identified services and their interfaces in the appropriate interface columns in the profile-components matrix.

If an activity has more than one associated API, protocol, or other interface, all the interfaces should be entered in the appropriate columns. Profiles, as well as standards, may be entered in the matrix. If there are no look and feels, APIs, formats, or protocols for a specific usage type, then entering *None* indicates the lack of standards in those areas, or a lack of need for such standards. If the need exists, but corresponding standards do not, you might want to think of products that your company might want to standardize around to fill the gap. A product is not usually a specified interface, but it might be expedient to make a note in the appropriate column of this matrix of a product that will become a standard for your company.

If there are interfaces required that do not fit into the existing interface columns, enter the interface in the Other column.

Table 7.6 shows one possible set of entries identified by a company using the EWOS profile components matrix to develop two application area profiles—for distributed-transaction processing and for electronic spreadsheet-data interchange.

Table 7.6 OSE Profile Components Matrix Example

Application/ or Scenario	Look & Feel	APIs	Formats	Protocols	Other

Transaction Processing	U—None
	S—None
	I—None
	C—None
	CC—None
		U—None
		S—ISO Cobol
		  —ANSI C
		  —C++ (Future)
		  —POSIX.1
		  —P1003.1c (Threads)
		I—ISO SQL
		  —X/Open SQL RDA
		    (Remote Database
		    Access)
		  —X/Open SQL Call
		    Level Interface (CLI)
		  —X/Open TX API
		  —X/Open TxRPC API
		  —X/Open XA API
		  —SQL Level 2
		  —Embedded SQL
		    (Cobol)
		C—X/Open XAP
		  —P1238 FTAM API
		  —P1003.12 XTI API
		  —X/Open CPI-C
		CC—P1387.4 Print Mgt.
		CC—IEEE P1003.6
		  DAC Security
		CC—X/Open C213
		  Supplementary
		  Definitions
			U—None
			S—None
			I—None
			C—None
			CC—None
				U—None
				S—None
				I—ISO 10026 DTP
				C—X.500
				  —ISO FTAM
				  —ISO ISP 10608-2
				CC—ISO CMIP
					—X/Open S302
					Internationalization
					of Interworking
					Specifications
					—CORBA
					Interoperability
					Objects (Future)

Electronic Spreadsheet	U—Windows
	  X-Windows
	S—None
	I—Proprietary
	C—None
	CC—None
		U—None
		S—None
		I—None
		C—None
		CC—None
			U—None
			S—None
			I—DIF
			  —WK1
			  —WK3
			  —WKS
			CC—None
				U—None
				S—None
				I—ISO WD 8613
				  (ODA/ODIF)
				C—(PC)NFS
				  —OSI or TCP/IP
				  —ISO CSMA/CD
				CC—None
					None

Source: Emerging Technologies Group.

Key: U—User   S—System   I—Information   C—Communications   CC—Cross Category

CMIP—Common Management Information Protocol
CPI-C—Common Programming Interface for Communications (mainframes)
DAC—Discretionary Access Control
DTP—Distributed Transaction Processing
ISP—International Standardized Profile
FTAM—File Transfer, Access and Management

ODA—Office Document Architecture
ODIF—Office Document Interchange Format
(PC)NFS—Network File System (for PCs)
TX—Transaction Demarcation Specification
XAP—XA-to-Protocol API
XTI—X/Open Transport Interface

159

Meeting Special Needs

The EWOS OSE profile components matrix can be tailored in many ways to accommodate the different ways organizations think about a problem. Two organizations, for example, defined an enterprisewide architectural model based on a hybrid of the IEEE P1003.0 model and the Emerging Technologies Group model (shown in Chapter 1), and added some additional architectural features of their own. These organizations then used the group brainstorm technique to define and populate the architectural model with required services and standards.

Having developed an open Client/Server systems planning database throughout their planning processes, the organizations retrieved the pertinent data from their databases in order to develop several profiles. Two of these profiles—for electronic mail and for PCs in an automated office—are described in the following sections.

A Miniprofile for Electronic Mail

Seventeen service requirements that were defined in one organization for an enterprisewide electronic mail system are listed below.

1. Send and receive mail between people in local work groups, and between local work groups and other company work groups, corporate personnel, and people external to the organization.
2. Store and forward mail so that messages can be sent and held if the destined recipient is not active, or forwarded to a designated recipient if the recipient is away.
3. Send electronic mail with document enclosures.
4. Send electronic mail to groups of people, or broadcast mail to all people.
5. Send binary code, various fonts, graphics, and images via electronic mail.
6. Send and receive arbitrarily long electronic-mail documents (compression/decompression).
7. Locate the address of destination recipients.
8. Post persistent messages on a bulletin board for everyone to see.
9. Combine EDI with electronic mail so predefined EDI transactions can be exchanged between applications using the X.400 message handling system.
10. Cause any electronic-mail document to be printed on any connected printer from within the electronic-mail system.
11. Queue electronic-mail documents to be printed on any specialized printer, regardless of the location of the printer.
12. Address electronic-mail destinations by a logical, intuitive name, rather than an address.
13. Send electronic mail by whatever type of network or communications that exists within a department.

14. Send electronic-mail documents to specified recipients with some assurance that unauthorized people cannot read the mail.

15. Participate in an electronic-mail system with some assurance that unauthorized people cannot navigate and snoop in other mail users' directories and files.

16. Send, read, and print mail using a graphical user interface and icons.

17. Install, configure, modify, and otherwise manage the electronic-mail system.

Having defined these service requirements, the next step was to specify the standards and specifications for the profile. The organization defining the profile found it convenient to use a variant of the EWOS profile components matrix to define and check the look and feel, APIs, formats, and protocols for this application area, as well as to identify gaps in the standards, and areas that are implementation dependent and must be filled by applications (Table 7.7).

One difference between this organization's profile matrix and the original EWOS definition is that the variant matrix's lefthand column identifies required services for a particular application, instead of a broader-based type of usage or application area. Also, the righthand column, called *Other*, is a catch-all column for specifications that did not seem to fit into the other columns, such as the data-encryption standard algorithm and proprietary products.

Which of the network transport and electronic-mail standards and/or specifications is accepted is specific to an organization. The organization defining the electronic-mail miniprofile used a combination of the Internet Suite's Simple Mail Transfer Protocol (SMTP), CCITT's X.400, SVID UUCP, and Lotus Development Corporation's cc Mail, running on TCP/IP and a variety of PC networks. OSI is planned for the future, but has not been implemented.

The matrix's standards and specifications for look and feels, APIs, formats, protocols, and so on, were then mapped onto a miniversion of the organization's architectural model to be used for communicating with management and with the other open Client/Server planning teams.

A Platform Profile for Desktop PCs

Using similar methods, one company developed what is known as a *platform profile* for desktop PCs in an office environment. As the name implies, a platform profile is a profile geared to a particular platform. The PC-based platform profile for office automation, shown in Tables 7.8 and 7.9, is based on the company's architectural model, infrastructure services, and applicable standards.

Like the organization that developed the electronic-mail profile, the company defining the PC-based office-automation profile used a variant of the OSE profile

Table 7.7 OSE Profile Components for an Electronic Mail Profile

Services	Look & Feel	APIs	Formats	Protocols	Other
–Underlying Transport	None	–P1003.1g XTI API (formerly P1003.12)	None	–TCP/IP –ISO OSI Transport –(ISO ISP 10608-2) –XTI	
–Send/Receive –E-mail; –Store-and- Forward Mail; –Enclosures; –Broadcast	None	–X/Open/APIA API –IEEE P1327.1X.400 API (C binding) –X/Open XOM (Common Object Svc.) –P1327 API (XOM) –SVID UUCP	X.400	–X.400 –SMTP –SVR4 UUCP –(Honey Danber)	
–Locate Addresses	None	–X/Open/APIA XDS –P1327.2 API (X.500: C binding) –X/Open XOM –P1327 API (XOM)	ISO X.500	ISO X.500	
–Distributed Naming Service	None	–Internet DNS –OSF DCE DNS	–Internet DNS –OSF DCE DNS	N.A.	
–Compression/ Decompression	None	–X/Open, SVID, and OSF/1 compress/ uncompress/zcat	Algorithm stds. in progress	Application	
–Send binary code, fonts, graphics, etc.	None	–IEEE P1003.2 uuencode/ uudecode	IEEE P1003.2 uuencode/ uudecode	N.A.	
–Security –Encryption –Authentication –Authorization	None None None	–X/Open, SVID, & OSF/1 crypt/ encrypt/setkey –OSF DCE –Kerberos –P1003.1e ACLs	None None P1003.1e ACLs	None None None	DES Algorithm N.A. N.A.
Bulletin Board	Impl.-Dep.	None	N.A.	N.A.	Application

Table 7.7 OSE Profile Components for an Electronic Mail Profile (Continued)

Services	Look & Feel	APIs	Formats	Protocols	Other
EDI Via E-Mail	None	X/Open EDI Messaging	CCITT X.435 X/Open EDI Messg.	CCITT X.435	
Printing in E-mail	None	None	None	None	Application or Operating System
Print Queuing	None	IEEE P1387.4	None	IEEE P1387.4	
GUI	None	Vendor Agent-Specific	N.A.	N.A.	Impl.-Dep.
Mail Mgt.	None	None	N.A.	None	Impl.-Dep.

Source: Emerging Technologies Group.

Key:

N.A.—Not Applicable

Impl.-Dep.: Implementation Dependent

10608-2—ISP International Standardized Profile for Connection-mode Transport Service over connectionless-mode network service using CSMA/CD (Ethernet) LANs

XTI—X/Open Transport-independent Interface, which is the basis for the IEEE P1003.12 protocol-independent interface standard

X/Open X.400 API—An API to X.400 Message Handling Services (jointly developed by the X.400 API Association), which is the basis for the IEEE P1224.1 X.400 API Standard

XDS—X/Open Directory Services API (jointly developed by X/Open and the X.400 API Association), which is the basic for the IEEE P1224.2 Directory Services Standard

XOM—X/Open API to object-management services

UUCP—UNIX to UNIX Communication (Copy) Protocol: UUCP is ubiquitous, having been shipped for years with every copy of System V Unix and Berkeley BSD UNIX. It was included in early drafts of the POSIX.2 standard, but was ousted from the standard after Draft 9 and is not part of the final standard.

Honey Danber—The USL SVR4 version of UUCP

uuencode and uudecode—POSIX/Unix services that translate binary and other non-ASCII code into ASCII code for transmission, and then decode the transmitted data back to binary, etc.

compress, uncompress, and zcat—Ubiquitous compression and decompression routines that were included in early POSIX.2 draft standards, are not part of the final POSIX.2 standard, but are included in the SVID, SVR4, OSF/1, and X/Open's XPG

DES—Data Encryption Standard

ACL—Access Control Lists

DNS—Distributed Naming Service

Table 7.8 A Profile for Desktop PCs: General Facilities

Services	Look & Feel	APIs	Formats	Protocols	Other
Window Mgr. & GUI Tools	MS Windows NT (Future)	MS Windows NT Future	N.A.	N.A.	
Icon-oriented desktop metaphor	MS Windows	MS Windows	None	None	Impl.-Dep.
Cut-and-Paste	MS Windows Clipboard	Microsoft DDE (Dynamic Data Exchange)	None	DDE	
Command-line metaphor	N.A.	MS Windows DOS	None	None	
On-line documentation	N.A.	N.A.	N.A.	N.A.	Application Specific
Hypertext	None	None	None	None	Proprietary
Multiple/Outline Fonts	–Adobe Type I –HP's Intellifont –Apple's TrueType	Adobe Type I HP's Intellifont Apple's TrueType	Adobe Type I HP's Intellifont Apple's TrueType	N.A.	
Presentation Graphics	None	CGM, GKS	CGM, GKS, Lotus PIC, McDraw PICT, PICT2	None	
Spreadsheet	None	None	DIF, CSV, WK4, XLS	None	
Revisable Document Interchange	None	None	ODA/ODIF	ODA/ODIF	
Import/Export	None	None	CGM, DIF, CSV, WK4, PICT, PICT2	None	
Database Front End	None	SQL SQL Access ODBC	None	None	
Departmental DBMS	None	None	Rbase	None	
EDI	None	X.12, Edifact	X.12	X.12	Proprietary
Compression	None	None	None	None	Proprietary
Virus Protection	None	None	None	None	Proprietary

Source: Emerging Technologies Group.

Table 7.9 A Profile for Desktop PCs: Communications Facilities

Services	Look & Feel	APIs	Formats	Protocols	Other
Electronic Mail (Message Transfer Agent)	None	P1327.1 API (C binding)	X.400	X.400	
File Transfer & Sharing	None	PC/NFS Netware	None	PC/NFS Netware	Proprietary
Directory Svc.	None	P1327.2 API to X.500 (C binding)	X.500	X.500	
Client/Server Protocol	None	None	None	None	Proprietary
RPC	None	OSF DCE RPC	None	OSF DCE RPC	Proprietary
Terminal Emulation	None	None	None	Telnet VT 100	
Dial-up Protocol	None	None	None	Kermit X-Modem Y-Modem	
Transport Provider	None	None	None	TCP/IP Netware	Proprietary PC LANs
Printing	None	MS Windows	None	None	Proprietary
Remote Printing	None	Netware NT	None	Netware NT	
Backup	None	None	None	None	Proprietary
PC Mgt.	None	OSF DME Netware NT SMS	None	SNMP Netware	
License Mgt.	None	OSF DME NLS	None	SNMP Netware	

Source: Emerging Technologies Group.

Key:

4GL—Fourth generation language

DME—OSF's distributed management environment

NLS—Network Licensing System (An OSF DME service for controlling organization-oriented software licensing policies)

(Continued)

Table 7.9 A Profile for Desktop PCs: Communications Facilities (Continued)

Rbase—An SQL-compatible PC database management system manufactured by Microrim

ODA/ODIF—Office Document Architecture/Office Document Interchange Format (ISO IS 8613)

PICT, PICT2—Apple Macintosh graphics and imaging formats and compression systems

CGM—Computer Graphics Metafile (ISO IS 8632)

GKS—Graphical Kernel System (ISO IS 7942 standard for 2-D graphics)

DIF, WK4—Vendor-developed spreadsheet exchange formats that are *de facto* standards

SMTP—TCP/IP Internet Suite's simple mail transfer Protocol

PC/NFS—A version of Sun Microsystems' network file system for PCs to access servers and mainframes

Telnet—TCP/IP's virtual terminal application protocol

P1327.1 API—An IEEE API for X.400 message handling services, based on the message handling API developed by X/Open and the X.400 API Association

P1327.2 API—An IEEE API for Directory Services, based on the Directory Services API developed by X/Open and the X.400 API Association

DCE RPC—OSF distributed computing environment's remote procedure call

DDE—Dynamic data exchange

Netware—Novell's PC LAN software

8802.2—IEEE's data link protocol standard (identical to ISO IS 8802/2)

8802.3—IEEE's CSMA/CD media access standard (identical to ISO IS 8802/3 and almost, but not quite, equivalent to Ethernet)

components matrix that lists the required office automation services in the matrix's lefthand column. Also, the righthand Other column is a catch-all column for product standards and proprietary specifications. Proprietary products are intentionally omitted from the matrix.

The desktop PC profile discussed here is one possible platform profile for desktop PCs. Many organizations will develop different profiles to suit their needs. This profile, however, is typical of profiles for PCs used in an office environment.

An organization might require a desktop PC to support any of the following types of applications: word processing, spreadsheet, drawing, presentation graphics, desktop publishing, electronic mail, bulletin-board support, file transfer, a departmental database, an SQL front-end to obtain data from corporate databases, and a windowing-based graphical user interface (GUI).

The GUI would be expected to provide desktop facilities such as drag and drop, the ability to cut and paste between applications, GUI libraries for building GUI-based applications, a calendar, clock, calculator, a drawing tool, and perhaps some games. Electronic mail would require security, particularly authentication and authorization. The SQL front end implies interoperability with various company databases. This interoperability requires, in turn, an underlying transport method (network, modem, or both), and probably a virtual terminal protocol to access mainframes. Also required by this networking is a way to manage the PC and any PC networks from the company's backbone network and server platforms.

All the software, including the windows software and the applications, require clearly written hard-copy documentation, and also on-line documentation. The on-line documentation should support hypertext facilities to maximize the usefulness of the on-line help that the application can provide.

The desktop PC Platform functional components are, theoretically, a subset of the functional components identified by the architecture, infrastructure, and application experts planning teams in the development of the enterprise architectural model. As often happens, the process of defining an actual profile targeted at a specific area uncovered a few items omitted from the original set of identified services. These were added to the original model and the open Client/Server planning database.

Attempts to make a direct match between the functional components and service requirements in a miniversion of an organization's architectural-reference model and the standards identified to provide those services and functional components will reveal that there are more items in the functional components model than in the populated standards model. This is due to the lack of standards in certain areas. Since functionality is needed in the real world (what good is a portable, interoperable system that can't do useful work?), these functional areas must be filled by *de facto* standards, proprietary products, or any other types of specifications that rank low in the standards preference hierarchy.

Moving from Generic to Specific OSE Planning

The open-profile development methodology is intended to provide guidance for open Client/Server environment planners. Open-system profiles, however, even if they are geared to a particular application area, provide an idea of the *de jure* and *de facto* standards to aim for to achieve maximum interoperability and portability. Rarely, however, is a standards-based profile suited in its generic form to all organizations. Many vendor-specific, product-specific, cost, performance, and other nonstandard attributes must be taken into account at deployment time.

Beginning with the next chapter, the open Client/Server planning methodology moves out of the conceptual planning world into the real-world information technology environment. The rest of this book focuses on deployment issues such as business process reengineering, distributing applications, choosing initial applications, assessing the role of the mainframe, planning how to manage the Client/Server environment, determining the Client/Server environment's cost, and developing a migration strategy.

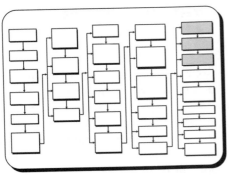

Chapter 8

Phase Seven: Planning for Deployment

Introduction

By the end of Phase Six, the standards for your project should be selected and fairly well prioritized, the Client/Server requirements determined, and the Client/Server application areas, and possibly platforms, selected and prioritized. With the major open system and Client/Server system planning tasks completed, the time has come for the application expert, architecture, and infrastructure teams to turn a good deal of open Client/Server planning work over to the deployment team and subteams.

In Phase Seven, Client/Server planners begin to plan for deployment. During this phase, Client/Server planners decide whether or not to reengineer their applications for Client/Server computing, choose the initial functional application area(s) to implement and the initial platforms to use to support open Client/Server applications, and address a number of Client/Server and open system issues that must be resolved before actual migration can begin (Figure 8.1).

Client/Server Issues

The major technical issues and challenges that users must face and decide on before migrating to open Client/Server environments include:

- Whether or not to reengineer existing applications
- How to distribute the applications
- What to do about the mainframe
- Selection of initial applications to migrate
- Choice of appropriate servers

Decide whether or not to reengineer existing applications for Client/Server computing.

Decide how to distribute the applications.

Decide how to protect legacy mainframe investments.

Choose the initial functional application area and platforms that you will implement using open-systems technology and a Client/Server architecture.

Select scalable servers appropriate to the application.

Figure 8.1 Planning for deployment.

Three other important issues—selection of appropriate middleware for the Client/Server applications and architecture, determining how to manage the Client/Server environment, and determining the cost of the open Client/Server environment—are discussed later in this book.

Re-engineering: More Bang for the Bit

Client/Server computing allows users to create a more flexible and scalable computing infrastructure than is possible with traditional monolithic mainframe-computing architectures. It allows knowledge workers to more easily and simultaneously access the data they need when they need it, because they need not depend on overworked technology-oriented MIS professionals and wait in an application backlog queue.

Client/Server computing also allows computing to become more business-results oriented. Results-oriented computing, in turn, allows organizations to more quickly respond to events and market changes, and to better compete globally. It allows the reduction of paper pushing because Client/Server systems allow work to automatically and concurrently flow, electronically, to the people and places where they are needed.

Most users have read about these benefits. Users must bear in mind, however, that these benefits are not automatic. Most existing applications were written for traditional centralized environments. Many of these applications, in their present form, do not readily lend themselves to Client/Server processing. Consequently, only incremental improvements can be achieved if users simply reimplement their existing systems using new software technology (a process called software re-engineering), and don't also change the basic business processes to take full advantage of Client/Server computing (a process called business-process re-engineering).

Business-process re-engineering is defined as the rethinking and redesign of basic business processes, organizational structures, and values in order to achieve new goals. In Client/Server environments, the goals in question are those possible with Client/Server systems. Examples of business processes that organizations have re-engineered include revamping the way they deal with customers, run their field offices, handle service and delivery schedules, deal with taxpayers and legislators, and redesign actual product development and manufacturing systems.

This kind of business-process re-engineering should not be confused with software reengineering, which is limited to the reautomation of old business procedures. The benefits of business-process re-engineering to take advantage of Client/Server capabilities benefits are often dramatic improvements in performance, costs, quality, and service.

To cite one example, several organizations that have redesigned their business processes and applications for Client/Server processing report significantly decreased computing costs compared to the costs incurred for running comparable processes on traditional centralized mainframes. These experiences run contrary to the many stories that talk about the high costs of Client/Server computing.

In addition, several of the companies that re-engineered their business processes and applications report increased revenues for existing and/or new services that would not have been possible without Client/Server computing. Other companies report competitive advantages since they can offer new services that bring in new revenues, where such offerings would have taken two to four times longer to bring to market under traditional centralized mainframes.

The problem with business-process re-engineering is that a change in an organization's business processes inevitably ripples through many aspects of an organization, both business oriented and information-technology oriented. For example, job definitions, the business-management structure, the management of various business or information-technology processes, training, compensation, and many people's beliefs about what is important to an organization, are among the things affected. What this means is that cooperative processing requires cooperation not only between computer applications, but between people in the enterprise. Unfortunately, many people in an organization resist these kinds of changes.

Because business-process re-engineering can affect so many people in an organization, in order to get support for this kind of change business process re-engineering must be led by a strong-minded, persuasive senior manager. This manager should have a vision of how the organization should look in the future and how to get there.

State of Minnesota Re-engineering Example

No one wants to pay taxes. Since the law says that taxes must be paid, there are ways that Client/Server computing can help make the paying of taxes more palatable. The state of Minnesota Department of Revenues (DOR), provides an example of how this can be done.

Like all states, Minnesota has computer programs to ensure that taxpayers pay their taxes on time, to notify the taxpayers if they fail to do so, and to deposit the taxes in a bank. But the Minnesota DOR has re-engineered its sales-tax system to use Client/Server computing to increase taxpayer compliance with the tax laws, reduce taxpaying stress in times of trouble, show the taxpayers that the state is providing something for their tax dollars, and to notify state legislators about taxpayer problems that should concern the legislators, as well as the taxpayers and the DOR (Figure 8.2).

The state of Minnesota DOR's Client/Server system is essentially a workflow program based largely on Lotus Notes and SQL data access from a Sybase database. The Client/Server-based sales-tax system has 1300 client systems directly attached to its servers and thousands of users statewide.

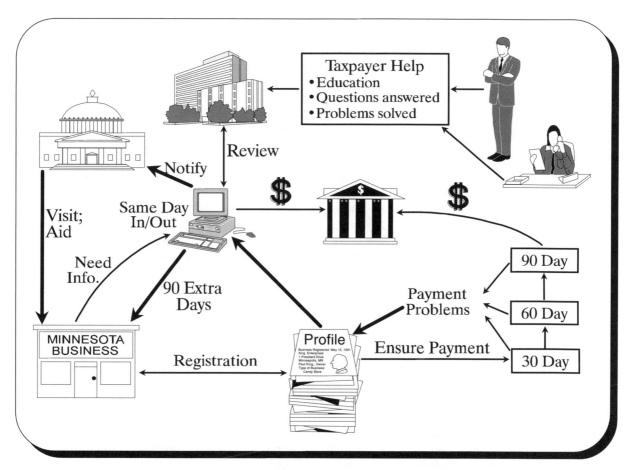

Figure 8.2 Minnesota re-engineered Client/Server sales-tax system. Source: Emerging Technologies Group and state of Minnesota Dept. of Revenues.

At the core of its Client/Server-based sales-tax system, the DOR maintains a profile of all taxpayers. The profiles include such items as descriptions of the taxpayers' businesses, the taxes they should pay, and their geographic locations. These profiles can be used to tailor services for individuals or groups of taxpayers.

To show one way in which this Client/Server system is used, when a crisis such as the midwest floods of 1993 occurs, the state recognizes that business owners are more concerned with their business's survival than with paying taxes. Automatic dunning tax letters merely serve to antagonize the taxpayers and make them nervous. In this kind of crisis situation, the dunning letters do not, generally, make them pay their taxes faster. So, why waste money and energy and generate hard feelings trying to enforce the unenforceable?

To address this situation, a DOR user keys information about the geographical regions hit by the flood into the Minnesota Client/Server-based sales-tax system. The sales-tax system reacts instantly matching the flood region with the taxpayers in that region. The system then sends letters to the taxpayers telling them that the Department of Revenues is aware of the problems caused by the flood, and thus 90 extra days of grace are granted before payment is due.

The information about the taxpayers hit by the flood is also sent to legislators from the district in question. Alternatively, the legislators can access the Client/Server sales-tax system for information about which taxpayers are affected by the flood. The legislators use this information for many purposes, ranging from visiting their constituents to assessing the monetary problems and requesting immediate federal aid. The taxpayers themselves can also access the sales tax system for a variety of reasons. Some taxpayers' reasons for accessing the system are problems to be solved and questions to be answered.

The Client/Server sales-tax system uses four different server-platform operating systems (AIX, OS/2, NetWare, and MVS), with the major client-operating system being Windows. The various clients and servers are connected locally and remotely by Novell's IPX, TCP/IP, and SNA, in token ring, Ethernet, T-1, Frame Relay, and STAR topologies.

The Client/Server architecture is largely a two-tier one, although some mainframe interactions are necessary. The Client/Server database runs on UNIX servers. The applications themselves, such as Lotus Notes, data entry, and others, run on NetWare-based workgroup servers or on client systems. The server applications are accessed using a graphical user interface, which is located on the client PC.

The applications are developed using C and SQL, with PowerBuilder for client GUI development and two-tier application distribution. CPI-C (IBM's Common Programming Interface for Communications) is the major interface to get to the mainframe.

The reengineering process required changes in the DOR's business processes, organizational culture, and application development. Tables 8.1 and 8.2 show some of the business/organizational and application development changes that were made as part of the reengineering process, many of which are typical of reengineering changes made in all kinds of organizations.

Table 8.1   Business and Organizational Changes Due to Reengineering

Old	New
Inward focus, on taxpayer	External focus, on customer
Assessment/collections priority	Win compliance priority
Emphasis on protecting your turf	Value on supporting each other
Customary to keep information to yourself	Policy is to share information
Practice is to report on policy changes after they occur	Practice is to solicit input during the policy process
Tell the customers what they need to comply	Ask the customers what they need to comply
Generic, one size fits all	Customize to industry groups
Decisions made by formal leaders	Decisions made where work is done
Managers manage functions	Managers manage business processes
Single-function jobs	Multifunctional jobs
Paper	Electronic (future)
Media—reactive	Media—outreach

Source: State of Minnesota, Department of Revenues.

Table 8.2   Application Development Changes Due to Client/Server Systems

Old	New
Traditional system development methods and backlog	Accelerated application development
All requirements and development work is done behind the scenes and suddenly it appears	Ongoing interaction and development
Years of requirements definition	Months of requirements definition
Application design is locked in up-front	Application is adapted during design, prototyped, and adapted again
Hard coded and inflexible	Code generation and tables make applications flexible
User unfriendly (3270 screens)	Easy to use because of GUIs, on-line help, etc.
Applications written in Cobol	Applications written using PowerBuilder

Source: State of Minnesota, Department of Revenues.

How to Distribute Client/Server Applications

To efficiently implement a multitiered Client/Server architecture, the following questions must be answered:

- On which tier (or tiers) should data be located?
- On which tier (or tiers) should application logic be located?
- On which tier (or tiers) should a user interface be located?

The answers to these questions reflect the interactions among application components. They are decided by examining such factors as the quantity of data relevant to individual applications, the number of users concurrently running applications against this data, the technical characteristics of the applications, and the technical characteristics of the client and server platforms. The availability of applications on certain platforms also affects how and where applications are distributed.

Many people envision the user interface being located at the lowest tier on desktop clients. Desktop machines provide fast response, interactivity, and bit-mapped graphics. Modern desktop machines also support a number of multimedia capabilities. Consequently, the desktop client is usually selected to handle functions such as presenting the results of applications, formatting data, data-entry procedures, reporting, and so on.

Application logic and/or data can be placed on the bottom, middle, or top tier, or possibly all tiers. Applications encoding business rules and personal-productivity applications/tools usually reside on the lowest tier. Workflow applications are usually implemented on middle-tier workgroup servers. High-volume transaction-oriented applications would be implemented either on a middle-tier high-end information processing server or a top-tier traditional mainframe.

Mainframes make excellent database servers (this is discussed in this chapter in "What to Do About the Mainframe"). However, UNIX also has very good database-management systems which are usually relational. UNIX machines are therefore commonly used as data servers.

Table 3.4 in Chapter 3, on guidelines for choosing a two-Tier or three-Tier Architecture, the text accompanying this guidelines table and much of the material in the sections on Client/Server architectures, is devoted to detailed suggestions on, and examples of, how to distribute applications in a Client/Server environment. Readers with further questions on distributing applications in a Client/Server environment are advised to review this material.

What to Do About the Mainframe

The question of what to do about the mainframe invariably arises during Client/Server and open-system environment planning. Since the mainframe issue can affect planners' Client/Server and open-system migration decisions, and the time for migrating, it is necessary to briefly address the mainframe issue here.

Legacy Mainframes: Here Today, Here Tomorrow

Most organizations do not want to scrap their working mainframes and all the legacy applications that have been built up over many years. The mainframe is an example of an expensive, highly competent legacy system on which many of an organization's critical data and applications reside. Many MIS professionals who know the tools, security, archiving, and other capabilities available for mainframes, compared to those available for emerging open system platforms, are downright fearful of the impact of scrapping the mainframe.

However, the ownership of a legacy system does not necessarily mean it is a good investment. In fact, the maintenance of some legacy computers and applications might actually be an overly burdensome expense, requiring a good deal of the organization's cost structure. So Client/Server and open-system planners need to look closely at legacy applications to determine which ones are more of a cost and resource drain on the organization rather than an investment, and chose which ones should stay and which should be replaced by newer, more interoperable servers.

In general, many users who have begun moving to, or planning for, open systems are not planning to unplug their mainframes (although many will not buy any more mainframes). There are several reasons for this decision.

First, the mainframe is a good data-management server and can have an ongoing role in a Client/Server system. Second, it is one of a number of working legacy systems that are going to stay around for a long time in many organizations because it is not cost-effective to replace them.

Some users integrate the mainframe into a three-tiered Client/Server architecture where the mainframe has an ongoing role running its traditional applications, while data is distributed on smaller UNIX-based servers, close to certain local sites that are most interested in that data. In other cases, users keep the corporate data on the mainframe and distribute the traditional mainframe applications on UNIX-based middle-tier servers.

In many cases, it is a good idea to move almost anything off the mainframe except corporate data. Database navigation is a time-consuming, compute-intensive operation. It is not unusual for a database search to require several hours. Data also is the key to many businesses' and organizations' revenues. It needs to be treasured, guarded, and given kid-glove care.

All in all, mainframes are exceptionally good data-management servers. They handle data management better than almost any other platform. At present, mainframes have a lot of sophisticated capabilities related to data management (e.g., security, backup and archiving, maintenance of data integrity, and performance) that have yet to be made available on UNIX servers.

It is true that UNIX is gaining more and more of these capabilities. In general, corporate data, as well as applications with high-security, mission-critical requirements should be kept on the mainframe, at least for the short term. However, there are a number of traditional mainframe applications that can be moved onto small networked servers located close to the physical site that is most concerned with them. These servers would run the applications, provide information to authorized users, and use the mainframe as still another server to access the data they need.

There also is a need for middle-tier data servers. Locked-up data that is accessible only to a small number of MIS people is no longer the appropriate model for a good deal of data. Many kinds of data must be easily available to authorized people who need to analyze it and to make timely decisions based on their analysis. In a Client/ Server environment, this kind of data is generally located on middle-tier servers. The data may be implemented specifically for Client/Server work. Or the mid-tier data server may contain a subset of the mainframe enterprise data. In the latter case, the mid-tier data server may be updated periodically by the mainframe.

Choosing the First Application

A move to open systems and/or Client/Server systems requires an organization to undergo a lot of change, which can be difficult. While change may solve some problems, it often happens that the chief cause of new problems within an organization is the solutions to old problems. Therefore, the open Client/Server system areas implemented first should be those which solve immediate problems, have fast payoff, and are quick and easy to implement. It is wise to start with a pilot implementation. Implementing multiple open-system areas at one time is not recommended. Doing so makes it difficult to determine why applications that should be compatible aren't.

The initial open-systems–based application will be many users' (planners, implementors, and end users) first experience with open or Client/Server systems. Therefore, the open Client/Server environment planning teams should choose a functional area that is easy enough to be successful and can provide a good learning experience. However, they should also make sure their application is important enough to have value to the organization, and is not so trivial that it provokes a so what reaction. Also, it makes sense to choose an application that has a reasonably high visibility so it can gain further open system support in the organization.

Electronic mail is often a traditional choice for a first open and Client/Server systems experience, followed by file access and sharing, data access, sharing of PC productivity-tool data, and workflow applications. Virtual-terminal applications also are important to Client/Server computing because virtual-terminal provides access to the mainframes.

The desire to connect organizations' many PCs to servers in order to provide PC users with the information they need in a timely manner is a major factor driving the selection of these applications for initial Client/Server activities. Electronic mail is sometimes implemented on numerous vendors' midsize UNIX servers and accessed by the organization's PCs running DOS or Windows. In other organizations, electronic mail is implemented on Intel-based PCs, running Netware (and more recently, NT) and accessed by other Intel-based PCs.

Data-access Client/Server applications, on the other hand, more commonly involve a UNIX-based database (e.g., Sybase, Oracle, Informix) running on a midsize

UNIX server and accessed by Intel-based PCs running DOS or Windows. Workflow applications commonly involve PCs running a network operating system like Netware or NT, but they can also use UNIX-based servers. Certain traditional machines, such as the AS/400, have also shown very good performance for workflow applications.

Users should understand that it is just as important to the success of a new technology like open systems technology or Client/Server technology, not to make enemies as it is to have strong supporters, and possibly more so. Open systems is still tenuous enough at most companies that if a few people believe that it was a serious mistake, development efforts might grind to a halt. Because a failure can make many enemies, mission-critical and bet-your-business applications should wait until later phases for migration.

Implementation Criteria

Figure 8.3 sums up some criteria for choosing which applications to migrate to open Client/Server technology, and whether to migrate them in the short, medium, or long term. The problem of deciding how and when to use these criteria is illustrated by one Emerging Technologies Group study of users moving to open systems. Responses to this study showed that users ranked some high-priority requirements relatively low on their purchasing plans not because standards were a low-priority requirement, but because the users doing the ranking knew that approved standards were not generally available in products.

Although many vendors offered interim versions of these standards in progress, users shied away from using them because they did not want to jeopardize their chances of future compatibility with other vendors' equipment. Although many users would like to try out some of the nonstandardized versions of standards functionality,

- How easy or difficult is the application to migrate?
- How critical is the application to the company's business?
- How visible is the application area to users in various departments?
- Is the application stable, or likely to change?
- Does the application require a lot of external interaction and communications?
- What computer system services (e.g., operating system, data management, data interchange, graphics) does the application require, and do standards exist for these services?

Figure 8.3 Some criteria for choosing open system applications.
Source: Emerging Technologies Group.

they were not willing to go through two application implementations—one for the interim version of the standard and another for the final standard.

In general, if a standard or other consensus specification has been in progress for a while or is imminent, logic suggests that open-system planners consider waiting until the standard is completed. If, however, no standards efforts are underway in a certain functional area, or if an approved standard is three to four years away with implementation even farther off but the functionality is required now, then use of a vendor product must be considered.

In the latter case, the objection that the use of a vendor product will require reimplementation in five years, using an open-systems technology has minimal significance because in five years even standards change. Consider, as evidence, the fact that the SQL 2 standard developers have already begun work on SQL 3, which will handle object databases. SQL 3 will not be completed for some time. Vendors will not wait for SQL 3—instead, they have already begun implementing (or have implemented) SQL 2 because SQL 2 functionality is essential to database management.

Although all formal standards are required to undergo a review for revision every five years, most standards do not change all that much. Often, a revision consists of the addition of a few new capabilities, clarification of terms, and some bug fixes. Other standards, however, undergo massive changes during their review. Examples are the changes to the Cobol standard as it progressed in 1961, 1968, 1974, and 1985; the Fortran standard between 1977 and 1990, and, possibly, the SQL 3 standard because of the desire to standardize and integrate SQL and object databases.

Another important criterion in selecting applications for open-systems implementation is the stability of the application in question. Applications that frequently change, and need constant reimplementing on different platforms, have the potential for faster payback if they are migrated to open-systems technology than do highly stable applications because, with open-systems technology, the cost both of reimplementation and of training is reduced.

A third consideration when choosing an open-systems application is the amount of external interaction and communications required by the application. Applications that require a lot of external interaction and communications have the potential for a faster payback because the cost of constantly updating interfaces to multiple applications and communicating equipment can be reduced or eliminated.

Case Studies: Choosing Open-Systems Applications

A good idea of how to apply some of the criteria for choosing targeted open-system applications can be gained by studying some real users' experiences. As is often the case in the real world, the answers to questions and the decisions made, are not simple and straightforward. Instead, they tend to be fuzzy and to combine the attributes of open-systems and nonstandard systems. Often, the ability to satisfy immediately required functionality, while also satisfying open-systems goals, requires the implementation of nonstandard systems in the short term, with the vendors of these currently nonstandard systems required to demonstrate a timely migration plan to open systems.

Two case studies of real users' experiences in selecting initial open-systems application targets are described in Figures 8.4 and 8.5. Both users are industrial companies, but comparable situations based on different applications could just as well have arisen in any other type of organization.

Company A, an industrial "metals" company, made the decision to move to open systems two years ago. No less than the company's chairman announced that "All persons in A should have available the data or information they require to enable them to excel in performing their work."

A's computing environment, which comprised non-networked, non-integrated, heterogeneous systems, could not achieve this vision at an acceptable price. Hence, the company considered it business mission-critical to establish a worldwide Information Systems architecture, which facilitates information availability and transfer. Within the architecture, the company would procure standards-based products for networks, database management systems, data interchange, graphics, programming languages, and operating systems, all sitting on Unix, and POSIX as it became available. So the company came up with a plan and a time-scale.

In the midst of this transition, software developers in the firm's industrial plants were faced with the task of upgrading computers. The upgrade would force them to rewrite certain critical applications that were used for real-time furnace control in the ingot plant, as well as for certain other real-time process applications.

Since these applications had to be rewritten for a different computer, it seemed ideal to redo them under real-time Unix and POSIX. Unix was considered the closest thing to an operating system standard until full-blown POSIX was available. Some plants were already using Modcomp's real-time Unix for other critical real-time applications. So the use of Unix would not result in company culture shock.

The application developers in the plants disagreed. They argued that they had to produce results that met bottom-line expectations. Meeting bottom-line expectations was more important than moving to open systems. These application developers were used to working with Digital Equipment Corporation's VMS operating system, and they knew what it could do and could not do. Furthermore, they knew from first-hand experience that VMS was reliable, robust, and trustworthy, while Unix-based open systems were just emerging.

Unix and POSIX proponents, and the corporate MIS open systems teams argued that if the company rewrote the applications now in VMS for the new machines, in five years, when the entire company was moving to Unix, the applications would have to be rewritten again.

Figure 8.4 The proprietary versus open systems issue (Continued).

Questioning of Company A's plant development people revealed that this particular application was a real-time application with very demanding, time-critical real-time response requirements. Vanilla POSIX.1 could not satisfy these requirements. And real-time POSIX was not close enough to completion at the time to be considered.

This real-time issue was puzzling because VMS was not a real-time system, and was not deterministic enough to satisfy this application's real-time requirements. It turned out, however, that some time ago, the company had developed a fully pre-emptable, highly-deterministic version of the VMS kernel, which has, since then, operated reliably providing the real-time responsiveness needed by this and other real-time applications.

After listening to the discussions about Unix, POSIX, and VMS, Emerging Technologies Group discerned three critical points to clarify:

1. How critical is the application to the company's business?

2. How stable is the application?

3. Does the application require a lot of external interaction and communications?

The answer to question 1 was easy. Some of the applications in question were among the most critical to Company A's business, and its ability to perform the operations directly resulted in revenues for the company.

Question 2's answer was that the applications involved are very stable. They hadn't changed in the past five years, and they were not (or were barely) expected to change in the next five.

Finally, question 3's answer was that the applications in question were mostly standalone applications, controlled by a single computer. The applications have few requirements for interaction or communications with the outside world.

Decision

Company A decided to rewrite these particular real-time applications for VMS. This seemed prudent since there was no real-time POSIX standard yet. Furthermore, these applications were so critical to the company's business that they were considered too risky to be an early target for the emerging open systems technologies. Finally, since the applications involved were very stable, and had few requirements for external communications, they did not need Unix or POSIX to help provide interoperability or portability.

Figure 8.4 The proprietary versus open systems issue (Continued).

As for the problem of having to rewrite the applications again for Unix or POSIX in five years, it was agreed that, at the time, operating system standards were in such a state of transition that even if a pro-POSIX/Unix decision were made, in all likelihood, the applications would have to be rewritten in five years anyway.

It should be noted that this decision was made a few years ago. If the same decision were to be made after the IEEE P1003.4 Real-Time Extensions to the POSIX standard was approved and available in products, or even if it was only a few months away from final approval, the decision might be very different.

Company A's Second Open Systems Decision

Readers should also note that a similar issue arose at this same company concerning a "Shop Floor" application. Shop floor applications are concerned with managing the plant floor as a whole. Toward this end, they perform a lot of data collection and transaction processing, concerned with lot control, work-in-process, employee time and activities, etc.

Real-time is not a big issue for shop floor applications. Parts of shop floor applications, however, may be subject to constant change to reflect changes in business and production techniques. Also, shop floor applications have connections to many different systems on the plant floor and interact with many other systems. Shop floor applications, however, are not directly critical to the company's ability to generate revenues. Finally, some, although not all, of the major required standards needed for shop floor applications were approved standards that were available in products. Even though all the standards required for the shop floor application did not yet exist, it was considered feasible to gradually evolve and upgrade the Unix/POSIX-based shop floor application to the emerging standards, without disrupting business operations.

Unlike the case with the real-time applications, when all these factors were considered, the company decided that shop floor control was a good open systems target application. The company is now in the process of interviewing vendors and designing and implementing the shop floor application for a Unix-based open systems environment.

Figure 8.4 The proprietary versus open systems issue (Continued).

One idea that characterizes both these case studies also characterizes most organizations today. Most organizations are polarized into two factions. One faction wants to move to open systems; the other wants to stay with proprietary systems. The faction that wants to stay with proprietary systems is usually directly responsible for the organization's daily operations (e.g., production, billing). The people within that faction want to retain the status quo because they know it works. To these people, moving to any new technology is a high-risk proposition. It is such operations people that will have to bear the blame for decreased production, fouled-up billing, and more, if something goes wrong.

Company B, a large process company, with both Digital Equipment Corporation VMS systems and Hewlett-Packard HP-UX and MPE systems, wants to move to open systems, including Unix and POSIX. The company is polarized around VMS and HP-UX. It is currently making plans to move to Unix and POSIX, including for hard real-time process control programs. They are starting their migration with a particular process control application with demanding real-time constraints.

The VMS camp, led by a VMS consultant who developed many programs for Company B, doesn't think the present real-time HP-UX can handle Company B's real-time requirements. Company B's experience, however, was with HP's discontinued real-time HP-UX. HP's newer real-time HP-UX version (called HP-RT) can handle critical real-time because it embeds Lynx Real-Time Systems' LynxOS kernel inside HP-UX. But HP-RT wasn't ready at decision time.

The HP camp doesn't want VMS because they want their real-time applications to be independent of the operating system. Not only is VMS not isolated from its applications, but it cannot handle critical real-time constraints without customizing its kernel.

This application might be a good DECelx target. DECelx is Digital's hard open real-time operating system which embeds the Wind River Systems' real-time executive in DEC UNIX (based on the OSF/1 operating system). Unfortunately, neither the VMS nor the HP camps had heard of DECelx, so they vetoed this suggestion.

Decision

In the end, Company B decided to use VMS as an interim solution for the application in question, and plan a migration strategy to HP-RT for the future. This seemed prudent since they had to have the application now, and there was no approved real-time POSIX standard or product available. HP-RT could not be used at the time because it was still under development and, therefore, did not yet exist as a product. DECelx could not be used, even if the company's polarized factions could be convinced that it could do the job, because insufficient associated tools were ready, and Digital was vague about when the full systems, with tools, networking, and integration hooks would be available.

Since the company was in the process of planning its movement to open systems, it had to buy what it needed for its day-to-day operations. As a result, suppliers' open systems migration strategies became one of the major purchasing criteria for Company B.

Figure 8.5 The second proprietary versus open systems issue.

In contrast, the people who want open systems are the strategic planners whose job it is to have a long- and medium-term vision. These are the people who will bear the blame for losing market share to competitors who gain a technological edge, and for not preparing the company for the twenty-first century.

Resolving these two factions requires a great deal of political skill, as well as technical expertise. Good boundary persons, with one foot in the management and political camp and the other in the technical camp, and who communicate between them, are an asset to companies planning and migrating to open Client/Server environments.

Downsizing, Rightsizing, or Fantasizing?

Many users' major reasons for moving from proprietary mainframes and minicomputers to open Client/Server systems involve the overall downsizing of their information systems. Such downsizing is intended to save money by moving to smaller-scale computers.

Downsizing also allows organizations to automate, and interoperate with, departments and branches that cannot justify the cost of a mainframe. The different size sites within a single organization result in the use of different size computers. For example, headquarters is likely to retain their legacy mainframes. Large remote sites will probably use large servers, while smaller sites will probably use smaller servers.

A goal of all this downsizing is to use open-systems–based software and interfaces to run the same vertical applications and tools on all the heterogeneous, possibly multivendor platforms across the enterprise, and to integrate all the computers in an enterprise, regardless of their size. If this goal is satisfied, everyone in the enterprise can access and use the data, applications, and other resources they need to do their jobs.

Unfortunately, in the early stages of open Client/Server systems, many user companies think that they can supply their entire companies with "Little Computer" models, often from "The Tiny Computer Corporation." Their idea is to connect large numbers of these Little Computer models into a Client/Server network. Since the Little Computer models are getting faster and faster, the organization hopes to get equivalent performance to what was available on mainframes at substantially reduced costs, and also disperse computing intelligence among more people. This concept is commonly called *downsizing* or *rightsizing*.

There are many examples of companies that have successfully downsized. Unfortunately, the hype surrounding downsizing has raised many people's expectations of downsizing to a misleading level, which can wreak havoc with an organization, not to mention with people's careers. The result is neither downsizing nor rightsizing, but "fantasizing." Downsizing only works if the organization planning the downsizing has a sound idea of the right platform for the job, understands which applications lend themselves to downsizing, and knows which of the downsizing benchmarks, which almost every vendor touts, apply to its applications.

A Downsizing Case Study

Figure 8.6 presents a case study of a construction company that learned its downsizing reality lesson the hard way. The company involved was misled by vendors

The company described in this case study is a company that designs, constructs, and manages shopping centers around the world. Before the downsizing decision, the company was running its applications on an IBM 4381, which was running a CICS Cobol environment. The company had just passed the $1 billion mark and needed to move up to a 3090.

The company asked for a quote on the 3090. The quote turned out to be in the order of several million dollars. As a result, the company's information planners decided that perhaps the time had come to look into an open systems alternative.

In an open bid for a 3090 alternative system, the company asked for the following guarantees:

- Support for 60 or 70 users simultaneous, maximum.

- A total of 2 1/2 transactions per second generated by the users together (which is considered a mild requirement for a transaction processing system); and

- A maximum delay time on a commit of 2 1/2 seconds (which is also considered to be quite mild, especially since subsecond delay times are fairly common in transaction processing applications).

In answer to the open bid, the company received quotes ranging from PCs to a half-million dollar multiprocessing system—all guaranteeing the required performance. That all these different machines could meet the same requirements as the company mainframe was somewhat disconcerting to the company. The company's information planners decided that, guarantee or no guarantee, PCs probably couldn't do the job. On the other hand, the company figured that if all these machines could meet the performance requirements, there was no need to spend $500,000. So they choose a system costing about $175,000.

The system was installed, and put into production. It ran the first 10 simultaneous users acceptably well. Then the performance began to degrade. And at about 15 simultaneous users, it took minutes for a commit.

Then the fun and games started. The company asked themselves what they did wrong. They brought the company's MIS resources to bear on the problem, and also brought in a set of consultants to help them figure it out.

Six months later, the company had its answer. The bidder companies who guaranteed that their systems could meet the construction company's performance requirements guaranteed this performance based on the TPC-A benchmarks. The TPC-A benchmarks are good benchmarks for certain purposes. They use real, rather than simulated users. The benchmarks are audited.

Figure 8.6 OLTP downsizing: A case study (Continued).

However, the TPC-A benchmarks pertain to certain type of transaction processing application—debit/credit benchmarks, such as those used in banking transactions. Debit/credit transactions are relatively simple transactions. The picture which finally emerged after the six months of study is that the construction company's transactions were actually quite complex—perhaps 10 times as complex as TPC-A and other banking transactions which are quoted as being "normal."

By definition, one million instructions executed per second equals one MIP. In this case, measurements showed that it took on the order of 9/10th of a MIP-second to parse and execute a single SQL statement, which means about 900,000 instructions. This sounds very inefficient. But we accept this inefficiency because no one wants to perform database operations by writing assembly language code. Information processing today is dominated by the cost of automation and software development.

Using this starting figure, arithmetic shows that the theoretical cost for a single transaction was 36 MIP-seconds. And on the 7-MIP CPU that the construction company initially bought, that implied 5.2 seconds per transaction—which is already twice the maximum commit time acceptable.

Interestingly, even to support a single user required a 14-MIP single processor. And to support 7 users, generating a total of 2 1/2 transactions per second, required 90 MIPS. So a seemingly mild environment generates very big requirements.

The construction company ended up buying a multiprocessing system manufactured by Pyramid Technology. The multiprocessing system was twice as large as the largest system bid in the first bidding round. But the company was very happy because the multiprocessing system still cost a fraction of what the proprietary 3090 system would have cost.

Figure 8.6 OLTP downsizing: A case study (Continued).

guaranteeing performance requirements based on the TPC-A benchmarks. The TPC-A benchmarks are good benchmarks, are audited, and require the use of real, rather than simulated users. But the TPC-A benchmarks are good only for certain applications. In particular, the TPC-A benchmarks measure debit/credit transactions, such as those common in banking operations.

Debit/credit benchmarks are simple transactions. Simple transactions tend to be heavily update oriented. These transactions comprise only about 10 percent of the transactions performed in the real world.

A second common transaction category is *decision-support transactions*. Decision-support transaction queries tend to be undisciplined and extraordinarily complex. A single user can often tie up and bog down an entire machine. Decision-support transactions comprise about 20 percent of the real-world transactions.

The third and last category of transactions, is *run-your-business transactions*. These transactions are fairly complex, and certainly much more complex than the simple debit/credit transactions. Run-your-business transactions comprise the bulk of the transactions performed in the real world—about 70 percent. The construction company's transactions fell into this class. And the TPC-A benchmarks were inadequate to provide performance information for such transactions.

Before making a decision about the platform to buy, Client/Server planners and application experts should require the final bidders to code a portion of the real application. Furthermore, the purchasing company should choose the application portion to code—not the vendor. Executing this application portion on the machine is the most accurate, and possibly the only, way to demonstrate the real performance achievable with a downsized system. Certain companies have always imposed such requirements on their bidders.

What Does It All Mean?

As the construction company example shows, seemingly mild environments can generate large transaction requirements. PC-based servers may not be powerful enough to handle these transaction-processing jobs, nor are some other workstations and computers that users think of when they think of downsizing. The complex nature of database applications requires big CPUs. This will be even more true for object-oriented databases.

What should be done with all the super PCs and workstations that users are planning for their interconnected downsized platforms? The answer is to use them, but for appropriate applications. For some applications, they are fine. Other applications require minicomputer-type servers, multiprocessing machines, or mainframes.

Downsizing Guidelines

Successful downsizing doesn't happen by itself. Before downsizing, organizations should build an infrastructure. The infrastructure should consist of a companywide network that allows all PCs, workstations, servers, minicomputers, and mainframes to communicate. Also necessary to this infrastructure are a variety of data interchange and data-access standards (*de jure* or *de facto*) that allow users to access and exchange data. Finally, for this infrastructure to be successful it is necessary for the organization to have some knowledge of how to build distributed applications.

When analyzing and choosing platform options, look past the central processing unit. Consider the total system, including the hardware, operating system, system management, and application software. Remember that even though processors are becoming faster and faster, the computers that contain the processors are often limited by their I/O capabilities. Furthermore, some operating systems are better designed for GUIs and certain types of applications, while others are designed specifically for multitasking, multiuser, or computer-intensive operations.

Choose appropriate applications to downsize. As mentioned earlier, the mainframe is an exceptionally good data-management server. But there are many applications that do not need to reside on mainframes. These can be placed on less expensive platforms. Good candidates for downsizing are applications that involve data entry and editing, highly interactive applications, many statistical and mathematical analyses, and many (but not all) decision-support applications. Certain traditional mainframe applications, such as accounts payable and receivable can also be placed on downsized platforms in a Client/Server environment, provided there are good data-access and data-interchange capabilities across a network.

Wherever possible, don't choose a downsized platform without trying it by running a critical portion of the application targeted at that machine to make sure the platform is appropriate. Don't rely on benchmarks, vendor claims, or hearsay from other users. Their applications are not yours. Downsizing mistakes can result in missed schedules, unmet business requirements, or canceled projects. Therefore, it is critical to allot sufficient time and resources to investigate, design, and test the downsized platforms.

Migration

This chapter focused on deployment issues related to applications, such as reengineering; distribution; choosing the initial applications; and choosing appropriate platforms for the applications; whether the platforms are mainframes, multiprocessing systems, desktop workstations, or traditional servers. The next chapter addresses middleware, a relatively new type of software developed for distributed Client/Server computing and necessary to most Client/Server implementations.

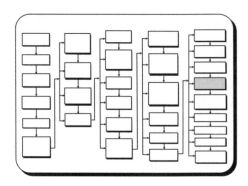

Chapter 9

Middleware

Middleware: The Go-Between Software

Interoperability in distributed Client/Server environments means much more than hardware, wiring, local area networks, and protocol stacks. It also means software connectivity, application interoperability, and data portability. Middleware is key to achieving these capabilities.

There is by no means unanimous agreement on the meaning of middleware. Middleware is often thought of as the glue that binds the front end and the back end of a Client/Server application. Other people see it as a translator between heterogeneous parts of a Client/Server system.

What middleware is intended to be, however, is a new class of Client/Server software that facilitates Client/Server interactions, application-to-application communications, and remote database access. As the name implies, middleware sits in the middle of Client/Server components—between the operating system and protocol stack at one side, and the actual database and user applications at the other side (Figure 9.1).

Why Middleware?

Although middleware is considered to be at the heart of Client/Server systems, it is not, strictly speaking, essential to Client/Server computing. Anything that middleware can do, programmers can also do using traditional methods. But they won't, normally, because to do so won't be worth it to them or to management. The labor-intensive task, for example, of writing C-language programs directly to network protocols, or to networking facilities such as Berkeley Sockets (which is built into most UNIX versions) was practical in the past when relatively simple networking for small numbers of computers was involved. At that time, applications were generally monolithic and computing environments were centralized. Heterogeneous networking entailed usually two, or at the most three, heterogeneous computers. The most common networked applications were file transfer, transaction or database

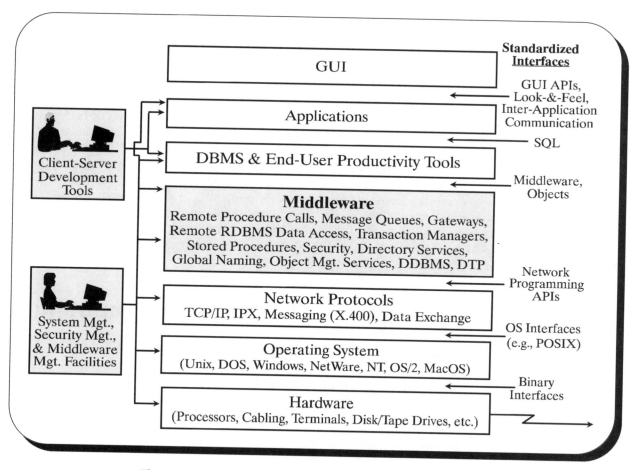

Figure 9.1 The anatomy of middleware. *Source: Emerging Technologies Group.*

Note: The shaded areas represent middleware, or areas related to middleware, such as middleware management and Client/Server middleware tools.

updates, and terminal emulation. File and print sharing was also done, but usually in homogeneous environments such as UNIX-based engineering environments and PC networks.

In contrast, today's Client/Server environments are highly complex. Client/Server environments connect tens of thousands of PCs, many interconnected through PC networks to one or multiple UNIX-based servers. The UNIX-based servers often come from multiple vendors. The UNIX servers, in turn, are connected to legacy mainframe computers. Users are constantly moving to different computer addresses at different nodes or networks.

Client/Server applications today typically include data and file sharing, electronic mail, revisable document transfer, interactive data access and updates, product data exchange with user annotations, and cooperative processing. Application logic may be split across two or more machines. This is a far more complex programming situation than networking monolithic applications.

In this kind of Client/Server environment, it is not cost effective to use the same manual programming methods that were used in centralized, monolithic, relatively homogeneous environments. Writing directly for native network protocols is a time-consuming, error-prone process. It results in thousands of lines of hacked-out, network-specific, and database-specific code that is difficult to maintain and difficult to port to other operating environments in the enterprise.

Middleware's advantage is its ability to insulate programmers from the complexity of networked Client/Server environments. It allows the interconnection of heterogeneous hardware platforms, network protocols, LAN environments, databases, operating systems, and legacy applications, while hiding many of the differences between these systems. As a result, users, programmers, and computers need not speak multiple protocols, database languages, operating system syntaxes, and so on, in order to communicate with the different systems.

Middleware Approaches to Client/Server Computing

Overall, middleware can be classified into four main categories:

- Communications/networking middleware
- Data management middleware
- Gateways
- Standardized APIs (Application Programming Interfaces)

Communications/networking middleware is software that helps connect clients to servers over networks. *Data-management middleware* is software that requests data from database-management systems residing on interconnected servers. *Gateways* serve as translators between different database-management languages and between different protocols. *APIs* are standardized interfaces between applications and information processing services.

Each type of middleware consists of a diversity of technologies, services, and interfaces. Table 9.1 identifies a number of middleware technologies, services, and interfaces, along with some examples of each. Each category of middleware has advantages and disadvantages that will be explained in the following sections.

The Gateway Approach to Interoperability

Gateways are of two main types—network gateways and database gateways (Figure 9.2). Network gateways convert between different network protocols at the

Table 9.1 Representative Middleware Technologies, Services, and Interfaces

Communications/Networking Middleware

- Remote Procedure Calls (e.g., OSF DCE [Distributing Computing Environment] RPC, Sun ONC RPC, Gradient Technologies Inc.'s PC DCE)
- Message Queuing Services (e.g., IBM's MQSeries (developed by Apertus Technologies Inc. [formerly System Strategies] in conjunction with IBM), Apertus Technologies' MQ View, DEC MessageQ, Peer Logic Inc.'s Pipes Platform, Covia's Communications Integrator)
- Transparent Distributed File Access (e.g., IEEE TFA [Transparent File Access], Sun NFS [Network File System] [also Internet RFC 1094], CMU Andrew File System [AFS], OSF DCE Distributed File System [DFS])
- Directory Services (ISO X.500, DCE Global Directory Services)
- Global Naming Services
- Objects and Object Management Services (e.g., OMG ORB, IBM SOM, Sun DOMF)

Data-Management Middleware

- Remote Database Access Services (e.g., ISO Remote Database Access [RDA], X/Open and SQL Access Group Remote Database Access [RDA] and X/Open CLI [Call-Level Interface])
- Distributed database and Federated database services
- Distributed Transaction Management Services (e.g., X/Open's Distributed Transaction Processing [DTP] XA Interface [for Transaction Demarcation], X/Open XA+, interface between the Transaction Manager and the Communication Manager; X/Open TX Interface between the Transaction Manager and the Application, Transarc/IBM Encina)
- ISO 10026:1992 Distributed Transaction Processing protocol and format (DTP)

Gateways

- Database gateways and translators to convert source SQL into a target data manipulation language (e.g., Sybase Open Server)

Standardized APIs

- Standardized Client/Server application programming interfaces (APIs) to be used by applications to access new types of communications middleware software such as RPCs and message queuing software
- APIs to database front-end and back-end software, and database APIs such as SQL, Microsoft's Open Database Connectivity (ODBC), and the Borland/IBM/Novell Coalition's Integrated Database Application Programming Interface (IDAPI)
- APIs to access traditional networking standards (e.g., the IEEE P1327.1, and P1327.2 APIs to X.400 Message Handling Service and X.500 Directory Service [with C language bindings]) and APIs to the operating system (e.g., P1003.1 POSIX API)

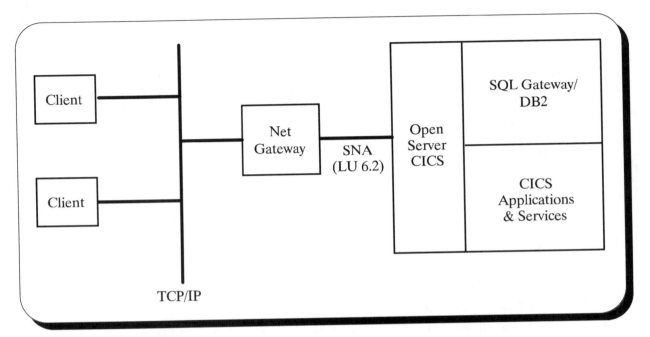

Figure 9.2 Example of Three Gateways. *Source: Sybase.*

Note: This figure illustrates three different gateways, two of which are communications gateways, and one of which is a database gateway.

The Net Gateway provides translation from the open systems network protocol (TCP/IP) used by the open systems clients, to the proprietary network protocol used by the mainframe.

The Open Server/CICS, in this case, acts as an RPC-based gateway that allows access to any CICS application. The CICS application may retrieve data from any data source accessible from the CICS environment and return the data to the client. Open Server also has an API function. It is a toolkit that assists developers in enabling any data source or service in a Client/Server environment (shown here for CICS) to become a multithreaded server. It makes the data source or service look like SQL Server so it can be used by clients with ODBC or Sybase OpenClient.

The SQL Gateway/DB2 provides a target-specific gateway for dynamic SQL access to DB2 data. The client can use the full capabilities of the DB2 SQL dialect. This provides the ability to generate ad hoc queries from client applications.

application level. Database gateways typically convert source SQL into a target data-manipulation language.

Database gateways are important because the ISO SQL 1989 standard, although well accepted, has relatively minimal functionality. Consequently, every database vendor has had to add nonstandard functionality to its database to make it useful in a real-world environment. Since the functionality added was nonstandard, almost no two SQLs were compatible without gateways.

To alleviate this problem, a new SQL standard (SQL 2: 1992) was approved. SQL 2 has a much larger core of standardized functionality, intended to obviate the need for database vendors to define nonstandard functionality, and increase the chances of compatibility between different vendors' SQLs. However, SQL 2 is not yet in common use. Moreover, it still requires vendor-added extensions in a real-world environment, either for functionality or performance reasons. Vendor extensions lead to incompatibilities between databases.

Database gateways are designed to solve the incompatibility problem. The big advantage to the gateway approach to interoperability is that the gateway is designed to translate between specific hardware, system software, and database-management systems (DBMSs). Therefore, the gateway provides the full capabilities of the vendor's hardware, system software, and/or DBMS to interconnected users.

Another advantage to database gateways is their ability to translate between SQL and existing proprietary non-SQL DBMSs. This is important because conversion from one database management system to another is probably the most expensive operation in a real-world computing environment. Vendors and users are therefore very concerned with compatibility between standardized DBMS interfaces and existing DBMSs.

The disadvantage of gateways is that they consist of nonportable, custom interfaces to networks, DBMSs, and applications. Application code and data that depend on gateways are not portable to, or interoperable with, other clients or servers unless another gateway is written for each client and/or server. The writing, upgrading, and maintaining of multiple custom interfaces is costly.

Weighing these advantages and disadvantages, the following recommendations can be made. If short-term migration from a proprietary version of SQL to an open version of SQL 2, or from a proprietary network to an open one like TCP/IP, is a goal, then the gateway approach to interoperability may not be the right approach. On the other hand, for access to proprietary data and applications, the gateway approach may be necessary.

The Standardized API Approach to Interoperability

Standardized application programming interfaces (APIs) are high-level programming interfaces between applications and various types of system software. They have the advantage of supporting application interoperability, portability, and scalability across other standards-conformant systems. Consequently, standardized APIs provide access to data on all standards-conformant systems from any standards-conformant systems. Moreover, the potentially widespread data access and interoperability possible through the use of standardized APIs does not require the constant costly updating of custom interfaces whenever a vendor modifies its software.

The application portability and interoperability that results from the use of standardized APIs allows users to run and access the same application on multiple heterogeneous machines, so no retraining is necessary whether the user works in one location using minicomputer-based servers, in another using UNIX workstations, and in a third using Intel-based PCs (Figure 9.3).

SQL is the dominant standardized database-access language API. It allows databases to be split into a front-end data query, and front-end application development tools, and a back-end SQL database engine. SQL is the middleware that connects the front-end and back-end parts of the database. Clients request data using SQL. The server then translates or compiles the SQL query into a database language that the DBMS can use to navigate the database, find the requested data, and send it to the client.

Nothing is perfect, and standardized APIs have some disadvantages. Unlike the gateway approach to interoperability, the standardized API approach may not provide access to all database capabilities because APIs are generic, rather than specific to a DBMS. Also, standards are frequently less functional than proprietary systems because of the needs for vendors, users, and others with diverse interests to compromise in order to reach a consensus. Finally, because of the difficulty of achieving a consensus, standardized APIs may not be available in a timely manner.

In addition to standardized-database APIs, some proprietary APIs to proprietary database extensions have been published, or are available. These APIs include Mi-

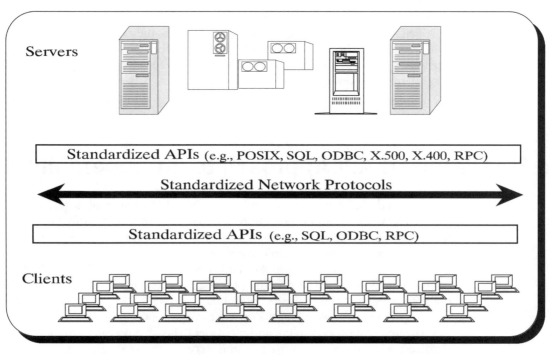

Figure 9.3 Standardized APIs. *Source: Emerging Technologies Group.*

crosoft's Open Data Base Connectivity (ODBC) specification, and the Lotus-Borland-and-others coalition to specify IDAPI (Interface to Database API). The publication of these APIs make them more open than a totally proprietary product would be. Unfortunately, these APIs don't have the universal acceptance that a formal standardized API would have. Consequently, ODBC and IDAPI provide access to particular databases only. And, even so, supposedly compliant software from different vendors may support different database functionality and, therefore, be incompatible with one another.

Communications Middleware

Communications middleware is software that facilitates connections across a network between clients and servers. Communications middleware sits between the applications and the traditional network protocols. This middleware offers application programmers a more straightforward way to connect clients and servers and to partition application logic across clients and servers without having to program complex networking protocols.

Communications middleware does not include network-protocol stacks. Network-protocol stacks are a traditional component of networked environments. Writing applications directly to native network protocols requires very savvy network programmers. Most business-application programmers, however, do not know the various details of pipes, sockets, sessions, tokens, and so on, that are embedded in network protocols. What is more, they are not paid to know such details; they are paid to develop business-application programs.

There is a wide variety of communications middleware, including remote procedure calls (RPC), message-queuing services, transparent distributed file-access services, directory services, global-naming services, object management services, and more.

Remote Procedure Calls

A remote procedure call (RPC) facility allows an application to make an ordinary programming-language procedure call on one machine and have it answered or executed by a remote machine. If the RPC facility works with a directory-services facility, the fact that the procedure being called is located on a remote machine, instead of locally, is transparent to the application and programmer (Figure 9.4).

RPCs are important to a variety of networking and Client/Server applications. They are used in partitioning applications across clients and servers. In such cases, the part of the application running on the client calls the part of the application running on the server just as it would call a local subroutine. Distributed system-management facilities use RPCs, in conjunction with directory services, to route system-management requests to the computer that houses the requested system-management service. Distributed-file systems (e.g., Sun's NFS) also require an RPC

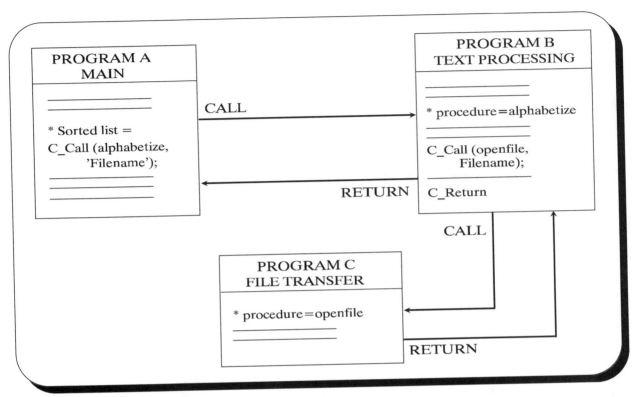

Figure 9.4 How remote procedure calls work. *Source: Emerging Technologies Group.*

mechanism. The NFS RPC, however, although ubiquitous, was developed for use with the NFS, and is tightly integrated with NFS. Its interfaces are not normally exposed for general use by other applications (although they can be used by savvy programmers).

There is not yet an approved and accepted formal RPC standard. Two RPCs, however, are becoming *de facto* standards. One is OSF's RPC. OSF's RPC is part of OSF's Distributed Computing environment. It is also published by X/Open. Thus, it has the approval of two consortia. In addition, the OSF RPC also is implemented for PCs by Gradient Technologies Inc. in its PC DCE.

The other *de facto* RPC standard is Sun Microsystems RPC. Sun's RPC is based on one developed by NetWise, Inc., and is incorporated by Sun in its Open Network Computing (ONC) environment—a distributed-computing environment and collection of middleware services comparable to OSF's DCE.

RPC Tools

The remote procedure call concept is simple. In practice, however, without the aid of special tools such as an RPC interface definition language and associated compiler, the use of remote procedures calls can turn out to be more work than many application developers are willing to devote to the task. Client/Server planners and application developers should, therefore, include RPC tools in their list of required services and specifications.

The greatest amount of work that remote procedure call users normally must perform is the creation of pairs of stub procedures for each remote procedure call to be performed. *Stub procedures* contain a procedure's input statements (which accept an application's request for procedure execution) and output statements (which return execution results to the application). But stub procedures do not contain the body of the procedure. The body is located on the remote machine.

One stub in each pair resides on the same machine as the application. To the application, this stub looks like the procedure being called. The other stub in the pair resides on the same machine as the remote procedure. To the remote procedure, that stub looks like the calling application.

By themselves, stubs are not difficult to write, but they can be a nuisance and a source of errors. RPC vendors often supply a compiler that automatically generates the stubs. With this compiler, application developers need specify only minimal information, such as the names of the remote procedures to be called, their arguments and argument datatypes, and some other optional pieces of interface information. This information is specified in a high-level language.

The RPC interface definition language is the interface to the stub compiler and it is a key component of an RPC interface. Application developers specify remote procedure calls using the RPC interface definition language. The interface definition language specification can then be processed by a stub compiler, which generates stubs.

A second RPC interface is an API to the RPC run-time system. In any RPC implementation, this run-time system handles the RPC networking, and performs tasks such as binding to a naming service, binding to a directory service that finds an instance of a particular procedure on some server, binding to a remote server, and announcing a new server.

RPCs: The Good and the Bad

RPCs are good in that they hide the network from the programmer. The major disadvantage to RPCs is that they normally support only synchronous communications. This means that they block further processing until the procedure called has completed and returned control to the calling program. Vendors get around this problem by implementing RPCs in a multithreaded operating system. A multithreaded operating system has multiple threads of control within a single process, so each RPC call goes out on one thread. That thread only waits for the RPC return. Meanwhile, other threads can continue their work. Users must bear in mind, however, that RPC performance may be slow unless their operating system is multithreaded. Vanilla UNIX is single threaded. Most vendors implementing RPCs under UNIX, however, have implemented threads in their UNIX systems. Similarly, IBM has implemented threads in OS/400 in order to host the DCE RPC.

The other problem with RPCs is their lack of transactional semantics to handle transaction processing. *Transactional semantics* refers to the ability to lock data in a database and not commit an update until a transaction completes, as well as being able to roll back a transaction in the event of a computer failure, so it appears as if the transaction never happened. This procedure entails the exchange of a number of messages, such as "Prepare to Commit," "Acknowledge Data Update in a Temporary Log," and "Ready to Commit."

Transactional semantics have been added to several RPCs. The performance of RPCs in transaction-processing environments is still unclear. Consequently, RPCs are mostly used in simpler request-reply Client/Server applications.

Message-Oriented Middleware

Message-oriented middleware hides the network from applications and programmers. In addition, it supports asynchronous communications. This means that it allows clients and servers to communicate by sending messages to each other, and it queues the messages for delivery at a later time if the intended recipient is not available. In this respect, the message queues act like voice mail (Figure 9.5).

Message queues can be persistent or nonpersistent. Persistent message queues are stored on disk, and can survive system failures. Nonpersistent queues reside in main memory, and can be lost if a system fails.

Message-queuing software has traditionally been used in transaction processing. For this purpose, message-queuing software has transactional semantics (such as database commits and roll backs), and the stored messages are persistent. The difference between traditional and modern Client/Server message-queuing software is that traditional message-queuing software had proprietary interfaces and was tied to proprietary networks, operating systems, and hardware. In contrast, modern message-queuing software is network, operating-system, and hardware independent and the interfaces are published and available to other vendors for use with their applications.

There are several advantages to message-oriented software. First is the benefit of asynchronous communications support. Message-queuing software enables applications to exchange messages with assurance that the data will be delivered. A sending system needs not sit idle until it receives a response to its message.

The second advantage is the message-queuing software's ability to ensure data integrity just as databases do. Databases must be capable of ensuring data integrity to preserve the data's value. Messages, however, are works in progress, and are as valuable as database data. Therefore, message-queuing software is designed to ensure not only that data will not be lost, but also the data will not be duplicated or delivered out of order. The transactional capabilities also ensures the integrity of transactions.

In the financial industry, these data-integrity capabilities are important to money transfers and stock trades. The manufacturing and industrial-process community uses these capabilities to ensure that the sequence of steps in a critical manufacturing

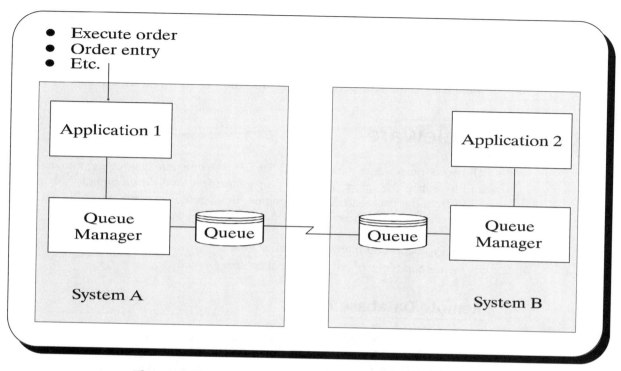

Figure 9.5 How message queues work. *Source: Apertus Technologies.*
Note: When a user makes a request to an application (Application 1), the application invokes the queue manager. The queue manager writes the message to a local queue designated for transfers to the remote system and delivers the data across the network to the remote destination queue. The target application (Application 2) reads the destination queue and gains access to the message.

process is transferred in the correct order. And, in a retail system, message-queuing software might be used to send sequences of messages to control warehouse inventory or to handle customers' orders.

There are no message-oriented middleware standards yet. In 1994, however, a message-oriented middleware association, appropriately called Message-Oriented Middleware Association (MOMA) was formed. The organization counts just about every message-oriented middleware vendor as a member. Its goals are to promote message-queuing technology and to educate potential users about the technology's benefits. Although not a standards organization, MOMA promotes interoperability among competing message-oriented middleware products.

IBM has submitted its Message Queuing Interface (MQI), the interface to its MQSeries product (based on Apertus Technologies' technology), to X/Open as a proposed standard. In addition, some MOMA vendors are privately developing links between their message-queuing software. One example is an IBM link between MQSeries and PeerLogic's Pipes Platforms.

Other software vendors have begun licensing technology from message-oriented middleware vendors to provide their software with messaging capabilities. All this could lead to the emergence of a *de facto* message-queuing standard.

Database Middleware

The major purposes of database middleware is to integrate heterogeneous databases, and to isolate the query, forms, report generation, and development tools on the client from the back-end database engine. Besides the gateways and APIs discussed earlier, there are two main types of database middleware:

- Protocols and interface specifications
- Certain types of database architectures

Remote Database Access

The major database middleware protocol and interface is the Remote Database Access (RDA) specification. It was developed to fill a big gap in the functionality specified by the SQL and SQL 2 standards, as well as by most proprietary databases. The problem with SQL and SQL 2 is that they are designed for standalone, single environment databases, and do not readily accommodate Client/Server environments.

The Remote Database Access specifications are extensions to the SQL data language to allow remote access to a database in a Client/Server environment. The Remote Database Access specifications include protocols, formats, and interfaces needed to allow remote database access in a Client/Server environment, where the databases may be heterogeneous and from multiple vendors.

There are two main Remote Database Access specifications—the ISO 9579 standard and the remote Database Access specification developed by the SQL Access Group and published by X/Open. The SQL Access Group (SAG) was initially formed by members of the ISO RDA standards group with the aim of putting more distributed functionality into RDA and accelerating the work of the ISO RDA Group.

The X/Open specification is consistent with the ISO RDA standard, but is a superset of it. I strongly recommend that Client/Server planners specify the X/Open RDA specification, for the following reasons.

First, although ISO's RDA provides a protocol for remote data access in a Client/Server environment, it only specifies the service and protocol between a single client and server. It does not consider multiple connections and, therefore, does not specify distributed database access. This ISO RDA deficiency is one factor that caused the formation of the SQL Access Group.

Second, the X/Open-SAG RDA specification contains more standardized functionality, such as some of the functionality specified by SQL 2. Users are not likely to obtain this functionality in a standardized form from SQL 2 because SQL 2 is seg-mented into levels (Entry Level, Intermediate Level, and Full Level). Vendors have begun their implementation with Entry Level SQL 2. Entry Level SQL 2, although more functional than SQL 1989, is still not sufficient for a real-world production environment. By the time vendors get around to implementing the Intermediate- or Full-Level SQL 2, however, it will almost be time for SQL 3 to arrive. Consequently, vendors may never implement the Intermediate and Full-Level SQL 2.

The X/Open RDA offers a nice balance between the Full-Level SQL 2 features and what users need now in a Client/Server environment. The X/Open RDA speci-fications, for example, include connection-management capabilities (which are part of SQL 2's Full Level), and schema manipulation and the CHARACTER VARYING data type (which are in SQL 2's Intermediate Level. X/Open's RDA also specifies features not included in any SQL 2 conformance level, such as the CREATE INDEX and DROP INDEX statements.

A third reason to favor X/Open's RDA is that ISO's RDA specifies only a protocol, but no APIs or formats. In contrast, the X/Open specifications include both an API and formats, in addition to a Remote Data Access protocol.

The X/Open API specification is known as the call level interface (CLI) speci-fication. It allows an application program to call an SQL program directly, without having to embed the SQL program in a third-generation language, and without re-quiring a preprocessor for each language in which SQL is embedded. The CLI is particularly useful for the execution of dynamic SQL—a capability that allows the execution of SQL statements that cannot be compiled ahead of time.

Among other things, dynamic SQL allows the execution of SQL statements that vary with time or with the execution environment, where the time or execution environment can only be determined at run time, a situation that occurs in Client/Server environments.

Dynamic SQL is specified in intermediate-level SQL 2. So important is dynamic SQL, however, that it is implemented in many vendors' proprietary SQLs. Dynamic SQL is one of a vendor's value-added database features that make different SQLs in-compatible, thereby making heterogeneous Client/Server computing more difficult.

Database Architectures

Three major database architectures and services act as middleware because they can integrate multiple, possibly heterogeneous, databases at multiple sites:

- Distributed databases
- Federated databases
- Distributed transaction processing

Distributed Databases

True distributed databases allow a database administrator to partition a single co-herent database and its control system, and distribute the database partitions across multiple, geographically dispersed, autonomous nodes. The partitioning is done in such a way that the location of any particular set of data is transparent both to users and applications. In the best case, the data is also synchronized (Figure 9.6).

There are many benefits to distributed DBMSs. They include the ability to reflect an organization's structure, reference data locally, improve response time and data availability, decrease communications costs, and support disaster recovery. A DDBMS allows users to join data tables across platforms transparently, at multiple sites. DDBMSs also transparently support multisite updates within a single transaction.

Having databases replicated at different sites but maintained so the data at all sites is always synchronized, is one form of a distributed-database management system (DDBMS). But partitioning data is really what DDBMSs are all about.

A distributed DDBMS can be partitioned so that the database tables (relations) are distributed at different locations. Regardless of the data's location, users see only a single logical database. They can create a view that is a join or union of tables in different databases without being aware that the data tables span multiple locations. Knowledge of where requested data is located resides in a smart data dictionary. The DDBMS routes requests to the proper location(s) and returns the requested data.

Besides distributing data tables, a DDBMS can allow users to fragment individual database tables and distribute the fragments across different nodes. In a horizontal-fragmentation scheme, different rows, or records, of a table are distributed to different sites. In a vertical-fragmentation scheme, the columns, or field attributes, would reside in different places. In either case, the application and DDBMS handles the table fragments at the various locations as if they were a single relation.

Flexibility, the need for intelligence in applications, and the ability to simplify the complexity of distributed environments are the advantages to fragmenting tables. To cite one example, suppose a company with regional offices in Chicago and Detroit has a Chicago employees relation and a Detroit employees relation. If, as part of a cost-cutting move, the company combines these offices, it would be illogical to continue to maintain two separate employee tables. Unfortunately, combining them into a single employee table for the new regional office requires changing every application that references the Chicago or Detroit employee tables. However, if employees was a single table, fragmented horizontally, the only change necessary would be to inform the data dictionary that the Detroit and Chicago employee data are located in a new site. Similarly, use of a vertically fragmented table would eliminate the need to modify applications if a company changes a manufacturing process and brings in a new machine that combines two processes into one.

Figure 9.6   Not all distributed databases are equal.

These benefits must be balanced against the high cost and overhead that can occur if applications require large numbers of data accesses to multiple remote sites. The costs and overhead problems are compounded if distributed-update capabilities, with resulting synchronization requirements, are needed. For this reason, many initial DDBMS product introductions support distributed queries, but plan full distributed-update facilities for later releases.

DDBMSs have three main problems—communications, political, and heterogeneous database access. The communications problem is largely due to the locking coordination activity needed to keep databases at multiple sites synchronized. Keeping the dispersed databases synchronized is very expensive due to the large amount of communications involved between the databases at the different sites. The large amount of communications required also causes performance problems.

Many communications and performance problems are alleviated by distributing the data so that most accesses are local. Query-optimization software is another way to minimize the amount of communications needed to respond to a query. To do this job, the query-optimization software plans a data-access path based on the cardinality of the relations needed to respond to the query, the distribution of attributes in the relations, the size of intermediate results generated during a multistage join, an estimation of the network traffic involved, and disk access costs.

In a hypothetical example, two different processing sequences can be used to find the identifiers of projects in Detroit that use 10-inch bolts (Figure 9.7). One processing sequence searches through all part numbers (say, 100,000), transmitted from a parts table in Rochester, NY to a projects table in Detroit to see which parts correspond to 10-inch bolts. The other is to transmit only the numbers for the various types (say 10) of 10-inch bolts, for joining with the projects and supply tables in Detroit. As the figure shows, the second technique is an order of magnitude faster than the first.

Another DDBMS problem is the difficulty of heterogeneous database access. DDBMSs require the same relational DBMSs on each platform to make all the databases appear as a single coherent database. Database gateways are generally needed to access heterogeneous databases.

One reason for the heterogeneous access difficulty is that SQL is not an automatic panacea for database compatibility. Even if SQL statements are identical, subtle differences at the internal level make it necessary to map a database's SQL statements into the call to which each individual implementation responds. Data types must be converted. Also, relations and attributes must appear the same.

A more serious problem can occur if the meaning and identity of the data between different systems are different because the databases were designed without some central data administration. Pieces of data may have the same name but mean different things. Or one database may use a "0" meaning no value in a field, while another database may use a "null" symbol. In either case, users will receive wrong answers to their queries, and may not be able to recognize that the answers are wrong.

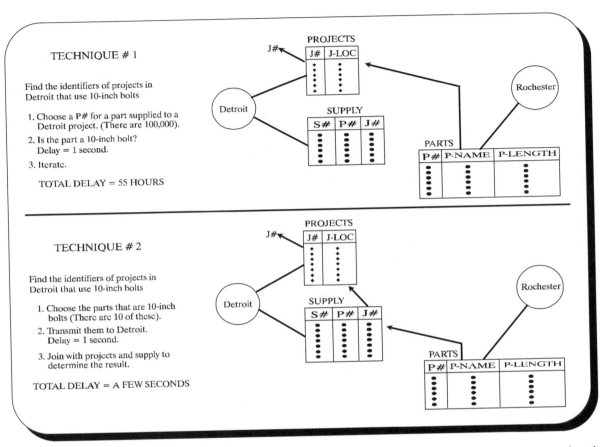

Figure 9.7 Two distributed query techniques. *Source: Emerging Technologies Group.*

Federated Databases

Federated databases are an alternative to DDBMSs. A *federated database* is a collection of loosely integrated, autonomous, heterogeneous databases. The databases can be stored in a variety of data structures, including relational and nonrelational databases, and indexed files. Federated-database–middleware services, in addition to communications middleware, provide read/write access to these databases and files at multiple sites, over LANs and WANs.

The database-middleware services required to implement federated databases provide data translations between different data representations, data types, and data encodings. Federated-database services should also provide a federated-naming protocol that allows the DBMSs to resolve differences between names for similar fields in the heterogeneous databases. Depending on the particular federated-database services' functionality, the database-middleware services also may optimize distributed queries and permit heterogeneous database updates without sacrificing the local autonomy of each database.

Needless to say, an organization using federated databases for its Client/Server environment should require a single interface, standardized at least within the organization, to the federated-database services.

Because federated databases are heterogeneous, federated-database access is not as transparent as a DDBMS environment. Table 9.2 shows some of the advantages and disadvantages of typical federated databases, as well as the difference between federated databases and distributed databases.

Federated database technology is evolving. Some vendors, however, claim to have developed, or to be developing, federated database services that provide a single view of records partitioned across multiple databases. These services store a description of all the heterogeneous databases in a data dictionary/directory. Database administrators can then define federated data *views*, which include data from multiple heterogeneous databases.

Table 9.2 Distributed Databases versus Federated Databases

Distributed Databases	Federated Databases
Supports remote database access	Supports remote database access
Supports a high level of data-access transparency because data at all sites looks like a single, coherent database	Data access is not totally transparent
Allows users to transparently join tables across multiple platforms and sites	Does not normally allow users to join tables across multiple platforms and sites
Supports transparent, multiple site updates within a single transaction	Does not allow multiple site updates within a single transaction, except through a distributed transaction manager
Requires the same database at all sites	Works with relational and nonrelational data
Requires application redesign and/or gateways to access legacy databases	Allows applications to access legacy databases without application redesign
Coordinates 2-phase commit and data recovery if a system or disk crashes at one or more sites	Does not coordinate 2-phase commit or data recovery after a system or disk crash, except through a distributed transaction manager
Difficult to migrate data into a DDBMS and distribute the data so that most accesses are local	Database migration is not necessary
Difficult to manage the DDBMS environment	Easier to manage

Source: Emerging Technologies Group.

Distributed-Transaction Processing

Despite the fact that distributed-transaction processing (DTP) technology and standards are still emerging, DTP systems promise to help integrate heterogeneous computing environments and heterogeneous databases. Distributed-transaction processing architectures, services, and interfaces are, therefore, considered a very important form of middleware.

Distributed-transaction processing allows an organization to distribute transactions and transaction data across multiple, geographically dispersed, autonomous nodes in such a way that a node anywhere in a network can initiate or process a transaction on any one or more network nodes. The location of the transaction manager that manages a transaction, and the data required for the transaction, are transparent to users and applications. In the best case, a single transaction may require multiple updates involving data, which is, itself, transparently distributed across multiple nodes.

DTP requires a more modular architecture than that used in centralized-transaction processing. It also requires specialized standardized transaction-processing interfaces, protocols, and formats to allow the different parts of the DTP system to communicate with one another. Use of the appropriate architecture, interfaces, formats, and protocols allows users to gain heterogeneous transaction-processing system interoperability, independent of the operating system, network, or database being used.

X/Open has defined the dominant distributed-transaction–processing architectural model, and the interfaces between the components of an open distributed-transaction–processing system. ISO has defined the transaction-communications protocol for communicating between transaction-processing systems, and the format for the transaction data that is transmitted across a network.

The X/Open-ISO DTP Model   The components of an open distributed-transaction–processing system are the:

- Application
- Resource manager (RM)
- Transaction manager (TM)
- Communications manager (CM)
- Distributed transaction processing (DTP) protocol

In the X/Open model, a DTP system has at least, the first four of these components (Figure 9.8).

The *application* defines a transaction by specifying actions that constitute a transaction and transaction boundaries. The application also uses resources (e.g., data).

The *resource manager* (RM) manages, and provides access to, shared resources. Most often, but not necessarily, an RM is a DBMS. An RM, for example, could manage resources such as print queues, rather than a DBMS.

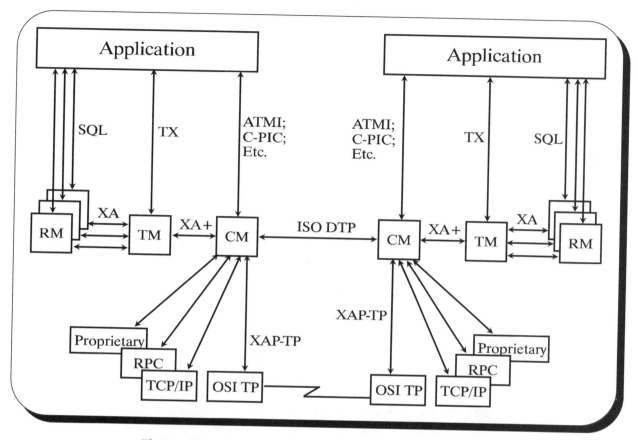

Figure 9.8 The X/Open-ISO DTP model and how it works. *Source: Emerging Technologies Group. Based on the X/Open DTP Model.*
Key: RM—Resource Manager; TM—Transaction Manager; CM—Communications Manager; XAP—X/Open Access Protocol (to the OSI protocol stack)

The *transaction manager* (TM) controls the transaction, communicates with the RM, and manages and coordinates global transactions which are distributed among different computers connected across a network. As part of these functions, the TM monitors the progress of transactions, determines whether a transaction can be committed, maintains data integrity across multiple databases located on multiple interconnected computers, and performs failure recovery. TMs also communicate with remote TMs. The RMs communicate with other RMs only through the TMs.

The *communications manager* (CM) provides access to a communications mechanism when cooperating transaction-processing applications need to communicate with one another. The communications mechanism can be an OSI or TCP/IP protocol stack, a remote procedure call facility, a message-queuing facility, a proprietary network, or something else. It matters not what the actual communications mechanism is because the CM insulates the transaction-processing system from the communications system.

It is very important that the interface between the TM and RM is standardized to ensure that distributed-transaction processing can occur with heterogeneous databases. It is equally important that the interface between the TM and CM is standardized to ensure that distributed-transaction processing can occur, regardless of the network or communications system used. Such interface standardization are among X/Open's most valuable DTP contributions. X/Open has standardized the interface between the TM and RM (XA), and between the TM and the CM (XA+).

X/Open has also standardized the interface between the application and the TM (TX). The TX interface is important because software vendors balked at implementing fourth-generation languages for DTP application development until a standard was available. In addition, X/Open standardized an interface between the CM and the OSI protocol stack (XAP). In the future, X/Open may define interfaces between the CM and other communications protocols and mechanisms.

For transaction-processing applications that require remote resources, the CMs must support transaction semantics, preferably in a standardized manner. The ISO distributed transaction processing protocol (ISO DTP 10026) supports transaction semantics, and provides the protocols and transaction request formats for OSI networks. With this standard, heterogeneous DTP systems can communicate. In the not formally standardized arena, message-queuing facilities, which are traditionally used with OLTP systems, generally support transaction semantics. Transaction semantics also have been added to remote procedure calls.

DTP's Client/Server Organization

In a DTP implementation, the DTP model's components are organized into a Client/Server architecture. In this Client/Server architecture, clients are processes that define the look and feel of the application to the user, and gather input from end users at workstations or terminals. The clients send this input, in the form of a service request, to the TM. The TM routes the request to the appropriate server. Servers are processes that access RM resources, such as a DBMS, on the client's behalf.

The TM handles the routing of a client's request to an appropriate server process regardless of where that server is on the network. The server receives and processes the request and sends a reply back to the client. If a transaction-processing application requires remote resources, the TM sends the communications request to the CM.

Transaction Managers and Transaction Monitors

In defining a TM for DTP, a major question that had to be answered was who controls the transaction. Does the database control it? The transaction monitor? Teleprocessing monitor? Or something else? The classic transaction monitor for many people is CICS. CICS performs multiple functions: It controls the terminals and user access to terminal resources, provides a screen mapping and formatting facility, and a database access facility, and controls the scheduling of the database.

But today, people are moving toward Client/Server computing with workstations or PCs on their desks. As a result, many traditional transaction-monitor functions such as managing terminals, controlling terminal access, and controlling screen manipulation are no longer relevant because these functions are now being done on workstations or PCs. Accessing and scheduling the database can be done by the database.

What the TM does that a transaction monitor does not do, is coordinate transaction processing in a distributed environment. This means performing distributed functions such as the coordination of locking at geographically dispersed databases, and deciding whether and when to commit a transaction using a protocol called the *two-phase commit* (to be described shortly).

When to Use DTP in a Client/Server Environment   Whether or not to use DTP in a Client/Server environment depends on an application's requirements. DTP systems have many of the same problems as distributed databases. In particular, distributed databases and distributed-transaction processing share the problem of communications overhead because of the need to keep different databases synchronized during distributed updates. The large amount of communications needed for this synchronization could result in reduced performance.

The key concern in distributed updates is to keep the data at different sites synchronized in the face of multiple users and possible network or node failures. Also, users must be prevented from updating the same data at the same time and interfering with one another.

The classic example of a distributed transaction is the transfer of money from a savings account at one site to a checking account at another. This transaction requires two discrete updates: debiting the savings account and crediting the checking account. If the two updates are performed within a single transaction, in order to ensure than no one winds up with a loss either both of the updates must be completed or the transaction must abort so that neither update is carried out.

The usual solution is to lock the data in the database until the entire transaction (both updates) is completed. The database keeps a log of database transactions and changes made to records in the database.

The actual update is performed in two stages. In the first stage, the transaction updates a log. In the second stage, it updates the database. In the event of a computer failure or illegal update, the log is used to back out the transaction so it appears as though the transaction never happened.

In a centralized transaction-processing system, all the information and control software pertaining to an update is in one memory. Failures cause all processing to stop, and locking and rolling back transactions are simple matters.

The problem in a distributed environment is that once a machine initiates an update, it assumes the update will be done. It may be unaware that a remote machine failed before completing its work. Consequently, it may allow other transactions to read the now-inconsistent information.

Distributed DBMSs avoid this inconsistency by using a protocol called *two-phase commit*. As is the case in a centralized database, the two-phase commit updates a log in the first phase, then commits the update to the database in the second phase. With a distributed update, however, there are two databases and two logs, and each database and log set is located on a different computer. To ensure that both computers update their logs and databases at the same time, the two-phase commit involves a lot of messages, overhead, and communications traffic among lock managers, data items, and updating of nodes.

For example, a node must obtain a lock mechanism from the node acting as the lock manager for a particular data item. Data may be locked at several sites. During both phases of the protocol, all the sites involved in the update exchange messages equivalent to "Are you ready to commit the transaction?" "Prepare to commit," "Yes I am," "No I am not," "Ready to commit," "Acknowledge the commit," and "Abort."

The exchange of so many messages provides coordination between sites and resistance to failure, but during the message exchange, the data being updated is locked at all nodes involved, and remains locked until all the nodes have completed their processing and communications exchanges. Consequently, maintaining synchronized data is expensive, not only in terms of the communications required by the protocol, but also in terms of reduced availability of the data being updated.

Someone Else in Your Seat?   There are several possible solutions that exist to solve this overhead problem. One is to support multiple synchronized updates within a single transaction only if they all occur at a single site. Another is to decompose transactions that update multiple nodes into smaller separate transactions so that they do not keep data locked for long.

A third solution, called a *reliable-update–propagation mechanism*, ensures that all updates get to all copies of the data in questions. However, the DBMS is not required to perform all the updates in a single transaction at the same time. Consequently, the locking that occurs could be local to only one site and consume a short period of time relative to communications delays. This would make the data more available.

This reliable-update–propagation scheme is used by several airline-reservation systems. Airline-reservation systems have huge DBMSs that allow people anywhere in the world to make reservations with several airlines for a specified seat on a flight to a particular destination. To the busy airline reservation systems, high data availability is more important than data consistency at all times.

To satisfy their high data availability requirements, airline agents' reservation systems, whether centralized or distributed, issue updates to be handled on an as-soon-as-possible basis. As a result, conflicting updates for the same seat may cross each other in transit, and both may, unfortunately, update the same seat in the database.

TP Application Requirements   Whether performance concerns are valid or not depends on the application. Table 9.3 shows some typical requirements for TP applications, gathered by surveying a number of users. If Client/Server application planners are concerned about performance, availability, security, and other transaction-processing requirements in a Client/Server environment, they have several choices.

Table 9.3 Typical Transaction Processing Requirements

Application	Throughput (In TPS per # of users)	Response Time	Peak Load Handling	Capacity	Fault Tolerance (Availability)	Data Integrity	Robustness	Security	MIPS Consumed	Platform Types
Airline Reservations	Very High	Very Fast	Very High	Very High	Very High	Medium	Very High	Medium	Very High	Mainframes, Multiprocessing machines
Financial (Fund transfer, ATM, debit-credit, customer updates)	High	Medium	High	High	Very High	Very High	Very High	Very High	Medium	Mainframes, Fault-tolerant minicomputers, Multiprocessors
Financial Instrument Trading	High	Fast	High	High	Very High	Very High	Very High	Very High	Very High	Mainframes, Fault-tolerant minicomputers
Database Update	Medium	Medium	Low	Low/Medium	Medium	Medium	Medium	Medium/High	Medium	Mid-range Servers, PCs
Status	Medium/High	Medium	Low/Medium	Low/Medium	Medium	Medium/High	High	High	Medium	Mid-range Servers
Order Entry	Medium/High	Low/Medium	Low	Low	Medium	High	Medium/High	High	High	Mid-range Servers, PCs
Ad Hoc Report Generation	Medium	Low/Medium	Low	Low	Medium	Medium/High	Medium/High	Medium/High	Medium	Mid-range Servers, PCs

(Continued)

Table 9.3 Typical Transaction Processing Requirements (Continued)

Application	Throughput (In TPS per # of users)	Response Time	Peak Load Handling	Capacity	Fault Tolerance (Availability)	Data Integrity	Robustness	Security	MIPS Consumed	Platform Types
MRP	—	High	High	—	Medium	Medium	—	—	—	—
Shop Floor	High	Medium/High (5 sec. or less)	High	Medium	High to Very High	Medium	Very	High	High	Mainframes,
Decision Support	Low	Low	—	Medium	Low	High	Medium	High	Very High	Mainframes, Superminicomputers, Multiprocessors Parallel Processors, Mid-range Servers
Inventory Control	Medium/High	Medium	Medium	Medium/High	Medium	High	Medium/High	High	—	—
Facilities Mgt. & Maintenance	Medium/High	Medium	Medium/High	Medium/High	Medium	Medium	Medium/High	Medium	—	—
Service Reservations	Medium (20 to 200 200 tps)	Medium (2–3 sec.)	Low	Medium (e.g., 20 concurrent users)	Very High	Very High	Very High	Very High	Burst Mode Very High; Steady State: Low	Large minicomputers, SMP machines
Customer Service & Support	Medium/High	Medium	Medium/High	High	High	Medium	High	—	—	—

Source: Emerging Technologies Group.
Note: A "—" in a cell means data could not be obtained.

One is to design the DTP applications so that most accesses are local. Another is to buy faster multiprocessing machines. A third way to speed performance is to design DTP applications with the database RM and the transaction manager on the same machine. A fourth choice is to stay with centralized OLTP for the time being.

Keeping the Systems Up and Running

The best planned systems in the world does no one any good if they don't work. The next chapter will therefore address the systems management and control of the entire set of resources that will comprise an open Client/Server environment.

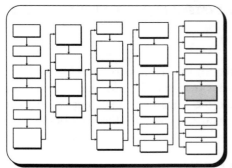

Chapter 10

Managing the Open Client/Server Systems

The Big Gap in Open Client/Server Systems

Distributing a computing environment containing hardware and software in seemingly endless varieties requires complicated management software for managing the distributed systems. The management software must be able to monitor, manage, and administer heterogeneous, multivendor computers, networks, diverse devices, system software, and a variety of Client/Server applications. All this network and system management must be accomplished without necessarily hiring more administrators.

Unfortunately, the lack of distributed system-management tools and utilities is becoming the biggest barrier to open Client/Server computing. This chapter examines the major system-management issues that open Client/Server planners must consider, and helps readers identify the system-management solutions that will deliver the highest return.

Before and After

Until recently, most system management was geared to centralized, proprietary, host-centric environments, and was fairly straightforward. These centralized environments were simple environments consisting of a centralized computer with a lot of attached terminals (Figure 10.1).

The terminals are I/O devices. Even the PCs access the mainframe through terminal emulation, and thus are just other I/O devices. In this environment, you installed a piece of software once, and 512–1024 users could use it. Similarly, you customized, patched, and upgraded it once for all these uses. If a problem developed, you knew it was in that computer because it was the only computer in question. There was no need to send messages to other computers about events on a third.

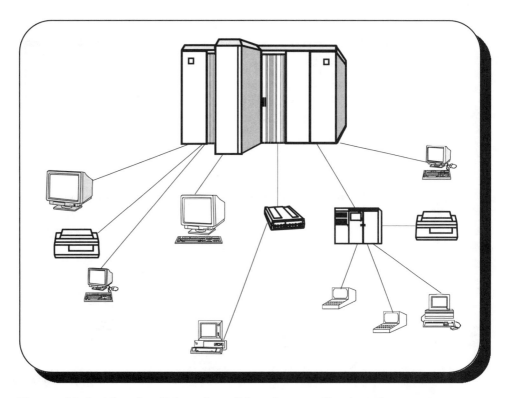

Figure 10.1 The simplicity of traditional, centralized environments.

What makes system management in a Client/Server environment difficult is the complexity of the environment. Client/Server environments typically contain multivendor, heterogeneous servers; hundreds to thousands of PCs; and remote heterogeneous, multivendor, interconnected LANs, WANs, routers, bridges, hubs, and so on. Legacy mainframe applications also are an integral part of Client/Server environments because most users are not trashing their legacy systems to move to Client/Server computing all at once (Figure 10.2).

The computers, hubs, routers, bridges, operating systems, DBMSs, applications, and network-management and system-administration software interact. Consequently, if a problem occurs, it often appears to be in multiple places. The root cause of the problem, however, is buried under layers of interacting, interdependent systems.

Software distribution also cannot be handled in a Client/Server environment the way it was in a simple mainframe-terminal environment. It would be ridiculous to install software separately on 512 or 1,024 different client workstations, possibly at different sites, then go to these sites to customize each person's software, then repeat the process to patch and fix, and, later, upgrade the software.

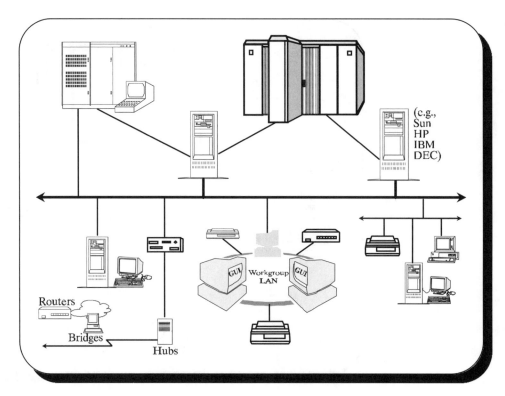

Figure 10.2 The complexity of Client/Server environments.

System Management Transmogrified

System management is a catch-all term that includes network management, system administration, and operations management. System management is currently going through multiple paradigm shifts in order to be able to handle the complexity of heterogeneous, multivendor, Client/Server environments. The paradigm shifts that users should target first to achieve cost-effective system-management include the integration of network management and system administration and the integration of system management solutions.

There are other system-management paradigm shifts, such as the use of object-oriented capabilities to make system management more intuitive, GUIs to simplify Client/Server system management, and middleware to transparently connect managed and managing systems. These paradigms, however, affect vendors first because users cannot use them until vendors have implemented them.

Integrating Network and System Management

In the future, network and systems management will be integrated. System management, along with the network, must become the infrastructure for emerging system management applications.

Systems and network management have been traditionally viewed both by users and vendors as separate domains. Network managers tend to concentrate on the network, and view the systems as just attached devices that the network binds together. System managers tend to concentrate on the systems aspects, and view the network as the glue that binds their systems together.

The result is numerous system-management solutions that are product- and vendor-specific, are difficult to use in a Client/Server environment, and that each have different human interfaces, data representations, and protocols. In reality, both the system and network domains are concerned with similar issues to which similar techniques can be applied (Table 10.1). The integration of system and network management will begin to eliminate the need for an expert in each different piece of managed equipment. Currently, system management requires separate experts to manage a Cisco router, a Cabletron hub, an HP-UX system, an IBM AIX SMIT system, and so on.

Table 10.1 Network and System-Management Requirements Compared

Network Management	System Management
Fault Management	Fault Management
Monitoring	Monitoring
Detection	Detection
Diagnostics	Diagnostics
Reporting	Reporting
Logging	Logging
Fault Avoidance	Fault Avoidance
N.A.	Software Safety
Security Management	Security Management
Authentication	Authentication
Access Control	Access Control
Auditing	Auditing
Performance Management	Performance Management
Monitoring	Monitoring
Tuning	Tuning
Capacity Management	Capacity Management
Configuration Management	Configuration Management
Hardware Device	Hardware Device
Network	File System
	Kernel Configuration

(Continued)

Table 10.1 Network and System-Management Requirements Compared (Continued)

Network Management	System Management

Accounting Management
  Chargeback and Billing
  Apportion Resource Usage
  Asset Monitoring
  Asset Reporting
  Asset Planning
	Accounting Management
	  Chargeback and Billing
	  Apportion Resource Usage
	  Asset Monitoring
	  Asset Reporting
	  Asset Planning

System Initialization and Shutdown	System Initialization and Shutdown
N.A.	Backup and Restore
N.A.	Storage Device Management
N.A.	Software Licensing Management
N.A.	Batch Job Scheduling

Distribution Services
  Local Directory Service
  Global Directory Service
  Distributed Name Service
  Distributed Naming Configuration Mgt.
  Distributed Time Service
  Local versus Remote Determination
  Transparent Location Determination
  Distributed Access Service
  Object Manager
	Distribution Services
	  Local Directory Service
	  Global Directory Service
	  Distributed Name Service
	  Distributed Naming Configuration Mgt.
	  Distributed Time Service
	  Local versus Remote Determination
	  Transparent Location Determination
	  Distributed Access Service
	  Object Manager

Software Distribution Services
  Distributed Network Software Installation
  Distributed Network Software Upgrades
  Distributed Network Software Customization
  Network Operating System Installation
  Network Operating System Upgrade
  Network Operating System Customization
	Software Distribution Services
	  Distributed System Software Installation
	  Distributed System Software Upgrades
	  Distributed Application Installation
	  Distributed Application Upgrade
	  Distributed Application Customization
	  Networked Operating System Upgrade
	  Distributed Software Management

Source: Emerging Technologies Group.

No matter how excellent a vendor's system management capabilities are, if each system in a mix-and-match Client/Server environment has different system-management services, features, and interfaces, users will gain little for their money except chaos.

Integrating System Administration Solutions

Integrated system-administration solutions provide a way to reduce system-management complexity in a Client/Server environment, and to make system administrators more productive. As will be seen in the next sections, providing tools to make people more productive is a high priority system-management requirement in Client/Server environments.

People Costs Are Dominant

Due to the complexity of Client/Server environments, system-management people costs dominate the overall costs in a Client/Server environment (Figure 10.3). The data in this figure is based on an Emerging Technologies Group nine-month in-depth study of the cost of system management in Client/Server environments. During this

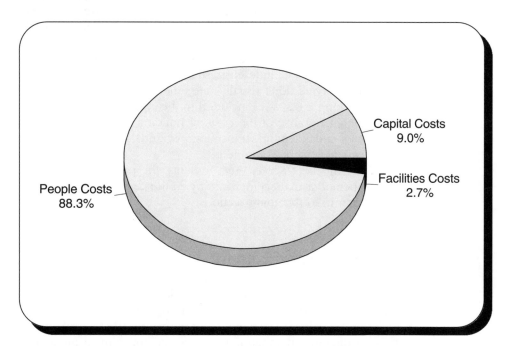

Figure 10.3   The cost of system administration and operations management. *Source: Emerging Technologies Group.*

study, ETG conducted in-depth interviews with 17 Fortune 1000 organizations and government agencies. The interviewees included 3 banks, 1 insurance company, 3 process industrial companies, 1 aerospace company, 1 engineering company, 1 department store chain, 1 network services company, 1 computer company, 3 government agencies, and 2 universities.

These organizations had 2-to-850 UNIX servers, NetWare workgroup servers, NT servers, or some combination of these. They also had 50,000 users, and nearly 200 system administrators. These organizations were selected for the study with an eye to choosing Client/Server environments using different approaches to system management. Three system management approaches were investigated. These approaches include "do it yourself" solutions (e.g., UNIX scripts), point solutions (e.g., specialized backup, job scheduling, print mgt., security management, etc. solutions from different vendors), and integrated system administration solutions (e.g., CA Unicenter, Tivoli Systems).

Figure 10.3 shows how system-management money is spent in the Client/Server organizations interviewed. The data includes only system-administration and operations-management costs. It does not include the cost of the network or other types of Client/Server costs. (Comprehensive Client/Server costs are covered in Chapter 12.)

Note that the capital-equipment costs for system administration and operations management in a Client/Server environment is very small compared to the people costs. The capital costs are mostly for software. Client/Server system administration does not generally need expensive platforms to run the system-administration software.

Facilities costs for Client/Server system administration are almost negligible. Facilities costs include costs such as dial-up lines and archived-tape storage. Clients and servers don't usually need air-conditioned, humidity-controlled rooms. If networking costs were included in this figure, the capital and facilities costs would be higher because of the costs of building wiring, routers, hubs, wide-area networks, wide-area–network transmissions, and, sometimes, special facilities to house the larger network equipment.

In Client/Server environments, the people costs for system administration and operations management are by far the largest cost category. The reasons will become clear in forthcoming sections.

Advise and Lament

Although well documented, the dominance of system-management people costs in Client/Server environments has not yet made an impression on management in many organizations. The lament that permeates the Client/Server and system-management communities is that as the management domain increases in size and complexity, the number of people that organizations have in relationship to that growth in management complexity is decreasing. And, if the management domain remains constant, companies are being pressured to reduce the number of people managing that particular environment.

The Responsible Culprits

Several factors contribute to the dominance of system-management people costs in Client/Server environments.

- **Number of Heterogeneous Nodes.** In the past, many system administrators managed a single system. Today, system administrators often struggle to manage 30–50 nodes, or more. The nodes are smaller than mainframes, but in a networked environment, each node is about as complicated to administer as a mainframe. The problem is compounded because the nodes are heterogeneous.

- **Tools.** Client/Server system-management tools exist, but they are often difficult to use, not integrated with one another, require system administrators to learn different interfaces, and need different types of system-management expertise for each type of tool used.

- **Lack of Experience and Learning Time.** Most system administrators' experience with Client/Server systems is minimal, so a great deal of time goes into learning how to best use the new software and hardware. Learning new paradigms to administer and manage a distributed Client/Server environment is like learning a new programming language. Within a week, the learner can build a system to perform some simple management tasks. Three months of work will render the learner able to manage a reasonable-sized, somewhat diverse, Client/Server environment. But six months to three years are necessary to reach virtuoso levels, where system administrators are facile and intuitive at planning, designing, administering, diagnosing, and troubleshooting all, or most, of the aspects of the Client/Server environment which fall under their responsibility.

- **Distributed System-Management Files.** Many of the tasks that must be done to administer and manage a system involve multiple steps spread out over different files. In distributed Client/Server environments, the files are on different systems. The distribution of the files used in system management makes networked heterogeneous and multivendor systems very complex to learn. Even after learning, editing, and changing the various distributed configurations, and other system management files can be an error-prone task.

- **Counterintuitive.** Traditional system management approaches require a system manager to perform a task like moving a user from a node on one department's subnetwork to another node on a different department's subnetwork, by editing a file. This is not an intuitive approach. As environments become more distributed, and, hence, more complex, this kind of system-management approach becomes increasingly difficult to learn and to use because it is not intuitive.

Don't Make Comparisons with TCP/IP

Extrapolating from the amount and kind of system management needed in a centralized environment (where a few centralized hosts were networked) to determine the amount and kind of system management needed in a Client/Server environment provides an erroneous idea of the complexity of managing Client/Server environments. It is equally dangerous to compare the system management needed for TCP/IP environments that use mostly FTP (File Transfer Protocol), SMTP (Simple Mail Transfer Protocol) and Telnet (for terminal emulation) to the system management needed in full-fledged Client/Server environments.

The difference is that file transfer, mail transfer, and terminal emulation are simple services. TCP/IP networks running FTP, SMTP, and Telnet need hardly any management. It's a different story for today's emerging Client/Server environments which use a lot of distributed services. As soon as the environment begins to use distributed services, it needs a lot of management. As applications become more critical in this distributed environment, there is a need to manage applications.

Types of People Costs

What do these system administrators do that consumes so much time and money? The people costs are largely split among three categories—training, setup, and operations (Figure 10.4).

Setup and/or development of system-management programs, along with training, constitute the up-front, or initial, people system management costs. Some of the initial costs in some organizations are management application-development costs. These development costs occur primarily in organizations that believed that writing their own system-administration software costs nothing because they already had UNIX. Unfortunately, some of the organizations forgot about the cost of the people who had to write these UNIX system-administration scripts.

To determine the total initial costs, the cost of purchased software and hardware must be added to the up-front people costs. Once the software and hardware is purchased and set up or developed, presumably costs decline. This lower cost, however, may be higher than just the operations costs because many organizations have ongoing training, and ongoing costs for moving users to different locations.

System-Management Tasks

Figure 10.5 shows the most commonly performed system-management tasks. The shaded boxes represent tasks that are more commonly performed than the others and/or that are the most important to the greatest number of organizations.

Problem Management

Problem management includes fault management, help desk, and troubleshooting. Problem management is where most of the system management money goes in most Client/Server organizations, and, certainly, in all the Client/Server environments

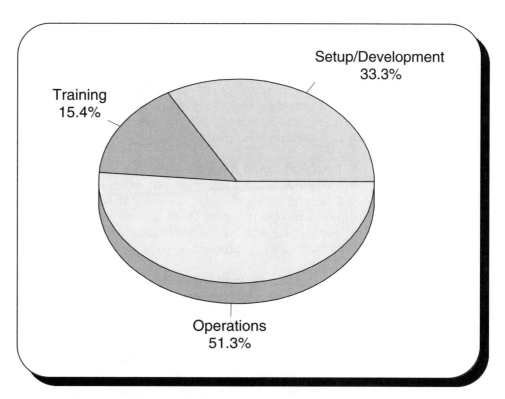

Figure 10.4 Types of people costs. *Source: Emerging Technologies Group.*

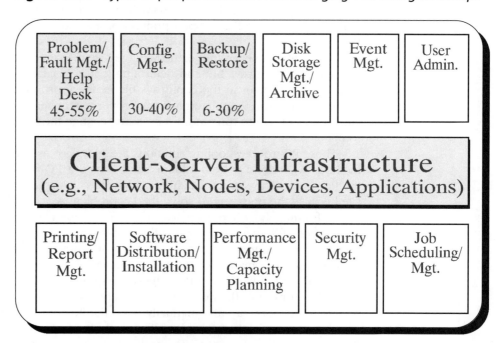

Figure 10.5 System-administration tasks. *Source: Emerging Technologies Group.*

interviewed for the ETG cost of system management study. On average, problem management represents 45–55 percent of system management costs, but it could run as high as 80 percent. PC problem management often tends to cost more than UNIX-system problem management.

PC Troubleshooting Is People-intensive   PC problem management consumes the largest amount of PC system managers' time. Consequently, both Novell's ManageWise and Microsoft's SMS (Systems Management Server) endeavor to provide help-desk tools and remote PC diagnostic aids. Unfortunately, although very helpful, neither ManageWise nor SMS can provide full fault management. The problem is not with either companies' management software. The problem is in the nature of PCs.

To facilitate PC troubleshooting, both ManageWise and SMS provide tools to allow system managers to remotely look at individual PCs, individual workgroup servers, and groups of PCs and servers. Both companies' diagnostics programs can take over the screen, the keyboard, the mouse, and so on, so the remote expert can determine the problem and help the PC users get their PCs up and running again. Sometimes, the PC-management programs can perform these functions when the PC user is not present.

In the SMS case, for example, the management software can determine who might be having a problem because of an old application version. SMS can then automatically distribute the new version across the network. SMS can also determine things like a remote PC stopped printing or a screen saver did not power down a PC.

To quote another example, the ManageWise management software can remotely examine the config.sys file and determine that a program is not running properly because a parameter in the config.sys file is not appropriate for a program that is trying to run. It can then determine the proper parameter, change the config.sys file, allow the program to run, and, if necessary, change the config.sys file to its original form.

These PC-troubleshooting solutions are orders of magnitude better than earlier methods whereby a system administrator solved a PC problem by walking across the floor, across the street, catching a train, or catching a plane to the troubled PC site because the only way to solve the PC problem was to solve it in person.

Unfortunately, when it comes to remote or automated PC troubleshooting, all bets are off if something happens that locks up the PC, or if an error occurs that requires an operator to press a key. These are not uncommon events. Often, the only way to cure many PC problems is to manually reboot the machine. For this reason, the only thing that a PC-diagnostics program can do if a problem takes the PC off line, or out of the network, is to notify a service person who is on call at the remote site to show up and manually press the key or reboot the machine.

The reasons for these problems in troubleshooting networked PCs is simply that PCs are PCs. They are not UNIX machines or proprietary mainframes. And, unlike UNIX platforms and proprietary mainframe, PCs are not designed for unattended operation.

Since Client/Server environments tend to be made up largely of PCs (and many Client/Server environments are networking hundreds to tens of thousands of PCs), the need for manual intervention for PC problems must be taken into account when planning how to manage a Client/Server environment.

At present, most PC-based Client/Server environments do fairly little system management. Fault management dominates all PC system-management tasks. But PC fault management cannot be easily automated or remotely controlled. Therefore, when planning for PC system management, plan to dedicate extra people to the PC fault-management task.

Configuration Management

Configuration management includes the time and cost to set up a system when it is first delivered, and perhaps to reconfigure it later to accommodate new disks, memory, users, software upgrades, and so on. Configuration management is important because if you don't set up the software or hardware system properly, you can't use it properly.

Initial configuration management when equipment is first delivered and networks, nodes, clients, and servers are configured for the first time, can range from 30–40 percent of initial system-management costs. After the systems are initially configured, configuration-management costs decrease. Configuration management, however, remains a costly ongoing task because of the need for reconfiguration whenever a user is moved from one location or subnetwork to another. Major reconfiguration may be needed if an environment moves to a different operating system or a new technology.

Backup and Restore

Users could, conceivably, buy a computer without a network, or without some of the system-administration tasks shown in Figure 10.5. In a production environment, however, they would rarely buy a computer without a good backup system.

Actually, most users couldn't care less about backup. What they care about is restore. But you can't have restore unless you first have backup. Therefore, unless decent software is available to perform backup, users will not buy the computer.

Backup and restore ranks third in system management importance. It represents six to 30 percent of system-administration costs and time. The importance of backup, and the cost and percent of time doing backup, varies depending on how critical the data is to the organization, and also on whether the environment is a dynamic or a static one.

For example, if a manager is trying out some preliminary ideas on a spreadsheet, if that spreadsheet misses a backup one night, it will get backed up the next night. If, on the other hand, the organization is an insurance company, and all the billing is on a database, the organization cares very much about losing any data. Consequently, the organization is likely to make sure that its data is backed up every night. If, on a random morning, the system administrator discovers that the backup stopped in the middle or skipped some files, he or she must spend the day figuring out why.

The other factor that affects the importance of backups, and the cost of backing up files and data, is whether the environment is a dynamic or a static one. *Dynamic environments* are environments that constantly add and modify users and computers. Examples are networking and communications companies. Dynamic companies run between 15–30 percent of system administration time and cost for backup operations.

Static organizations have stable environments. Static organizations, dealing with files that are not critical, consume between 10–15 percent of system administrators' time for backup, and sometimes as little as three to six percent.

A relatively small amount of time is required for backup operations because most organizations automate their backups. Most backup time spent is devoted to recovering files and determining why a backup failed, or, in the UNIX world, to writing shell scripts to automate backup operations.

Writing UNIX backup scripts is not a difficult task. If the environment, however, is one that cannot afford to lose data, and it is necessary to determine the cause of a backup failure or recover lost files, the use of UNIX shell scripts can become time consuming and expensive. For these and other reasons, most organizations that use UNIX scripts for system administration buy specialized backup and restore software.

Backup software is not overly expensive. However, if an organization plans to install separate backup systems for all the clients in a Client/Server environment backup costs mounts up. Typical costs are $120 per workstation/PC just for the backup software, plus about $250 more per workstation for backup hardware. The hardware and software costs are even greater if backup is to be combined with archiving and hierarchical storage capabilities. The result may be an investment from $500–$1,000 for hardware and software, multiplied by the number of workstations/PCs in a Client/Server environment.

One way to keep costs down is to handle all backups through the servers. At night, client workstations are backed up across the network to the server. The server is backed up to tape. Hierarchical storage and archive facilities belong only to the server.

Users can, if they wish, store their data on their workstation, but they know that this data may be endangered because system administrators only back up the servers.

Disk Storage and Management

Disk management is important to enable users to work productively without the possibility of losing data because a disk is full.

PCs perform disk management by sensing that a disk system has become full. The next time you try to save data to disk, you get a message saying, in these or similar words, "Sorry, disk full. Please remove some files." So you do. But you cannot save the file you are working on, so you lose it.

How much better it would be if hierarchical storage-management/archiving software sensed that the disk was becoming full. Then when the disk reached a certain percent of fullness, it would archive some of the data on the disk to tape.

When the user needs that data again, the disk-storage management software would automatically put it back on the disk. The user need never know it was gone.

Besides eliminating the potential to lose data because of a full disk, this kind of disk-storage management software eliminates the need for the system administrator to search many tapes to see which one contains the data that must be recovered. Manually searching tapes to find data is time consuming, tedious, and messy.

Hierarchical disk storage management also improves disk and network performance. It improves computer performance by maintaining a larger workspace on the disk. It also improves network performance because it ensures that there is enough free disk space to store data on the appropriate server. Hence, there is no need to spend overhead cross mounting NFS data on multiple servers.

Software Distribution and Installation

Software-distribution-and-installation software is software that distributes, installs, upgrades, customizes, and patches applications across a network. Software-distribution programs are important because they eliminate the need to make multiple trips to 512 computers to install, customize, patch, and then upgrade an application.

Software-distribution packages are an important capability for organizations to have if the organization runs applications on individual users' workstations. Some organizations, however, do not have a need for software-distribution packages because they install software only on their servers. Users access and download the applications they need from the server. This approach to installing software eliminates the need for software-distribution packages because the system administrator only installs, upgrades, and so on, each application once, on the server. This approach to installing applications is not, however, suitable for all environments. For example, it may not be suitable for highly distributed environments with numerous servers and users in remote locations, where network traffic and response time is a problem.

Printing Management

Traditional print systems cannot generally support the printing and management of documents in a multivendor, heterogeneous, distributed-computing environment. Managing print jobs in a distributed, multivendor computing environment requires such capabilities as being able to accept printing requests; queue and schedule print jobs; and perform requested printing on the most suitable and/or available printer for a particular job; manage multiple printers and printer queues; change a printer's queue; and more.

Most Client/Server users claim that distributed print management is a difficult task. Neither the current generation of PCs, nor UNIX with its "lpd" and "lpr" print commands, are designed for remote or distributed printing.

Many UNIX administrators have written their own print management programs, but they claim that writing a clean print-management program is a lot of work.

It is not the command telling the computer to "go to" a certain printer that causes print-management problems, nor is the problem one of seeing queues for each printer. The problem is the "came from" when something goes wrong. With ordinary PC or UNIX facilities, it is difficult to tell where a stopped print job originated. The second problem is print jobs that disappear into a black hole: There is no indication or notification if a user submits a job for printing but the job never shows up at the printer.

Job Scheduling

Job scheduling includes tasks like scheduling a job to run at a particular time each night, determining the right place to run a job, and workload balancing. These kinds of job-scheduling capabilities are commonly used for batch-processing jobs. At present, the majority of existing Client/Server environments do little or no batch processing, and therefore have little need for job-scheduling capabilities.

Most Client/Server environments that do job scheduling do it for very simple tasks. Job scheduling in PC networks, for example, mostly consists of writing a DOS batch file to backup a PC to its own tape or to a server at night.

UNIX systems provide a facility and command, known as *cron*, to schedule jobs. The UNIX cron command is extremely limited. It schedules a job, and that is all. It does not notify users as to whether their submitted scheduled jobs were actually run. If the server scheduled to run the job fails, cron does not tell you. Nor does cron restart a scheduled job after the server is back on line.

Cron also does not take into account other jobs using the same resource, the load on the server intended to run the job, the load on the client, the network traffic, nighttime audit/journal activity, nighttime report activity, batch-database update activity, and so on. These kinds of capabilities are important not only to programs like payroll, that people traditionally associate with batch processing, but also to the scheduling of disk-to-tape archiving activity in an environment with lots of backup activity. In such an environment, for example, it is important to schedule backups based on whether other jobs are using the tape drives at that time, the load on the tape server, any other backup (or heavy disk use), reporting activities, and so on.

If job scheduling is needed for anything but the simplest activities, a separate job-scheduling package should be purchased. Job-scheduling facilities also are included in some of the integrated system-administration packages.

Performance Management and Capacity Planning

Performance-management tools allow organizations to tune individual systems and subnetworks to meet their individual performance requirements. The performance management tools should provide the ability to:

- Track computing activity to determine system state
- Collect activity data in a performance database
- Analyze performance data with applications to identify bottlenecks
- Tune performance to eliminate or minimize bottlenecks by adjusting hardware, operating system parameters, application distribution, or load balancing

- Characterize workload statistically for resource consumption predictions
- Forecast workload for resource-requirements predictions (capacity planning)

While tools to perform many of these performance-management chores are well-known in the mainframe environment, some are literally unknown in the world of distributed computing. LAN-based systems for PCs are notorious, for example, for few performance tools, and little or no capacity planning tools.

Even where performance-management tools exist, such tools are few and far between, especially for the multivendor/platform/operating system environment. Performance management tends to be specific to a vendor's operating system and hardware.

PC-based workgroups connected in PC networks tend to do very little performance management. In other environments, however, where performance management is important, it is an ongoing activity, often with an associated high cost.

There are a variety of performance metrics available today that were initially developed to provide a general guide to internal system, memory, and disk usage, or to processor capabilities, often when the processor is under no load. As such, these metrics are no longer adequate for today's problems.

User Management

User-management utilities are concerned with the creation or deletion of a users, the ability to disable a user account, and the allocation of system resources to a user. In UNIX systems, user management also provides such services as the creation of home directories with options for NFS mounting of directories, and the setting up of authorization and authentication attributes for users.

User-administration capabilities are available in the operating system, be it an NT, OS/2, or UNIX operating system. Most organizations use the user-administration capabilities that come with the operating system.

Security Administration

Security in a Client/Server environment is concerned with three major issues:

- Who are you? (e.g., user identification name, password, and authentication)
- What are you allowed to do? (e.g., authorization, access control)
- What did you do, or who did it? (e.g., audit)

Security administration is intimately related to user management because at the time a user is defined to a computer system, the user is granted permission to access specified local or remote data, use particular local or remote physical assets, or perform specific operations on particular local or remote data or objects, or execute programs.

To provide true security, security considerations must be applied at the operating-system, database, application, and network levels. There are multiple methods for achieving different levels of security at each of these levels.

The simplest method of achieving security is through the assignment of passwords. Assigning or modifying passwords or other security protection is a mundane task. Depending on the system, however, the assignment or modification of security protection requires a high-priced system administrator because of the need for root or system-administrator status. The use of many third-party security software programs provides an easy way for an organization to save system-management money, because these programs provide graphical forms for the entry or modification of passwords, access-control information, and so on, without the need to be root. Therefore, a lower-priced system manager or junior system administrator can do the job.

A problem related to security, especially in networked environments, is the proliferation of viruses. About 100 new viruses are emerging every month, according to the National Computer Security Center. With such growth, it is almost impossible to rely only on programs that detect and kill viruses. Many organizations avoid viruses by waiting to move new software onto an organization's computers until after that software has been tested on an isolated computer for a period of time.

Security in Heterogeneous Environments   Heterogeneous environments have unique security problems because of the number of different human and software security managers that exist. Often, different departments are each responsible for administering the security of a different resource, platform, operating system, and LAN.

Unfortunately, often neither the human security managers, nor the software security managers implemented on the different platforms, operating systems, applications, and LANs, are coordinated with one another. As a result, the heterogeneous security managers may have different user-ID naming conventions, different password-management rules, and different security defaults. Where users must sign in to each platform, application, and so on, with a different user ID and password, they often end up with so many different user IDs and passwords that they write them down. All these problems can compromise an organization's security.

There are several steps an organization can take to alleviate these security problems:

- Develop an enterprisewide security management policy.
- Provide a single user ID and password for a user, regardless of the platform, data, or other resource the user must access.
- Provide a single user ID and password for a user to log into a system once, and for the rest of that session, any other systems, resources, or network the user connected to would check with a security database to determine the user's rights and privileges. Unfortunately, the single sign-on approach to security is difficult to implement in a heterogeneous platform, heterogeneous operating system, multiprotocol networked environment.
- If passwords are changed, apply the same password change rules to all systems.

- Encrypt sensitive data transmitted over the network.
- Instead of sending passwords over a network, transmit a cryptographic representation of it using a one-time encryption key. This technique should result in an access code that cannot be "sniffed" and contains no reusable information.
- If dial-in calling to the networked systems is allowed, use callback modems, and permit external access only through a firewall system. A *firewall* is a hardware device that electrically and logically isolates the network from the caller until the caller is correctly authenticated.

Event Management

Event-management services generate information for messages that are generated as the result of an event. The event services notify appropriate applications and/or system managers that a particular event of interest, concerning a system, network, device, file, application, or other managed object occurred. Typical events that warrant a notification message are warnings, error conditions, or security violations.

In a distributed environment, when an event of interest occurs, event services generally forward the event notification between systems. Such event services also allow the filtering of events based on system-administrator–defined thresholds (e.g., notify a management application of an event only if it occurs a certain number of times).

Event management underlies almost all operations management. This includes problem management, help desk, monitoring, maintaining availability, workload management, storage management, and automated operations.

Systems without event-notification capabilities generally obtain information about managed objects by polling. Continuous polling is a higher overhead process, and can be a less reliable means of getting timely information about system objects.

System-Administration/Management Approaches

There are three main approaches to system administration/operations management:

- Do-it-yourself solutions (e.g., UNIX scripts)
- Point solutions (e.g., specialized backup, job scheduling, print management, security, solutions each from a different vendor)
- Integrated system-management/system-administration solutions

The most common do-it-yourself system-management solutions are those written using UNIX scripts, although DOS batch scripts, VMS programs, and so on are also used. UNIX scripts have the advantage of no extra initial capital software costs because the UNIX system already exists, but this solution often carries with it high personnel costs.

Point solutions have the advantage of being developed by vendors who are expert in a particular area of functionality (e.g., backup, disk storage, print management). The disadvantage is that acquiring tools incrementally means that each tool has its own unique characteristics, which makes the use of a variety of tools quite a challenge. Imagine, for example, the number of different kinds of system-management experts that an organization would need to manage a Legato backup system, an HP PerfView performance-management system, a Unison-Tymlabs batch-job scheduler, Secure Computing Corporation's security-management software, and BGS systems capacity planning software, not to mention the UNIX experts needed for various tasks.

Point solutions are not generally integrated with each other. Nonintegrated tools usually mean more labor-intensive support and management.

It would be helpful to have a single interface and paradigm for managing the different aspects of a Client/Server environment. This is an advantage of integrated system-management solutions.

Integrated system management solutions provide a basic system administration architecture and common services. They have a single interface for all of the system management applications, just as MS Windows and OS/2 provide for their applications. Different management applications can use the same data to perform their functions such as common calendarying and user management. Integrated system management solutions also provide a software backplane (conceptually equivalent to a hardware backplane, but made of software) that allows various third-party solutions to be plugged in and integrated.

An example of integrated systems management is Computer Associates' CA-Unicenter, which provides a set of integrated system administration solutions with common shared repositories, and a software developer kit that allows for third-party integration. An example of a system management framework is Tivoli Systems' Tivoli Management Environment (TME), which is a set of APIs that allow third-party integration through event trapping and management.

During the cost of system-management study (described earlier in this chapter), some users reported a 30–50 percent savings from an integrated system management solution as compared to point solutions, and a decrease in system-management costs compared to system management on the mainframe. Other users reported that the use of an integrated system-management solution enabled their organization's quality assurance people and help desk to provide better service, because of the integrated system's ability to show what is happening throughout a system (not just on part of the system) using a single interface and paradigm.

The reason for both of these benefits is that integrated solutions simplify Client/Server complexity, and, therefore, reduce people costs and improve ease of use.

Integrated system-management tools benefit organizations that are downsizing system-management departments (through layoffs or natural attrition) or that are expanding the Client/Server environment without hiring more system administrators. In either of these cases, the organization needs to make the remaining system administrators more productive so they can handle more computers, more users, and more tasks more easily. This is the justification used by two organizations shopping for an integrated system-management tool. Their argument is that the organization must make a capital investment to replace the labor investment. If it is possible to increase the number of machines managed per system administrators, that is more profit to the company.

Dollars and Cents

Much has been written about the high costs of system management in a Client/Server environment. Costs need not be high. Although system management is one of the highest Client/Server costs, there are numerous examples of organizations that have significantly reduced their computing costs as well as their system-management costs, in moving to Client/Server computing. Examples of such organizations are discussed in this book in Chapter 12.

To estimate the system-management costs for your environment, it is important to realize that the system-management activities discussed thus far constitute primarily the technical system-administration and operations-management activities performed during the operations phase of the system-management life cycle. In terms of time spent and cost, however, these activities account for only the tip of the iceberg. The only meaningful system-management cost metric is the cost of ownership.

A cost-of-ownership analysis must include capital equipment expenses (e.g., software, hardware, and related support costs), people costs (salary plus fringe benefits), and facilities costs (includes the facilities for managing the Client/Server systems and for housing the personnel). Each type of cost must be calculated for all the Client/Server system management life-cycle phases.

The system-management life cycle can be divided into three phases. Phase One is initial acquisition, covering the initial development and/or product and installation costs. Phase Two is the operations phase, covering backup, job scheduling, fault management, and all the other activities discussed in this chapter. Phase Three is the change phase, covering the acquisition, people, and facilities costs during a technology upgrade or future transition.

As part of an Emerging Technologies Group cost-of-system management study, these costs, for all the system-management life-cycle phases, were collected and analyzed for 17 organizations. The results were shown in Figures 10.3 and 10.4.

In calculating people costs, which are by far the largest system management cost, a variety of business, as well as technical costs, had to be taken into account. Many of the business costs are not immediately obvious, and are consistently underestimated.

A breakdown of costs, and the methodology for calculating Client/Server costs or system management costs, is given in detail in Chapter 12.

Figure 10.6 shows many of the activities in a system-management–solution life cycle that must be planned for as part of Client/Server environment planning, and whose costs must be taken into account in a system-management cost-of-ownership analysis. This plan was developed by a system administrator in an investment bank-

I. Planning.

    A. Determine need.

    B. Determine functionality/features.

    C. Select method of acquisition.

        1. Home grown.

        2. Outsourced (either integrated package or multivendor solution).

    D. Create design specs (home grown) or select vendor (outsourced).

    E. Determine need for additional resources (facility planning).

    F. Lock down full requirements.

II. Acquisition

    A. In-house development.

    B. Vendor procurement.

    C. Maintenance agreements.

III. Installation

    A. Acquisition and setup of required additional resources before installation (facilities setup).

    B. In-house or outsourced installation.

    C. Training of maintainers and users.

        1. Outsourced classes (either in-house or at vendor location).

        2. In-house manual reading/experimentation.

    D. System configuration for local requirements, may involve using vendor/developer-supplied tools or locally developed tools/software.

    E. Installation problem resolution.

        1. Hardware failure (DOA or broken equipment).

        2. Software bugs that occur locally due to specific needs of customer, not foreseen by vendor/developer.

        3. Vendor/developer support (help desk) to get novice maintainer up to speed.

    F. Effect of system down time (to do installation or to resolve problems) on user base.

    G. Determination of insufficient resources after installation, including lost productivity while waiting for additional resources.

Figure 10.6 Management solution life cycle. *Source: Bruce Barton (Long Island, New York).*

IV. Routine operation
   A. Prime shift (frequency and duration, to perform the system mgt. operations activities).
   B. Alternate shift(s) (frequency and duration).
V. Non-routine operation
   A. Maintenance.
   B. Hardware failure repair.
   C. Software failure resolution.
   D. Beeper duty—scheduling, overtime costs.
   E. Modification of configuration (e.g., add a new user).
   F. Modification of environment (e.g., add a disk drive to a mgt. station, move equipment, etc.).
   G. Hardware/software upgrades.
VI. Disaster planning
   A. Off-site data storage.
   B. Off-site hardware (hot spare site).
   C. On-site hot spare (e.g., disk drive replacement).

Figure 10.6 Management solution life cycle (Continued).

ing company. Although developed for system-administration and operations management, most of this plan also pertains to planning network management.

This system-management life-cycle plan can be used for planning or estimating system-management costs. It includes the straightforward system-management activities and costs, as well as some activities that planners often overlook and cost areas that are consistently underestimated (often termed *hidden costs*).

Integrate System and Network Management Through SNMP

How to fully integrate system administration, operations management, and network management is still an unsolved problem. Vendors and consortia are working on the problem. At present, however, Client/Server planners can begin to integrate system and network management by standardizing around a common protocol for communicating all kinds of management information. At present, it is recommended that users standardize around the Internet Suite's (TCP/IP) Simple Network Management Protocol (SNMP) for communicating management information. SNMP is important because most open system-management products, running on most platforms, communicate management data using SNMP.

The SNMP network-management protocol is a simple request-and-reply protocol. Rather than defining a large set of commands, SNMP performs all its operations using a fetch-and-store paradigm. Effectively, the SNMP network manager is restricted to only two commands that are performed on the MIB (Management Information Base) data items (elements to be managed)—*set* and *get*. Variables are retrieved (get) or modified (set). All other operations are defined as side effects of the set operation.

The chief advantages of a fetch-and-store paradigm are simplicity and stability. SNMP is simple because of its limited number of commands and options. It is stable because there is little to change since new operations are defined as side effects of storing new data items into the MIB.

SNMP Version 2 (SNMPv2) was developed to provide privacy, authentication, and access control. This development eliminates one of the most glaring SNMP deficiencies, which was its lack of security. SNMPv1, for example, provided no effective way to prevent an unauthorized third party from acting as a manager and performing get and set operations for an agent. To prevent this security breach, many SNMPv1 users disabled the set function. Unfortunately, this limited SNMP to more of a monitoring/data-gathering capability than a management function.

SNMP's chief disadvantage is the fact that its simplicity severely limits the protocol's ability to satisfy users' requirements for event reporting, sufficient control, extensibility, and consistent or extensive addressing. SNMP accommodates only limited event reporting by means of the trap mechanism. Other events must be discovered by the managing node through periodic polling.

Cost is another SNMP concern, particularly where extensibility is required. The first implementation of SNMP is relatively inexpensive. But SNMP's simplicity so severely limits its extensibility that future SNMP developments are more likely to occur in the form of new MIBs—both proprietary and standard—rather than as SNMP enhancements. Each additional MIB will require changes and additions to the existing MIB-specific applications, in order to support new functions. New MIBs also will require unique application code to be developed, documented, and supported. MIB development and maintenance can result in a high cost to both users and vendors.

Despite its limitations, SNMP does an adequate job of managing existing networks because most existing networks are simple.

SNMP versus CMIS/CMIP

ISO CMIS/CMIP has more functionality than SNMP, such as support for automatic event notification, filters, and threshold-driven notification. CMIP also is less restrictive than SNMP because it supports commands to direct the performance of complex operations. In addition, because it is based on object-oriented technology, CMIS/CMIP is easier and less expensive to extend than SNMP. Even though CMIS/CMIP's initial cost is higher, it allows additional objects to be added, and an associated level of management provided, at a small incremental cost (Table 10.2).

Table 10.2 Comparison of SNMP and CMIP

Attribute or Function	SNMP	CMIS/CMIP
Type of Standard	Defacto standard	Formal standard
Programming Interface	Request/Reply, Traps	Request/Multiple Reply, Event notification
MIB	Collection of objects that a network management protocol can address	Repository of all the information needed for management of a system or network
Initial Cost of Implementation	Inexpensive	Relatively expensive
Cost of Maintenance	High: Each added MIB requires unique or altered application code	Inexpensive: Additional objects can be easily added
Object-Oriented	No	Yes
Monitoring the State of the Network	Primarily by polling, Limited number of traps	Event notifications, autonomously emitted by managed objects
Overhead	High, because monitoring depends on continuous polling	May be low because monitoring can be through event notification
Control	Get and set variables on data items in the MIB	Transmission of operations to be performed on managed objects
Event Discovery	Events primarily discovered by the managing node via periodic polling; Restricted event reporting facility associated with traps.	Event notification mechanism
Discrimination	No	Yes
Fault Notification	Limited traps	Events
Performance (threshold) Notification	Indirectly—side effects of set operations on MIB items	Events
Log Control	Specific by MIB	Built into CMIS architecture

Source: Emerging Technologies Group.

CMIS/CMIP's functionality is needed for distributed computing. Distributed computing, however, is still emerging, and relatively little of it exists today. Moreover, even though CMIP's maintenance cost is much less than that of SNMP, its initial cost is much higher. Most commercial organizations see little need to spend that higher initial cost to manage today's limited-functionality TCP/IP networks, so SNMP continues to be patched and enhanced. SNMP is actually the only choice for a network/system management protocol in a heterogeneous environment because no other management protocol runs on many platforms.

SNMP versus SMP

An intended revision to the SNMP specification, called the Simple Management Protocol (SMP), promises to overcome many of SNMP's limitations. Among other improvements, SMP will offer event notification (instead of just polling), bulk file transfer, improved network-element management, and the ability to manage applications on hosts and personal computers. Current SNMP lacks these features.

SMP, however, has several problems. First, SMP was developed outside the IETF, and is not accepted by the IETF. Second, like SNMP, SMP is expensive to extend. Like SNMP, this is largely due to SMP's lack of object orientation. New functionality generally requires changes to SNMP which ripple through the implementing software. Alternatively, new functionality or extensibility can be implemented by defining new MIBs. Unfortunately, however, every new MIB requires a new application or changes to existing applications.

Because there is no easy way to extend SMP, for cost reasons vendors moving to SMP will most likely develop new SMP products, rather than retooling existing SNMP products. Will vendors, however, want to develop new products for a protocol that still has most of SNMP's problems, adds only a small amount of extra functionality, as SNMP, is not easily extensible, and is not accepted by the IETF?

What's Integrated with SNMP?

Most major vendors' UNIX systems run TCP/IP and support SNMP for communicating management information. These vendors' management applications are integrated with SNMP. Most vendors' proprietary systems also run TCP/IP and often support SNMP.

Of the third-party vendors who supply most of the management applications for UNIX systems, support for SNMP varies. Some third-party management applications are integrated with SNMP; others use proprietary protocols. It is up to the user to determine which third-party management applications are integrated with SNMP, and then decide how much SNMP support means to them for the application in question.

PC SNMP Support

On the PC-management front, Novell's NetWare supports both TCP/IP and SNMP. The NetWare management console, called the NetWare Management System, can monitor SNMP-based applications. A range of available third-party management solutions are integrated with SNMP services of NetWare 4, NetWare 3, the NetWare Client, and/or the NetWare management System. Some of these SNMP-integrated applications are described in the company's *NetWare Management System Solutions Guide*. For the user, this integration means that these applications and products can be monitored by SNMP management consoles.

Microsoft's SNMP story is a schizophrenic one. NT supports TCP/IP and comes with an SNMP agent. NT, however, also uses its built in Microsoft-developed OSF DCE RPC-compliant remote procedure call (RPC) to communicate management information. Finally, Microsoft's SMS (System Management Solution) uses IPC, rather than SNMP, to exchange management data.

NT's SNMP agent is a sample reference program to demonstrate how an NT-based management application can take an arbitrary event, such as an SMS alert, and catch it in an SNMP trap. System-management developers can use this SNMP agent support to develop management applications suited to SNMP. Microsoft, however, chose not to use SNMP for its SMS because, the company claims, SNMP is really optimized for a different problem than that which SMS is trying to solve.

Microsoft has a point. SNMP is, traditionally, best suited for network-management applications that need a low-level protocol to manage fine-grained network devices, such as routers, hubs, and so on. SMS, which is an integrated package of management tools for software distribution, inventory, and PC diagnostics deals with higher-level objects, such as the operating system, applications, files and directories, and users. It's difficult to determine when it is appropriate to have SNMP handle these kinds of objects, and when an RPC is more suitable. It also is not clear when it is appropriate to use an SNMP-based API to interface to these kinds of objects, and when a higher-level API is more suited for management-application development and integration.

Microsoft provides its own higher-level SMS APIs for system management. An SMS agent runs on NT management servers that knows how to talk to the SMS API. The SMS agent communicates over the Microsoft RPC to NetView, OpenView, and other vendors' platforms, provided these vendors' platforms understand the Microsoft RPC and know how to talk to the SMS APIs.

Similarly, almost every major vendor has integrated its system-management applications with Novell's Netware.

The 15 Commandments of System Management

There is no simple recipe for efficiently managing open Client/Server systems. The following guidelines, however, will help Client/Server planners to address the major system-management issues, improve quality of service, and reduce costs and risks.

1. Think twice before writing all solutions yourself to save initial acquisition costs. You may end up spending more on people costs.

2. To simplify system management and reduce system-management life-cycle costs, choose system-management tools designed to reduce complexity. Examples of such tools are integrated system-management solutions.

3. Since Client/Server environments are intrinsically heterogeneous, multivendor environments, choose system-management software that runs on multiple platforms. This avoids the problem of learning multiple-management systems.

4. Wherever possible, use tools that automate system- and network-management processes without requiring human intervention. Automating these processes will make system managers more productive and effective.

5. Because networks are growing in size, implement system and network-management solutions that can scale across large networks.

6. Consolidate small systems into large ones. This minimizes the number of sites to be managed, and addresses system-management costs and software-distribution costs.

7. Because networks are growing in complexity as well as size, use tools that distribute management functions, rather than running all management functions on a centralized platform.

8. Minimize your number of network protocols. Multiple disparate protocols increase management complexity and create performance problems.

9. Improve performance by retiring your older PCs. The use of 286- and 386-based PCs with 8-bit I/O boards creates bottlenecks in getting information through the network adapter and to and from the network.

10. Save money by avoiding the backup of desktop machines to their own tapes.

11. Save money by using a system-management package that allows junior people to add users because knowledge of the root/system password is not needed.

12. Use distributed system-management techniques to manage Client/Server systems wherever possible. If, instead, you manage your Client/Server systems like a mainframe and proprietary network, your Client/Server systems will behave and incur costs like a mainframe and proprietary network. Many traditional techniques for managing routers, bridges, gateways, and modems, or for administering centralized mainframes, are not as suitable for managing complex distributed services across heterogeneous systems.

13. Combine network management, system administration, operations management, and database administration.

14. Work with a company that provides good service and support. If your system management's personnel are new to Client/Server computing and UNIX, reduce everyone's frustration level by getting a good book on the subject. One recommended book about UNIX, with a focus on distributed computing, is *UNIX System Administration Handbook*, Second Edition, by Evi Nemeth and others, Prentice Hall, Englewood Cliffs, New Jersey 07632, 1995.

15. Make the network a corporate resource, with common administration, common management, and common capacity planning.

The last commandment is important to effectively manage and maintain interoperability. At present, different departments within many organizations, and different groups within departments, are responsible for running various parts of the Client/Server infrastructure. Corporate accounting may run the mainframe-based accounting systems and Novell NetWare servers, while engineering runs the UNIX workstations and a TCP/IP local network. Sales may run AppleTalk, while business planning runs UNIX database servers connected to NetWare (but is moving to NT and TCP/IP). Within each department, the servers may be under the control of the operating-system group, while the clients are under the control of the applications group. The backbone TCP/IP network, however, which all the departments share, may be under the control of one or more telecommunications groups.

The end result is conflicting islands of system and network management. This is bad because one dysfunctional island in a distributed, Client/Server environment can impact other islands. Also, in a distributed environment the distinction between the networking/telecommunications, operating systems, platforms, and applications is blurred, because applications are distributed across the enterprise's networks, platforms, and operating systems.

When failures occur in such a decentralized management environment, it is difficult to tell whether the failure is in the server code, the client code, the network, or some combination of these. Before the cause of a failure can be discovered, it is necessary to find the appropriate system-management people from the different departments just to determine basic information about the network, clients, servers, applications, and other resources, as well as the ways in which they all interact.

For example, problems such as network-hardware failures, and intermittent NFS failures that cause clients to drop out, may be caused by the network load. The network load is impacted by various departments' server applications and server loads. This is a capacity-planning problem. Unfortunately, in a Client/Server environment without coherent management and administration, there is no easy way to capacity plan for current systems or for future growth.

Users who are sitting at a computer trying to perform their jobs don't care how loaded a network, server, or router, is. They care that they aren't getting their cursor back, their screen has turned gray, and that they cannot receive their electronic mail. To provide quality of network and Client/Server system service (which is the job of the network and system managers), it is necessary to treat the network as a corporate resource, not an individual department possession.

Questions to Ask Yourself and Your Vendors

Moving to any new technology is regarded as high risk. To lend confidence and credibility to a potentially risky venture, there are several questions you should ask yourself, your vendor, system integrator, or outsourcing organization.

1. How will you monitor and manage home-grown applications that are, or will become, critical parts of the Client/Server system? Many products help monitor different aspects of Client/Server systems, but what if packaged products are not available to monitor in-house written applications?

2. How will you make the Client/Server system reliable?

3. How will you secure the Client/Server system, and how will you prevent the introduction of viruses?

4. How quickly can you restore critical files that a user deletes? How quickly will you be able to restore a disk after a disk crash?

5. How will you accelerate change to meet your corporate goals, but also control change so you don't spend most of your time fighting fires?

6. How will you make the transition from your current centralized, proprietary environment to an open distributed one? How will you bring your present policies, procedures, and people into the open, distributed Client/Server world?

7. How will you integrate multivendor system and network management facilities?

8. How will you manage multivendor platforms, devices, operating systems, networks, databases, and applications?

9. How will you add new services in the future?

10. Are your vendors delivering open system-management solutions? Are their solutions hardware independent?

11. How do you support an organization's business requirements from a data-center and operations-management point of view?

12. Should you hire new UNIX, NetWare, or NT gurus, or will you retrain your existing staff? Is it easier to teach mainframe people how to manage open Client/Server systems than it is to teach UNIX and PC people the discipline needed to support mission critical applications?

13. What happens if you are so successful that you end up with double the number of users that you had a year ago?

The last question is both the dream and nightmare of almost every Client/Server planner and system manager. Some related questions include, "What happens if your Client/Server systems make users so productive that they generate a great deal more network traffic?" Or, what happens to your network and servers if the users start asking queries that are much more difficult than previously because the users have easy access to so much more data?

Planning for Deployment

With most of the initial open Client/Server planning completed, it is time to think about how to migrate to the targeted environment. The next chapter addresses the various migration strategies.

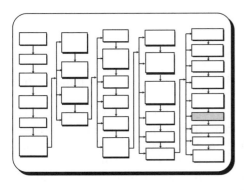

Phase Eight: Migration Strategies

Introduction

In the last chapter, this book discussed some of the major Client/Server issues and questions that must be resolved before actual migration can begin. The major open Client/Server planning tasks remaining are the development of a migration strategy, the choosing of vendors, procurement of products, the installation and integration of these products, the internal development of open Client/Server applications, and a plan for managing the open Client/Server environment.

This chapter provides a summary of the most common migration strategies that users employ to move to open systems.

Top–Down, Bottom–Up, and Middle–Out Migration

There are three approaches that organizations take to migrate to open Client/Server systems: Top-down, Bottom-up, and Middle-out.

Organizations that migrate using a *top–down approach* create an overall infrastructure as well as profiles for different domains and platforms. They define application-specific and platform-specific profiles before they build the profile components. As is the case with top–down programming, as the design progresses the planners fill in more and more details, and gradually build the lower-level components incrementally.

The idea of this top–down approach is to ensure, at each step of the planning process, that the infrastructure is designed so that all its parts can work well together.

243

If there is a possibility that they may not work well together, then the infrastructure is fixed before continuing on to the details.

The problem with a top–down approach is that it often turns out to be of theoretical use only because most organizations do not start with a clean slate—they have an installed base of legacy systems that they are not about to trash. Development tools for 3-tier Client/Server applications are first emerging now. Furthermore, many of the standards needed, and products implementing standards, are not yet available or are not yet sufficiently functional or robust. As a result, many exceptions to the original plans must be made. The result is disappointing portability, interoperability, and scalability, and limited Client/Server capabilities, at least for the short term.

A *bottom–up approach* involves people in various groups and departments creating individual components or small groups of open Client/Server components. After they are sure that each group of open Client/Server components works well, they try to integrate the different components.

Unfortunately, this bottom–up approach fell into some disrepute in the 1980s when a number of people, thinking to move to open interoperable systems, ended up creating open-systems–based islands of automation that did not work well together. A bottom–up approach could have equally poor results in a Client/Server environment where Client/Server components in various departments must cooperate to accomplish a goal. Furthermore, the Client/Server systems must be extendible to accommodate new systems, technologies, and applications that also must cooperate with the initial systems and applications. Few organizations use a totally bottom–up approach, unless they are implementing only a standalone Client/Server system in a single department.

The most common and practical approach used today is what can best be described as a *middle–out approach*. A middle–out approach is in some ways a combination of the top–down and the bottom–up approaches. Much of the middle–out planning procedures are done as though the organization were approaching open systems from a top–down perspective. This planning provides a target to aim for and to bear in mind during the migration and implementation phases.

The top–down and middle–out approaches differ when it comes to their implementation. Implementors using a middle–out approach tend to begin their implementation with a small number of bottom-level components. The bottom–level components that are implemented first are backbone components that are found in many or all departments, and that can provide a basic infrastructure to tie together the organization in the future. At implementation time, planners tend to choose a minimum set of standards that work together (e.g., a protocol stack, file transfer, and a network file service). These standards, by their nature, are ubiquitous throughout the organization, and will be required regardless of specific future open Client/Server directions. The Client/Server applications that planners implement initially are those that use these fundamental standards, such as data-access and workflow applications.

Unlike the bottom–up approach, the middle–out approach to open systems does not begin by implementing components for individual functional areas that must be integrated later. Thus, no islands of automation are created.

Which Approach to Choose

To maximize interoperability and portability for now and the future, many users moving to open Client/Server systems are planning their open systems from the top down, but their actual move to open systems is occurring from the middle out.

The way this works is that regardless of the migration approach chosen, users planning open Client/Server environments develop a generic architecture for their organization and populate it first with the services they need, and second with the standards and specifications that interface to those services. This is equivalent to developing an organization-specific, enterprisewide profile.

The development of this organization-specific profile may or may not be a formal process. It may consist of a small group of planners with a vision talking to various users in the organization to determine their requirements. It may result in choosing a common networking scheme, network-operating system, file-transfer system, database, electronic mail, productivity tools, and workgroup products. Or, it may involve the identification of the targeted distributed functionality and activities, as well as the whole gamut of applicable standards and specifications.

The planners may then subset the components and standards in this generic organization-specific profile in order to develop subprofiles for different application areas and platforms (e.g., transaction processing, the automated office, desktop computers). This process also may or may not be a formal one, but the development of profiles for targeted Client/Server platforms and application areas is done formally or informally because it is a logical next step in the planning process.

At implementation time, organizations tend to do one of two things:

- Organizations employing a top–down approach to open Client/Server systems migration choose a specific initial application type to implement (e.g., electronic mail), develop a profile for that application area, and begin their implementation. As the implementation of this initial application nears completion, the users begin to implement one or more open Client/Server systems applications based on other profiles they have developed. As they implement these applications, they constantly check to see that the different profiles and, consequently, applications, are harmonized with each other. If they are not, then phased implementations provide a chance to discover any incompatibility problems.
- Users choosing a middle–out approach to open systems migration choose a minimum set of standards that work together (e.g., a protocol stack, file transfer, and a network file service), are ubiquitous throughout the organization, and will be required regardless of specific future open Client/Server standards directions.

Open systems today are important because a move to open systems usually is coupled with a move to a Client/Server distributed environment. Most users consider interoperability as more basic to this environment than portability. Consequently, most users' highest priority open-systems directions focus on networks (OSI or TCP/IP), Client/Server computing (though different users have different definitions of Client/Server computing) and, supposedly, PCs. The advantage of PCs for Client/Server systems is their low price and ubiquity. The problem with PCs as a Client/Server focus is the difficulty of managing them, and the fact that they don't scale well to the enterprise. The problem with PCs as an open-systems focus is that few standards exist, and the integration and management of PCs with heterogeneous computers in an enterprise is currently chaotic.

It will neither be possible, nor necessary, to standardize all systems in an organization so that they work cooperatively. Migration to open Client/Server systems is an evolutionary process. The average company moving to enterprisewide open Client/Server systems has a three-year, five-year, or 10-year plan—and three-year plans are tenuous, except for individual systems in parts of the enterprise.

It is, however, important early on for an organization moving to open Client/Server systems to have a vision of where it wants to be in five years and how it will get there. This vision helps in planning an open Client/Server environment that is extendible as new standards are approved, and as new technologies and Client/Server tools emerge, and that will support changing business requirements. Many times, this vision also helps later on in making some of the tactical decisions that are needed to get the job done.

Migration Approaches

After you decide to migrate to an open Client/Server environment, and you have determined what applications you will reengineer to take advantage of Client/Server computing, you will need to understand the technical differences between open systems and your current proprietary operating environment. At this point, you need to consider the best methodology for conducting the migration. No two migrations are the same, and the key to a successful migration is a well-thought-out migration plan. It is vital to handle all the details systematically and to monitor progress throughout the process.

The migration process is a multistep procedure. It involves setting objectives, performing a system and application inventory for the systems to be migrated, and examining the migration methods. Setting objectives and performing a system and application inventory are organization-specific activities. There are four major open system environment migration strategies:

- Coexistence via networking, gateways, and data interchange
- Application-programming interfaces (APIs)
- Compatibility libraries
- Code conversion

The most commonly used of these approaches is the network, gateways, and data interchange strategy. The last, code conversion, is the most expensive and time-consuming migration strategy. On the other hand, several users' experience has shown that if reengineering of applications is done in conjunction with code conversion, the result is often an environment that is less expensive to operate and provides greater business benefits.

Coexistence Strategy

The network, gateways, and data interchange migration strategy is essentially a coexistence strategy. It is the most common open Client/Server system migration strategy because most organizations have an installed base of legacy platforms, networks, databases, applications, and so on, which are perfectly functional. Even if all the standards and products needed for open systems were available, it would be very difficult to justify the trashing of these earlier systems for the latest style platform, network, database, application, and other system software.

What users can expect vendors to offer much of the time is a coexistence strategy. With this strategy, open-systems networks and software are procured when a new system is needed to satisfy new Client/Server functionality, or when a new system is needed because the legacy system is due for replacement. In these cases, when the new standards-based open systems are brought in, they are set up to interact and otherwise work with other legacy systems.

This coexistence strategy is accomplished through the use of networking, gateways, and other data-interchange software and hardware facilities. Such facilities allow new systems to be based on standards and provide Client/Server capabilities, while legacy systems run existing applications, and also allow the new and the existing systems to be integrated. Integration means that the standards-based systems and the legacy systems can exchange and access data, and remotely execute applications (Figure 11.1).

Most users migrate to standards-based open systems via this kind of coexistence strategy.

Compatibility Libraries Strategy

A number of user and independent software vendor (ISV) software developers are achieving open-systems portability through the use of library routines. Examples include vendors who are providing POSIX and X/Open system software and applications, as well as X Windows and Motif applications.

To achieve open systems portability in this way, developers design their applications only for the standard POSIX features (or for the Motif GUI). They then use library routines to provide additional services. This method requires fewer application rewrites for portability.

In the case of POSIX-based libraries, the libraries contain a routine to execute the extended operating-system feature, or an interface to the extended feature. The

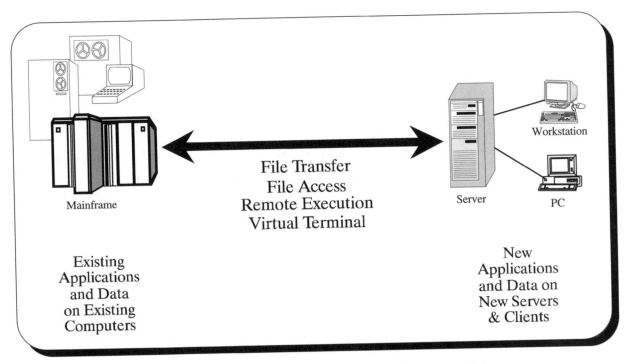

Figure 11.1   Networking and data-interchange strategy.

library routines interface to the core POSIX standard on one side. The other side interfaces to the application (Figure 11.2).

The application issues certain calls to the POSIX interface directly. These calls do not affect application portability because POSIX is standard and the same core is present in every POSIX-based operating system.

Each system library performs the same function, but each performs the function in its own way. In the case of a POSIX-compliant UNIX system that does not perform a particular function at all, the system call is sent to a separate operating-system library. This library will contain additional vendor- or user-written service routines able to perform the function.

An application might require a specialized routine that is not part of any POSIX or UNIX system. To insure maximum portability, that specialized routine would be written, placed in the system library, and documented. To port that application to System V, BSD UNIX, SCO UNIX, or another POSIX-based system, an application developer would see from the documentation that a specialized routine is required. That routine would be rewritten for the new target POSIX system and placed in the target POSIX system library. Since the library routine, regardless of computer or operating system, would recognize the same system calls to perform the service, the application would be portable.

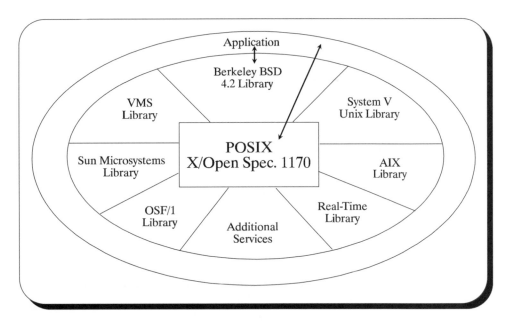

Figure 11.2   Compatibility libraries strategy.

Application-Programming Interfaces Strategy

The third migration strategy is through application-programming interfaces (APIs). This is the strategy that vendors use when they make their proprietary-operating systems and database-management systems compatible with the IEEE POSIX and X/Open XPG (X/Open Portability Guide) standards and the ISO/ANSI SQL standards. Example of vendors supporting this strategy are Digital Equipment Corporation, IBM, Hewlett Packard, Unisys, Tandem Computer, and others.

With this API strategy, vendors develop their traditional system software with dual APIs. One API is the proprietary API (such as VMS, MVS, or MPE XL). The other interface is the POSIX-interface standard.

The POSIX and proprietary interfaces sit side by side on top of the base proprietary system (Figure 11.3). Proprietary applications run just as they always have because the same VMS, MVS, or MPE interfaces are still present to recognize the calls. POSIX applications also run because the base operating system provides a POSIX interface which recognizes the calls.

Vendors claim that extending VMS, MVS, MPE XL, and so on will not affect the internal performance of applications because POSIX specifies only the interfaces and not the internal implementation of the underlying system. The advantage of this strategy is that the addition of POSIX compatibility to the proprietary operating system means that proprietary system users will have access to new software standards and technologies that are built on top of POSIX as they become available.

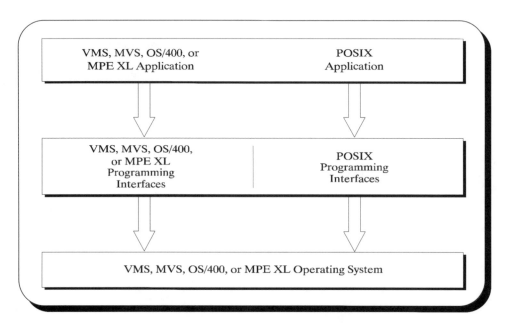

Figure 11.3 Proprietary operating systems with standardized APIs.

Note that this dual API technique is different from past approaches where vendors merely layered a UNIX interface on top of a non-UNIX system. With a layered approach, all the UNIX file formats, system calls, methods of handling processes, and so on, would have to be translated into proprietary system formats, system calls, and so forth. Translation is a very slow task, which would make application execution very slow.

Instead, what the vendors are doing today is implementing their proprietary system with two interfaces—POSIX and the proprietary one. This eliminates time-consuming conversion operations. In some cases, only one file system is provided. For example, OpenVMS provides only the VMS file system. Digital Equipment Corp. claims that having a single file system eliminates time-consuming file conversion operations. In other cases, such as with POSIX-compatible MVS, both the POSIX and MVS file systems are provided. MVS and POSIX applications each use the file system that is most natural for them. An advantage of this approach is that UNIX programmers are familiar with POSIX file system operations because of their similarity to UNIX.

At present, POSIX-compatible proprietary operating systems are new and are mainly useful as an opportunity for proprietary system users to gain some experience with POSIX, to run certain POSIX applications that they would not otherwise be able to, and to begin to migrate to an open-systems environment.

Code-Conversion Strategy*

The fourth major method for migration to open systems is code conversion. Whether or not to actually convert working proprietary code to standards-based code depends on several factors. One driving factor might be if the proprietary code is going away because a proprietary system has been discontinued and no longer performs the functions that an organization needs. Another reason governing whether or not to convert code depends on the amount and size of existing code to move. Still another major reason is the reengineering of existing applications for Client/Server computing.

The code-conversion process is multistep. It requires first performing a source-code inventory and examining data and program transport methods. Next, the code conversions and data conversions must be done, followed by functional testing, and finally performance tuning.

To make all this happen in an efficient manner, users should arrange for vendor support. Such support should include planning assistance, media-conversion service, and the provision of software tools and programmer consultation. The vendor will also need to help accommodate custom features in the data or applications, and accomplish performance tuning. Vendor support is necessary regardless of whether the code conversion is outsourced to a consulting organization.

Note that some of the steps in the code-conversion process described in the following sections apply to all applications being converted. Other steps apply only to applications whose existing code is being converted to run on a different system (e.g., on a UNIX system, rather than a proprietary one), rather than to applications being reengineered.

Source-Code Issues

Any sizable migration project should begin by setting objectives and establishing a way to determine when these objectives have been met. For open Client/Server systems migration, a reasonable set of objectives includes a list of applications to be moved, peripherals to be supported, and performance goals to be reached.

A source-code inventory is necessary for applications being converted to run on a different system. Depending on an organization's maintenance practices, a source-code inventory could be a major or minor effort. For each application to be migrated, application developers will need a list of all program modules, data files, and documentation required to construct the product. The developers then should examine each of these to determine the level of effort required for migration.

In most cases, the source-code modules do not contain the entire application. There will also be control files and on-line documentation to convert, and these should be included in the inventory and in the migration plan. Job control files will almost certainly have to be completely rewritten.

---

*A significant portion of the information on code conversion was developed by Charles Watkins for Texas Instruments' *VAR Guide to UNIX Migration.*

For source-code modules that will be migrated, application developers should note the number of lines of code the modules contain. They should then scan the code looking for statements that may require special attention.

Attention may be required for statements that make assumptions about initialization, statements that use nonstandard syntax or compiler-unique features, statements that use terminal-specific procedures, or statements that make assumptions about storage allocation. Statements that perform screen processing using menus or forms, use indexed file management, use calls to assembly language routines, have dependencies on other user- or vendor-written programs, or use operating system service calls will also require consideration.

Getting Code Off the Old System and On to the New

One of the basic problems that must be solved in the course of code migration is how to get the data and source code off the old machine and on to the new one. There are three main options:

- Protocol-based file transfer
- Compatible tape transfer
- Networking

The advantages of protocol-based file transfer, such as IBM 3780/2780 communications, are error-checking and long-distance capabilities. The error-checking service of a good file-transfer package is crucial when moving large volumes of code and data. Long-distance transfers may or may not be a concern.

Tape transfer is fast and convenient, but requires the host and destination machines to agree on the tape format and data layout. You will want to move entire directories at a time, not just individual files, so there must be some agreement or translation of directory contents as well. In moving files and directories, incompatibilities have caused problems for users moving files and directories from platforms using a flat-file system to POSIX or UNIX platforms that employ a hierarchical-directory structure.

If open-systems migration involves a POSIX or X/Open platform as the destination platform, the transfer of code and data will be greatly facilitated if the proprietary platform can write a tape in tar format. The *tar* format is the traditional UNIX transport utility. Although it has many shortcomings, it was standardized by POSIX due to its widespread use.

Your vendor should be able offer some media-conversion support. Some vendors, for example, have developed their own tools to help move code from proprietary platforms to a tape with a tar format. Also, if your proprietary platform supports older tapes (e.g., 3200-bpi tape) and you are planning to use cartridge tape on the new platform, your vendor should either loan you a tape drive or translate your tapes for you.

Probably the ideal environment for moving code and data to the UNIX system is a local-area network that supports both machines. That way, the information can be moved incrementally between systems, and in some cases, the application can be run on both systems simultaneously to assure that the conversion is correct.

In the best case, such a networking product should not only permit file transfer between proprietary and open-system platforms, it should also allow users to log in from one machine to the other and allow programs to access data across the network at the record level. With such an arrangement, the migrated application can be run with data still residing on the original machine, allowing a smooth changeover to the new system.

Develop Tools to Automate the Code Conversion

Most of the effort that goes into a typical migration is spent in code conversion and syntax debugging. The more this process can be automated the better, since it is exacting, repetitive work.

It is very important to take the time to develop tools to automate the code-conversion process, or to work with a vendor that provides such tools. Although it may seem appealing to skip this step and just run your source code through the new compiler, then fix the errors the compiler reports, in practice this method causes you to return to the same source modules again and again as the solution to one problem uncovers the next. If you take the time to scope out the work ahead, you will have the opportunity to develop tools to solve several problems at once. You will also be able to schedule the work and monitor your progress.

Converting the Code

There are three possible approaches to code conversion.

The first is to go through every source file and make the necessary changes using your favorite text editor. This is a lengthy, iterative process, and is usually abandoned when the programmer realizes the scope of the task and the need for conversion tools.

The second approach is to review the list of changes and make some generic string substitutions aimed at eliminating most of the repetitive work. This approach also is lengthy because the source-code review and the string substitutions involve a good deal of manual work.

The third method is to develop a syntax translator that comprehends an organization's specific migration needs. By refining the translator, rather than your source code, you will need to solve each problem only once.

Data conversion is as complex as code conversion, and often more so. It can be complicated by the need to maintain a single, correct set of data during the changeover to the new system. It is highly desirable to operate the old and new versions of the application in tandem for some period after the conversion—both as a fallback in case unforeseen problems appear in the new system and as an assurance that the new version works the same way as the old. During the time of parallel execution, new data will have to be fed into both versions. An example of why maintaining two systems is important is shown by one organization that rid itself of its old systems too early after a conversion. As a result, it could neither pay its bills nor invoice customers until it determined and fixed its problems.

Functional Testing

Most of the code-conversion work will center on the compiler, using test data obtained or constructed as needed to exercise the new code. Functional testing is another lengthy, laborious process that can be facilitated by the right set of tools.

If automated test suites have been developed for the application, they should be included in the list of programs to be converted.

Performance Tuning

After the application has proven its correctness and stability by running in tandem with the original for some period of time, application developers can turn to the final task of tuning the application and the system to work together for the best performance. Really bad performance problems will probably show up in the functional-testing period, but others may not appear until the system is placed under an operational workload.

The most important tool for system tuning is a performance tool that lets the developer observe the system at work. Developers must be able to see potential bottlenecks such as buffer shortages, bus contention, and excess paging. It is desirable to work with a vendor who can provide a performance monitor with graphical as well as statistical displays for major system components, plus a history and replay facility for capturing performance data over time.

The Programmer's Responsibility

Standards make portability and interoperability possible, but they do not guarantee either. A certain amount of responsibility in achieving portability and interoperability rests with the application's programmers.

A poor or standards-resistant programmer can make any program nonportable and non-interoperable. In order to achieve portability and interoperability, programmers must migrate their applications, and design new ones with portability and interoperability in mind. This is particularly important because most standards-based products contain certain vendor-specific value-added features.

There are several reasons for incorporating these nonstandard features. First, standards are usually incomplete because compromises had to be made to reach consensus, and also because standards cannot perfectly anticipate future technology. Second, vendors try to differentiate their products by extending standard features. Although these nonstandard features are often valuable and sometimes necessary, many vendors also add facilities that restrict portability and interoperability without providing sufficient benefits in return. In addition, vendors often retain some nonstandard interfaces to provide compatibility with legacy systems. Indiscriminate use of these extensions may lock an organization in to a particular "open system." On the other hand, it may be very handy to use these extensions.

To ensure open systems, application developers and their managers must make decisions to manage their work, leverage the extensions that warrant use, and design their applications for portability and interoperability.

Design Guidelines for Portability and Interoperability

To maximize portability and interoperability, programmers must first of all write as much as possible of the application to standardized APIs, such as SQL for data management; POSIX APIs to request operating system services, GKS, PHIGS, or other graphics standard APIs for graphics; and so on. Sometimes this is not possible. For example, there may be no standards in a certain area. Or, for performance reasons or to accommodate a legacy system, it may be necessary to bypass a particular API.

In cases like this, where there are no standards or where it is necessary to bypass the standardized interface, there are methods by which application developers can still maximize portability. Toward this end, the second design-for-portability-and-interoperability rule to follow is to separate, into different modules, the code written to the standard API from the code written to the nonstandard implementation-specific interfaces.

The third rule to follow is to thoroughly document the nonstandard parts of the program.

The fourth design-for-portability-and-interoperability technique is to mask off the nonstandard code from the standards-based code. This technique, which will be described in the next section, facilitates application portability because it ensures that an application always remains the same from system to system, regardless of its use of nonstandard extensions.

If these portability guidelines are followed, large parts of an application using nonstandard features will be portable. To move the application to a different system, or to migrate to a standard when the standard is approved and a product implementing that standard is available, application developers need only rewrite some pieces of the application—not all of it. In particular, developers should need to rewrite only the nonstandard code.

Masking Off Nonstandard Code

One way to maximize application portability in cases where nonstandard software features must be used is to mask off nonstandard code. *Masking off* nonstandard code is a programming technique to isolate a nonstandard function via an interface. The interface is known as a *mask* because it masks off, or shields, the nonstandard function from the application (Figure 11.4).

One side of the mask, or interface, interfaces to the nonstandard function. The other side interfaces to the application. The mask's job is to translate an application's calls issued using a standardized syntax, arguments, order, type, and so on, to the

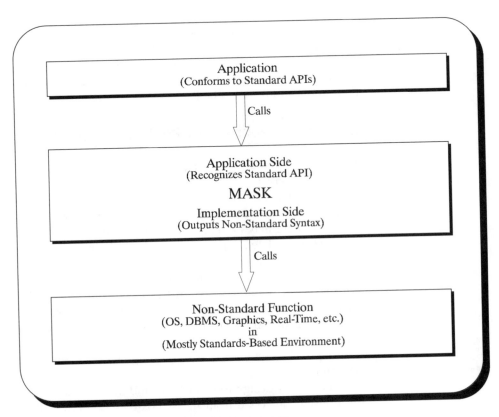

Figure 11.4 Masking off nonstandard code.

syntax, arguments, order, type, and so on recognized by a nonstandard service in another application environment. The mask, or interface, is stored in the system library as a library routine.

To use this mask, if an application needs a nonstandard service, the application simply calls the service at a high abstracted-syntax level that is as free as possible from implementation details. The side of the mask that interfaces to the application recognizes the application's high-level calls. This side never changes. The other side interfaces to the nonstandard extension.

To port an application to another environment, the library-routine mask travels with the application. The application need not be changed because it always issues its calls to a function in the same way. Nor must the side of the mask that interfaces to the application be changed because it maintains the same interface to the application regardless of the target environment.

Only the side of the mask that interfaces to the nonstandard function in the original environment, and calls the equivalent function in the new target environment, must be modified. This is simpler and more straightforward than rewriting complex nonstandard code or applications. Moreover, it does not require the application developer to get involved with the detailed code of a specific implementation.

In practice, implementing masks may be more work than many application developers are willing to do. This feeling, however, may last until the first time they have to port an application and realize how much more work they have created by ignoring the mask as a portability-management technique.

Vendor Support

Many migration chores will benefit from (or need) a certain amount of vendor support. One of the greatest assets in planning and executing an organization's migration to an open Client/Server environment is the support its vendor(s) can provide.

Many vendors offer some sort of media-conversion support. Your vendor should also be able to furnish software tools for converting source code and data. Translators, debuggers, cross-compilers, and various networking arrangements are reasonable to expect from a vendor with migration experience. An exceptional vendor will develop custom tools for you, drawing on a base of experience with other system integrators and their applications.

Some vendors don't offer such support, and some value-added resellers, system integrators, and very large-scale users are able to make it on their own. But most successful migrations are the result of user and vendor cooperation. For this reason, a number of mainstream user companies have partnered with one or two vendors to help them move to open systems.

There are many things a vendor can do to support an open Client/Server migration effort, and these should be factored into an organization's vendor selection. A word of caution, however, is necessary. It is a common ploy in the industry today for a would-be vendor to "prove" that migration will be easy by offering to migrate some portion of your application for you. Some even say they will do the whole job if you will just buy their product.

The problem with the sample migration is that the code chosen for conversion is almost never as complicated as the rest of the application you will be left to do yourself. Vendor often try to choose the simplest conversion, and rarely do more than get it to recompile on new hardware. There is a good chance that there will still be much to be done to get the required performance, and you may find your own people cannot match the productivity of the vendor's experts doing the conversion.

Even if everything is done for you, you may be worse off than doing it all by yourself. If your people are not involved in the migration, how can they support the product? And do you really suppose the vendor understands your customers' requirements as well as your own people do? If these concerns are real to you, you should be looking for a vendor who will work *with* you.

Planning Assistance

A vendor who has done open system and Client/Server system migrations before should be able to help you plan your own. Your vendor will know and anticipate problems in the migration plan encountered by other users and workarounds for these problems. Technical barriers to implementing your application should be visible to your vendor, and the effort required to develop or customize conversion tools should be understood.

Your vendor may also be able to put you in touch with other users who are in the process of migrating to open systems and who would be willing to share their experiences with you. Your vendor should certainly be able to point out the best way over obstacles that others have encountered.

As you complete your migration plan, you may realize that to complete the effort successfully, you will need a short-term infusion of skilled programmers. Once the migration is complete, you can return to a normal staffing level. But even the easiest conversion is likely to tax the capabilities of an organization's existing people. Remember, most people are new to the standards-and-distributed-systems game and will not be fully productive for some time.

If you present a large enough business opportunity to your prospective vendor, you may be able to arrange for the vendor to send programmers to your site to help with the project. These people are best used as consultants, trainers, and troubleshooters to help you educate your own staff as quickly as possible. If you need to assemble a migration team of experienced programmers skilled in open Client/Server systems, your vendor may be able to help you find them.

Custom Features

If some of your applications happen to be built around a feature that is available in your proprietary environment but has not it been implemented in a standards-based product, you may need to test your vendor's commitment to your account by asking for that feature to be implemented on the new system. Most of the time, vendors will look for a workaround. In some cases, however, they will be willing to modify their standard product on your behalf.

Beware of specials, however. Remember that unless a feature becomes part of the vendor's standard offering, you will not be able to count on future enhancements or ongoing support.

Paying the Bills

At this time, we have completed the initial plans for implementing Client/Server systems that are interoperable, portable, and scalable. No matter how well thought out these plans are, the Client/Server systems planned cannot be successful if there is no way to pay for them. The next chapter addresses the cost of open Client/Server systems, and how to determine Client/Server costs for your environment.

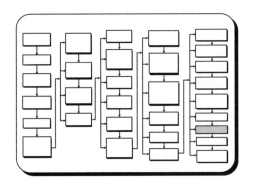

Chapter 12

How Much Will It Cost?

The Cost Factor

Don't believe the hype—whether the hype says that Client/Server systems are more expensive, or less expensive, than traditional computing. Your costs will depend on:

- The type of applications running in your environment.
- The number of servers and clients you purchase.
- How many heterogeneous servers and clients you support in your environment.
- Whether your physical organization must be rewired.
- Whether applications were reengineered for Client/Server computing.
- How your applications are distributed.
- The amount, and quality, of training provided for your Client/Server staff.
- Your accounting methods and methods of calculating overhead.

It is a poor idea, businesswise, to plunge into a new technology, paradigm, or environment without having some idea of its costs. But only you know your computing environment and your organization's accounting procedures—only you can estimate your costs.

This chapter shows you what others in the industry are spending, what the consistently underestimated major cost items are, and how to determine your Client/Server costs. Cost determination is not part of the DOSEE methodology. It is, however, essential to successful Client/Server planning.

259

Proceed with Caution

The economics of Client/Server computing are compelling. The costs involved in Client/Server computing are less than those associated with traditional centralized mainframes and minicomputers. The differences are apparent in the costs of processors, operating systems, DBMSs, networks, and software development. Who can resist faster, cheaper hardware and software at a time when resources are scarce and so many jobs are threatened by downsizing and retrenchment?

The problem is estimating the true costs. Initial costs are easy to estimate because they are straightforward. Vendors can provide the initial price of a piece of hardware or software, but estimating the cost of maintenance, operations, support, and future growth is difficult.

Vendors sometimes opt to offer attractive hardware prices, knowing that expensive service and support will be required later. Consequently, the great hardware buy's cost savings disappear into high-priced maintenance and support. For this reason, users must consider the *total* cost of ownership.

Users also should realize that open Client/Server environments are the most complex computing environments that MIS managers, infrastructure managers, and system administrators have yet experienced. Maintaining highly functional applications and reasonably low costs in such a complex, heterogeneous environment generally requires good advance planning for change, architecting of the environment for integration, and engineering applications for Client/Server computing.

Organizations who have done their planning and reengineering jobs well maintain that their Client/Server environment costs, including the operational and system management costs, are less than they paid for traditional mainframe computing.

Cost savings is not the only reason for moving to Client/Server computing. Several organizations have found that the ability of Client/Server computing to increase their customer services, and consequently their number of customers quickly, more than outweighed their up-front costs of buying new servers and rewiring buildings for Client/Server networks.

To make the most cost-effective case for Client/Server computing, plan well; reengineer your applications for Client/Server computing; consider the total cost of ownership, not just the up-front costs; and consider the benefits of Client/Server, too.

Where Does the Money Go?

To determine where the money goes, it is necessary to identify all the cost items involved in your Client/Server environment. It is helpful to determine whether your costs are normal or out of line with the rest of your industry, and if they are out of line, which cost items should be corrected. One way to understand whether your costs are reasonable is to learn what organizations with comparable Client/Server environments pay, then analyze your cost items to see which, if any, are out of line.

Comparing costs must always be done with the idea of taking into account another organization's physical size, business nature, applications, and so on, relative to its costs, because no two organizations are exactly alike.

Information about organizations' Client/Server costs can be gathered from an Emerging Technologies Group (ETG) extensive study of Client/Server life-cycle costs. As part of this study, ETG conducted in-depth interviews with 22 Fortune 1000 companies, organizations, and government agencies. The interviewees included 4 banks, 3 process industrial companies, 1 heavy manufacturing company, 1 defense contractor, 1 instrumentation company, 1 engineering firm, 1 software company, 1 networking company, 1 retail chain, 1 distributor, 1 wholesale food raiser, 1 city government, 3 state governments, and 2 universities. In total, these organizations had 2-to-1000 servers (UNIX, NetWare, NT, AS/400, or some combination of these), and nearly 80,000 users. These organizations were selected for the study with an eye to choosing Client/Server environments that are representative of those existing in the large-scale business population.

The goal of the interviews was to determine all possible Client/Server costs. These costs include interoperability, system management, and business-related costs. Although the study targeted the entire Client/Server life cycle, the study could only be conducted for a one-year period for each participant, because most users have not been running Client/Server environments for longer than that.

The results of this study can serve as a baseline for organizations trying to get a handle on their Client/Server costs. Once the overall costs are understood, it is necessary for the organization to identify its individual cost items to see where the bulk of its money is going, and to determine which costs can be reduced.

The ETG cost study showed that, on average, people costs, including support-staff–loaded costs (salaries, benefits, overhead, etc.), the cost of hired consultants, and outsourcing costs account for approximately 64 percent of the Client/Server life-cycle costs (Figure 12.1).

Capital-equipment costs, representing 30 percent of the Client/Server costs, accounted for the next largest chunk of money spent. Most of that money was spent on rewiring buildings for networking, followed by servers, network hubs, routers, and the like.

Facilities costs, which include ongoing costs like premises, WAN transmissions, dial-up lines, archived tape storage, power consumption, and air conditioning are almost negligible in Client/Server environments compared to other costs, because Client/Server systems don't require expensive computing centers, air conditioning, and high power consumption.

Types of People Costs

What do people do that consumes so much money in a Client/Server environment? Figure 12.2 shows that for the 22 organizations interviewed as part of the ETG Client/Server-cost study, the people costs are largely split among three categories—

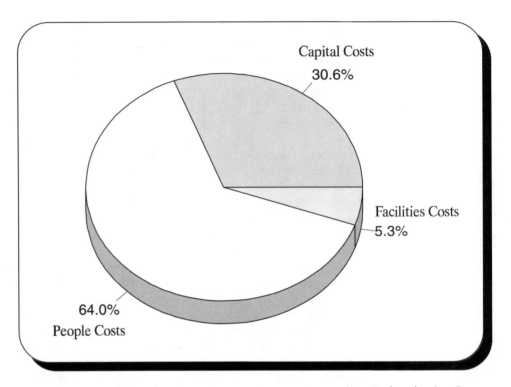

Figure 12.1 Where the money goes. *Source: Emerging Technologies Group.*

training, set up, and operations. The numbers given for each of these individual costs represent the average for all the organizations.

Operating costs consume the largest percentage of people costs in a Client/ Server environment. By far the largest operating cost item is problem management, which constitutes the activities needed to keep the network, interconnected nodes, and software up and running and interoperable. The cost of keeping PCs up and running and troublefree is greater than the cost of comparable tasks for UNIX servers. Similarly, set-up costs for PCs also exceed those for UNIX servers.

Training costs will vary with the organization. Some organizations place great stock in training, while others do very little.

The Price of Client/Server Systems

The study indicates that the average Client/Server life-cycle cost per server is about $75,000, while the average Client/Server life-cycle cost per user is about $2,300. There is a great deal of variation, however, in what organizations pay for their Client/Server environments. Your Client/Server environment also can turn out to be very cost effective or very costly.

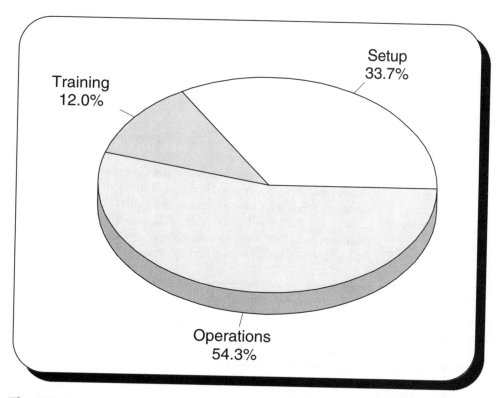

Figure 12.2 Types of people costs. *Source: Emerging Technologies Group.*

The first way to get a handle on Client/Server costs is to take a look at the cost items associated with Client/Server environments. Understand these costs, because they will become the basis for a matrix used to calculate (or estimate) your own Client/Server costs. How to set up this matrix, based on various cost items, will be shown later in this chapter.

The Major Cost Issues

The major Client/Server costs occur in two areas:

- Technically oriented
- Business related

The costs in these areas are not just due to the initial cost of equipment. Instead, as this chapter will show, the costs tend to be people costs, overhead, and a lot of gotchas. Many Client/Server costs are not immediately obvious. Each of the major costs within the technical and business-related cost areas will be discussed in the next sections.

Technically Oriented Costs

Most technically oriented Client/Server costs can be classified in two main areas:

- Interoperability
- System management

Figure 12.3, a diagram of a networked node, shows the major technical-cost areas in Client/Server computing. To help categorize these cost areas, the figure shows the layers of software necessary for Client/Server computing, the tools needed to develop Client/Server applications and to manage the Client/Server environment, and connections to other networked nodes.

The unshaded boxes in the diagram show computing areas whose cost is well understood. The shaded areas show emerging Client/Server functionalities whose costs are not well known and often underestimated. The less-understood function-

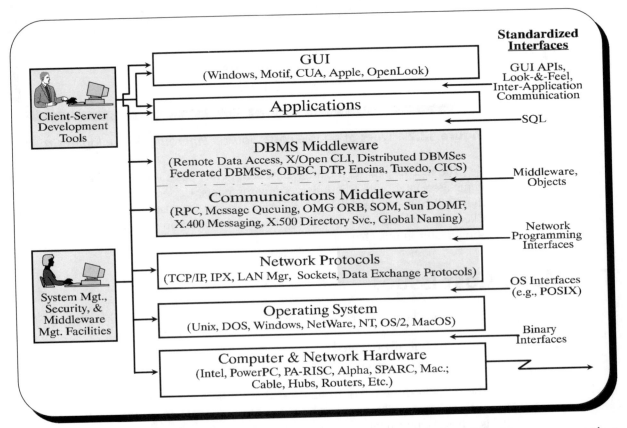

Figure 12.3 Underestimated technical costs for Client/Server computing. *Source: Emerging Technologies Group.*

alities mainly concern interoperability (middleware and some networking), system management, and Client/Server application development).

The Well-Understood Costs

The functionalities indicated in unshaded boxes in Figure 12.3 are straightforward, easy-to-determine costs.

Computer Hardware and Their Operating Systems
Thousands to tens of thousands of PCs currently exist in various organizations. PCs can be had at bargain prices. They are the major target for client computers in Client/Server environments. Servers are a newer phenomenon. Many organizations are spending a good deal of their Client/Server capital costs on servers.

The client operating systems are DOS, Windows, Windows 95, OS/2, and MacOS. Server operating systems are typically UNIX, NetWare, and sometimes OS/2, depending on the server applications, with NT coming down the road. All these operating systems cost much less to purchase, operate, and maintain than operating systems like MVS, VMS, and other proprietary mainframe and minicomputer operating systems.

Network Hardware
Communications and network hardware includes such equipment as routers, hubs, muxes, cables, and local area networks.

Communications and network hardware constitute a very large up-front cost for users migrating to Client/Server environments. For example, if users don't already have cabling in place to connect their computers and networks, or if their existing wiring is not adequate, they must install the appropriate wiring. An eight-month Emerging Technologies Group study of the cost of Client/Server computing showed that organizations that needed to wire or rewire their sites typically spent two to six million dollars just for the wiring and its installation.

This is not a cost unique to Client/Server computing. Networks also connected centralized computing sites, although Client/Server environments are likely to have a larger number of small networks. If you want networks, whether in a centralized or Client/Server environment, you need to install the appropriate wiring.

GUIs
GUIs are a relatively new phenomenon, but they are fairly well understood. The desire for GUIs is among the reasons for downsizing to PCs.

The Underestimated Client/Server Costs

Between the hardware and operating system at the bottom of Figure 12.3 and the applications and GUI at the top of the figure, are a number of poorly understood, emerging, and often costly functionalities. These functionalities are shown in the shaded boxes in Figure 12.3. These functionalities mainly concern interoperability (middleware and networking), system management, and Client/Server application development.

Network and Data-Exchange Protocols Half of the network-protocols box in Figure 12.3 is shaded; the other half is unshaded. Network protocol stacks and low-level communications facilities are not new. They are a well-understood component of traditional networks. Why, then, should half of the box be shaded?

The reason for shading half the Network Protocols box is that two different kinds of network protocols are represented in the Network Protocols box. Only one type is the traditional, well-understood protocol stack and low-level communications facilities.

Other, newer types of protocols sit on top of the protocol stack. These are largely the data-interchange protocols. Data-interchange protocols include protocols, services, and formats designed to support capabilities such as revisable document exchange, spreadsheet exchange, and graphics exchange. Other data interchange protocols include specifications for image interchange, multimedia interchange, hardware-description interchange, product-data exchange, bibliographic-data interchange, and the exchange of almost any other type of data imaginable.

Data interchange protocols are not as well understood as TCP/IP or IPX protocols. The use of data-interchange protocols often requires more time and more savvy technical personnel to understand how to use them. The result is greater people costs.

Middleware Most people, when asked how they are achieving interoperability, usually respond with the type of networking they have, such as Ethernet or TCP/IP. But meaningful networking and interoperability means more than hardware connectivity and protocol stacks. Interoperability also means software connectivity, application interoperability, and data portability. Many of these requirements are achieved through middleware.

Above the network-protocols box is a large, two-part box representing middleware. Middleware, as the figure shows, consists of a lot of acronyms (e.g., RPC, MAPI, OMG ORB, and DOMF), plus directory services, messaging, distributed database, distributed-transaction processing, and other middleware functionalities discussed in Chapter 9. The many acronyms contribute to the complexity of a meaningful, workable, Client/Server environment.

DBMSs are included in the middleware box. It is true that DBMSs have always been part of a data-processing environment, but the DBMS in a Client/Server environment is a networked DBMS that handles remote-database access. Although some standards exist for remote-database access, they are not always sufficient. Remote database, therefore, involves nonstandard vendor extensions. Nonstandard extensions mean the labor-intensive writing of different applications, using different programming interfaces for each vendor's extensions.

Client/Server Development Tools Two shaded boxes are on the left side of the layers of Client/Server components. One box represents Client/Server development tools. Such tools facilitate the development of graphical user interfaces for the client side of the application. Client/Server development tools also have the job of taking an application (new or existing), and allowing developers to identify which parts should run on a server and which parts on the client. The tool then compiles the code so that the appropriate pieces of code segments run on the correct platform for interactive Client/Server applications.

Unfortunately, few such tools exist. Existing Client/Server development tools are mostly used to facilitate the development of client-application GUIs. A sprinkling of tools can help distribute applications, but they do so mostly for two-tier Client/ Server environments. A few tools have been introduced or announced that can help distribute applications in three-tier Client/Server environments, but these are still emerging.

All this means that Client/Server development is a labor-intensive process without adequate tools. This is changing, but it will take time. Meanwhile, people costs for Client/Server development are high.

System Management   The second shaded box on the left side of Figure 12.3 represents system management. System management consists of the facilities necessary to manage the Client/Server environment. It is a catch-all term for network management, system administration, and middleware management facilities.

System management is currently the big gap in open Client/Server systems. Many Client/Server projects fail due to the lack of a good way to manage the Client/Server system. It costs more per year to manage a $5,000 workstation than to purchase it.

The reasons for the potentially high cost of system management have to do with the diversity and complexity of the Client/Server environment. Client/Server environments generally involve legacy systems, UNIX servers, workgroup servers (e.g., NetWare- or NT-based), and thousands of client computers running DOS, Windows, and sometimes UNIX.

Because of the diversity and complexity of the Client/Server environment, system management in a distributed networked Client/Server environment can be very difficult and expensive. Due to the environment's complexity, staffing costs dominate the overall system management costs in a Client/Server environment.

Client/Server system-management tools exist. Unfortunately, they are often difficult to use, not integrated with one another, require system administrators to learn different interfaces for each tool, and need different types of system-management expertise for each type of tool used. Many users, developers, and some vendors underestimate the complexity of the system-management problem.

Two time-consuming, labor-intensive system-management tasks consume the most time in a Client/Server environment. But both tasks are essential to a Client/ Server environment (or any other environment, for that matter).

The first of these tasks is problem and fault management for networks, computers, and software. Emerging Technologies Group studies show problem and fault management consumes about 50 percent of system managers' time, but it can be as high as 75 percent. Problem and fault management is important because if the software or hardware system goes down, it can't be used, and the people who need to use it may be idle.

The other time-consuming task is configuration management. Configuration management includes the time and cost to set up a system when it is first delivered, and perhaps to reconfigure it later on to accommodate new disks, memory, users, software upgrades, and so forth. Configuration management is important because if the software or hardware system is not set up, it can't be used. Configuration management consumes, on average, about 22–33 percent of system managers' time, with the number rising to as high as 50–70 percent for PC environments. PC environments tend to be more difficult to configure than UNIX environments.

Configuration management in the context of system management should not be confused with configuration management as a software-development capability.

The third most important system-management task, according to users, is backup and restore. Users tend to buy point-backup solutions that automate the backup. The major backup cost is, therefore, capital costs, rather than labor-intensive costs.

Other system-management tasks include disk-storage management, user administration, security management, performance management, printing management, job scheduling, event management, and software distribution.

An Emerging Technologies Group study on the cost of system management did not show system management costing as much as trade-press stories would have people believe. One reason is that most Client/Server environments are in their early stages, are mostly PC-based, run simple applications, and don't do very much system management.

The majority of clients in these workflow environments are PCs running DOS and/or Windows. The servers are mostly workgroup servers running NetWare, with some NT servers planned. Usually these environments also had one or a small number of UNIX servers, often being used as a database server. Workflow, as exemplified by the capabilities of Lotus Notes, constituted the most common type of Client/Server application.

System-management costs are relatively small in this kind of environment because this kind of environment does relatively little system management. The major system management task is to set up the networks and the UNIX and/or NetWare (or NT) servers.

Once installed, the two chief system-management cost items, and sometimes the only system-management cost items, are problem/fault management, with backup a distant third. Usually, the organizations purchase a backup solution.

There are few other system-management costs in this environment. User administration and disk-storage management are typically done using whatever operating facilities are available. Because workflow environments are almost paperless, they don't need print management. Since no batch processing is involved, workflow environments don't do job scheduling. Security is a concern, but although most system managers in a workflow environment are worried about it, they spend little operations time doing security management.

When all the system-management costs in a PC-based workflow environment are considered, once the environment is set up, the cost of system management is essentially the cost of problem management, along with the capital costs and labor costs for the initial configuration of backup systems.

Not all Client/Server environments are PC-based workflow environments. Several organizations running more sophisticated Client/Server environments were interviewed during ETG's cost of system-management study. The individual organizations tended to have 20 to 120 UNIX servers, up to 100 workgroup servers and thousands of clients. The clients ran mostly DOS and Windows, although several organizations had a large number of UNIX clients too.

These sophisticated Client/Server environments ran a variety of applications, including transaction processing, decision support, general ledger, capital tracking, human resources, CAD/CAM, and purchasing. The management staff at these environments tended to be technically knowledgeable people with organizational skills and visions of the future. The applications were generally reengineered, rather than patched legacy applications. As the number of applications and the complexity of these environments grew, many organizations tended to migrate to integrated system-management solutions, rather than using homegrown scripts and a diversity of point solutions.

These organizations reported significantly decreased system-management costs compared to those incurred with traditional centralized computing systems.

See Chapter 11 for more detailed system-management information.

Standardized Interfaces   On the righthand side of the diagram in Figure 12.3 are a series of standardized interfaces. The standardized interfaces are necessary because Client/Server environments generally involve connecting UNIX-based servers, PCs running DOS or Windows, mainframes, and TCP/IP or NetWare networks.

It would be easier to learn, develop, and manage a Client/Server environment if the environment was homogeneous, and from the same vendor. However, this does not generally happen in Client/Server or distributed enterprisewide environments. As explained in Chapter 1, as organizations hook up the enterprise, they end up with *de facto* heterogeneous, multivendor environments. Also, all computers cannot be the same because enterprise environments cannot consist only of clones.

Writing every application for a multitude of diverse operating systems, GUIs, network protocols, DBMSs, graphics systems, communications and database-middleware software, objects, and so on, can rapidly become an intractable, costly, labor-intensive problem. What is needed is a common interface for each type of functionality that all applications write to. The common interface helps users achieve compatibility between their heterogeneous computer software. Standards provide that common interface.

Common interfaces can reduce Client/Server development labor costs, and help users and developers to cost effectively develop Client/Server applications that can run transparently anywhere in the network. For this reason, it is generally recognized that open systems, including many of the standardized interfaces on the right side of Figure 12.3, are at the core of Client/Server computing.

Business-Related Costs

Business-related costs include the largest number of cost items that come as a surprise to Client/Server planners, who tend to focus on the technical and planning aspects of Client/Server computing. Such nonbudgeted expenses are often estimated to be as high as 25 percent of the true total IT spending in some companies.

Business-related issues include:

- Overhead charges
- Corporate politics delays
- Negotiation of maintenance agreements
- Vendor management
- Consultants
- Customer relationship management
- R&D
- Downtime
- User training
- Throwaway costs
- Dead-on-arrival costs
- Miscellaneous

Overhead Charges

Overhead charges include the cost of premises, such as space for servers or local and remote office space. Also included in overhead costs are the cost of utilities, human resources, recruitment, financial departments, and corporate management allocated to Client/Server maintenance, and support departments.

Delays Due to Corporate Politics

Corporate politics in the Client/Server environment often center around friction between the mainframe support staff and the Client/Server staff. Dealing with this friction is often a problem because both sides have valid points. The mainframe support staff wants something that they know works. The Client/Server personnel want to move ahead while they can do it at a reasonable pace, rather than being frantically pressured into moving ahead when management discovers that planned Client/Server milestones and deadlines are not being met.

Friction can also develop between different department managers who are responsible for their department's P&L statements and the Client/Server staff. The problem is that information technology is frequently essential to a department's P&L statement. With the introduction of Client/Server computing, however, department managers, who supposedly own a piece of the Client/Server network, discover that they are no longer in control of that network. These managers may feel that Client/Server computing may be good for the company, but does not serve them well.

The problem is that all the people involved in this kind of a situation have valid points. Unfortunately, this can result in extra meetings and paperwork, which can delay the implementation of a Client/Server system for a long time.

Negotiation of Maintenance Agreements

Most people realize that the identification and investigation of available products, and meeting to decide what to buy, is a necessary, time-consuming part of the open Client/Server planning and deployment process. Many people are less likely to realize that it also takes time to negotiate maintenance agreements.

Negotiating maintenance agreements is often an important part of buying products, especially when the products implement new technologies in highly complex heterogeneous environments. It may take time to negotiate a good maintenance agreement. This is part of the cost of doing business.

Vendor Management

Even after the maintenance agreements are in place, there is often a lot of finger pointing between vendors. This is not a conspiracy. The problem is that determining whether a fault lies in the network, the node hardware, or the software, or determining whose interacting platform hardware or software is responsible for the fault is a difficult task.

An added problem has to do with today's prevalence of voice mail. The telephone of yesteryear often becomes a "Problem-Solving Prevention Machine" due to people being unavailable, and sometimes due to the inability to reach the voice mail because it is full. Repeated abortive, unproductive, telephone calls are time consuming and labor intensive. Voice mail problems are more likely to affect small-to-medium size companies. Large companies can often negotiate special support agreements.

Users interviewed in the Emerging Technologies Group study report vendor management costs ranging from $50,000 per year for medium-size companies, to a few hundred thousand dollars per year for large companies.

Consultants

Consulting costs are the payments to hired consultants who work as nonpermanent employees. In implementing many new technologies, especially those dealing with heterogeneous environments, there has always been a tendency among vendors and users to underestimate the technology's complexity. There is also a tendency to underestimate the size of the staff needed to keep a complex technology up and running. Consequently, the cost of consultants, usually hired on contract for a certain number of months, should be planned for in the open Client/Server deployment budget.

Customer-Relationship Management Costs

Customer-relationship management costs are the costs involved in interfacing with customers. In Client/Server environments, customer-relationship management frequently concerns external customers who buy services that are available because of an organization's Client/Server capabilities, but they could also be customers internal to the organization. These customers cannot use the services they bought unless their network connections to the Client/Server environment, and the Client/Server services, are maintained and available.

The customer-relationship management staff acts as managerial-level go-betweens who coordinate the activities between the customers and Client/Server operations staff. Coordination involves such tasks as tracking service requests, tracking performance, ensuring that the network and Client/Server services are available when needed, and making sure the customers' business, network, and Client/Server needs are being met.

Since customers are everything to a company, customer-relationship management is an important job that should not be overlooked. Of the organizations interviewed, customer-relationship management expenses ranged from a few hundred thousand dollars to a half a million dollars per year. Some of these organizations' Client/Server environments are shown in Table 12.3—see where you fit in.

Training Users

Much has been written about training people who must support the Client/Server environment. Much less is written about training the user base.

Some people call user training a hidden Client/Server computing cost, and many organizations spend a great deal on user training. Other organizations disclaim this cost. They say that most users today are well acquainted with Windows, and that the Client/Server environment simply adds an icon or two to the environment.

The advent of Windows '95, with its different interface and paradigms, has been cited by some as a hidden Client/Server training cost. But Windows '95 training is not a Client/Server issue—it is a Windows '95 training issue. It would be necessary regardless of whether the PCs were standalone or networked.

Downtime

Downtime means that users are idle, planned work cannot proceed, and, often, revenues are lost.

Downtime may be caused by the need to upgrade systems. More often, downtime is caused by the need to resolve system problems. The complexity and newness of the Client/Server environment contributes to downtime. Additional downtime may occur because of the multivendor environment. When one vendor dominates an environment, resolving problems is relatively straightforward. When multiple vendors are involved, expect more downtime while the vendors work together to determine responsibility.

Unfortunately, downtime is a true hidden cost because the real effect of downtime on the user base is almost impossible to estimate.

Throwaway Costs

No matter how carefully you plan your open Client/Server systems, some systems may just not work out. In some cases, the system can be put on hold for a while, and used in the future. If the system, however, includes hardware, it may not be possible to use the hardware later because the hardware may be practically worthless a few years after its purchase. In that case, the system may have to be abandoned.

When dealing with a new technology that must be integrated with multiple other systems at a hardware, system-software, and application level, there is probably no way to make all your first plans a total success.

Dead on Arrival

Have you ever had a computer, network, peripheral device, or piece of software be dead on arrival? If not, you can imagine the frustration and ramifications. This problem is likely to happen more than once if you are buying and setting up a new environment with lots of new servers, clients, networks, and associated software.

Research and Development

Research and development (R&D) is the expense dedicated to doing upfront and ongoing Client/Server exploration in different areas. Such exploration ranges from testing new software, new system-administration tools, and new applications; and determining what kind of compatibility issues exist.

Miscellaneous

There can be a variety of other unanticipated miscellaneous costs. Perhaps the worst of them include hardware and/or software purchased and charged to a miscellaneous category. The miscellaneous category is the bane of accounting methods because it results in a lack of financial accountability.

The problem with miscellaneous category costs is their potential to become hidden Client/Server costs. For example, suppose some information-technology people in a company division migrating to Client/Server computing decide they need several dozen more PCs. Unfortunately, the information-technology budget was approved months ago, and the capital expenditures portion of the budget did not allocate money for more PCs. However, the information-technology people can still purchase the PCs and account for their cost under a miscellaneous item in their division's budget.

This is like getting extra PCs free of charge. No money is charged to the information-technology budget. Money is, of course, charged to the division. But people sometimes fail to take into account the companywide impact of their purchases. They feel that if the budget item is not in their budget, it doesn't matter what they buy. And, to some extent, it doesn't matter—until one day the company's chief financial officer revises the accounting procedures to more effectively track costs. Then the PCs and their associated software become part of the information-technology budget. As a result of these miscellaneous costs, the Client/Server costs turn out to be higher than projected.

The Big Surprises

The most surprising cost to most organizations migrating to Client/Server environments is the discovery that their staff knows about mainframes, CICS, and Cobol, but lacks Client/Server expertise. A related surprise is the cost of managing and administering the Client/Server networks and computers. Managing Client/Server networks and software is different from managing centralized mainframe computers.

Figure 12.4 shows the biggest surprise costs, prioritized. These prioritized items were obtained as a result of the ETG Client/Server cost study.

The problem is that there is a scarcity of Client/Server knowledge because it is new. Information technology took 30 years to reach its present mainframe-based state of maturity. Organizations are trying to provide all of mainframe computing at once on downsized Client/Server systems, and add many more capabilities besides. This will take time. Until tools mature, standards gaps are filled, and the staff becomes more experienced with Client/Server systems, the development, maintenance, and management of these systems will be labor intensive, resulting in high people costs.

The Business-Enhancing Move

The best business-enhancing move is to make sure you don't get caught short by surprise costs. Know your costs. Remember that you can get burned if you focus on easy-to-determine acquisitions costs. The only really meaningful Client/Server cost metric is the cost of ownership, not the initial cost.

1. Staff with no Client/Server expertise
2. Lack of a good way to manage Client/Server networks
3. Lack of a good way to administer Client/Server software
4. Need to fill gaps in standards and in vendor offerings
5. Immature Client/Server application software and tools
6. Training of the technical staff
7. Training users to get involved with new Client/Server systems
8. The cost of server database software

Figure 12.4   The biggest cost surprises, prioritized. *Source: Emerging Technologies Group.*

Cost-of-Ownership Analysis

A Client/Server cost-of-ownership analysis must include three types of costs—capital equipment, people costs, and facilities. Capital-equipment expenses include the purchase price of hardware and software. People costs are the loaded cost of personnel to the company, meaning salary plus fringe benefits and employee overhead. People costs must also include the cost of hired consultants and the cost of outsourcing. Facilities costs include the cost of the building space for operating and managing the Client/Server system and housing the Client/Server personnel, and ongoing costs like transmission and dial-up costs, and air conditioning.

These costs must be calculated for all the phases of the Client/Server life cycle. The Client/Server life cycle includes three distinct phases—initial acquisition, operations, and change. Initial acquisition costs are the costs for initial product installation and set up, development costs for homegrown software, and training costs. Operational costs include the operation, management, and administration of the organization's Client/Server networks, platforms, and software. Change refers to acquisition, people, and facilities costs as a result of a technology upgrade or future transition.

To perform the cost-of-ownership analysis, users must determine how much their organization spends for the three major types of cost items—capital equipment, people, and facilities—for all three life-cycle phases. The cost data is totaled and entered into a matrix such as that shown in Table 12.1.

The three major types of cost items in this matrix actually represent almost 100 individual line items corresponding to the various kinds of apparent and hidden costs that we have discussed. Aside from obvious costs, the cost items include such things as delays due to corporate politics, overhead, where to put extra system administrators (a problem that is fading, since many organizations are not hiring extra system administrators), and software that comes in DOA (Table 12.2).

Formulas are used to determine the cost per year for each of these items, based on the number of people allocated to certain tasks, the time required to accomplish the task, and a variety of other factors. The individual cost-item numbers in each category, for each life-cycle phase, can then be totaled for entry into the Table 12.1 matrix to get an idea of overall costs. Or they can be studied in their more granular form to see where the major costs occur and whether they can be reduced.

Table 12.1 ETG Cost-of-Ownership Model

	Life Cycle Phases		
Types of Costs	**Initial Acquisition**	**Operational Phase**	**Change Phase**
Capital Equipment	$AA	$BB	$CC
People Costs	$DD	$EE	$FF
Facilities Costs	$GG	$HH	$JJ

Source: Emerging Technologies Group.

Table 12.2   Representative Line Items in the Cost Model

Capital	People	Facilities
• Server hardware • Desktop PCs • Local network (TCP/IP) • PC LAN • Backup hardware • Server DBMS • Middleware (e.g., RPC) • Purchased system administration software • Central & remote router hardware & software	• Client/Server planning & product evaluation • Initial configuration • Reconfiguration as users and nodes are moved • Operating system installation • Setup costs for purchased software • Development of homegrown system administration software for different system administration tasks (e.g., backup, security mgt., print mgt., event mgt.) • Support staff training • User training • Outsourcing/Consulting • Vendor management	• Dial-up lines • WAN transmissions • Archived tape storage • Premises • Power supply • Air conditioning

Source: Emerging Technologies Group.

The data in the cost-of-ownership model can also be used with other information gathered during the study, such as the information in Table 12.3, to identify, calculate, and correlate other metrics that are more meaningful to you. For example, banks that are providing services to external customers find the cost per user most meaningful to them. Many manufacturing companies find the cost per server more meaningful to justify each department's costs.

Table 12.3 also provides a good way to understand what's happening in the real world with Client/Server costs. It shows the Client/Server cost breakdown along with ancillary information, for seven representative organizations.

The metrics in this table cannot be viewed on an absolute basis for comparative purposes because they are affected by combinations of factors unique to each organization, such as geographical location, the nature of an organization's business, the type of applications they are running, and their system management solutions. For example, consider an organization located in the southwestern United States. The support staff and system administration salaries in many areas of the southwest and midwest are often comparable to a good secretary's salary in New York or San Francisco.

The bank has the highest cost per server and the largest number of system administrators and network managers. This is not surprising. In general, banks run far more support-intensive operations than do most industrial companies, government agencies, and other types of businesses and institutions. Banks run a large number of

Table 12.3   Client/Server Cost Breakdown for Eight Organizations

Organization	# of Unix Servers	# of Workgroup Servers	Server OS	Client OS	# of Users	# of Sys. Admins	# of Network Mgr.	Cost Per Server	Cost Per User
Aerospace Co.	16	5	HP-UX NT (Future) Solaris	Windows 3.1 Windows 95 MacOS	450	5	1	$60,000	$651
Bank	150	54	Solaris	Windows 3.1 UNIX	1,100	64	20	$98,200	$910
City Gov't	34	31	AIX HP-UX MVS NetWare OS/400 Solaris VMS	Windows SunOS	1,500	15	6	$15,928	$613
Engineering Firm	4	2	HP-UX	HP-UX	54	2	2	$105,088	$3,135
Insurance Company	2	1	AIX OS/2	Windows 3.1 OS/2	70	2	2	$47,900	$914
Process Industrial Plant	6	17	NT OSF/1 VMS	NT Windows 3.1	3,000	15	5	$106,852	$850
State Gov't	2	75	AIX OS/2 Netware MVS	Windows 3.1	8,000	27	32.5	$93,560	$941
University	44	0	AIX SunOS	Windows 3.1	1,200	13	4	$92,388	$1,614

Source: Emerging Technologies Group.

mission-critical applications. A few seconds of downtime can result in lost revenues and lost opportunities. In contrast, comparable downtime in a university might result in irate students. The downtime effects would be more consequential in an industrial plant or government agency, but they would not be likely to have the unrecoverable disastrous effects as it would have in the bank.

In any case, the bank claims to have rapidly instituted new services and picked up new customers that would not have been possible without Client/Server capabilities. And the bank's cost per user is average, right in there with other companies.

Some companies have a low cost per user because their Client/Server environments are relatively new and perform few functions beyond electronic mail and data access. One surprise is the engineering company, which has a relatively high cost per server and cost per user, and an average cost per system administrator, despite the fact that it runs a homogeneous environment.

The most heterogenous environment interviewed is the city government, which runs seven different server operating systems and two different client operating systems, as well as the highest Client/Server functionality of any of the other organizations. Yet this city government has one of the lowest costs per system administrator, as well as the lowest cost per server and cost per user.

One reason for the city government's low system administration costs might be its use of an integrated system management program, rather than a home-grown one or a group of point solutions. Two other organizations—the bank and the insurance company—are using integrated system administration solutions. When the system administration-specific costs for these three organizations are extracted from the rest of the Client/Server costs, these organizations have the lowest overall costs for system administration, as well as the lowest system administration costs per user. Is this a trend? Possibly, notably in heterogenous environments, and especially when the environment's Client/Server functionality and number and diversity of system administration tasks that are performed are very high. High functionality means numerous Client/Server applications other than workflow, including transaction processing and batch processing and 3-tier Client/Server processing. High number and diversity of system administration tasks system administration tasks like event and console management, mainframe type of job scheduling (not just scheduling backups), distributed print management, hierarchical disk storage management, and so on. All three organizations using integrated system management solutions have these kinds of system management requirements.

Another Client/Server cost difference noted between the organizations depends on whether they use a lot of WANs, compared to LANs. WANs tend to be more expensive than LANs, especially if the organization is an international one. Therefore, LANs and WANs must be separate cost items in determining cost of ownership, and not combined into a single network cost.

Client/Server Cost versus Functionality Trends

The purchase and setup cost of networks, servers, server software, and client hardware and software, along with the setup and/or development of Client/Server applications, associated system management programs, and training, constitute the up-front, or initial, Client/Server costs. Once the capital equipment is purchased and set up, or developed, presumably costs decline to a lower level, during the operations phase. Besides the normal operations costs, however, the operations phase may still include some training costs because many organizations have ongoing training. The operations phase also includes ongoing costs of moving users to different locations.

Figure 12.5 represents one type of experience with Client/Server cost and functionality. A set of graphs representing another experience, where costs greatly decline as a result of the move to Client/Server computing, is shown shortly, along with real-world numbers.

Figure 12.5 has two curves and one baseline reference. The two curves represent Client/Server costs and functionality with their associated benefits. The baseline reference represents the cost and functionality of centralized, mainframe environments. There is no scale in the Figure 12.5 graph. The graph is a representation of costs versus functionality and benefits that is intended to show the trends of each of these items, and to show each of these items relative to the other.

As the left side of the graph shows, when the move to Client/Server computing begins, costs are at their highest. This part of the curve represents the up-front costs.

The right side of the graph shows the decline in costs after all the equipment is purchased and set up, and software is developed. There still are perturbations on the graph representing times when costs briefly increase. A larger perturbation is expected further out on the timeline when a major upgrade or technology transition occurs.

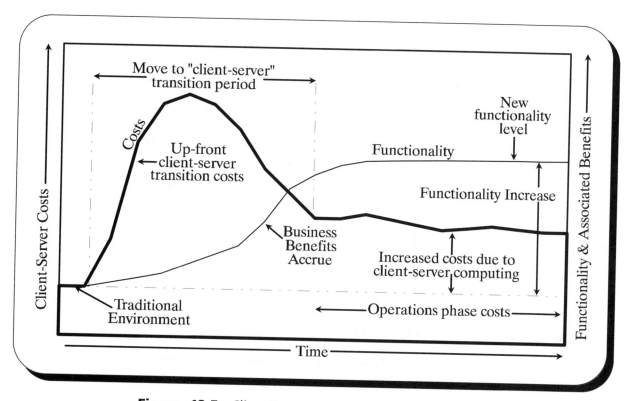

Figure 12.5 Client/Server cost versus functionality and benefits trends. *Source: Emerging Technologies Group.*

Although the Client/Server costs decline after the migration period, Figure 12.5 shows that Client/Server costs may still be higher than the cost of operating a centralized mainframe environment. This rise in cost does not necessarily occur. If a cost increase does occur, it is often due to a Client/Server environment design that merely adds the new Client/Server costs to all the traditional mainframe costs, and supports only minimal sharing of Client/Server applications. Most organizations who experience a reduction in costs have redesigned their business processes to take advantage of Client/Server computing and gain economies of sharing. As a result, they greatly reduce their mainframe needs and Clinet/Server costs. The Client/Server costs that replace the mainframe costs are significantly lower. And through sharing of applications and data, Client/Server computing achieves cost savings.

Even in cases like that represented by the Figure 12.5 graph, however, where the costs of the Client/Server environment are higher that the costs incurred in a mainframe environment, the cost increase is more than made up for by an increase in functionality and productivity.

As the Client/Server environment is set up and begins to operate, functionality begins to increase. It is not the increase in functionality that is important, but the business benefits that accrue from this increase in functionality. The increased functionality that Client/Server environments provide, however, should manifest itself in increased revenues or cash flow, which are the real benefits. The curve in Figure 12.5 labeled "functionality" actually represents both functionality and associated business benefits, as indicated on the right-hand vertical axis.

How do functionality and business benefits increase? The automation possible because of a distributed Client/Server environment, and the immediate access that authorized people have to information that they need when they need it, makes it possible for companies to take on fast turnaround jobs that pay much more than routine business jobs. The use of Client/Server systems also allows companies to respond faster to changes in the marketplace and to quickly seize new business opportunities. This gives the companies extra competitive leverage.

A wide difference between the functionality and cost curves in the operations phase part of the diagram (represented by this area between them) is what makes Client/Server systems cost effective. If the difference between the curves is small, meaning that the Client/Server operations costs are too high, and/or the cost benefits from the increased functionality too low, it is necessary to examine how you are using your Client/Server systems, and if all the expended monies are really necessary. Then you must decide what to do to increase the difference between the curves.

Improve the Bottom Line

There are several things that an organization can do to reduce its costs and improve its bottom line:

- Outsource integration, operations, and system management.
- Move more slowly to Client/Server systems.

- Consolidate small systems into large ones.
- Choose products designed to reduce complexity.
- Reduce the number of vendors.
- Concentrate on managing the servers, not the clients.
- Use corporate-standard software where possible.

Some companies are planning to outsource their integration, operations, and/or system management because they say that outsourcing costs less than doing it themselves. On the other side of the coin, some companies who outsourced these activities a few years ago are now bringing the operations and system management back in house.

The problem with outsourcing is not the price, which can be substantially less expensive than doing similar tasks internally. The issue that organizations must be aware of is the quality of the service provided by the outsourcing company. Outsourcing companies may not provide the availability, knowledge of company requirements and priorities, and service quality that internal people can provide.

However, some organizations view outsourcing as a good way to get started in Client/Server computing because another company takes a lot of the hit for the up-front costs. This scheme is comparable to buying a used car instead of a new one.

Moving more slowly to Client/Server systems slows down the payment of some of the initial costs until the Client/Server systems reach a critical point where they begin to produce benefits for the organization.

Consolidating small systems by combining multiple small LANs into a larger LAN, or by consolidating E-mail systems, is a way to simplify the complexity of the Client/ Server network. Less complexity usually results in reduced costs. The consolidated networks also minimize the number of sites to be managed, and, consequently, minimize network and system-management costs.

Products designed to reduce Client/Server complexity should be high priority because they can reduce costs. Complexity-reducing products include integrated system-management solutions that simplify and/or automate system-administration tasks. One bank using such an integrated system-management product reports 50 percent lower costs than it could obtain with either homegrown (e.g., UNIX scripts) or point solutions. Small organizations that use little of an integrated-system management program's functionality, however, may find it less expensive to use UNIX scripts.

Since Client/Server environments are intrinsically heterogeneous, multivendor environments, when you purchase packaged system management solutions it is helpful to choose system-management software that runs on multiple platforms. This avoids the problem of having to learn multiple interfaces and paradigms.

Complexity can also be reduced by curtailing the number of vendor-suppliers. Many organizations try to make do with a maximum of three vendors. This minimizes the cost of system management, interoperability, and incompatibility diagnosis.

Another Client/Server cost-reduction method that organizations use is to perform many system-management tasks for servers only. For example, users' pricing research showed that backup hardware costs about $300 per desktop workstation, plus an additional $120 per workstation for software. Add to this labor costs for each workstation and the backup costs rise between $500 and $1,000 for each workstation. Some organizations keep down costs by backing up only the servers. Users can still store their data on their own workstations, but they are responsible for maintaining that data. The organization's system administrators only back up the data stored on the server.

Similarly, many organizations have eliminated the software distribution problem by only installing software (e.g., word processing, electronic spreadsheets, graphics, vertical business software) on servers. When the users need the particular software, they downline-load it from the server. When a package is upgraded, it only needs to be upgraded on the server.

Finally, it goes without saying that standardized software, whether based on formal standards or corporate standards, can reduce the time spent writing and updating custom interfaces. Writing and updating custom interfaces is a labor-intensive task—such tasks should be avoided wherever possible. This is particularly true since, unlike capital equipment costs for equipment already purchased, salaries and benefits packages have the potential to increase over time.

Has Anyone Improved the Bottom Line?

The state of Minnesota Department of Revenues, is a good example of an organization that reduced its costs by moving to Client/Server computing. Figure 12.6 shows the Minnesota Department of Revenues' (DOR) and its Information Systems Division (ISD) budget history for 1983 to 1994.

The light bars in the figure indicate the total budget, in millions of dollars, for the DOR. The dark bars in the figure represent the base budget cost for running the Information Systems Division.

As the figure shows, in 1983, the DOR's total base budget (exclusive of special funding items) was $31.2 million. In the next 11 years, it more than doubled, bring the total DOR base budget to $77.57 million.

An examination of ISD's base budget for the same time period shows that in 1983, ISD's base budget was about $1 million. It peaked at $12 million in 1991. Since then it has dropped, so that in 1994, it was $9.39 million.

Why did the ISD budget costs go down from 1991 to 1994? The state of Minnesota says the costs went down because it implemented Client/Server technology. True, some of its cost reductions occurred because the cost of mainframe computing decreased. But the state of Minnesota DOR asserts that the decreases in mainframe computing doesn't account for all, or even most, of its cost reductions. Furthermore, the DOR takes issue with people who definitively believe that Client/Server technology is as costly, if not more costly, than traditional centralized computing.

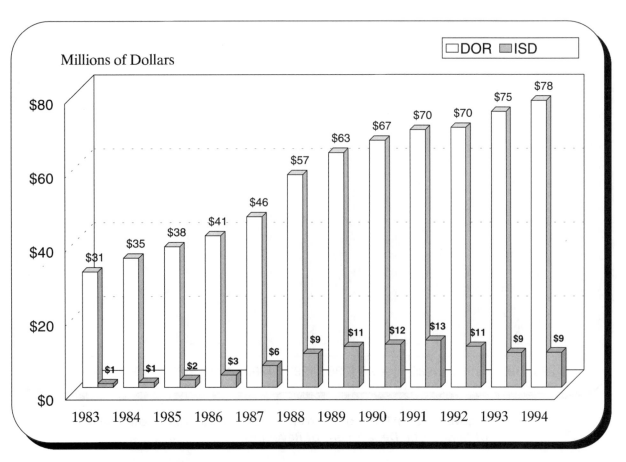

Figure 12.6 State of Minnesota DOR/ISD budget history. *Source: State of Minnesota, Department of Revenues.*

The DOR has been charting its ISD costs in detail since 1983, not only in dollars (as shown in Figure 12.6), but in terms of ISD's budget percent of the total DOR budget (Figure 12.7). What Figure 12.7 shows is that between 1983 and 1991, ISD's budget, as a percentage of the DOR's budget, has varied from a low of about three percent in 1983 to a high of about 18 percent in 1991, increasing at an overall average rate of 11 percent per year. Until 1991, ISD's costs were based almost totally on mainframe computing. In 1991, ISD projected a comparable continuing annual cost increase to 1995. At that time, the DOR realized that if it continued to experience the same increase it had been experiencing during the previous seven years, by 1995 it would be spending $13 million a year for mainframe computing alone.

Therein lies the Minnesota DOR ISD's motivation for its Client/Server technology decision. Minnesota DOR's goal in moving to Client/Server computing was to reverse its annual ISD budget increases. It was a wise decision. Since 1991, ISD's budget, as

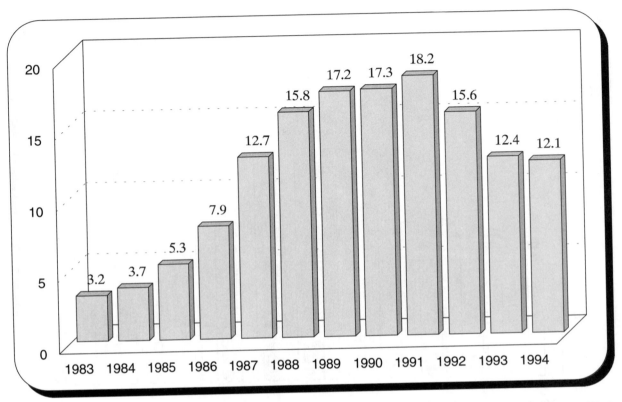

Figure 12.7 ISD budget percent of the state of Minnesota DOR. *Source: State of Minnesota, Department of Revenues.*

a percentage of the DOR's budget, has declined to 12 percent. The 1991 to 1994 ISD budget total (in dollars and in percent of the DOR budget) represents a combination of Client/Server computing and mainframe computing. Mainframes are still used for many functions, but Client/Server systems have taken over some functions. This fairly steady decline in total ISD costs, from 18 to 12 percent, represents a 33 percent reduction in costs from the 1991 peak. And instead of having to spend $13 million a year on the mainframe (as projected for 1995), the state of Minnesota DOR's ISD mainframe costs are currently less than $3 million.

The state of Minnesota is not alone in experiencing cost reductions that it believes result from Client/Server computing. The bank, whose Client/Server environment and metrics were indicated in Table 12.3, compares its present computing costs with Client/Server computing, to its earlier costs in a centralized environment where 200 people, each making $50,000 a year (a direct, not loaded, salary figure) were employed just to perform system management for the mainframes. It also concluded, after analyzing its figures for Client/Server and mainframe environments, that the move to open Client/Server computing reduced its computing costs, besides opening up new business opportunities.

These two views of Client/Server costs gain substance from a Texas Instruments Client/Server cost and benefits study. As part of its study, Texas Instruments (TI) consulted a variety of companies that had already made the transition. The companies included vendors such as Ameritech, Apple, Hewlett Packard, Intel, Kodak, Motorola, and Sun.

According to Texas Instruments, "before migrating to Client/Server, these companies were spending on average 6% of their annual revenues on computing costs, including IT. Their IT budgets ranged from 40 to 70% of total computing costs. After migrating to Client/Server environments, that figure dropped to 3 to 4% of revenues. TI says that among the 10 companies that migrated to Client/Server computing, none reported IT costs increases, some realized minor cost savings, and a few reported substantial reductions in IT costs."

The state of Minnesota DOR ISD asserts that it has had the same experience. It has reduced its information technology costs by moving to Client/Server computing.

What's Next

We have now concluded the actual open Client/Server planning process. It is time to begin implementing.

Begin by implementing the easy and noncritical applications. Only when you have gotten the major bugs out of the system, have a fully trained support staff, and are confident that your Client/Server systems work and provide benefits for your organization, should you start thinking about Client/Server versions of mission-critical systems.

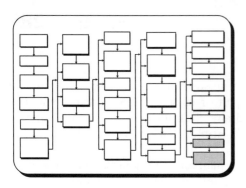

Implementation at Last

What Does Success Look Like?

If the 1970s were the age of huge, proprietary computers and the eighties were the age of open desktop workstations, then the nineties are the age of integration and distribution. We are now able to build enterprisewide, integrated solutions that are distributed across different vendors' heterogeneous but integrated hardware and software. These distributed solutions empower users to access the data and information they require, when they require it. They empower the users to develop applications to meet their needs without waiting on a long MIS queue. And they enable the users to do collaborative computing, unhindered by organizational or geographical boundaries.

This user empowerment allows users and their organizations to take advantage of opportunities as they arise, respond to events in a timely manner, and generally perform better-quality work than was possible without Client/Server capabilities.

Despite the need for new technologies whose early product versions may not work as well as anticipated, or be ready at the expected time, and the need for open systems that may take a long time to develop and agree on, many organizations have been quite successful with open Client/Server implementations. These successes are characterized by several elements and features:

- Horizontal and vertical integration
- Local- and wide-area networking
- Modularity
- Standards—*de jure*, consortia based, and *de facto*
- Servers—UNIX-based, NetWare-based, NT-based, and traditional minicomputer- and mainframe-based

- Hundreds to thousands of interconnected DOS, Windows, and Macintosh PCs, moving to tens of thousands of PCs, as well as hundreds to thousands of desktop UNIX workstations
- The ability to perform ad hoc database queries
- The ability to circulate and comment on documents, and recirculate them for further comments

Having the biggest and best computer isn't always necessary to Client/Server computing; having computers that can meaningfully interoperate is always necessary.

Having a single database is not essential to Client/Server computing as long as a single access language is available for users and applications, and the network coordinates delivery of all information to appropriate areas.

Having only formal standards is not essential, as long as consortia specifications and *de facto* standards are available to make the heterogeneous, multivendor systems sufficiently open to support interoperability, scalability, portability, and consistent user and programmer interfaces.

User enthusiasm plays a major role at organizations that have been successful. In these organizations, users understand why Client/Server technology is important, what the technology can do for them, and, to a degree, they understand the technology itself. Most users appreciate their empowerment. They appreciate not having to go hat in hand to ask MIS for the data and applications they need, then wait in a backlog queue to get it. Consequently, users are comfortable with their roles in a Client/Server environment.

Ensuring Success

The key to an organization's successful migration to open Client/Server computing is the development of a comprehensive plan based on the organization's goals and activities, and an understanding of open systems as well as the role of legacy systems. This book's methodology describes the detailed business-oriented and technically oriented steps for planning how to design, develop, and use heterogeneous, multivendor systems in distributed Client/Server environments.

Whether this methodology, or any other, is used, the actual development and carrying out of this plan requires disciplined planning, estimating, scheduling, and monitoring, as well as carefully thought-out people communications strategies.

To ensure Client/Server system success, it is also essential to have an effective Client/Server technology champion. Such individuals are not the kind of people easily hired, nor can they be picked by senior management based on seniority, regardless of their loyalty, work quality, or technical expertise. An effective Client/Server champion must be someone who knows how to effectively employ technology, sell the system to upper management, gain the cooperation of middle management, and communicate with users.

Change in the Wind

Achieving the benefits of Client/Server computing goes hand in hand with a number of organizational changes.

The technical staff, including MIS professionals, programmers, systems engineers, and network architects, will have to be able to communicate effectively with the business people in the organization. No longer can the technical people just be concerned with software code or network packets. They must understand software and hardware issues in the context of the overall business goals, and be able to develop a system to effectively enhance business performance.

Similarly, the business staff, be they CEOs, CFOs, or business planners (or have comparable roles in government agencies), will have to able to communicate effectively with the information-technology staff. No longer can the business staff just be concerned with numbers and financial statements. To achieve the benefits of Client/Server computing, they must be willing to invite the information-technology people to their business-planning meetings, and be able to explain their business goals so the technical staff can develop a system that effectively enhances business performance.

A tougher issue will face numerous technical managers, company programmers, and MIS professionals in the coming years. A variety of new technologies like client-and-server PCs, graphical user interfaces, Client/Server development tools, easy data access methods, and easy Client/Server network-access techniques, will become commonplace, just as surely as Client/Server networks will. As a result, application-interoperability tasks that were thought to be too much work to computerize will become amenable to computer solutions. Increasingly, other tasks, such as application development, that were thought to be beyond the ken of users and user departments, will be routinely done by them.

The advent of these technologies, combined with the downsizing trend, will cause certain jobs to disappear or be changed radically, and individuals will have to adapt. The wise technical manager, MIS professional, programmer, or network architect will want to anticipate these changes, plan for them, and, if necessary, considered new or related careers. If your work, or the work of those who report to you, depends on Cobol, SNA, DOS/VSE, VMS, and so on, you should begin to consider some alternatives. You may want to position yourself as the architect of open Client/Server systems, or you may decide that you want to acquire a broader base of skills in order to integrate existing Cobol programs with C and C++ systems, or SNA with TCP/IP and NetWare networks. As with past technologies, those individuals that can blend the power of the emerging technologies with the existing technologies, and with the goals and constraints of their organizations, will be the winners.

What's Next

The commonly implemented two-tier Client/Server systems will not end the evolution of data sharing, collaborative computing, or distributed networks. The next evolutionary steps will be three-tier Client/Server architectures, and more sophisticated applications that need three-tier architectures (e.g., transaction processing and data warehousing). More types of collaborative computing will evolve using, for example, multimedia technologies.

The next generation of Client/Server tools will make the development of three-tier Client/Server applications practical. Emerging technologies, such as object-oriented programming, object-request brokers, and message-queuing techniques and standards, also make increased Client/Server capabilities amenable to users and applications.

Bear in mind that Client/Server computing, and the open systems that lie at the core of Client/Server environments, are still new fields. Migration, as well as new Client/Server technology developments, will be evolutionary, not revolutionary. But the process is dynamic, the implications for business exciting, and the need for early education, experimentation, and insight, imperative.

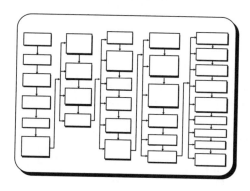

Appendix **A**

Types of Standards and Specifications

Introduction

Open system profiles are built as much as possible from standards. It is not generally possible to build a real-world environment totally from standards. However, the greater the number of standards chosen, the greater the degree of portability and interoperability. Therefore, it is necessary to understand something about the types of standards that can be specified for an organization's open-systems environment, who defines these standards, how the status of the different types of standards is identified, the priorities to use in selecting standards, and a general means for evaluating a standard.

Types of Standards

There are four major categories of open system standards:

- Formal standards
- Informal standards
- *De facto* standards
- Public domain specifications

Formal (or *de jure*) standards are standards defined by formally recognized standards bodies. These include international, national, and regional standards groups, and some professional and technical standards organizations.

Informal standards are defined by informal standards bodies. These are typically created by suppliers or users of information technology, often using a consensus method, to enable the implementation of specifications that support portability and/or interoperability. Informal standards bodies produce specifications known as *industry standards* or, simply, *specifications*. Example of informal standards bodies include certain trade associations, industry groups, vendor consortia, and user groups. Informal standards groups typically submit their specifications to formal standards organizations for approval as international or national standards.

De facto standards are not generally consensus standards. The term *de facto standard* is sometimes applied to popular vendor-defined products or specifications. Microsoft's DOS, Windows, and ODBC (Open Data Base Connectivity), IBM's CICS, and Novell's System V Interface Specification (SVID) are examples of *de facto* standards. *De facto* usage may make it necessary for other vendors to make their hardware and software compatible with a vendor-controlled *de facto* standard. *De facto* product standards and vendor-defined specifications, however, are closed systems, often controlled in a proprietary fashion. A vendor's unilateral change to a *de facto* standards-based product may result in incompatibility with other vendors' products and applications.

It is not possible for standards groups to anticipate users' requirements in all aspects of computing, and to define standards to satisfy these requirements in a timely manner. Increasingly, however, informal standards bodies, vendors, and academic institutions are defining specifications which provide needed extensions to the international standards, and can meet users' open-systems needs in advance of the completion of the formal standards process. Some of these informal and *de facto* specifications have achieved broad consensus outside the formal standards process. Furthermore, although initially developed by a single vendor, consortium, or trade organization, many of these standards are maintained by a consensus process.

A new class of standards, called *public specifications,* has therefore been recognized. Public-domain specifications are specifications that:

- Are available
- Do not overlap with, or conflict with, an existing formal standard or formal standard under development
- Exercise no restraint on who can use the specifications and how they can be used
- Have achieved consensus outside of the formal standards-making bodies
- Are maintained by a consensus process.

MIT-developed X-Windows and TCP/IP are examples of public-domain specifications. The important thing to note about public-domain specifications is the fact that they are "maintained" by a consensus process, regardless of who initially developed them. Such maintenance decreases the chances of their suddenly making applications and platforms incompatible.

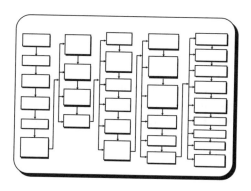

Who Standardizes the Standards?

International Standards Organizations*

At the center of the open-systems standardization efforts is the International Standards Organization (ISO), which is made up of delegations from various countries. ISO is a general standards organization that represents all industries. Other international standards groups include the International Electrotechnical Commission (IEC), which is the equivalent of ISO for electrotechnical standards, and the International Telecommunications Union Telecommunication Standardization Bureau (ITU-T), which is concerned with telecommunications standards. ISO solicits comments from international and national standards bodies, and standards groups such as European Computer Manufacturers Association (ECMA), Institute of Electrical and Electronic Engineers (IEEE), and National Institute of Standards and Technology (NIST).

The international standards groups coordinate their efforts. To avoid the possibility of incompatible standards, in 1987 ISO and the IEC agreed to merge many of their information-technology efforts. Toward this end, they established the ISO/IEC Joint Technical Committee 1 (JTC-1). Most information technology standards that most people think of as ISO standards are now really JTC-1 standards.

National Standards Organizations

National standards bodies, such as the American National Standards Institute (ANSI), British Standards Institute (BSI), and the Deutches Institut fur Normung (DIN) are voting members in ISO. Membership in national standards groups is open to vendors, trade associations, professional organizations, user groups, consortia, individu-

---

*Portions of this appendix were written by the author and contributed to the *IEEEP1003.0 Guide to the POSIX Open System Environment*.

als, and communications carriers. Rather than developing standards themselves, the national standards bodies usually delegate other groups to develop their standards. For example, X3 and the IEEE are development arms for ANSI (see Figure B.1).

Consortia

Many vendors have banded together into consortia to fill gaps in standards. The consortia, often working with users, identify the gaps, define implementable requirements, and define specifications in different functional or interoperability areas. The most influential consortia include X/Open, Open Software Foundation (OSF), the

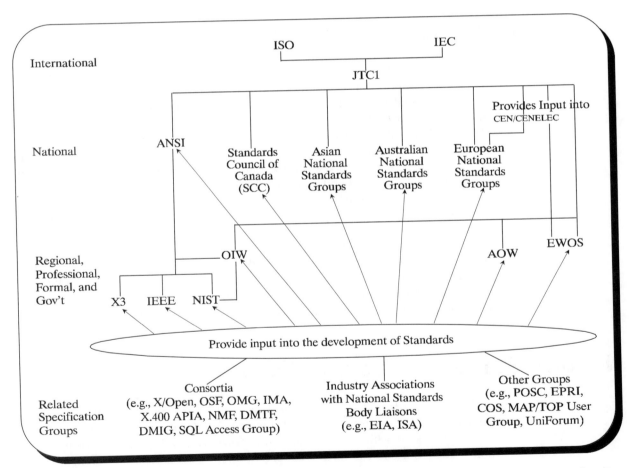

Figure B.1 Selected standards bodies and standards influencing bodies. *Source: Emerging Technologies Group, Contributed.*

Network Management Forum (NMF), the X.400 Application Programming Interface Association (APIA), the SQL Access Group, the Object Management Group (OMG), and the Desktop Management Task Force (DMTF). Many of the consortia provide input into the formal standards groups, and often contribute their specifications to these groups for standardization as ISO, ANSI, IEEE standards, for example.

The OSE Implementors Workshop

The Open System Environment (OSE) Implementors Workshop (OIW) is actually an expansion of the earlier OIW (OSI Implementors Workshop) which, through a series of workshops, generated Implementor Agreements for OSI standards. Through a similar series of workshops, the current OIW is now identifying the details necessary to implement the various standards for a comprehensive open systems environment, and create a new series of Implementor Agreements for these standards. As part of its process, the OIW will also, where necessary, identify public-domain specifications to fill the gaps in the formal standards.

Regional Standards Bodies

Regional standards bodies exist mainly in Europe and Asia. For example, the Comité European de Normalisation (CEN), Comité European de Normalisation Electrotechnique (CENELEC), European Committee for Post and Telecommunications Administration (CEPT), and European Telecommunications Standards Institute (ETSI) are regional standards groups responsible for developing European regional standards. These groups are considered the European regional equivalent of ISO. They are associations of the European Community (EC) and the European Free Trade Association (EFTA), and/or have as members the national standards bodies of their eighteen EC and EFTA member states.

CEN is active in making its members' national standards into ISO standards. CENELEC is the CEN counterpart dealing with electrotechnical matters. CEPT and ETSI are the CEN counterparts dealing with telecommunications matters.

There is no regional standards counterpart in the United States.

Industry/User Groups

Many industry and user groups, such as the Instrument Society of America (ISA) and the Robotics Institute of America (RIA) have long been active in defining and promoting standards for their industries. More recently, several industry and user groups have formed with the aim of facilitating the use of open-systems technology in, and defining open-system profiles for, their industries. The Petrotechnical Open

Software Corporation (POSC), for example, founded by a group of major oil companies, is developing an Application Environment Profile (AEP) for the exploration and production (E & P) segment of the international petroleum industry. Its interests focus on an integrated-data model, a common look and feel for a user interface, networking, and test suites. The Electric Power Research Institute (EPRI), supported by the electric power utilities, focuses on communications. Its open system interests, however, span real-time UNIX, database access using SQL and RDA (remote data access), and expert system technology.

The Movers and Shakers

Three standards organizations deserve special mention here because of their special influence on standards and industry. These groups are the Internet Society (a *de facto* standards group producing public-domain standards), X/Open (a consortium), and the IEEE Computer Society's Portable Applications Standards Committee (PASC), a formal standards group.

The Internet Society

The Internet Society provides the focus for most of the research, development, review, and production of TCP/IP protocols and network applications. The TCP/IP protocols, which include the TCP/IP protocol stack, Simple Mail Transfer Protocol (SMTP), File Transfer Protocol (FTP), Telnet, Simple Network Management Protocol (SNMP), and more, are collective known as the Internet Protocols Suite (IPS). These protocols and network applications run on the Internet (a global public-domain network), and were initially developed for the Internet. Today, various TCP/IP software is shipped with almost every UNIX system, and runs on most proprietary systems as well.

The major, completed Internet standards documents are known as RFCs (request for comment). RFCs are *de facto*, public-domain standards, based on proven and interoperable implementations. Other Internet documents are Information RFCs, Experimental RFCs, and Internet Drafts.

The Internet Society is the umbrella organization for the Internet Architecture Board (IAB) and Internet Engineering Task Force (IETF). The IAB, once the public-domain network standardization body, now performs a more advisory role. The Internet Engineering Steering Group (IESG) authorizes Internet standards (RFCs).

The Internet Engineering Task Force (IETF) is the standardization arm of the Internet Society. It is the Internet protocol-engineering body that develops, produces, reviews, and finally documents Internet protocol and network-application technology. It meets three times a year; its members communicate electronically for the rest of the year. The final IETF RFC documents are available electronically or in hard copy from the Network Information Systems Center at SRI International, 333 Ravenswood Avenue, Menlo Park, California, E-Mail: TCP-IP-CD@NISC.SRI.COM.

Although best known for TCP/IP, the IETF has produced more than one thousand standards. It currently is organized into ten areas, each consisting of a number of working groups. Current areas in which the IETF is developing and/or enhancing standards include next-generation protocols, network management, network operations, security, remote-procedure calls, naming, routing, directory services, interactive-mail access, Electronic Data Interchange (EDI), hypertext, audio/video transport, multimedia session control, benchmarking, and integration of the Internet Protocols with underlying communications, ranging from AppleTalk to ATM.

X/Open

X/Open is an independent, nonprofit, vendor-neutral consortium formed in 1984. It was the first of the consortia and other standards groups to define an architecture and guide for a comprehensive, source-level–portable open-systems environment, and has been a leader in defining APIs, models, and guides for almost all the capabilities needed for a comprehensive open-systems environment since 1984. Although its members were initially vendors, X/Open's membership now encompasses users, system integrators, value-added resellers, government agencies worldwide, other industry standards groups, and academic and research institutions.

X/Open's goal is to promote the practical and timely implementation of open systems. To achieve its goal, X/Open produces five types of products:

- Specifications
- Guides to the use of standards and specifications
- Descriptions of market requirements
- Conformance test suites
- X/Open branding licenses

Published specifications are X/Open's core products. X/Open does not normally define specifications itself, instead, it chooses from existing and emerging standards. An X/Open market-research program, in conjunction with an open user requirements forum, identifies and prioritizes user and market requirements, based on input solicited from users. These prioritized requirements, published in a document known as the *Open Systems Directive*, help drive the X/Open specification process.

X/Open conformance test suites are available to verify that vendors' products comply with the X/Open specifications, and to assure users that their software is open and will be interoperable and/or portable within the still evolving open Client/Server environment. Products that comply can be licensed with an X/Open "brand."

X/Open has multiple specifications and guides in multiple interoperability and portability areas. Figure B.2 shows a selected subset of X/Open's published documents.

Newer X/Open work programs and projects have been formed to develop specifications and guides in the areas of multimedia, repository, application-development architectures, and open-systems architectures, distributed software installation and interoperability, a backup-and-restore services API, as well as enhancements to its existing specifications.

Some of X/Open's specifications have been submitted to the IEEE and approved as IEEE formal standards. Examples of X/Open specifications approved as IEEE formal standards are the APIs to X.400 Electronic Mail, X.500 Directory Services, OSI

- Operating System Interface: (e.g., Single UNIX Specification (Spec. 1170), which includes POSIX and XPG System Interfaces and Headers and Commands and Utilities, and X/Open Internationalized Terminal Interfaces (XCURSES).
- Internetworking: (e.g., APIs to X.400 electronic mail, X.500 directory services (XDS); OSI File Transfer, Access and Management (XFTAM), and Object Management (XOM) (which simplifies the use of X.400 and X.500); Network File System for internetworking PCs with NFS platforms ((PC)NFS), SMB protocol and mechanism for PC networking, Electronic Data Interchange (EDI) using X.400, Federated Naming (XFN), Multiprotocol Transport Networking (MPTN), X/Open Transport Interface (XTI); and CPI-C Mainframe Data Access.
- Distributed Computing: (e.g., OSF Distributed Computing Environment's (DCE) Remote Procedure Call (RPC), DCE Time Service, DCE Directory Services, Document Interchange Formats (including between personal word-processing programs and large-scale technical publishing), and CD-ROM Support Component (XCDR).
- Data Management: (e.g., SQL, Remote Data Access (RDA); Call Level Interface (CLI); RDA Mapping for TCP/IP, and Indexed Sequential Access Method (ISAM), with SQL2 in progress).
- Distributed Transaction Processing: (e.g., Transaction Demarcation (TX), Interface between the Transaction Manager and Resource Manager (XA), Interface between the Transaction Manager and the Communications System (XA+), Interface between the Transaction Manager and the OSI Protocol Stack (XAP-TP), API between the Application and the Transaction Manager (XATMI), Remote Procedure Call with transactional semantics (TxRPC).
- Desktop Services: (e.g., Graphical User Interfaces (GUI), such as the X-Windows system, Motif Toolkit API, and the Common Desktop Environment (CDE), Desktop Security, and various specifications for PC internetworking).
- Distributed Systems Management: (e.g., Managed Object Guide (XMOG), Management Protocol Profiles (XMPP), API to both the CMIP and SNMP management protocols (XMP), Universal Measurement Layer Interface (MLI) used for performance measurement, Universal Measurement Architecture Data Capture Interface, Universal Measurement Architecture Data Pool Definitions (DPD), Monitoring Level Interface, ISO GDMO to XOM Translation Algorithm (XOM)).

Figure B.2 Selected X/Open specifications and guides.

- Internationalization: (Focuses on internationalization specifications for developing applications and internationalization of internetworking specifications, rather than just internationalization of the operating system. Specifications include Internationalization Guide, Locale Registry Procedures, Distributed Internationalization Services, Internationalization of Internetworking Specifications, File System Safe UCS Transformation Format (FSS-UTF) (important for historical operating systems to handle the standard Universal Character Set), and support for multilingual text within a single encoding. Support for multilingual text is needed to produce internationalized application programs with native language application messages and prompts for users who may not speak US English (represented by 7-bit ASCII code)).
- Object-Oriented Technology: Common Object Services, Common Object Request Broker (CORBA).
- Security: (Security Guide, Security Interface Specifications for Auditing and Authentication, Generic Security Service (GSS), GSS-API Security Attribute and Delegation Extensions, and Desktop Security).

Figure B.2 Selected X/Open specifications and guides (continued).

FTAM, and OSI Object Management (XOM). These standards are now ISO work items, striving for approval as international standards.

Many of X/Open's APIs and profiles were initially developed by other consortia or vendors. X/Open's ability to collaborate with vendors and other consortia is responsible for its large number of specifications, including the following:

- X/Open's RDA (Remote Data Access) and CLI (Call Level Interface) were developed by the SQL Access Group.
- The initial version of Spec. 1170 was developed by COSE.
- The X/Open APIs to X.400 and X.500, (now IEEE-approved formal standards) were developed in conjunction with the X.400 API Association (XAPIA).
- X/Open's Management Protocol Profiles references the Network Management Forum's (NMF) work.
- XMP, X/Open's common management API to SNMP and CMIP was developed by Bull and adapted in conjunction with OSF.
- The DCE's RPC, time, directory services, and Motif were developed by OSF members, as a result of OSF's RFT (Request for Technology) process.
- CPI-C, the mainframe-access interface, was developed, initially by IBM.
- (PC)NFS is based on work initially done by Sun Microsystems.
- The XATMI API between a transaction processing application and a transaction manager is based on the application API to Novell's Tuxedo (at the time it was adopted, AT&T's and USL's).

- X/Open has adopted OMG (Object Management Group) Common Object Request Broker Architecture (CORBA) model and OMG's object services. It has offered to OMG its work on object-based system management services. An X/Open object-oriented test development tool is currently under development. The tool will use OMG's Interface Definition Language (IDL) as an Assertion Development Language. The first test suite will be for CORBA.

The CORBA work is an example of true collaboration. The X/Open-OMG relationship is complementary and reciprocal. There is no duplication of effort and resources are used effectively.

Strengths

X/Open has three major strengths:

- Proven ability to get things done
- Branding program
- Neutrality

Anyone with doubts about X/Open's ability to develop, complete, approve, and publish specifications need only look at the list of specifications mentioned earlier.

X/Open's branding program allows users to identify X/Open-conformant products.

X/Open has always been regarded as the most neutral of all consortia. Because it has maintained its neutrality while piloting a course toward achieving practical goals, X/Open has been able to coordinate and publish the work of many consortia. This is responsible, in large part, for X/Open's ability to rapidly turn out the large number of specifications listed in Figure B.2 to fill the gaps in open Client/Server standards.

Consortia come and consortia go, but X/Open seems to endure. Perhaps as a result of X/Open's user requirements forum and its market research program, in almost all areas of open Client/Server computing X/Open is where the action is. If you have a specification that should be made available to the public, or are looking for timely, approved, accepted, and usable standards, for practical purposes, X/Open is the only game in town.

For further information contact X/Open Company Ltd., Apex Plaza, Forbury Road, Reading, Berkshire RG1 1AX United Kingdom, Telephone: +44 734 508 311, or X/Open, 1010 El Camino Real, Menlo Park, CA 94025, Telephone: (415) 323-7992.

IEEE Portable Applications Standards Committee

The IEEE Portable Applications Standards Committee (PASC) is a formal, accredited standards group chartered by the IEEE Computer Society, one of several IEEE technical societies. The IEEE, in turn, is accredited by ANSI (American National Standards Institute).

PASC is responsible for spearheading the movement to a standardized UNIX-like operating system interface called POSIX, and the movement to Application Environment Profiles. POSIX's goal was to support source code portability of POSIX-compliant application programs across diverse machines and facilitate the use of distributed systems. As will be seen shortly, to accomplish its goal PASC interface-specification work has long since branched out into related system-software areas, including networking and graphical user interfaces. PASC's goal in its profiles work was to make POSIX and other standards more practical to use.

PASC's portability and interoperability API work, its POSIX *Open System Environment Guide*, and its pioneer profile work, lie at the heart of distributed Client/Server computing.

The Safe Buy

PASC's accreditation by ANSI as a formal standards group through its IEEE Computer Society charter, allows all new and revised standards to be automatically submitted to ANSI for review and adoption as ANSI standards. This direct route to becoming an ANSI standard reflects ANSI's approval of the IEEE's standards development procedures. To become accredited, a standards body must show that its standards represents a true consensus of the widest possible diversity of interests. Therefore, participants in the PASC standards efforts come from large and small organizations; vendor and user organizations; consulting, commercial, and industrial organizations; and from government agencies.

Because the PASC standards are a set of specifications on which so many diverse vendors, users, and industry standards groups agree, POSIX is considered the "safe buy." Almost all vendors and application-environment specifiers worldwide are committed to conformance with POSIX.

Misconceptions

There is a misconception among some people that users are specifying, and vendors are providing, X/Open's XPG specifications and Spec. 1170, rather than POSIX. X/Open's XPG specifications and Spec. 1170 contain POSIX. They differ in going beyond POSIX and specifying additional functionalities. Some of these additional functionalities were not specified by the POSIX groups because they were considered beyond its scope. Others were not specified by the POSIX groups simply for lack of time and the impossibility of doing everything at once. A formal standard takes time because of the need to achieve consensus among a diversity of constituencies.

Consortia like X/Open fill the gaps that practical issues like time and resources create in standards. But every vote for, and procurement of, X/Open's operating system specifications is also a vote for, and procurement of, POSIX.

In the Beginning, There Was One

The initial POSIX group, called P1003, was formed in January 1985 to standardize the interface to the operating-system kernel. Users were very vocal, however, about regarding this core interface only as a first step along to portability. The lack of a shell and the operating-system utilities made POSIX insufficient for their needs.

To overcome these deficiencies, a new POSIX group, called P1003.2, was formed in January 1986 to standardize the POSIX Shell and Tools. The P1003 group was renamed P1003.1.

To ensure the compliance of individual implementations with POSIX, still another group, dubbed P1003.3, was formed to develop POSIX conformance test methods.

As the conformance test standards began shaping up, users and vendors realized that portability and connectivity required standardization of other operating-system functions, as well as of related functionalities.

System administration, for example, differs from system to system, even among *de facto* standard System V and/or Berkeley UNIX system-administration facilities. Security, real time, and batch scheduling were three areas for which neither formal nor *de facto* standards are defined. And, with the growth of Client/Server computing, the need also grew for distributed file systems, graphical user interfaces for desktop computers, electronic mail, and directory services.

In addition, when the ANSI and ISO committees standardized the Fortran, COBOL, and Ada programming languages, the Open Systems Interconnection (OSI) networking protocols, X.400 messaging services, and X.500 directory services, they focused on the language or protocol services. They did not standardize the interfaces, formats, and input/output libraries (known collectively as the *bindings*) required for programming languages or networking protocols to access POSIX services.

Initially, the POSIX groups also focused only on POSIX interfaces and functionality. POSIX interfaces were defined, with the C programming language in mind—because POSIX is derived from UNIX, and UNIX is mostly written in C. So a lot of features exist in POSIX because they are supported by C. They may not exist, even conceptually, in other programming languages.

With no bindings except C, the recognition of still-emerging functionality to be standardized, and an increasing number of portability and interoperability requirements emerging, within the last five years more than 50 new POSIX groups have been formed. Some of them are standardizing APIs and bindings. Other groups are defining profiles for application areas and platforms, or defining generic open-system environments.

Table B.1 shows a snapshot taken in the last quarter of 1995 of the diverse PASC standards, along with their reference designation, status, approval (or expected approval) date, and, in some cases, additional information or comments. Many of the PASC standards are also submitted to ISO for review and balloting as international standards, often on a fast-track basis.

Standards, Guides, and Recommendations

The PASC working groups are chartered by the IEEE Computer Society's Standards Activities Board to produce standards. The IEEE is a professional scientific, engineering, and educational organization that develops and publishes consensus standards and other types of specifications as one of its activities.

The IEEE publishes three kinds of specification documents:

- **Standards.** Specifications with mandatory requirements.
- **Recommended Practices.** Specifications of procedures and positions preferred by the IEEE.
- **Guides.** Specifications which suggest multiple approaches for good practice but do not make any clear-cut recommendations.

Standards, recommended practices, and guides are balloted by an open-ballot group, and approved by the IEEE standards board. For a ballot to be effective, at least 75 percent of the ballots must be returned. To submit the standard, recommended practice, or guide to the standards board, a minimum of 75 percent of those who voted must approve the ballot.

As with any IEEE standards organization, members participate and vote as individuals, not as companies or organizations. IEEE membership is required for voting, but not for participating in the development of the specification.

Logistics

PASC and its working standards groups are embedded in the IEEE's overall standards structure. Within this structure, the IEEE Standards Board authorizes, coordinates, and approves all standards projects, and oversees cooperative activities with other standards organizations. Standards are proposed and sponsored by technical committees and Standards Coordinating Subcommittees (SCC) of various IEEE Societies, depending on the scope of the work. Management of the standards development and balloting is handled by the committees, with oversight and assistance from the Standards Department. The actual standards development takes place in working groups.

The IEEE Computer Society is one of the member societies of the IEEE. PASC is one of several IEEE Computer Society technical committees that sponsor the development of standards. PASC sponsored the development of all the standards in Table B.1.

For further information, contact IEEE, 345 East 47th Street, New York, NY 10017.

Table B.1 IEEE PASC Standards

Standard	Sponsor	Standard Reference	Status	Expected Approval	Comments
Guide					
POSIX Open Systems Guide	IEEE ISO	P1003.0 TR-14252	Std. DTR	1995 CD: 3Q94	
System Programming APIs					
POSIX: System (Kernel) Programming Interfaces	ISO/IEC IEEE	9945-1:1990 P1003.1-1990	IS Std.	1991 1990	
System API (Kernel) Additional Functions	IEEE ISO/IEC	P1003.1a	Draft CD/PDAM	4Q95	Includes checkpoint/restart, resource limits, time details
Real-Time Extensions to POSIX	IEEE ISO	P1003.1b-1993 (was P1003.4) 9945-1b:1993	Std. IS	1993 1993	
Threads	IEEE ISO	P1003.1c-1995 (Formerly P1003.4a) 9945-1c	Std. PDAM2	1995 PDAM 2: DIS-6/95	Because of ISO procedures, needs 6 extra months for ISO processing & preparation before the final standard can be published.
Addendum to P1003.4 Real-Time Extensions	IEEE	P1003.1d (was P1003.4b)	Draft	End '96 or early '97	Includes interfaces for multiprocessor synchronization, typed memory mgt., absolute nanosleep, and thread abortion.
Technical Corrections to P1003.1b	IEEE	P1003.1i-1995	Std.	1995	
Security Extensions to POSIX.1	IEEE ISO	P1003.1e (Formerly P1003.6) 9945-1e	Draft CD/PDAM	2H95	ACLs, Mandatory Access Control, Discretionary Access Control, Audits, Privilege
Standards Related to System Standards					
Distributed System Framework	IEEE	P1003.22	Draft	?	Guide

Standard	Sponsor	Standard Reference	Status	Expected Approval	Comments
Command Interfaces					
Shell & Utilities (was POSIX.2: application portability & POSIX.2a: User Portabiity Option)	ISO IEEE	9945-2:1993 P1003.2-1992	IS Std.	1993 1992	
Shell & Utilities Extensions revision	IEEE	P1003.2b	Draft	?	
Batch Computing Extensions	IEEE ISO	P1003.2d-1994 (Formerly P1003.15a) 9945-2 Amendment	Std. CD/PDAM DIS	1994 CD: 4Q94 1995	Group formed & chaired by Supercomputing Profile Group (P1003.10) but std. will be used in many areas.
POSIX Security Extensions to POSIX.2	IEEE	P1003.2c	Draft	Same as 1003.1e	
System Administration					
Print Management	IEEE ISO	P1387.4 (Formerly P1003.7.1) Was 9945-3d, #TBD	Draft CD/PDAM	mid-1996 CD: 4Q94	Object-based
Software Administration	IEEE ISO	P1387.2 (Formerly P1003.7.2) Was 9945-3b, New # TBD	IEEE Approved CD/PDAM	Published in 1996 CD DIS: 1996	Software distribution & software layout; Object-based
User and Group Management	IEEE ISO	P1387.3 (Formerly P1003.7.3) Was 9945-3c, New # TBD	Passed Ballot: Sept. 95 CD	DIS 1996	Officially, newly formed, but work was ongoing under 1003.7 since 1992
Placeholder for future system administration framework or model	IEEE	P1387.1 (Formerly P1003.7)	—	—	—
Language Bindings					
Fortran-77 Bindings to POSIX P1003.1	IEEE ISO	P1003.9-1992 ?	Std	1992 ?	ISO Fast Track
Fortran-90 Bindings to POSIX P1003.1	IEEE	P1003.19	Withdrawn	—	Insufficient Fortran-90 & POSIX expertise in 1992

Table B.1   IEEE PASC Standards (Continued)

Standard	Sponsor	Standard Reference	Status	Expected Approval	Comments
Ada Language Binding to POSIX P1003.1	IEEE ISO	P1003.5-1992 14519-1	Std. DIS	1992 1993	ISO Fast Track
Technical corrigenda to ISO Ada Std.	IEEE	P1003.5a	Draft	1996	
Ada Bindings to P1003.4 POSIX Real-Time	IEEE	P1003.5b (formerly P1003.20)	Draft	1,996	POSIX.5b will contain POSIX.5a.
C Bindings to P1003.1 (Because P1003.1 was supposed to be a Language-Independent Interface)	IEEE	P1003.16	Withdrawn	—	—
Windowing Interfaces					
User Interface APIs	IEEE	P1201.1	Draft	Withdrawn	
User Interface Driveability	IEEE	P1201.2	Draft	?	To be balloted as a Recommended Practice
MOTIF API	IEEE	1295-1993	Std.	1993	Equivalent to OSF Motif API
Profiles					
Supercomputing Profile	IEEE	P1003.10-1995	Std.	1995	Profile
Transaction Processing Profile	IEEE	P1003.11	Withdrawn	—	—
Multiprocessing Platform Profile	IEEE	P1003.14	Draft	1996	Profile
POSIX Platform Profile	IEEE	P1003.18	Draft	Early 1996	
Real-Time Application Environment Profiles	IEEE ISO	P1003.13 ?	Draft CD/PDAM	Early 1996 CD: 4Q94	4 profiles: Minimal embedded, process control, midrange, high end. The first two profiles use POSIX.1 subsets.

Table B.1   IEEE PASC Standards (Continued)

Standard	Sponsor	Standard Reference	Status	Expected Approval	Comments
Networking/Distributed Services					
Transparent File Access (TFA)	IEEE ISO	P1003.1f (Formerly P1003.8) 9945-1f	Draft CD/PDA M	1996 CD: 4Q95	Similar to, but more functional than, NFS
Protocol Independent Interfaces	IEEE ISO	P1003.1g (Formerly P1003.12) 9945-1g	Draft CD	Q495 CD: 1995	Based on Berkeley Sockets and X/Open XTI
Common Object Services for X.400 & X.500: Language Independent Interface	IEEE ISO	P1224-1993 14364	Std. DIS	1993 1994	Based on X/Open XOM
Common Object Services for X.400 & X.500: C Binding	IEEE ISO	P1327-1993 14365	Std. DIS	1993 1994	Based on X/Open XOM
X.400 Messaging Services API: Language Independent Interface	IEEE ISO	1224.1-1993 14360	Std. DIS	1993 1994	Based on X/Open & X.400 APIA Spec.
X.400 Messaging Services: C Binding	IEEE ISO	P1327.1-1993 14361	Std. DIS	1993 1994	Based on X/Open & X.400 APIA Spec.
X.500 Directory Services API: Language Independent Interface	IEEE ISO	P1224.2-1993 14392	Std. DIS	1993 1993	Based on X/Open & X.400 APIA Spec.
X.500 Directory Services API: C Binding	IEEE ISO	P1327.2-1993 (Was P1003.17) 14394	Std. DIS	1993 1993	Based on X/Open & X.400 APIA Spec.
ACSE & Presentation Layer API Language Independent Interface	IEEE ISO	P1351-1994 ?	Std. ?	1994 ?	ISO Fast Track
ACSE & Presentation Layer API: C Binding	IEEE ISO	P1353-1994 ?	Std. ?	1994 ?	ISO Fast Track
FTAM (File Transfer, Access & Mgt. API: C Binding	IEEE ISO	P1238.1-1994 ?	Std. ?	1994 ?	ISO Fast Track
Real-time Distributed System Communication	IEEE	P1003.21	Draft	1997	

Table B.1   IEEE PASC Standards (Continued)

Standard	Sponsor	Standard Reference	Status	Expected Approval	Comments
Conformance Test Methods and Assertions					
Generic Test Methods	IEEE	P2003 (Was P1003.3-1991)	Std	1991	
	ISO	13210	DIS	3Q94	
Test Methods for P1003.1 Kernel Interfaces	IEEE	P2003.1-1992 (Was P1003.3.1)	Std.	1992	
	ISO	14515-1	CD	1994	
Test Methods for P1003.2 Shell & Utilities	IEEE	P2003.2 (Was P1003.3.2)	Draft		
Test Methods for P1003.31b Real-Time	IEEE	2003.1b (was P2003.4)	Draft		
Test Methods for Threads	IEEE	P2003.1c			
Test Methods for P1003.5 Ada Bindings	IEEE	P2003.5			
Test Methods for P1003.5a Amendment	IEEE	P2003.5			
Test Methods for P1003.5b Ada binding to P1003.4 Real-Time	IEEE	P2003.5b			
Test Methods for Common Object Services: Lang. Ind.	IEEE ISO	P1326-1993 14362	Std. IS	1993 1994	
Test Methods for Common Object Services: C Binding	IEEE ISO	P1327-1993 14366	Std. IS	1993 1994	
Test Methods for P1224.1 X.400 Language Independent	IEEE	P1326.1-1993	Std.	1993	

Table B.1   IEEE PASC Standards (Continued)

Standard	Sponsor	Standard Reference	Status	Expected Approval	Comments
Test Methods for P1326.1 X400 API C Binding	IEEE	P1328.1-1993 14367	Std.	1993	
Test Methods for P1224.2 X.500 Language Independent	IEEE ISO	P1326.2-1993 14393	Std. IS	1993 1994	
Test Methods for P1326.2 X.500 API C Binding	IEEE ISO	P1328.2-1993 14395	Std. DIS	1993 1994	
Test Methods for ACSE & Pres. Layer API Language Independent	IEEE	P1353			
Test Methods for ACSE & Pres. API: C Binding	IEEE	P1354			

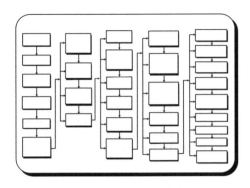

Understanding Standards' Status

Introduction

Most formal standards bodies support three status types for their standards or specifications:

- Approved
- Draft
- Work item

An *approved standard* is one which has been ratified by the approving standards body. A *draft standard* is one which has yet to be fully ratified. A *work item* is a catch-all phrase for everything else, such as immature specifications, proposed standards, and so on, which have not yet achieved draft status. Different standards bodies, however, use different terms to express the same status level. These terms do not necessarily apply to the informal standards groups or to product standards (Table C.1).

ISO's Three Standards' Status Levels

Each ISO protocol goes through three stages before it becomes an approved standard: a Committee Document (Draft Proposed Standard), Draft International Standard (DIS), and an International Standard (IS). ISO delegations from various countries vote on the documents produced at each stage.

Once a specification reaches the DIS status, some companies feel that they can begin their implementation with minimal risk. Others believe that a standard should not be implemented until it reaches IS status. While there may be some changes between the DIS and IS stages, they normally are few, not major, and often involve changes in the text of the document, rather than in what a vendor must implement.

Table C.1 Standards Status Terminology

Standards Group	Final Standard	In Progress
ANSI	Standard or Approved Standard (Standard name is followed by a year)	Draft Proposed Standard (DP) Working Documents
CCITT (Now disbanded, but standards still exist)	Recommendation	Draft Standard
IEEE	Standard or Approved Standard (Standard name is followed by a year)	Draft Standard (with a draft number) Working Documents
International Telecommunications Union Telecommunication Standardization Bureau (ITU-T)	Recommendation	Draft Standard
Internet Engineering Task Force (IETF)	Request for Comment (RFC)	Draft Standard Proposed Standard
ISO and ISO/IEC JTC-1	International Standard (IS)	Draft International Standard (DIS) Draft Proposed Standard (DP) (also called Committee Document (CD)) Working Paper
NIST	Federal Information Processing Standard (FIPS)	Initial FIPS Proposed FIPS
OSF	Application Environment Specification (AES) and Source Code	Snapshot Code Release Submitted Technologies Request for Technology
X/Open	Common Application Environment (CAE) Specification	Developers' Specification Preliminary Specification Snapshot Specification
Vendor Specifications	Available	N.A. or Under Development

Once a specification reaches the Draft International Standard stage, the technical content of a standard generally is mostly frozen and agreed upon, and changes are the exception. The final ballot, to reach the status of International Standard, is mostly a formality, and implementors can usually proceed with little risk.

ISO (and JTC-1) standards are defined by a standards document number and a date (e.g., Fortran-90 is ISO 1539:1991). The date is the publication date, not the date when ballot consensus is reached.

ITU-T Recommendations

The International Telecommunications Union Telecommunication Standardization Bureau (ITU-T) deals primarily with standards supporting the international interconnection and interoperability of telecommunications networks at interfaces with end-user systems, carriers, information and enhanced-service providers, and customer-premises equipment. Every four years, the ITU-T publishes the results of its work as "Recommendations." ITU-T Recommendations are law where communications in Europe are nationalized.

ANSI Standards and Working Papers

ANSI standards are generally called *approved ANSI standards* or just ANSI standards. ANSI standards are recognizable from ANSI draft standards under development because the standard number is followed by a date (e.g., ANSI C is ANSI X3.159-1989). If there is no date included, the standard is probably not completed and approved.

It is not common usage to refer to ANSI standards in progress as *draft proposals*. Instead, they are referred to by the name or number of the working group developing the standard. For example, ANSI C++, which is being developed by ANSI's X3 standards development arm, is referred to as the X3J16 standard. Before that, the standard is given a document number. The standards designation number by which the standard will ultimately be known is not usually assigned to ANSI standards until after they are approved.

IEEE Standards and Drafts

IEEE standards are referred to by the IEEE standard number, often followed by a date (e.g., IEEE 1003.1-1990). IEEE standards in progress are referred to by the designated standards document number (e.g., P1387.3), followed by the draft document number (e.g., Draft 9). This standards designation number is often the same as the working group name/number.

IEEE rules require a 75 percent vote for a specification to be approved as an IEEE standard. Voters cannot vote no because they don't like a specification. They must explain what they object to, and also specify how the offending area should be changed to make it acceptable to them. Supposedly, if the standards group accepts this change, the no vote should automatically change to a yes vote. To make certain that standards have achieved a true consensus, after making changes to fix the objections, the IEEE standards groups send out the ballots for a recirculation vote. As a result, IEEE specifications that become standards tend to achieve an 85 percent to 90 percent approval vote. This procedure, which is also followed by the international and national standards groups, is one of the major factors that differentiates formal from informal standards groups.

Contrary to what many people believe, the "P" in IEEE PASC standards designations stands for "Project," not "POSIX." When a standard is completed, the "P" is dropped (e.g., IEEE P1003.1 became IEEE 1003.1 after approval).

NIST FIPS

The NIST develops information-processing standards for federal government use. The standards are appropriately called "Federal Information Processing Standards" (FIPS). Where possible, the NIST uses ISO, ANSI, or IEEE standards. Because of the urgent U.S. government need for standards, the NIST may adopt as a FIPS an international or national standard which has not yet been completed and formally approved. Such standards are called *initial FIPS*. Before adopting an initial FIPS, the NIST identifies any features in the standard that are considered unstable, and explicitly omits these features from the initial FIPS. This makes it easy to align the final FIPS with the formal standard after that formal standard is approved.

Internet Specifications

The Internet Engineering Task Force, the standardization arm of the Internet Society, has a number of working groups that develop the Internet Suite (TCP/IP) of standards. When a proposed standard nears consensus in the working group, it is submitted to the Internet Engineering Steering Group (IESG).

The proposed standard is distributed, generally via the Internet, to Internet users. These users are allowed and encouraged to test its implementation. After six months, if two independent, interoperable implementations of the proposed standard can be shown, the proposed standard is considered for promotion to a draft standard.

After another six months, if all the draft standard's features have been implemented, and it can be shown that the standard has proven useful, the IESG revisits the standard to consider promoting it to a full standard. At this time, the IESG issues a final request for comment or objections to the entire IETF mailing list.

If there are no objections, or if comments and objections are successfully answered, the standard becomes an official Internet standard. The standard, known as a request for comment (RFC), can still be appealed to an independent body, the Internet Architecture Board.

After an RFC has been adopted by the IESG, the IETF makes the technical and implementation information available electronically (e.g., through its gopher site, WWW home page, or electronic mail) or in hard copy from the Network Information Systems Center at SRI International (Menlo Park, CA). These RFCs are the major source of accurate information about TCP/IP protocols and network applications.

Adoption by the IESG of an RFC does not guarantee compliance. The Internet Society and the IETF are voluntary organizations with no official membership. Therefore, enforcement of the RFC standard depends on voluntary compliance by vendors, and the push for interoperability by users.

OSF Specs, Software, and Snapshots

OSF produces both a set of specifications and software for an open-application environment. The specifications are defined, and software developed, using an open process into which vendors and users have input and access. Both members and nonmembers can submit technologies to OSF for consideration as an OSF specification or software offering.

OSF members are allowed access to the OSF software source code during development. Source code is released at various times during development. Each early source code release is known as *snapshot*.

When the specifications and code are completed, the OSF licenses its software to members and nonmembers under identical terms. The code is delivered for several reference ports.

At the same time, the final core set of interfaces is issued as an Application Environment Specification (AES). These specifications are available in the public domain. They are published in a book which indicates where each piece of technology had its origins (e.g. an ISO standard, in POSIX, from the SVID, from XPG3 or 4, produced by MIT, contributed by a named vendor).

X/Open's Four Specification Levels

X/Open produces four types of specifications:

- Formal Specifications
- Developers' Specifications
- Preliminary Specifications
- Snapshot Specifications

X/Open's *formal specifications* (which are not the same as formal standards produced by a formal standards group) are also called Common Application Environment (CAE) specifications. These specifications are identified by an XPG number (e.g., C436 for operating system Commands and Utilities and C190 for the API to Directory Services) and they form the basis for conformance tests and X/Open branding.

Developers' specifications are early releases of formal specifications. They are available to product developers so that they can plan and develop their products in time for the release of the formal XPG specifications. Conformance tests are not specified for Developers' specifications.

Preliminary specifications are early XPG specifications released in a controlled manner, usually for emerging technologies. Because the technologies they address are emerging, Preliminary specifications may change before being published as either an XPG Common Application Environment (CAE) or Developers' specification.

Snapshot specifications are draft documents that are distributed early to a limited audience in order to obtain feedback. Snapshots represent interim results of X/Open's technical groups' activities. User and X/Open members' feedback determines whether Snapshot documents will progress toward a specification.

Vendor Product Standards

Each vendor is responsible for its own design decisions and products. There is no consensus involved. Even though some vendor products are considered *de facto* standards because of their popularity, it only makes sense to talk about a vendor's product as available or under development.

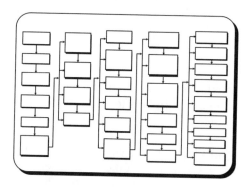

Appendix D

Investigate OSE Technology Basics

Introduction

The haphazard selection of standards that satisfy diverse functional requirements is likely to result in islands of standards that may not work together properly. To span the gap between requirements and a manageable interoperable and portable environment, it is necessary to integrate the standards into a coherent architecture.

To successfully plan an open Client/Server systems environment, it is necessary to understand what is an open system and what is an open-system model. It also is necessary to understand how these models are populated with standardized interfaces, and how standards-based profiles for specific application areas and platforms are developed from these models. These models and profiles are used as guides and productivity aids in planning an organization-specific open-systems environment.

What's an Open System?

A variety of definitions have been proposed for open systems. These include:

1. Published specifications for proprietary products (e.g., SNA).
2. Vendor products available from many vendors (e.g., DOS-based PCs).
3. Vendor products available for a range of computer systems (e.g., UNIX).
4. Public-domain *de facto* standards and code (e.g., TCP/IP, X Window System).
5. Consortia specifications (e.g., Motif, OSF DCE, X/Open CAE).
6. International or national standards (e.g., OSI, POSIX, SQL).

To a degree, all of these definitions define open systems. But some are more open than others, and some are more practical than others.

For example, published specifications for proprietary products allow other vendors to connect to the proprietary products. The problem with this definition is that

317

if every vendor publishes its own products' interfaces, the number of open systems in a user organization can be equal to the number of suppliers to that organization. This defeats the purpose of moving to open systems—that is, to achieve portability and/or interoperability.

The second definition, a vendor product available from many vendors, is the source of many people's misconceptions about open systems. Take DOS-based PCs, for example. Users can run the same binary software on any DOS-based PC. The problem with this definition is that PCs are clones—not open systems. In real-world organizations, users need a variety of heterogeneous platforms, ranging from PCs to mainframes and multiprocessors, to satisfy different requirements.

Vendor-defined-and-owned *de facto* product standards run on many types of computers. The problem with a vendor-owned *de facto* standard is the vendor owner's right to unilaterally change the standard or deny early access to the code to selected vendors. Hence, vendors do not like to be dependent on competitors.

Public-domain *de facto* standards and consortia specifications help close the gap between formal standards (which take a long time to develop) and proprietary functionality. Public-domain standards and consortia specifications are acceptable to a greater number of vendors than a "standard" controlled by a single vendor, because they do not give one vendor a competitive edge over others.

International and other formal standards have the greatest chance of acceptance by the most vendors and users. They therefore provide the greatest chance of interoperability and portability. The acceptance of formal standards stems from their requirement for approval from the greatest diversity of organizations (e.g., users, hardware and software vendors, system integrators, government agencies). The problem is the long amount of time necessary to achieve such consensus. Also, to achieve consensus, compromises usually must be made. As a result, formal standards tend to be minimal, or to specify multiple incompatible options for the same function.

Most users couldn't care less about open systems. They are indifferent to the particular standards, user interfaces, or networking protocols that standards organizations are defining. What users care about is portability, interoperability, and scalability among present and future heterogeneous computing systems. A good open systems definition is therefore one based on users' objectives. The IEEE P1003.0 Group's *Guide to a POSIX Open System Environment,* includes such an open-system definition (Figure D.1).

Open specifications in the IEEE definition are specifications that are maintained by an open public consensus to accommodate new technologies over time, and that are consistent with international standards. The open specifications need not be formal standards. X/Open specifications, and public-domain specifications such as TCP/IP, may be used. The important thing about open specifications is the fact that they are maintained by a consensus process, regardless of who initially developed them. Such maintenance decreases their chances of suddenly making applications and platforms incompatible. At the same time, the use of open specifications reduces the time before portability and interoperability specifications are available for implementation.

An open system is a system that implements sufficient open specifications for interfaces, services, and supporting formats to enable properly engineered applications software:

- to be ported with minimal changes across a wide range of systems.
- to interoperate with other applications on local and remote systems.
- to interact with users in a style that facilitates user portability.

Figure D.1 IEEE P1003.0 definition of open systems. *Source: IEEE P1003.0 Guide to the POSIX Open System Environment.*

Although standards provide great benefits, it is important to realize that standards do not eliminate all differences between heterogeneous multivendor systems. Conformance is not equal to interoperability. Open systems are not the same as clones.

Nevertheless, the standards community has made enormous progress toward open systems. Over the last several years, for example, standards groups have defined a core subset of standards that run on most vendors' equipment. Consortia are defining open specifications to fill functionality gaps in the standards, many of which have been submitted to ISO for formal standardization.

Components of an Open System

The major components of an open-systems environment include:

- Applications
- Hardware platform
- Operating system specific to the hardware platform
- System software implementations
- The external environment, which includes terminals, keyboards, mice, disk drives, cables, local devices, network connections, and so on
- Interfaces to all of these

What's Standard and What's Proprietary?

The hardware platform, operating system, and system software comprise an *application platform*. These application-platform components, and the external environment components are hardware specific and vendor specific. The applications also are vendor specific. What makes the environment open are the interfaces. It is the interfaces that standards groups and consortia are standardizing.

Location of Interfaces

The *POSIX.0 Guide to the POSIX Open System Environment* (OSE) depicts open system components in a generalized reference model that can accommodate a wide variety of general- and special-purpose systems and architectures. Among other things, this reference model shows the location of various types of interfaces. Figure D.2 shows a slightly expanded form of the POSIX OSE reference model.

As the figure shows, Application-Programming Interfaces (APIs) are located between applications and the application platform. Examples of APIs are the IEEE P1003.1 operating-system kernel interface standard, the SQL database-access standard, and the IEEE interfaces to X.400 message handling and X.500 directory services.

External-Environment Interfaces (EEIs) are interfaces between the application platform and the external environment. Examples of EEIs are the TCP/IP and OSI

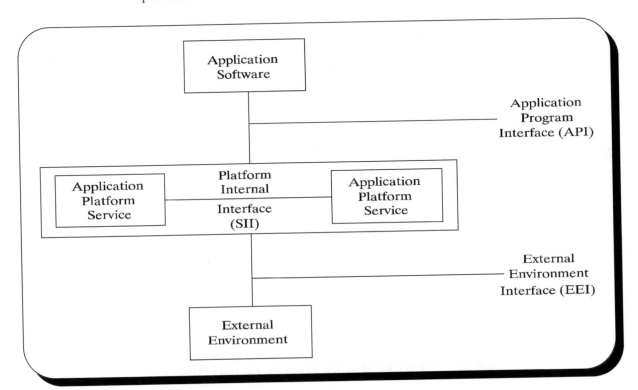

Figure D.2 POSIX OSE reference model, expanded. *Source: Emerging Technologies Group. Based on the IEEE P1003.0 Guide to POSIX Open System Environments: Reference Model.*

transport and network protocols, ISO Distributed Transaction Processing (DTP) (ISO 10026) standard (which standardizes the format and protocol for transaction data going from the application platform across the network) and the IEEE 1201.2 drivability standard (which standardizes end users' interactions with a mouse).

Hardware interfaces between an application platform and the external environment also can be considered examples of EEIs. Such hardware interfaces include disk-drive interfaces (e.g., SCSI), bus interfaces (e.g., VME), and RS-232 and RS-448 interfaces, which interface application platforms to a variety of peripheral devices. Hardware interfaces are not included in the P1003.0 Guide because the P1003.0 considers only software interfaces, thus hardware interface are considered beyond its scope.

Platform Internal Interfaces (PIIs) are interfaces between computing entities within a platform. These interfaces are not exposed to either application software or to the external environment. Nevertheless, they can affect portability and interoperability. X/Open's transaction-processing XA interface, which is the interface between a transaction manager and a resource manager (e.g., a database-management system) is a good example of a PII. PIIs are briefly discussed in the P1003.0 Guide, but they are not included in the P1003.0 Reference Model because PIIs are considered beyond P1003.0's scope.

In a real organization, the implementation of any given system component may differ from, and be more detailed than, that shown in the POSIX OSE model. The POSIX.0 Group's intention was to define a reference model that diverse application, implementation, and integration communities may assume as a starting point for their activities.

Types of Interfaces

The most important fact to be aware of in planning an open-systems environment is that open systems are based on standardized interfaces, not implementations. There are several types of interfaces that affect portability and interoperability. The most important interfaces in an open distributed (Client/Server) system that affect portability and interoperability are:

- Application-Programming Interfaces (APIs)
- Command-level interfaces
- Communications protocols
- Graphical user interfaces (GUIs)
- Formats

These interfaces are described below because they play a major role in planning an organization's open systems.

Application-Programming Interfaces

Application-Programming Interfaces (APIs) standardize the interface to the services that conforming software must provide to an application, and the syntax and the semantics of those services at the interface.

The IEEE P1003.1 standard, for example, specifies an API for an operating-system kernel. This API specifies such services as the ability to open a file and to change a file's permissions. It also specifies the name of the system call that provides the service (e.g., *chmod* to change a file's permissions), the data type of the *chmod* system call, the arguments that must be passed to *chmod* (such as the name of the file whose permissions will be changed and the new permissions), the order of the arguments, the data types of the arguments, applicable flags, return values, error messages, and required header files.

Two heterogeneous systems may support the same name for a system call, and both systems' system call may provide the same service. However, if the system calls differ in any of the detailed API elements, the application may not recognize or properly execute the system call. In that case, the two systems will be incompatible.

As the name implies, APIs are primarily used by applications and application developers. Common APIs are essential to application portability, and, to a degree, to interoperability.

Command-Level Interfaces

Command-level interfaces are interfaces that are typically used to invoke library routines. For example, the IEEE P1003.2 shell and utilities standard specifies such services as the ability to search for a pattern in a file, the name of the command used to search for the pattern (e.g., *grep*), and the options that conforming software must support. Even if two systems support the same commands, the systems may be incompatible if the command interfaces support different options.

Commands are used by programmers, system operators, system analysts, and users. If the commands are used in applications, they are important to application portability. Command-level interfaces also impact user portability because they allow users to move between systems without having to learn new commands for each system.

Graphical User Interfaces

Graphical user interfaces (GUIs) provide a graphical way to interact with a computer or software system. In some cases, GUIs replace command-level interfaces.

GUIs are used by end users, system operators, system managers, and application developers to interact with a platform or application. A consistent GUI style (look and feel) is important to user portability because it allows users to move between systems and use the same familiar interface. This reduces or eliminates the need for costly retraining for users who move between systems.

Besides the visual interface that is used to interact with a platform or application, GUIs also have an API. The API is used by application developers to develop graphical interfaces to applications. The major advantages to standardized GUI APIs are application portability and the ability to reduce programmer retraining.

Communications Protocols

Communications protocols are an interface between two communicating entities. The protocols specify the format of transmitted data to enable it to be understood by the communicating partner, as well as the rules (often called *handshaking routines*) that communicating entities must follow to ensure that they recognize each other.

Communications protocols are used by communications and network software, and, sometimes, by communicating applications and developers of end-user applications. It is the aim of technologists to ultimately make the communications and networking protocols transparent to end-user applications and application developers.

Formats

In open Client/Server systems, formats generally refer to data formats. Common formats are needed to ensure that data can be meaningfully exchanged between diverse applications and processors, each of which may represent the same data differently.

Porting data is as important as porting code, and is often more difficult. No longer is simple ASCII the only data exchanged between applications. Today's applications exchange character and formatted data, graphics, mixed text and graphics, spreadsheet data, product data, image data, and other kinds of multimedia data. For data to be exchanged meaningfully, it is necessary to standardize the encoding for various kinds of data and data types, or resolve the differences between them (e.g., through a standardized data format that applications recognize and can translate to).

Common formats are important to end users who need to exchange data with other users, or to use one application's or database's data in another application or database. Common formats also are important to system managers because they need to understand management-oriented data from diverse vendors' machines and applications. Finally, common formats are important to application developers who develop applications to process another application's data.

Functionality of Interfaces

The various interface standards can be grouped into five major functionality categories. (Figure D.3):

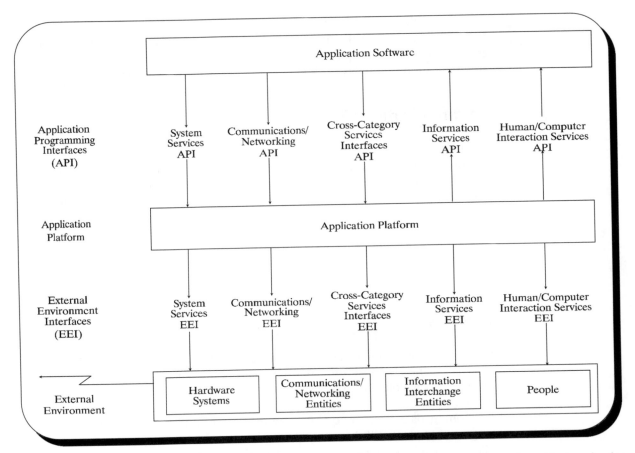

Figure D.3 Functionality of interfaces. *Source: Emerging Technologies Group. Based on a hybrid of IEEE P1003.0's and the DoD's OSE Reference Models.*

- Human/Computer Interaction interfaces
- System services interfaces
- Information services interfaces
- Communications interfaces
- Cross-category interfaces

Human/Computer Interaction interfaces encompass human/computer interface APIs, GUI toolkits, window managers, screen managers, look and feel (style guide), and command interfaces such as are found in Motif, Common User Access, MS Windows, the X-Window system, and the P1003.2 Commands and Utilities.

At the API level, on a bit-mapped display user interfaces are concerned with window-system services, program-script files, and application semantics. On a character-based terminal, user interface APIs address screen- and forms-management services. At the EEI level, user interfaces are concerned with physical interaction between the human using a computer or application and the application platform's input, output, and display devices. User interface EEIs include interfaces to CRT displays, keyboards, mice, audio input/output devices, and network-transport interfaces.

System-service interfaces provide access to services associated with the application platform's internal and attached resources, and to the services that create an execution environment for applications. System service interfaces include the P1003.1 operating-system kernel APIs, and interfaces to real-time services and multithreaded services.

Information services interfaces provide access to external storage, and to services that require the specification of formats and syntax needed to achieve data portability and interoperability, as well as application portability and interoperability. Information-system interfaces include SQL database management and data-interchange standards, for example, for document and graphics interchange, and transaction-processing demarcation interfaces, as well as the interfaces to disk drives, tape drives, and more.

Communications/networking interfaces provide access to services that support interactions between software on one application platform and software and/or hardware on other application platforms. Communications/networking interfaces include OSI and TCP/IP protocols, TCP/IP's FTP (File Transfer Protocol), ISO X.400 Electronic Mail, ISO X.500 Directory Services, and APIs to X.400 and X.500.

Cross-category services are services that affect multiple open-systems components. Examples of cross-category services are security, system management, and internationalization. Internationalization facilities, for example, contains facilities for features which vary with countries or geographical regions, such as coded character sets, local monetary systems, and the use of native languages for messages. These features affect DBMSs, GUIs, command interfaces, and programming languages. Similarly, security and system management are needed for operating systems, networks, DBMS, and more.

Profiles Put Standards Together

Although many standards requirements are common to numerous organizations, different organizations, application domains, and platforms either have some different standards requirements or they prioritize the standards differently. A good way to understand and communicate the requirements of each application area is to develop or specify a profile for these areas.

What's a Profile?

A profile is a subset or collection of one or more standards, along with applicable options, parameters, and environment values within standards, and, if necessary, additional defined nonstandard functionalities, needed to provide or support a particular function, application area, or platform.

Profiles are more practical to deal with than traditional standards. Standards are difficult to read because they specify functionality, syntax, protocols, data formats, and other interface details in sufficient depth to be implementable by a programmer. Standards also are large because they contain options to accommodate a variety of diverse application needs.

In contrast, profiles specify standards, or subsets of standards, at a high level, along with options, parameter, or environment values, that are applicable to the requirements of a particular application area or platform. Profiles may also specify other profiles that, themselves, identify relevant standards, options, and values. The ability to reference other profiles, as well as standards, facilitates the development of a profile.

Table D.1 shows one possible set of standards, specifications, options, and environment variables within standards, identified by one company in developing a profile for distributed-transaction processing.

Table D.1 An Example Transaction Processing Profile

Formal Standards	Consortia and De facto Specifications	Nonstandard Functionality
ISO Cobol and ANSI C	X/Open SQL RDA (Remote Data Access)	IBM CICS
C++ (Future)	X/Open SQL Call-Level Interface (CLI)	IBM Message Queuing Interface (MQI)
IEEE P1003.1 (POSIX Kernel)	X/Open TX API	
POSIX Option Identifiers	X/Open TxRPC API	
_POSIX-TP-C90 (C Language)	X/Open XA API	
_POSIX_TP_COBOL (Cobol)	X/Open CPI-C	
_POSIX_TP_RDBMS (Relational DBMS)	Internet TCP/IP	
_POSIX_TP_QUEUES	Internet SNMP (Network Mgt.)	
IEEE P1003.1c (Threads)	X/Open S302 Internationalization of Networking Specifications	
ISO SQL Level 2	CORBA Interoperability Objects (Future)	
IEEE P1387.4 Print Mgt.		
IEEE P1003.6 Security: Discretionary Access Control (DAC) option		
ISO CCR (Commitment, Concurrency, & Recovery) (Two-Phase Commit) as part of X/Open's XA interface		
ISO 10026 DTP (Distributed Transaction Processing protocol and format)		
ISO X.500 Directory Services		

Source: Emerging Technologies Group.

Benefits of Profiles

Profiles have a number of important benefits:

- Profiles simplify the use of standards because they identify, in one place, the standards, subsets, options, and parameters needed to achieve a particular goal.
- Profiles provide a clear method of communicating information about the standards need for a particular application domain or platform.
- Standardized profiles promote uniformity of the standards needed for particular environments so that conformance tests can be developed for the profile.
- Formal and industry-standard profiles increase the chances of product availability of groups of standards by identifying the standards that are expected to be components of large numbers of users' computing systems.

For further information about profiles and profiling organization, see Appendix F.

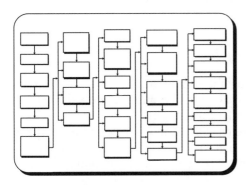

Advanced OSE Technology

What Creates Nonportable Applications

Most system software, such as operating systems, database-management systems, and network software perform a variety of the same or similar services for application programs. For operating systems, these services include input/output, memory management, file management, and more. Incompatibilities arise because every operating system performs these services differently. For example:

- The syntax of the system calls for services is different: read, get, and input (to get input), or allocate, alloc, and malloc (to allocate memory) are typical.
- The system calls require different parameters (bytes or sectors, for example).
- The parameters have different formats.
- The ordering of the parameters matters.
- Some operating systems refer to devices by logical names, while others use numeric indicators, data structures, or pointers.
- Different operating systems have different file formats.
- Different operating systems have different rules for naming files.
- Different operating systems have different error messages.
- Different versions of the same operating systems require different header files to be included with a system call.
- Different versions of the same operating system support different options for each command.

A similar list of incompatibilities can be compiled for database-management systems, network software, graphics, and so on. Each of these types of system software performs services specific to its intended functionality. Network software, for example, establishes connections, manages sessions, and performs handshaking routines to ensure that it is recognized by communicating partners. Database-management

329

systems translate user queries, access the database, and sort and summarize data for the user or application. CAD graphics systems rotate and scale objects, create shadows, and store graphics data in a particular format.

Two network, database, or graphics systems will be incompatible if they perform or provide any of these services differently (e.g., have different syntaxes or parameters, have different file-naming conventions, have different handshaking rules, or store data in different formats). In addition to these differences, heterogeneous network, database management, and graphics systems may provide different services.

The Open-Systems Solution

The method that is evolving to handle system-software incompatibilities is to insulate the system software from applications and from other system software with a standardized layer of software known as an *interface*. The standardized layer of software presents the user, programmer, and application with an interface that always looks the same, regardless of the underlying operating system.

This interface need not be a separate extra layer of software that sits on top of system-software code. Instead, the native system-software interface (for an operating system, database system, etc.) is modified to directly support a standardized interface.

How Standards Support Compatible Applications

To ensure application portability and interoperability across heterogeneous multivendor systems, standards specify two things:

- The functions and services that the system software must provide (e.g., operating-system standards specify operating system functions and services, database standards specify database functionality and services).
- The system interfaces that applications will recognize and respond to.

The P1003.1 and P1003.2 POSIX standards make uniform the services that an operating system should provide, the system calls and command names, their data types, the arguments, the arguments' data types, the order of the arguments, flags, modes, permissions, return behavior, symbolic error values, required header files, command options, and the content of the system's required header files. Networking-protocol standards make consistent the handshaking procedures necessary for communicating systems to establish an association, and the format of information to be communicated.

Types of Interfaces

Standards generally specify five different types of interfaces: application programming interfaces (APIs), command-level interfaces, graphical user interfaces

(GUIs), networking protocols, and formats. These interfaces may be located at the application-programming interface (API) level, which is the interface level between the application and the platform, or they may be located at the external-environment interface (EEI) level, which is between the platform and the external environment. These types of interfaces, their importance, and who uses them, are described and discussed in Appendix D. Other types of standards, such as object definitions, may become important in the future.

Figure E.1 graphically shows the operation of two interfaces—the P1003.1 API and the P1003.2 command-level interface. As the figure shows, there is a boundary between the applications developer (sitting at the computer above the boundary line) and the application platform (located below the boundary line). The boundary line represents the interface to services offered by a software system implemented below the boundary. A standard is created to satisfy application and user requirements for services at this interface (in this case, POSIX.1 and POSIX.2) in a portable way.

Table E.1 shows the details of the API for one UNIX system call as specified or implemented in P1003.1, OSF/1 Version 1.3, X/Open's SPEC 1170, and the SVID (System V Interface Definition). All four systems have the same system call for the same service. Differences in the technical details of the system call can, however, cause incompatibilities between UNIX-like systems under certain conditions.

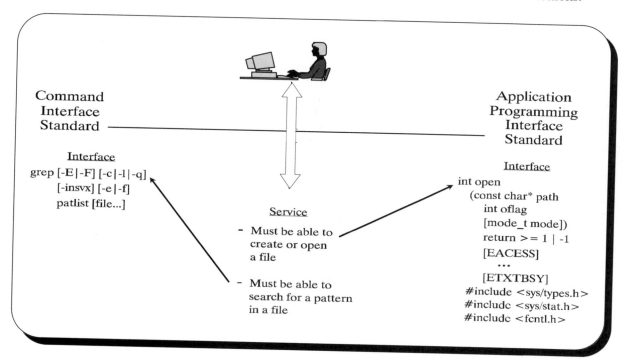

Figure E.1 Standards = interfaces, not implementations. *Source: Emerging Technologies Group.*

Table E.1 Example of a UNIX System Call API

File & Directory Operations		POSIX	OSF/1	X/Open Spec 1170	SVID
Change Owner & Group of a File **Change file owner/path**	**chown**	chown	chown	chown	chown
(Pathname of the file) (Numeric value of new owner ID) (Numeric value of new group ID)	int chown (const char * path, uid_t owner, gid_t, group)	✓	✓	✓	✓
Change file owner/fildes	**fchown**	—	fchown	—	fchown
(Pathname of the file) (Numeric value of new owner ID) (Numeric value of new group ID)	int fchown (const char * path uid_t owner, gid_t group)	Proposed for P1003.1 revision	✓	—	✓
Return Values					
Owner and group are changed; No change in owner; see erno.	return = 0 −1	✓	✓	✓	✓
Error Values					
Search permissions denied on path	errno= [EACCES]	✓	✓	✓	✓
"fildes" is not an open file descriptor (fchown)	[EBADF]	—	✓	—	✓
Invalid address for an argument	[EFAULT]	—	✓	Removed	—
Invalid or unsupported ID (if detected)	[EINVAL]	✓	✓	—	✓
Too many symbolic links in path	[ELOOP]	—	✓	✓	✓
Path or component name exceeds max	[ENAMETOOLONG]	✓	✓	✓	✓
Path component is not a directory	[ENOTDIR]	✓	✓	✓	✓
No such file (or empty path string)	[ENOENT]	✓	✓	✓	✓
Not owner, insufficient permission	[EPERM]	✓	✓	✓	✓
Read-only file system	[EROFS]	✓	✓	✓	✓
Required Header Files					
	#include <sys/types.h>	✓	✓	✓	✓
	#include <sys/stat.h>	—	—	—	—
	#include <sys/unistid.h>	—	—	✓	—

Source: Emerging Technologies Group Report "Comparison of Operating System Interfaces"

Key: ✓ means is explicitly specified — means not specified

Open Distributed Systems

In a distributed environment, multiple application platforms may interact with each other. Generally, when an application requests communication with a remote application or resource, the request is made at the API. System software on the requesting application platform translates the request into some appropriate action at the EEI. The APIs and EEIs hide the complexity of networking from the application.

The networking APIs and EEIs should hide the fact that requested data is remotely located. What is perceived as a single Application Platform may, actually, comprise several individual application platforms.

In reality, this concept is still a matter for the future. Multivendor interoperability between heterogeneous systems is a difficult goal to achieve. No one knows what the problems will be: Only two things are certain. First, conformance to a specification is not equivalent to interoperability. Second, the causes of interoperability failures appear to be related to a myriad of implementation details and timing parameters, rather than being traceable to a single fault that can be quickly fixed. Unfortunately, some of those implementation and interaction details that result in interoperability problems are often traceable to interactions between various kinds of system software, rather than being traceable to a network-protocol software issue.

APIs Interact Together

Standards alone will not ensure either highly interoperable or portable environments unless different standardized interfaces can work together in harmony. Harmonization is important because organizations typically consist of diverse environments (e.g., office, transaction processing, supercomputing, industrial-plant floor), each of which has different requirements. For enterprisewide distributed computing, however, the different environments must be able to work together cooperatively, without having conflicting services and interfaces. Lack of harmonization between the different environments will destroy the ability of the departments to cooperate, even if the departments all specify standards or open specifications.

Figure E.2 shows one of many possible API interaction scenarios when an application (or applications) calls multiple, distributed network services, as well as other services (e.g., an SQL database). Of necessity, the diagram is simplified, and does not show all the signal flows needed for a particular application and its service requests. The services requested, and signal flows shown are, however, typical interaction scenarios.

Consider the simplest signal flow that is shown in Figure E.2. An application, which does not need other services to execute, calls the IEEE PASC P1353 ACSE and presentation APIs to access an OSI protocol stack. The executed application then moves into the external environment and causes a disk drive to store data, a printer to run, and so forth.

Complicating matters somewhat, a user application may need the services of X.400-based electronic mail. To this end, as shown in the figure, the application

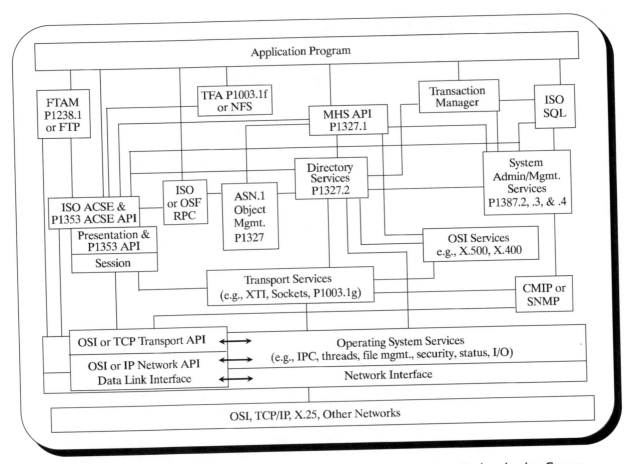

Figure E.2 APIs play together. Source: Emerging Technologies Group.

accesses the IEEE P1327.1 X.400 API to obtain X.400 services. The X.400 application services may directly access communications services. The interface to these services can be at the POSIX P1353 ACSE/Presentation Layer API. This API is protocol dependent: It is designed solely for the OSI stack.

To locate a mail recipient, the X.400 services may need to access Directory Services. For this purpose, in the figure, the application accesses the POSIX P1327.2 X.500 Directory Services API before accessing communications services.

As the figure shows, it is possible for the application and its associated X.400 services to use a Transport-protocol–independent API to access low-level communications services such as OSI, TCP/IP, X.25, and so on. At the lowest network level, network requests get out onto the network using the operating system, which controls I/O for the platform.

A similar signal-flow discussion applies to an application's use of FTAM or FTP services, an SQL-accessed database (as shown), or a transaction manager. An application that needs distributed-file access services can use IEEE P1003.1f Transparent

File Access (TFA) API and services or NFS (RFC 1094). Other services, such as SQL, can also use the TFA API or NFS. Finally, various network services, operating systems, SQL databases, and transaction-processing systems need to be managed, for example, by the IEEE P1387 standards, and/or by ISO CMIP or SNMP.

Depending on particular interests and requirements (e.g., requirements for document exchange using ISO ODA or SGML standards), readers will be able to fathom other interactions from a study of the figure. The figure is not definitive, but it represents one possible scope of the POSIX-distributed services APIs and other API interactions.

Interoperability May Depend on the Operating System

Although almost any of the interactions between components of a distributed system can interfere with interoperability, the operating system is often the culprit. The reason is that the operating system is intimately related to network problems because the operating system is the intermediary between the network and the networking software. The widespread diagrams of the OSI model, which show two parallel stacks connected by a cable and omit the role of the operating system, have been largely at fault in masking the dependence of communications on the operating system (Figure E.3). The operating system is the software that interfaces to the bare-bones hardware and takes care of input/output for a computing system. To the operating system, the network is just another input/output device.

The operating system does not allow any other software to take over its input/output function. Application processes that want to communicate with a remote

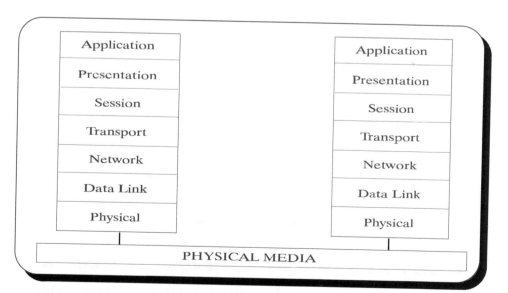

Figure E.3 The OSI model.

application or resource have two choices. They may pass service requests to the operating system which interfaces to a transport system and sends the request over the network, or the application can pass a request to OSI (or TCP/IP) application-layer protocols. In the latter case, the OSI (or TCP/IP) application protocols pass the request down the protocol stack (e.g., from FTAM to ACSE to Presentation to Session to Transport). Either at the Transport layer (layer 4) or the Data Link layer (layer 2), the protocol stack passes off the networking-communications request to the operating system. The operating system sends the request over the network. The operating system also has a listening process that listens for network transmissions that it should receive, so incoming transmissions must pass through the operating system (Figure E.4).

Besides interfacing to the network, networking software at various OSI levels makes several other requests of the operating system. For example, if an application wants to transfer a file to a remote computer, it invokes FTAM. FTAM, however, must perform functions such as determining if the file to be transferred really exists,

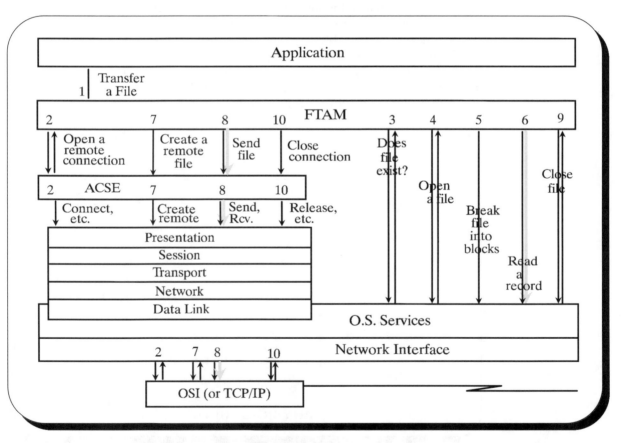

Figure E.4 Networking & operating system relationships in FTAM. *Source: Emerging Technologies Group.*

opening the file, reading the file, copying the file to a remote computer, and closing the file. The remote networking software must also determine if the file already exists. If not, it must create it. If the file does exist, the network software must determine if it should overwrite the file or append the transmitted data to the end of the file. All these file-related functions are operating-system functions.

Finally, the low-level communications process that puts a transmission onto a network is an operating-system construct, and it is managed by the operating-system kernel. Only higher-level networking services (e.g., Session services) are network constructs and managed by protocol software.

A walk through an FTAM or other file-transfer application shows the various operating-system interactions listed, which are also shown in Figure E.4. Operations shown with multiple arrows indicate operations that occur multiple times within a single file transfer. Operations showing arrows in two directions indicate operations that occur in the file-transfer–sending phase on the sending machine, as well as in the file-transfer–receiving phase on the receiving machine. All of the operations shown on the machine represented in Figure E.4 also occur on the machine's communicating partner.

The close coordination between networking software and the operating system can be a major source of interoperability problems in a distributed system. As Figure E.4 shows, more than 50 percent of the functions involved in transferring a file between computers are operating-system functions, performed by the operating system after it is invoked by the FTAM file-transfer software. Any little detail of any of the interactions between protocol software and the operating system can result in a failure to interoperate.

Users should therefore be aware that a platform's operating system can be a serious risk element, especially if the operating system and network-protocol software are procured separately.

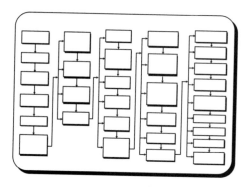

Appendix

Advanced Open-Systems Profile Technology

Introduction

The value of open-systems environments profiles as a way to present an integrated set of components has been recognized by many organizations. Open-systems profiles are, essentially, a catalog of standards, consortia or *de facto* specifications, and, where needed, proprietary product functionalities that are relevant to a particular industry, organization, application domain, or platform.

The idea of defining profiles is not new to commercial enterprises. In the past, companies defined profiles under the banner *corporate guidelines.* Profiles then were designed to satisfy an organization's functionality goals, and often to specify a particular vendor's products. Today's open-systems profiles differ from these corporate profiles in that open-systems profiles are designed not only to satisfy functionality goals, but also to satisfy the goals of portability and interoperability in Client/Server, heterogeneous, multivendor environments. Satisfying portability and interoperability goals means that open-systems profiles must be based on standards rather than proprietary products as much as is possible.

The existence of open-systems profiles eliminates the need for organizations planning open Client/Server systems to wade through many generic standards to find specifications relevant to a specific work environment. Profiles also allow users, vendors, system integrators, and procurement officers to focus on their business objectives, and to communicate their requirements to vendors. Finally, profiling facilitates companies' open-systems architecture and strategy planning.

Several standards bodies and industry groups are currently defining standardized profiles. Some of the profiles apply to broad application domains or to specific platform types. Others apply to a single type of interface in an OSE.

339

Types of Profiles

There are three types of profiles:

- Single-Interface–Type Profiles
- Platform Profiles
- Application Environment Profiles

A *Single-Interface–Type Profile* is a profile applicable to a single type of interface (e.g., communications, human-computer interface, or information services interface). This profile classification is based on the ISO TR 10000 taxonomy in which ISO classifies profiles in terms of the types of interfaces they specify. To define a Single-Interface–type Profile, profile developers specify one or more standards that address a single type of interface of the Open-Systems Environment (OSE) and options, parameters, and so on, within these standards that are applicable to the function that the profile is trying to accomplish.

Examples of Single-Interface–Type Profiles are ISO profiles for OSI Transport protocols used with different underlying networks, OSI FTAM (File Transfer, Access, and Management) profiles for use with different types of files to be transferred, and MAP, TOP, and GOSIP profiles, which are based on the ISO OSI standard but targeted at different environments (the industrial plant floor, the technical and business office, and government environments, respectively). Single-Interface–Type Profiles are created mostly by standards groups and vendor consortia, and are used by user organizations in their procurements.

A *Platform Profile* focuses on the functionality and interfaces needed for a particular type of platform, such as workstations, PCs, time-sharing systems, or symmetric multiprocessors. A Platform Profile could be created from one or more standards. Platform Profiles specify standards, options, gaps, and specifications to fill the gaps. Examples of platform profiles are the POSIX.14 Multiprocessing Profile and the POSIX.18 Traditional Multiuser UNIX System profile. Platform profiles are created either by standards groups or vendor consortia for use by user organizations in their procurements, or by user companies or government organizations (who define, for example, desktop or server profiles for their organization or division).

An *Application Environment Profile (AEP)* is created from multiple standards that specify multiple, diverse types of functionality (e.g. database, networking, graphics, operating system) necessary for a particular application area. AEP developers specify the diverse standards necessary for the application area in question. Within each standard, they identify mandatory options, functions and options that are not needed, standards gaps, and, if necessary, specifications to fill the gaps. An example of an AEP is the POSIX.10 profile for supercomputing environments. Application-Environment Profiles are created by users and vendors, companies and government organizations, standards groups and vendor consortia.

Who Creates Profiles?

Profiles are being developed by a variety of standards groups, industry groups, and commercial organizations (Figure F.1).

Standardized profiles, created by standards groups, are formal documents, based on ballots, that refer to formal standards only. Various formal standards groups are developing Single Interface Type, Platform, and Application-Environment Profiles (AEPs).

Industry-specific profiles tend to be Application-Environment Profiles based on an industry's needs, and are developed by industry groups. Examples of groups defining industry profiles are the Petrotechnical Open Software Corporation (POSC)

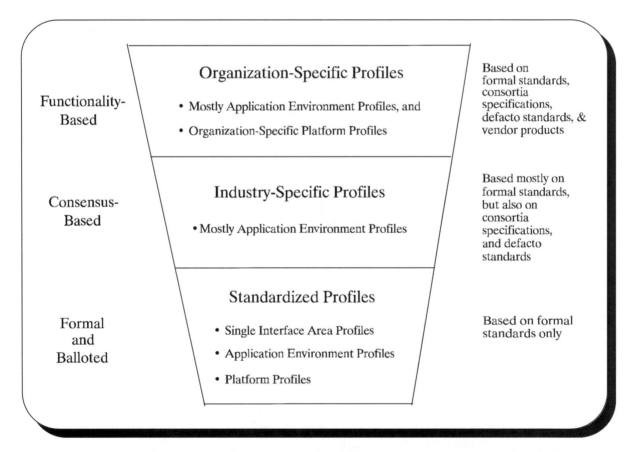

Figure F.1 The universe of profiles. *Source: Emerging Technologies Group. Based on information and diagrams contained in early drafts of the P1003.0 Guide.*

and the Electric Power Research Institute (EPRI). The profiles developed by such industry groups represent a consensus of the group as to the needs of their industry. To maximize portability and interoperability, industry profiles mostly specify formal standards. Where formal standards do not exist, industry profiles also stipulate consortia specifications and *de facto* standards (e.g., Motif, DCE, and TCP/IP).

Although more specific than standardized profiles, which apply to diverse industries, industry-specific profiles are too generic to fill the needs of individual organizations. Individual organizations may use industry-specific profiles as a starting point, a targeted goal, and a productivity tool. In the end, each organization must develop its own profile, or tailor the industry-specific profile, to fit its own needs.

Organization-specific profiles represent the largest number of profiles being developed. There are many more organizations developing profiles for their own systems than there are standards bodies or industry groups writing standardized profiles. Most organization-specific profiles are either Application Environment Profiles or Platform Profiles (for example, profiles for desktop workstations and PCs). The development of Single-Interface–Type Profiles, which requires a knowledge of the details of specific standards, is usually left to standards groups. Single-Interface–Type Profiles, however, should be specified as part of organization-specific profiles.

Individual organizations usually have a number of requirements that take precedence over the standards-based open-systems profiles specified by standards or industry groups. For example, besides providing portability and interoperability, real-world production environment systems must contain sufficient functionality to be able to perform users' business tasks. Performance also may be a major requirement for real-world applications. In addition, working legacy systems may be important to a commercial organization, either because of their functionality or because it may not be worthwhile to pay the cost for a new system. Because such requirements may be paramount, organization-specific profiles will likely specify a combination of formal standards, consortia specifications, *de facto* standards, and vendors' products.

Defining Standardized Profiles

The major standardized profile organizations include the ISO/IEC Joint Technical Committee 1 (JTC-1) Special Group on Functional Standards (SGFS) (In Europe, profiles are called *Functional Standards*), the European Workshop for Open Systems (EWOS), and the IEEE PASC Groups. All these groups are coordinating their work. The aim is to contribute the profile work occurring in these groups to ISO for international standardization.

Of these groups, ISO has written the definitive documents on standardized profiles. IEEE PASC pioneered the work in application environment profiles. EWOS pioneered the work in developing a methodology for defining profiles.

EWOS Profile Work

The European Workshop on Open Systems (EWOS) has been pioneering the development of a profiling methodology. Since EWOS began its work, I have personally, and quite effectively, used some of EWOS's methodology in planning open-systems environments with my own clients and incorporated some of EWOS's techniques in my firm's methodology. The major EWOS techniques that I have incorporated in the DOSEE are the determination of service requirements and standards through initial definition of attributes and attribute values, and the use of the profile components matrix.

EWOS applies attributes and attribute values to business scenarios in developing profiles. The DOSEE expands this work and applies the attributes-attribute value technique to the characterization of applications and interoperability interactions. DOSEE also uses EWOS's attribute-attribute value technique in planning an enterprisewide infrastructure before defining individual profiles.

The DOSEE methodology does not go directly from attributes and attribute values to identifying existing profiles (a big leap, and profiles may not yet have been defined). Instead, the DOSEE methodology uses the EWOS Profile Components Matrix to systematically identify standards and profiles, for each of the interfaces and functionalities needed in a profile.

The EWOS methodology and its attribute-attribute value technique are discussed in detail in Chapter 5. The EWOS attribute-attribute value application and business scenario characterization methodology is also discussed in Chapter 7.

ISO Profile Work

The most important ISO profile guiding document is known as Technical Report (TR) 10000. TR 10000 has 3 parts, known as TR 10000-1, TR 10000-2, and TR 10000-3.

TR 10000-1, "General Principles and Documentation Framework," outlines the concept profiles, the concept of taxonomy (or a classification scheme for profiles), and the format and the content to be included in International Standardized Profiles (ISPs).

TR 10000-2, "Principles and Taxonomy for OSI Profiles," deals with the principles of profiling and specifies the actual classification scheme used for OSI profiles that are registered and documented in International Standardized Profile documents. TR 10000-2 also describes a number of ISO ISPs based on OSI communications. This is an excellent document for people interested in using profiles as building blocks from which to form other profiles. Some of TR 10000-2's principles and descriptions of its taxonomy for communications profiles, are discussed later in this chapter.

TR 10000-3, "Principles and Taxonomy for OSE (Open Systems Environment) Profiles," contains the principles of profiling, and the meaning of conformance to a profile for Open Systems Environment (OSE) profiles. Although in its final form, TR 10000-3 is less mature than TR 10000-1 and -2. It uses model and interface information from the P1003.0 Guide, but it uses this information differently. Consequently, the author believes that TR 10000-3's basic premises do not explain many portability and interoperability considerations that the P1003.0 Guide explains.

Until now, ISO has constructed its profiles using the group brainstorm technique. According to TR 10000, an international standardized profile (ISP) is constructed by:

- Documenting the functional requirements and scenario in which the profile is required,
- Selecting the appropriate base specifications or profiles,
- Selecting the conforming sets of options, subsets, and so on,
- Combining compatible base specifications, by reference, to create the specification of an information technology function that meets the identified requirement,
- If necessary, adding further specification of the combined behavior in order to ensure that the specification is adequate.

It is expected that ISPs will, in general, be written, evaluated, and used by experts in specific areas of standardization. Considering the large number of information technology standards that have been defined, however, it will be very difficult for these experts, and next to impossible for semi-experts, to know what standards are available, and which ones apply to a particular business scenario. This confusing, almost unidentifiable, plethora of standards makes a strong case for identifying classes of profiles that correspond to particular areas of expertise and/or functionality.

For this reason, ISO SGFS has defined categories of profiles based on the types of interface they specify. ISO SGFS has then defined further subdivisions that indicate the main technical function area targeted by the profile. With this taxonomy, a Single-Interface–Type Profile might be classified first by the communications-system interface, because it is a profile concerned with the communication interface. All communications profiles might then be further classified according to whether they deal with Transport, File Transfer, and so on.

An OSE or AEP would have a more complex classification. OSE profiles and AEPs would address multiple interfaces, such as communications, human-computer, and information-services interfaces. It would therefore be classified as a profile for all these categories. However, an OSE profile might be further classified according to whether it deals with these interfaces in the medical, EDI, or transaction processing areas.

ISO OSI Profiles

Currently, most ISO profile work is communications-oriented profiles, related to OSI. TR 10000 divides OSI-related Profiles into the following classes.

T—Transport Profiles providing connection-mode Transport Service.
U—Transport Profiles providing connectionless-mode Transport Service.
R—Relay Profiles.

A—OSI Application Profiles requiring connection-mode Transport Service.

B—OSI Application Profiles requiring connectionless-mode Transport Service.

F—Interchange format and representation profiles.

M—Managed-object profiles.

Table F.1 shows selected OSI profiles that are international standards or close to becoming so. Since the profiles of concern are related to communications interfaces, they would all have a profile identifier beginning with the letter C. The associated numeric strings, such as TA, TB, TC, TD, TE, RA, AFT, AOM, and so on, indicate further levels of subdivision with the main functional area.

For example, TA in a profile title is a designation in which T indicates a Transport protocol profile and A indicates that the profile requires the Connection-mode Transport Service. FOD is the designation for open document format profiles, while AFT indicates File Transfer, Access, and Management profiles. The ISO taxonomy designation is included in the tables when it is part of a profile's title as an aid to obtaining a copy of the profile.

As Table F.1 shows, there are many OSI profiles. They are listed here because if a relevant profile is available, it is helpful to use profiles rather than individual standards as building blocks for Open-Systems Environment profiles. Use of these profiles can simplify open-systems planning because, otherwise, there are so many standards to be considered.

For example, there are more than 1,460 OSI Transport and Transport-related protocols, and thousands of possible combinations, depending on whether a connection-mode or connectionless Transport service is needed to run over a connection-mode or connectionless Network service, and whether the combination used for the Transport and Network service will use a particular media-access method, and so on.

Although Table F.1 profiles are OSI-specific profiles, they are listed here because many of the profiles and their standards that address application-layer networking (e.g., document transfer, graphics interchange, network management, electronic mail, distributed-transaction processing) have been (or will be) translated to also work with TCP/IP networks. Some OSI standards, such as X.400, are already in widespread use with TCP/IP. Except for file transfer and limited virtual terminal, equivalent network application-oriented standards do not exist for TCP/IP networks.

Besides the profiles listed in Table F.1, ISO plans, or has begun work on, a number of other profiles. One group of these is the message-handling profiles. The message-handling profiles are based on ISO/IEC 10021 Message-Oriented Text Interchange System (MOTIS). The first two MHS profiles initially reference the 1988 MOTIS versions. A third profile is based on the CCITT X.435 recommendation, which integrates Electronic-Data Interchange (EDI) and electronic mail.

Two other sets of ISO profiles are the Directory-Data–Definition Format profiles and the directory-access profiles. The Directory-Data–Definition Format profiles specify the properties of object classes, attribute types, and attribute syntaxes related to the use of the directory. Two types of usage are covered in these pro-

Table F.1   ISO OSI Profiles

TRANSPORT NETWORKING PROFILES ISO

International Standardized Profile (ISP) 10608-1:1992: Profile for Connection-mode Transport Service over Connectionless-mode Network Service—Part 1: General Overview and Subnetwork-Independent Requirements
Abstract: This International Standardized Profile (ISP) is applicable to Transport Class 4 connection-mode OSI end systems attached to any type of subnetwork from which the standardized connectionless-mode Network Service can be made available.

ISO/IEC/JTC 1 ISP 10608-2:1992: Profile for Connection-mode Transport Service over Connectionless-mode Network Service—Part 2: profile including subnetwork-dependent requirements for CSMA/CD Local Area Networks (LANs)
Abstract: Specifies subnetwork-type dependent requirements for end system operation when the end system is attached to a carrier-sense multiple access with collision detection (CSMA/CD) local area network.

ISO/IEC/JTC 1 ISP 10608-5:1992: Profile for Connection-mode Transport Service over CLNS—Part 5: Profiles Including Subnetwork-dependent Requirements for X.25 Packet Switched Data Networks Using Switched Virtual Circuits
Abstract: Specifies subnetwork-type dependent requirements for end system operation when the end system is attached to an X.25 packet-switched data network by a dedicated (permanent) access line and using switched virtual circuits.

ISO/IEC/JTC 1 ISP 10609-1:1992: Profiles for Connection-mode Transport Service over Connection-mode Network Service—Part 1: Subnetwork-type Independent Requirements for Group TB
Abstract: This part specifies the subnetwork-type independent requirements for OSI end systems using transport protocol Classes 0, 2 and 4.

ISO/IEC/JTC 1 ISP 10609-2:1992: Profiles for Connection-mode Transport Service over Connection-mode Network Service—Part 2: Subnetwork-type Independent Requirements for Group TC
Abstract: Specifies a combination of OSI standards which collectively provide the connection-mode Transport Service, Classes 0 and 2, using the connection-mode Network Service.

ISO/IEC/JTC 1 ISP 10609-3:1992: Profiles for Connection-mode Transport Service over Connection-mode Network Service—Part 3: Subnetwork-type Independent Requirements for Group TD
Abstract: This part specifies the subnetwork-type independent requirements for Transport protocol class 0 systems.

Table F.1   ISO OSI Profiles (Continued)

ISO/IEC ISP 10609-4:1992: Profiles for Connection-mode Transport Service over Connection-mode Network Service—Part 4: Subnetwork-type Independent Requirements for Group TE
Abstract: This part specifies the subnetwork-type independent requirements for Transport protocol class 2 systems.

ISO/IEC ISP 10609-5:1992: Profiles for Connection-mode Transport Service over Connection-mode Network Service—Part 5: Definition of Profiles TB1111/TB1121
Abstract: This part specifies the definition of Profiles with Permanent access to a Packet Switched Data Network (PSDN) via Public Switched Telephonic Network (PSTN) using virtual call, and Permanent access to a PSDN via Circuit-Switched Data Network (CSDN) using virtual call. These profiles use transport protocol classes 0,2 and 4.

ISO/IEC ISP 10609-6:1992: International Standardized Profiles TB, TC, TD and TE—Connection-mode Transport Service over Connection-mode Network Service—Part 6: Definition of Profiles TC1111/TC1121
Abstract: This part specifies the definition of Profiles with Permanent access to a PSDN via PSTN using virtual call, and Permanent access to a PSDN via CSDN using virtual call, and which use transport protocol classes 0 and 2.

ISO/IEC ISP 10609-7:1992: Profiles for Connection-mode Transport Service over Connection-mode Network Service—Part 7: Definition of Profiles TD1111/TD1121
Abstract: This part specifies the definition of Profiles with Permanent access to a PSDN via PSTN using virtual call, and with Permanent access to a PSDN via CSDN using virtual call, and which use transport protocol class 0.

ISO/IEC ISP 10609-8:1992: International Standardized Profiles TB, TC, TD and TE—Connection-mode Transport Service over Connection-mode Network Service—Part 8: Definition of Profiles TE1111/TE1121
Abstract: Specifies the definition of Profiles with Permanent access to a PSDN via PSTN using virtual call and Profiles with Permanent access to a PSDN via CSDN using virtual call, and which use transport protocol class 2.

ISO/IEC ISP 10609-9:1992: Profiles for COTS Over CONS—Part 9: Subnetwork-type Dependent Requirements for Network, Data Link and Physical Layers Concerning Permanent Access to a Packet Switched Data Network Using Virtual Call
Abstract: Specifies a combination of OSI standards, which collectively provide the connection-mode transport service using the connection-mode network service. Specifies Network Layer, Data Link Layer and Physical Layer requirements that apply specifically to configurations involving permanent access to a packet-switched data network using virtual call.

Table F.1 ISO OSI Profiles (Continued)

LOW-LEVEL NETWORK (LAYERS 1 AND 2)

ITU Recommendation X.28:1993: DTE/DCE Interface for a Start-Stop Mode Data Terminal Equipment Accessing the Packet Assembly/Disassembly Facility (PAD)in a Public Data Network Situated in the Same Country

Abstract: Defines the protocols for a start-stop DTE to use a PAD in accessing a PDN. Specifies Physical Layer electrical and mechanical characteristics; the procedures for exchange of control information, particularly PAD command signals and PAD service signals. Defines standard profiles of PAD parameters. Use with X.3 and X.29. Refers to T.50, V.21, V.22, V.23, V.24, V.25, V.28, X.4, X.20, and X.20 bis.

CCITT Recommendation X.351:1988: Special Requirements to be Met for Packet Assembly/ Disassembly Facilities (PADs) Located at or in Association with Coast Earth Stations in the Public Mobile Satellite Service

Abstract: Special procedures for a PAD in the maritime satellite service, including some additional PAD command/service signals and a profile of initial PAD parameter values. Refers to E.211, Q.60, T.50, V.21, V.22, V.23, V.24, X.3, X.4, X.28, X.29, and X.350.

CCITT Recommendation E.523: Standard Traffic Profiles for International Traffic Streams

Abstract: Concerns determining the number of circuits in automatic and semiautomatic operation. This Recommendation presents standardized 24-hour traffic profiles for international traffic streams, which are useful where streams are too small to obtain reliable measurements or where no measurements are available.

OSI REGISTRATION

ISO/IEC ISP 9834-4: Open Systems Interconnection—Procedures for the Operation of OSI Registration Authorities—Part 4: Registration of Virtual Terminal Environment (VTE) Profiles

Abstract: Specifies the contents of register entries for recording information about VTE-profiles and assigning unambiguous names of ASN.1-type object identifiers to VTE-profile definitions.

FACSIMILE DOCUMENT TRANSFER

CCITT Recommendation T.503: A Document Application Profile for the Interchange of Group 4 Facsimile Documents

Abstract: Specifies an interchange format suitable for the interchange of Group 4 facsimile documents that contain only raster graphics. Features which can be interchanged using this document application profile fall into the following categories: page format features; raster graphics layout and imaging features; and raster-graphics coding.

FILE TRANSFER

ISO/IEC ISP 10607-1:1990: File Transfer, Access and Management (FTAM)—Part 1: Specification of ACSE, Presentation and Session Protocols for the use by FTAM (AFTnn)
Abstract: Specifies how the OSI association control service element, the Presentation Layer, and the Session Layer standards shall be used to provide the FTAM functions for the International Standardized Profiles AFTnn.

ISO/IEC ISP 10607-2:1990: FTAM—Part 2: Definition of Document Types, Constraint Sets & Syntaxes (AFTnn)
Abstract: Contains the basic definitions of document types, constraint sets, abstract syntaxes, and transfer syntaxes as used and referenced in FTAM applications involving the transfer of simple (unstructured) files, positional (flat) files, and full (hierarchical) files.

ISO/IEC ISP 10607-2 Addendum 1 (AD1):1991: FTAM—Part 2: Definition of Document Types, Constant Sets and Syntaxes—Addendum 1: Additional Definitions (AFTnn)
Abstract: Defines additional document types, constraint sets, abstract syntaxes, and transfer syntaxes for FTAM implementations.

ISO/IEC ISP 10607-3:1990: FTAM—Part 3:—Simple File Transfer Service (Unstructured) (AFT 11)
Abstract: Covers transfer of files between two end systems' filestores, using the OSI connection-mode transport service. One end system acts in the initiator role and requests access to the file, the other acts in the responder role and provides access to the file in the virtual filestore.

ISO/IEC ISP 10607-4:1991: FTAM—Part 4—Positional File Transfer Service (Flat) (AFT 12)
Abstract: Specifies how OSI FTAM is used to transfer unstructured or flat files containing binary or character data between the filestores of two end systems by reading a complete file or by writing (replace, extend, or insert) to a file.

ISO/IEC ISP 10607-5:1991: FTAM—Part 5—Positional File Access Service (Flat) (AFT 22)
Abstract: Specifies how OSI FTAM provides access to unstructured or flat files containing binary or character data in order to read a File Access Data Unit (FADU) by node name, node number or position, to write (replace, extend, or insert) to a FADU, and to locate and erase within a file.

ISO/IEC ISP 10607-6:1991: FTAM—Part 6—File Management Service (AFT 3)
Abstract: Specifies how OSI FTAM is used to manage files between the filestores of two end systems, particularly to create or delete a file, and read and change the attributes of a file.

DOCUMENT TRANSFER

ISO/IEC ISP 8613-1:1994: Office Document Architecture (ODA) and Interchange Format—Part 1: Introduction and General Principles
Abstract: Facilitates interchange of office documents, such as reports, invoices, letters, and memoranda by means of data communications or the exchange of storage media. This part of 8613 gives an overview, presents the context, defines terms, describes interdependencies, gives rules for defining application profiles, and specifies conformance levels. (Equivalent to CCITT T.411)

ISO/IEC ISP 8613-4: Office Document Architecture (ODA) and Interchange Format—Part 4: Document Profile
Abstract: Defines the purpose and specifies the attributes that constitute the document profile. Contains an example of the document profile. (Equivalent to CCITT T.414)

ISO/IEC 8613-10 Draft Amendment (DAM) 1: Office Document Architecture (ODA) and Interchange Format—Part 10: Formal Specifications—Amendment 1: Formal Specification of the Document Profile
Abstract: Gives a formal specification of the document profile as described in ISO 8613 Part 4.

ISO/IEC ISP 11181-1:1993: Office Document Format—Enhanced Document Structure—Character, Raster Graphics and Geometric Graphics Content Architectures—Part 1: Document Application Profile (FOD 26)
Abstract: Specifies interchange formats for the transfer of structured documents between equipment designed for word or document processing of simple documents as well as highly structured technical reports, articles and typeset documents, such as brochures.

ITU-T Recommendation T.501:1993: A Document Application Profile MM for the Interchange of Formatted Mixed Mode Documents
Abstract: Specifies an interchange format for the interchange of mixed mode documents that contain characters and raster graphics. Documents are interchanged in a formatted form only, which enables the recipient to display or print the document as intended by the originator. Features that can be interchanged are: page format features; character content and raster-graphics layout and imaging features; character repertoire; and raster-graphics coding.

ITU-T Recommendation T.502:1991: Document Application Profile PM1 for the Interchange of Processable Form Documents
Abstract: Defines a document application profile referred to as PM1, which specifies interchange formats for the transfer of documents between word processors. The profile caters to the transfer of documents that contain characters only. Documents can be transferred in either processable form; formatted form; or formatted processable form.

Table F.1 ISO OSI Profiles (Continued)

ITU-T Recommendation T.505:1991: Document Application Profile PM-26 for the Interchange of Mixed Content Documents in Processable and Formatted Forms
Abstract: This Recommendation specifies interchange formats for the transfer of structured documents between equipment designed for word or document processing. Such documents may contain character, raster graphics, and geometric graphics content.

ECMA-101 VOLUME 1: Open Document Architecture (ODA) and Interchange Format—Volume 1—Part 1: Introduction and General Principles, Part 2: Document Structures, Part 3: Document Profile (Status: Final)
Abstract: Applies to documents interchanged via data communications or via the exchange of storage media. Describes the document architecture concepts and interdependencies of the parts; defines conformance; gives rules for defining document application profiles.

BULK DOCUMENT TRANSFER

CCITT Recommendation T.521:1992: Communication Application Profile for Document Bulk Transfer Based on the Session Service (According to the Rules Defined in T.62 bis)
Abstract: Defines the communication application profile for document bulk transfer using the session service defined in Recommendation T.62 bis in terms of: DTAM functional units used; DTAM service primitives and parameters used; lower layer X.215 session service mapping according to the rules of T.62 bis.

CCITT Recommendation T.522:1992: Communication Application Profile BT1 for Document Bulk Transfer
Abstract: Defines the communication-application profile for the document bulk transfer in terms of: DTAM functional units used; DTAM service primitives and parameters used.

GRAPHICS INTERCHANGE

ISO/IEC ISP 9636-1:1991: Computer Graphics—Interfacing Techniques for Dialogues with Graphical Devices (CGI)—Functional Specification—Part 1: Overview, Profiles, and Conformance
Abstract: This multipart standard describes sets of functions for control and data exchange over the interfaces between device-independent and device-dependent parts of a graphics system. Part 1 of this standard includes the graphics-standards reference model, and its relationship to other standards.

Table F.1 ISO OSI Profiles (Continued)

VIDEOTEX

CCITT Recommendation T.441:1988: Document Transfer & Manipulation (DTAM) Operational Structure

Abstract: Covers the needs of videotex interworking. It will be further developed as a set of rules for an interface between other T.400-based telematic services and an ODA document. Specifies how operational application profiles can be implemented.

ITU-T: Recommendation T.504:1993: Document Application Profile for Videotex Interworking

Abstract: Defines a document that conforms with the T.400 Recommendations and allows interworking between two videotex services using configuration 1 defined in Recommendations F.300 and T.564. The videotex documents are interchanged in formatted form, so the recipient can reproduce them as intended by the originator. This document application profile defines the features of the document structure that can be interchanged.

ITU-T: Recommendation T.523:1993: Communication Application Profile for Videotex Interworking.

Abstract: Defines a communication profile DM-1 for document unconfirmed manipulation to specify an interactive communication profile based on DTAM between videotex gateway systems. The ODA documents manipulated should be in formatted form.

ITU-T: Recommendation T.541:1993: Operational Application Profile for Videotex Interworking

Abstract: Defines an operational application profile that conforms with DTAM and allows operational structures to be interchanged for the purpose of international videotex interworking. Defines the features of the operational structure that can be interchanged.

GOSIP NETWORKING

NIST FIPS 146-1: Government Open Systems Interconnection Profile (GOSIP)

Abstract: This profile is the standard reference for all federal government agencies to use when acquiring and operating ADP systems or services, and communication systems or services, intended to conform to ISO Open Systems Interconnection (OSI) protocols. GOSIP addresses communication and interoperation among end systems and intermediate systems. It provides specific peer-level, process-to-process and terminal access functionality between computer system users within and across government agencies.

OSI NETWORK MANAGEMENT

ISO/IEC ISP 11183-1:1992: International Standardized Profiles AOMnn OSI Management—Management Communication Protocols—Part 1: Specification of ACSE, Presentation and Session Protocols for the Use by ROSE and CMISE

Abstract: Specifies how the Association Control Service Element, the Presentation Layer, and the Session Layer standards are used to provide the required upper-layer functions for the CMISE/ROSE functions.

ISO/IEC ISP 11183-2:1992: International Standardized Profiles AOMnn OSI Management—Management Communication Protocols—Part 2: AOM12—Enhanced Management Communications

Abstract: Specifies how the OSI Common Management Information Service Element (CMISE) combined with the OSI Remote Operations Service Element (ROSE) is used to provide the complete set of operation and notification services to the CMISE-service users of two end systems acting in both Manager and Agent roles. Defines the support level of all the OSI management communication features needed by Manager/Agent implementations. Specifies the (sub)sets of operations and notifications required by the different roles.

ISO/IEC ISP 11183-3:1992: International Standardized Profiles AOMnn OSI Management—Management Communication Protocols—Part 3: AOM11—Basic Management Communications

Abstract: Specifies how the OSI Common Management Information Service (CMISE) combined with the OSI Remote Operation Service Element (ROSE) is used to provide a basic subset of operation and notification services to the CMISE-service users of two systems acting in both Manager and Agent roles. Defines the support level of the OSI management features needed by Manager/Agent implementations for providing the kernel functional unit only. Specifies the (sub)set of operations and notifications required for each role.

ISO/IEC DISP 12060-3: Management Capabilities—Alarm Reporting Capabilities: AOM213

CONFORMANCE TESTING

ISO 9646-2 DAM 1: Information Technology—Open Systems Interconnection—Conformance Testing Methodology and Framework—Part 2: Abstract Test Suite Specification—Proposed Draft Amendment 1: Protocol Profile Testing Methodology

Abstract: This amendment expands ISO/IEC 9646-2 to include conformance to functional profiles.

ISO/IEC 9646-6:1994: Open Systems Interconnection—Conformance Testing Methodology and Framework—Part 6: Protocol Profile Test Specification

Abstract: Specifies the requirements and provides guidance for the production of Profile Test Specifications for conformance testing of functional profiles based on OSI protocols.

files. One is common usage, relevant to all systems using directory data. The other type is usage is specific usage relevant to particular application profiles. The first two directory-data profiles will cover Message-Handling Systems' (MHS) use of the directory and FTAM's use of the directory. The Directory-Access profiles specify services and protocols for accessing centralized as well as distributed directories. These profiles address the directory-user agent and the directory system agent in their support of distributed operations, for both the responder and initiator role.

ISO also is standardizing a number of Virtual-Terminal profiles that were originally defined as part of the GOSIP profile. The Virtual-Terminal profiles include profiles for scroll class, forms class, page class, enhanced forms class, enhanced page class, Telnet virtual terminals, and Basic Class VT virtual terminals. Among other things, the ISO profiles will define a number of types of information objects used by Virtual-Terminal application profiles, which are subject to registration.

Still another group of profiles targets industrial-plant–floor networking. These profiles are based on ISO/IEC 9506 Manufacturing Message Specification (MMS) for interworking computers and programmable devices in a manufacturing environment. MMS profiles defined include profiles for general applications, robot-controller applications, numerical-controller applications, programmable-logic–controller applications, process industries applications, and production-management applications.

Other ISO profiles include profiles for lower-level and application-level networking. Low-level networking include a number of relay profiles. Application-level networking profiles include profiles for remote database access, SGML (Standardized General Markup Language) data-interchange format, character sets, and distributed-transaction processing. The distributed-transaction–processing profiles are based on the ISO Distributed Transaction Processing standard (DTP) (IS 10026-1, -2, and -3). They cover polarized control and shared control for application-supported transactions, and provider-supported unchained and chained transactions.

Profiles as Building Blocks

The use of profiles as building blocks for other profiles is illustrated in Figure F.2. The example is taken from ISO/IEC TR 10000-1 Version 2 (TR 10000-1.2).

Figure F.3 shows a multipart profile, 999, which is used in defining Profiles X, Y, and Z. Profiles X, Y, and Z refer to the base standards p and q in exactly the same way, but in combination with different base standards (approved ISO standards or CCITT recommendations).

ISP 999-1 refers to base standards p and q, and contain contains text which is common to the definition of profiles X, Y, and Z. ISP 999-2 refers to base standards r and s, and contains text which is common to profiles X and Y. ISP 999-3 refers to base standard t, which is used in profile Z, as well as in other profiles not described here, such as ISP 888-9.

The documentation for profiles 999-1, 999-2, and 999-3 is short and understandable by open-systems planners and management because it needs not contain all the

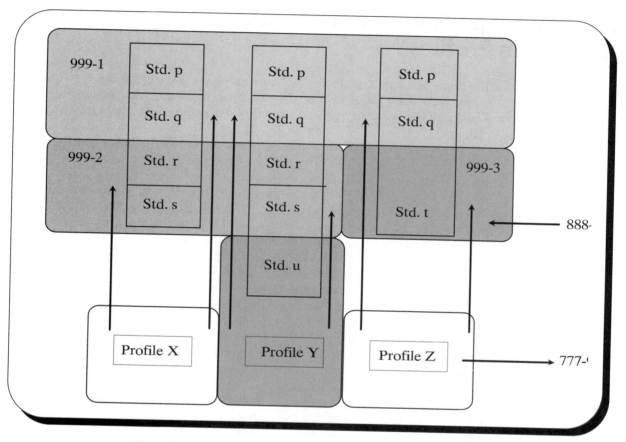

Figure F.2 Using profiles as building blocks for other profiles. *Source: ISO/IEC TR 10000-1.2.*

interface details. These details are contained in standards p, q, r, s, and t. The profiles may, however, contain some extra values and options relevant to their intended use.

Other profiles can now be built that use ISP 999-1, -2, and -3. For example, profile X is defined by referring to ISP 999-1 and 999-2.

Profile Y is defined by referring to ISP 999-1, ISP 999-2, with additional references to base standard u, which is specific to the domain of profile Y.

Profile Z is defined by referring to ISP 999-1, ISP 999-3, and ISP 777-9 (which is a part of still another profile not described in this example).

The documentation for profiles X, Y, and Z is brief and readable because it does not contain interface-specification details. Such details are contained in the referenced standards. Only the details that make the profiles X, Y, and Z different from the referenced standards and profiles need be included in the profile.

IEEE PASC Application Environment & Platform Profiles

The single-interface–type Profiles shown until now consist of standards and options in one particular type of interface area and functional area (i.e., communications). These profiles, however, can apply to every market segment, application area, and platform.

To help users and vendors understand, communicate, and acquire what is necessary for a comprehensive open systems environment that applies to specific application areas and platform types standards groups are developing an Open Systems Environment (OSE) profiles for specific application domains or platform types. Called *application environment profiles* (AEP) and *platform profiles,* these classes of profiles differ from single-interface–type profiles in that they specify standards and profiles in multiple, diverse functional and interface areas. An OSE profile for an application domain or platform contains the comprehensive set of interfaces, services, supporting formats, and user style guides to achieve interoperability, portability, scalability, and consistent user interfaces.

A comprehensive AEP for a particular application domain or platform type may specify services for application areas ranging from text processing, database retrieval, and electronic mail to distributed-transaction processing. The profiles might take into account an enterprise-wide distributed-computing system, including a backbone network, LAN subnetworks, and platforms ranging from PCs and technical workstations to multiprocessing servers.

The IEEE PASC groups pioneered the development of application environment profiles. IEEE PASC has defined two application-oriented profiles for supercomputing and four types of real-time applications, as well as two platform profiles for multiprocessing machines and traditional multiuser UNIX machines. These profiles are intended to give users, vendors, system integrators, program managers, and other profile developers a head start in understanding what is necessary for a variety of comprehensive OSE profiles that might apply to them.

The IEEE PASC profiles completed or in progress at the time of this publication are:

- P1003.10 Supercomputing Application Environment Profile
- P1003.13 Real-Time Application Environment Profiles (actually four different profiles for different types of real-time applications)
- P1003.14 Multiprocessing Platform Profile
- P1003.18 POSIX Interactive Multiuser Platform Profile

The P1003.10 and P1003.13 profiles are examples of application environment profiles. The P1003.14 and P1003.18 profiles are examples of platform profiles.

The IEEE application environment profiles and platform profiles are discussed here to provide organizations with an idea of what should be contained in a profile for these application and platform areas. Furthermore, much of the information specified by the IEEE profile groups is transferable to other application areas and platforms.

The IEEE Supercomputing Profile*

The IEEE P1003.10-1995 Supercomputing AEP is a profile designed to support application and programmer portability in POSIX-based supercomputer environments. This profile is needed because of the differences between supercomputing environments and traditional computing environments. In particular, supercomputing jobs are computationally intensive, very long running, and very demanding of resources. In addition, the cost of the supercomputer CPU and many of its peripheral resources is very high. Therefore, supercomputers need special standard capabilities.

POSIX-based standards alone are not sufficient for supercomputer environments because the historically derived functions in P1003.1 (ISO/IEC 9945-1) cannot adequately manage the use of, and accounting for, a supercomputer or its resources. Furthermore, supercomputers need better tape handling, multiprocessing, and other capabilities than POSIX, or even traditional time-sharing UNIX, initially supported.

The supercomputing profile reflects the portability, interoperability, and specialized needs of supercomputing users. Among other things, the supercomputing profile identifies the POSIX-based standards and other relevant standards that support supercomputing requirements. Where none exist, the supercomputing group defines the functionality itself, or instigates the formation of a new group to define it. The profile also identifies certain other specifications and/or functionality that are required for its application domain, regardless of whether these functions are approved formal standards. Since some of these nonstandard functions will be specific to an organization's targeted environment, the POSIX.10 Group specifies standardized configuration variables to indicate the organization-specific functionalities.

What's in the Supercomputing Profile?

The POSIX.10 supercomputing profile requires the following standards:

- C language
- FORTRAN-77 language
- P1003.9 FORTRAN-77 bindings
- POSIX.1 system API
- POSIX.2 shell and utilities
- The asynchronous I/O option from the POSIX.1b (formerly POSIX.4) real-time extension
- POSIX.15 batch extensions to the shell and utilities

*Much of the summaries and discussions of the POSIX Profiles shown in the rest of this appendix have been contributed to the IEEE P1003.0 Group for use in that group's document *A Guide to a POSIX Open Systems Environment*.

The POSIX.10 Supercomputing Profile also provides the following options:

- Ada language, and the POSIX.5 Ada language bindings
- Fortran-90 language
- P1224.2 directory services API (language-independent version)
- ISO labeled tapes as removable media

Besides the specifications, the supercomputing profile specifies a variety of P1003.1 and P1003.2 options, and indicates how to specify various types of configuration variables and optional functionality. Examples of these specifications are:

- More than one dozen base standard option indicators (to indicate various options used in the base standards, such as {_POSIX_JOB_CONTROL} {POSIX_NO_TRUNC});
- A number of configuration variables, to indicate particular supercomputing profile-specified options used in a specific system. Examples are {POSIX_SUPER_ADA} to indicate the use of the optional language Ada, and {POSIX_SUPER_ISO1001} to indicate the use of ISO Labeled Tapes.

The first version of the supercomputing profile does not include any graphics or data-storage standards. System-administration standards are not included either because these standards are just beginning to emerge, and there are very few implementations that could conform.

The only networking standards included in the profile are those emerging from the IEEE POSIX working groups. Unfortunately, some POSIX standards in progress, like P1003.1f (formerly P1003.8) for distributed transparent file access could not be included in the profile because P1003.1f was not completed in time for the profile.

Another problem in specifying networking protocols is that current supercomputing systems use mostly TCP/IP. Because the P1003.10 supercomputing AEP is a standardized profile, it can only include formal standards in the profile. Since TCP/IP is only a *de facto* standard, it, therefore, could not be included.

The language-independent version of the directory services API was specified because of different supercomputing users' requirements for diverse programming languages (e.g., C, FORTRAN-77, Fortran-90, and Ada). Hence, the group's consensus was to specify the language-independent API, and allow C-language users to require the C-language version.

The P1003.15 batch extensions is an IEEE PASC standard, whose development was instigated and coordinated by the P1003.10 Supercomputing Group to satisfy its specialized supercomputing requirements. For example, supercomputers have especially massive resource requirements, such as many hours or weeks of CPU time, gigabytes of disk storage, all the machine's memory, and expensive peripherals. UNIX's batch capabilities, such as at and cron, are inadequate for managing resources and scheduling jobs in supercomputer environments. Supercomputers do not run jobs in response to users or administrators instructing the machine to run a particular job as some particular time. Instead, a much more sophisticated batch-processing system is needed to optimally allocate and manage system resources among dozens of jobs and ensure that each job has the necessary resources and executes efficiently.

When the P1003.10 group began its work, no such scheduling standard existed. The group identified batch scheduling as a standards gap. It instigated the formation of a standards group (P1003.15) to define a batch scheduling standard. The members of the P1003.15 Group were primarily also Supercomputing Group members.

Besides the batch-scheduling standard, the POSIX.10 Group proposed a number of extensions to the POSIX.1 standard. These extensions include checkpoint/recovery (the capability of a user process or job to automatically checkpoint itself periodically and to restart at the latest checkpoint following a machine crash or shutdown) and resource limits extensions (to allow better management of resource limits). These extensions will become part of the next revision of P1003.1, as well as of the supercomputing profile's next revision.

The IEEE Multiprocessing Profile

The POSIX Multiprocessing Systems Profile (IEEE 1003.14) is a platform profile. It defines the functionality, standards, and options within standards that are needed for development and execution on a multiprocessing platform.

The multiprocessing systems profile is intended for use by multiprocessor vendors, application developers, users, and system administrators. It is designed to support portability of multiprocessing applications, as well as users and system administrators in multiprocessing environments.

The Multiprocessing Systems profile has two major goals. The first one is to make POSIX reliable for multiprocessing. This goal requires the 1003.14 group to identify and address the caveats, problems, and failings of POSIX for multiprocessing platforms. Examples of these failings range from reentrant function problems to potential problems with threads.

The second goal is to make POSIX useful for multiprocessing. This goal requires the P1003.14 Group to ensure that POSIX supports the functionality needed by multiprocessing platforms. Examples of such functionality include capabilities that allow vendors to implement software functions that can be executed in parallel. In the absence of parallelizing standards, the details of what happens when the same software functions are used on different multiprocessor systems currently may vary.

What's in the Multiprocessing Systems Profile?

The Multiprocessing Systems platform profile identifies standards, options, and gaps in the standards relevant to multiprocessing. It also identifies additional requirements not satisfied by existing standards and, in an informative annex, suggests interfaces to extended services that can satisfy some of these requirements. In addition, the POSIX.14 Multiprocessing Systems Group will propose changes and addenda to a variety of relevant standards in order to encourage the specifiers of these standards to add functions and options that accommodate multiprocessing requirements.

Standards particularly relevant to the Multiprocessing Systems profile include the POSIX Pthreads extension (IEEE 1003.1c), the supercomputing batch-scheduling standard (IEEE 1003.2d), and the supercomputing checkpoint and restart facilities proposed as extensions to ISO/IEC 9945-1 (POSIX.1).

The multiprocessing systems profile will specify both general-purpose and multiprocessor-specific standards. General-purpose standards planned or under consideration for the multiprocessing systems profile include:

- The IEEE P1003.18 POSIX interactive systems profile, which includes ISO/IEC 9945-1 (the POSIX.1 core POSIX system), and ISO 9945-2 (POSIX.2 Shell and Utilities)
- The IEEE 1003.1b POSIX real-time extension
- The IEEE 1003.1c: POSIX Pthreads extension
- The IEEE 1003.1e POSIX security standard
- The IEEE 1387 system-administration standard
- The IEEE P1003.5 ADA language bindings to POSIX
- The IEEE P1003.9 FORTRAN-77 language bindings to POSIX
- The IEEE 1003.10 Supercomputing Profile; and 1003.13 real-time applications profiles, when multiprocessing is applicable to these environments

As other relevant standards emerge, they will be incorporated in the Multiprocessing Systems profile. An annex to the profile will list relevant emerging standards to provide an idea of the multiprocessing systems profile's direction.

Multiprocessing-specific requirements identified by the 1003.14 Multiprocessing Group include:

- System-administration tools for multiprocessors
- Parallelizing compilers
- Explicit parallelism
- Threads
- Thread-safe libraries
- Message-passing IPC
- Parallel utilities (e.g. find, grep, make, etc.)
- Scheduler controls
- Processor allocation: mandatory/advisory
- Processor binding
- Degree of symmetry: I/O, computation, memory

Standards are needed for many of these requirements. Many of these requirements will, therefore, become the subject of a 1003.14 Group proposal for a new standardized function or an option in other standards.

POSIX Interactive Multiuser System Profile

The POSIX Interactive Multiuser Systems Profile (IEEE 1003.18) is a platform profile based on POSIX.1 (ISO/IEC 9945-1) and related standards. It defines the functionality and standards needed for a system that is as similar as possible to the traditional UNIX operating system's development and run-time environment.

The POSIX Interactive Systems profile is valuable for users, vendors, programmers, and program managers who have neither the time nor desire to analyze and specify all the individual interfaces for a system. This profile obviates the need for this analysis by enabling users and vendors to point to a single document that specifies exactly what they should order to obtain a system that looks like traditional UNIX systems (except that the POSIX Interactive Systems Profile will be totally based on formal standards).

What's in the POSIX Interactive Systems Profile?

The POSIX Platform Environment Profile consists of:

- ISO/IEC 9945-1 (P1003.1), with select options and parameter definitions
- All of ISO/IEC 9945-2 (IEEE P1003.2 Shell and Utilities) and the User Portability Utilities Option
- At least one of the following languages: ANSI C, ISO Ada, or ISO Fortran
- The language bindings to the POSIX services for the selected languages

To reflect the goals and intent of the 1003.18 Group, the POSIX platform profile document also commits to including future specifications when those specifications are completed and approved as standards. Such specifications include system administration, secure/trusted systems extensions, real-time facilities, verification testing facilities, graphical-user interfaces, and network-interface facilities.

Real-Time Profiles

The IEEE P1003.13 Group is defining profiles to address four types of real-time applications. These are:

- Minimal (Embedded) Real-Time System Profile (often known as *hard* real-time systems)
- Real-time Controller System Profile (also hard real-time systems)
- Dedicated Real-Time System Profile (with medium-level critical real-time constraints)
- Multipurpose (high-end) Real-Time System Profile

These profiles are mostly based on the IEEE P1003.1b real-time extensions to POSIX and the ISO/IEC 9945-1 (POSIX.1) operating-system kernel profile.

Minimal Embedded Real-Time Profiles

Embedded real-time systems, often known as *hard* real-time systems, are dedicated to the unattended control of one or more special I/O devices. They are embedded in standalone systems or buried deeply in the overall system electronics, and are typically used for robot controllers, instrumentation, high-speed data acquisition, satellite subsystem control, and flight control.

Time-critical responsiveness is a key requirement of embedded systems. In the absence of a standard, the real-time functionality required for embedded systems, and many controller systems, is generally provided by a proprietary real-time kernel or a simple home-grown monitor using memory-mapped I/O.

Embedded systems and real-time controller systems tend to need only minimal operating-system functionality. They have no requirements for a file system, multiple processes, user interaction, or I/O via specific device drivers. Including such features in an embedded real-time system could compromise its ability to satisfy its real-time requirements or to physically fit into the embedded system.

Since embedded systems need only minimal functionality, the P1003.13 embedded-systems profile subgroup identifies a relatively small number of P1003.1b (POSIX Real-Time) and ISO/IEC 9945-1 (POSIX.1) functions that are required for portable real-time embedded applications. Among other functions, the minimal embedded real-time profile specifies the P1003.1b binary semaphores, real-time signals, timers, and synchronized I/O for real-time responsiveness and synchronization; the P1003.1b Interprocess communication (IPC) interfaces for communications with like systems, and the P1003.1c threads extension to support multiple flows of control.

The minimum hardware required is a single processor with its memory. No memory management unit (MMU) or common I/O devices are required.

Although subsets of base standards were not allowed in the past, the IEEE has set up a process to allow the P1003.13 (and other profile groups) to develop profiles which contain subgroupings of the current POSIX.1 standard. The process will require profile groups whose requirements call for a POSIX.1 subset (e.g., the POSIX.13 Embedded Systems subgroup) to develop an authorized, special-purpose POSIX.1 subset. Although the profile group will develop the actual subset needed for the profile in question, the POSIX subset developers will coordinate their work with the IEEE P1003.1 Working Group.

Embedded real-time profile users (and other users and vendors using or providing a POSIX.1 subset) will not be allowed to claim conformance to the ISO/IEC 9945-1 (POSIX.1) standard. Instead, they will claim conformance to the POSIX.13 embedded real-time profile, or to a specific 9945-1 subset. This process is intended to prevent abuses, whereby vendors who offer a minimum of standardized functions could claim they comply with the POSIX.1 standard.

One of the mandatory POSIX.1 features that the Embedded-Systems Group wants to remove from its profile is the requirement for a file system. Another example of a POSIX.1 function that the POSIX.13 Group wants to eliminate from the POSIX.13 embedded systems profile is the fork system call. The *fork system call* is traditional in UNIX. It was a wonderful innovation for time-sharing systems in an era where system memory was very expensive, and systems had minimal memory. The fork allowed an operating system to have only a small number of essential processes present at any one time. Whenever a new process was needed, the parent process would fork (makes a copy of itself). The copy of the process (called a *child* process) would then be overlaid with the code for the new process invoked.

This fork procedure saves memory, because all processes are not required to be present in a system in advance. Such memory saving was important to a general-purpose time-sharing system because it was not known what users would do when they logged onto the system.

The fork system call, however, is time consuming because it requires a good deal of system overhead that cannot be interrupted. If used in a critical real-time application, the overhead required has the potential to cause the application to overrun its response time and possibly miss some critical event.

Real-Time Controller Systems

Real-time controller systems are another example of embedded real-time systems with time-critical response constraints. They are typically used in control systems, for example, in automated systems controllers and process control, and for some testing.

Real-time controller systems are similar to minimal embedded real-time systems. They differ in that they require a file system, character-by-character serial I/O interfaces, asynchronous (nonblocking) I/O interfaces, and POSIX.1 signals. Like minimal real-time systems, real-time controller systems require threads, but not multiple processes.

The minimum hardware required for minimal embedded real-time systems is a single processor with its memory, no memory management unit (MMU), and one or more RS-232-like serial channels (for downloading and debugging). Mass storage devices are not required; the file systems may, for example, be implemented in memory (RAM disk).

Dedicated Midrange Real-Time Profiles

Dedicated real-time profiles are designed for midrange real-time systems. Midrange real-time profiles are targeted at real-time computer-oriented applications that are typically used in avionics, radar systems, submarines, and medical-imaging equipment, as well as in controllers that control a group of robots or a subsystem on the factory floor. These applications tend to run on platforms that are dedicated to a single application set or mission mode.

The design complexity of such dedicated real-time applications varies from simple to complex to accommodate a range of requirements. Such requirements may include sophisticated signal-processing capabilities, but not necessarily a file system. A profile that satisfies these requirements would likely specify most of the IEEE POSIX.1b real-time functionality and ISO/IEC 9945-1 (POSIX.1) (except for hierarchical file-system facilities), along with relevant options from the P1003.1b and ISO/IEC 9945-1 standards and the P1003.1c threads extension. Since memory-management hardware may be provided, the functionality of memory locking is provided. There also is a common interface for device drivers and files (even though there is no file system).

The hardware model for the dedicated (midrange) system profile assumes one or more processors with or without MMUs in the same system.

High-End Real-Time Profiles

Multipurpose real-time profiles are applicable to complex high-end real-time systems. Such high-end, multipurpose, real-time systems are typically used in military command and control, space-station control systems, and systems that control robot or factory subsystems. Such real-time systems also are used as the operating system for high-end simulation systems, and in high-functionality real-time applications that are paced by operator interaction.

The current real-time multipurpose profile is geared to fully functional real-time systems, such as simulation applications, and embodies most of the existing real-time practice in the simulator world. Since high-end multipurpose systems have a greater design complexity than embedded or midrange systems, need much greater functionality, and generally support a mix of real-time and non-real–time processes, the high-end multipurpose real-time profile will require all of the P1003.1b and ISO/IEC 9945-1 standards. In addition, IEEE P1003.1c threads support is required so that multitasking may be done by threads, processes, or both.

Since high-end real-time applications may support interactive sessions with users, the high-end real-time profile supports two types of interactive user interface. ISO/IEC 9945-2 (POSIX.2 Shell and Utilities, including the User Portability Utilities Option) is specified as a command interface. In addition, the X-11 Window system is specified as the basis for a visual human-computer interface. Support for additional functionality is provided through options for networking and programming languages. This profile, however, does not require threads because multitasking may be done by processes.

The hardware model for this profile assumes processors with memory-management units, high-speed storage devices, special interfaces, network support, and display devices.

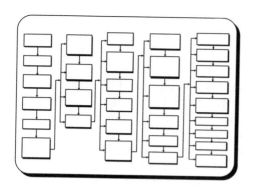

About the Software

What's on the CD-ROM?

The DOSEE Client/Server planning tool is used to plan the infrastructure for an open Client/Server environment. It incorporates the open Client/Server planning methodology described in the book "Distributed Open Systems Engineering: How to Plan and Develop Client/Server Systems." The tool contains much of the Client/Server planning database, and many of the methodology's templates, forms, and screens used to evolve the database.

The DOSEE planning software also contains a subset of the data in a DOSEE Client/Server planning database generated by one company for its office automation environment. You can modify or add to this database to reflect your own organization's Client/Server and open system needs and, thereby, use the software to help plan your own open Client/Server environment.

The software tool provides a way to organize planning and organization information concerning open Client/Server systems, as well as instant access to the information. With this DOSEE Client/Server planning tool, you can view, navigate, further evolve, print, and present any Client/Server planning information for your organization, provided, of course, that your Client/Server planning database is up to date. The tool will also automatically generate a list of formal and *de facto* standards information applicable to your organization's needs, and information concerning the practicality of those standards (e.g., standards deficiencies, portability and interoperability caveats).

Note that the software tool contained on this disk is a demonstration system—not a full system. The software does not contain all of the DOSEE methodology's templates, forms, screens, and database tables. The surveys used as part of the DOSEE methodology are not included in the software. The software does not contain all of the open systems services, standards, and standards practicality information. Although you can modify the Client/Server planning data, you may not modify the software.

The DOSEE Client/Server planning tool included with this book is part of an overall Client/Server planning methodology that includes business-level planning, applications planning, architectural tasks, infrastructure tasks, standards selection tasks, implementation planning tasks, planning for migration and deployment, and system maintenance based on feedback. The full DOSEE software also integrates business and application planning steps, and interactive surveys of user requirements and users' degree of infrastructure and standards acceptance.

The tool's software is based primarily on open systems and Client/Server planning work that the author and her company has done with its clients. Further information about the methodology is available from the author at Emerging Technologies Group, (516) 586-8810, or from wrauch@etg.com.

System Requirements

The DOSEE Client/Server planning software requires an 80386 or higher microprocessor, and 8 Mbytes of RAM, a hard disk with at least 13.5 Mbytes of free disk space to install the software and 8.5 Mbytes to run the system after it is installed. Also Microsoft Windows Version 3.1 or later and a mouse are required to run the DOSEE software. Further system requirements information and instructions is available in the DOSEE software's README file.

Installing the DOSEE Client/Server Planning Software

To install the DOSEE Client/Server Planning software tool on your hard drive, follow the instructions below.

1. Place the CD-ROM in your CD-ROM drive.
2. Go to the Program Manager in Windows.
3. Choose File | Run from the File menu of the Windows Program Manager.
4. In the command line, type in **<*drive*>:INSTALL\INSTALL**, where **<drive>** is the drive letter of your CD-ROM drive.
5. Click on OK to start the install process.
6. Follow the on-screen instructions in the installation program. By default, the files will be installed on your C drive in C:\DOSEE, C:\PFWRUN5, and c:\IDAPI unless you specify a different drive during the installation process.
7. When the install program asks for Disk 2 (to install your custom application), click on "Continue" or press "Enter."
8. Choose "Yes" to install a Program Group and the Program Icons to automatically start the DOSEE Client/Server planning software tool from an icon.

To install and run the DOSEE software tool under Windows '95, you must install and run it under Program Manager. To install and run it under OS/2, you must prepare a WIN-OS/2 Virtual DOS Machine (VDM). Further instructions for Windows '95 and OS/2 installation are found in the README file.

Using the Software

After all the installation steps are complete, double-click the DOSEE Open Client/Server Planning icon to start the DOSEE Open Client/Server Planning Tool. Double-clicking the DOSEE icon brings up a main menu of the Client/Server planning steps implemented in the software.

The DOSEE Software main menu selections are as follows:

- **Identify Applications:** List applications in your environment.
- **Identify Interoperations:** Identify interoperability among applications (in order to determine the targeted areas for interoperability).
- **Identify Attributes and Attribute Values:** Characterize the applications using predefined sets of attributes and attribute values (because these attributes and attribute values will be used to determine functional service requirements for which standards might be needed).
- **Identify New Attributes and Attribute Values:** Define your own attributes and attribute values if the predefined ones are insufficient or inadequate.
- **Determine Services:** Determine the service requirements that are applicable to your applications, interoperations, attributes, and attribute values.
- **View Applicable Standards:** View the formal, consortia, industry, and *de facto* standards and standards practicality information that the DOSEE software determined are applicable to your service requirements.

Press the Main Menu button for each task to initiate each task and to display the forms for each task. Most forms display the data initially in view mode. Press the Edit or Add/Edit button on the form to switch the form to the edit mode to add or change data. Scrollbars, push buttons, and icons, located at the top of each form, allow the user to navigate through the records and values in the table and the pages on the screen.

A Help button on each form provides an overview of each step in the planning process, and directions for using the software to perform that task. The Return to Main Menu button is used to return to the Main menu to save the session for the day or to continue to the next planning step.

User Assistance and Information

The software accompanying this book is being provided as-is without warranty or support of any kind. Should you require basic installation assistance, or if your media is defective, please call our product support number at (212) 850-6194 weekdays between 9 am and 4 pm Eastern Standard Time. Or, we can be reached via e-mail at: wprtusw@wiley.com.

To place additional orders or to request information about other Wiley products, please call (800) 879-4539.

For Further Reference

Chapter 1: Introduction

Adhikari, Richard, "Bringing Methodology to Client/Server Madness," *Software Magazine*, March 1995, pp. 35–46.

Atre, Shaku, "Twelve Steps to Successful Client/Server," *DBMS*, May 1994, pp. 70–76.

————, "Client/Server Culture Shock," *DBMS*, May 1995, pp. 87–91.

Azzara, Mike, "Let's Zero in on What 'Open' Really Means," *Open Systems Today*, September 26, 1994, p. 20.

Bruno, Lee, "A Prescription for Open Systems," *Open Systems Today*, November 23, 1992, p. 46.

Francis, Bob, "Client/Server: The Model for the '90s," *Datamation*, February 15, 1990, pp. 34–40.

Gantz, John, "Are Open Networks a Myth?" *Network Management*, May 1992, pp. 16–28.

Lewis, Ted G., "Where is Client/Server Software Headed?" *Computer*, April 1995, pp. 49–55.

Lytton, Nina, "Open Systems: More Than a Utopian Concept," *Open Systems Advisor*, Vol. III No. 12, May 15, 1992, pp. 1–10.

Moskowitz, Robert, "Overview: What Are Clients and Servers Anyway?" Client/Server Computing Supplement to *Network Computing*, May 1, 1993, pp. 10–12.

Rauch, Wendy, "Three Sides to the Story," *UNIX World*, March 1988, pp. 17–18.

————, "What's Ahead for the Computing World?" *UNIX Today*, August 6, 1990, pp. 68–69.

Scott, Karyl, "Groupware Must be Open at Its Core," *Open Systems Today*, October 10, 1994, pp. 1–63.

Shimberg, David, "Following a Client/Server Database Methodology," *DBMS*, May 1995, pp. 48–71.

Smith, William M., "A Client/Server Approach to Enterprise Information Access," *Data Management Review*, March 1995, pp. 48–56.

Willson, Jane R., "Strategies for Streamlining In-House Development," *Uniforum Monthly*, September 1994, pp. 32–36.

Winkler, Connie, "Driving a Successful Implementation," Client/Server '94, Supplement to *Information Week*, pp. 12–21.

Chapter 2: Phase One: Business-Oriented Tasks

Abels, David and Marie Lopinto, "Planning a Client/Server Strategy," *Beyond Computing*, May/June 1994, pp. 45–46.

Bartlett, Jeffrey, "Home Depot Builds on Big Box Boom," *Uniforum Monthly*, August 1994, pp. 30–34.

———, "Making Open Systems Make Business Sense," *Uniforum Monthly*, September 1994, pp. 26–30.

Bechtell, Michele L., *The Management Compass: Steering the Corporation Using Hoshin Planning*, New York: American Management Association, 1995.

Bloor, Robin, "Tactics for Downsizing," *DBMS*, December 1992, p. 14.

Brady, Sheila and Tom DeMarco, "Management-Aided Software Engineering," *IEEE Software*, November 1994, pp. 25–32.

Burden, Kevin, "The Client/Server Shuffle," *Computerworld*, September 26, 1994, pp. 97–98.

Connor, William D., "The Right Way to Rightsize," *UNIX Review*, May 1993, pp. 45–56.

Datamation Advertising Insert Articles, "Critical Success Factors in Downsizing," October 15, 1993, pp. S2–S16.

Detweiler, Richard A., "Make Your Plans Happen," *Information Week*, June 6, 1994, p. 108.

Elzey, Penny, "10 Easy Ways to Fail Miserably at Developing Client/Server Applications," Client/ Server '94 Supplement to *Information Week*, pp. 16–17.

Faden, Mike, "Move to Client-Server Paying Off for Insurer," *Open Systems Today*, April 12, 1993, pp. 72–74.

Garfinkel, Simson L., "Minding the Store," *RS/Magazine*, September 1994, pp. 39–46.

Gill, Philip J., "Insurers Discover Benefits of Unix," *UNIX Today*, September 2, 1991, p.42.

Gill, Philip J., "The Challenge of Managing Change," *Uniforum Monthly*, August 1994, pp. 26–29.

Industry Forum, "The New Corporate Posture: Managing Horizontally," *American Management Association*, May 1995, pp. 1–4.

Information Management Forum, "The Relation Between IS and Business Intelligence," *American Management Association*, April 1993, pp. 1–4.

———, "Information Technology and Organizational Change: What's Ahead," *American Management Association*, NY, July 1994, pp 1–3.

———, "Managing Resistance to External Technologym," *American Management Association*, October 1994, pp. 1–4.

———, "Trade-Offs with New Technologies," *American Management Association*, January 1995, pp 1–3.

Inmon, W.H., *Developing Client/Server Applications in an Architected Environment*, Boston: QED Technical Publishing Group, 1991.

LaPlante, Alice, "K-Mart's Client/Server Special," *DBMS*, December 1992, pp. 56–58.

Marshall, Edward M., "The Collaborative Workplace," *Management Review*, June 1995, pp. 13–17.

McGoveran, David and Collin J. White, "Clarifying Client-Server," *DBMS*, November 1990, pp. 78–90.

Monteleone, Frank, "Building by Consensus," *Information Week*, August 15, 1994, p. 70.

Morse, Stephen, "Tailoring the Applications and the Platforms," *Network Computing*, February 1993, pp. 63–78.

Rauch, Wendy, "What's SOS Mean?" *UNIX Today*, January 23, 1989, pp. 19–29.

Ricciuti, Mike, "The Best in Client/Server Computing," *Datamation*, March 1, 1994, pp. 26–33.

Richman, Dan, "Fidelity Investments Take Cross-Platform Plunge," *Open Systems Today*, August 1, 1994, pp. 62–63.

Russell, David Lee, "Hard-Learned Lessons," *Information Week*, September 26, 1994, p. 72.

Sashkin, Marshall and Molly G. Sashkin, *The New Teamwork: Developing and Using Cross-Function Teams*, New York: American Management Association, 1994.

Semich, J. William, "Where do C/S Apps go Wrong?" *Datamation*, January 21, 1994, pp. 30–36.

———, "Information Replaces Inventory at the Virtual Corp.," *Datamation*, July 15, 1994, pp. 37–42.

Sharp, Bill, "Where to Find Expert Help For Downsizing," *Datamation*, September 1, 1992, pp. 61–64.

Sinneck, Michael J., "It's All in the Implementation," *Information Week*, December 12, 1994, p. 87.

Thomas, George, "PC Networks? Not So Fast," *Information Week*, June 28, 1993, p. 112.

Wang, Charles B., *Techno Vision: The Executive's Survival Guide to Understanding and Managing Information Technology*, New York: R.R. Donnelley & Sons Company, 1994.

Wyatt, John, "Applying the Right Principles," *Information Week*, October 24, 1994, p. 84.

Chapter 3: Phase Two: Application Experts Tasks

Adler, Richard M., "Distributed Coordination Models for Client/Server Computing," *Computer*, April 1995, pp. 14–22.

Altman, Ross, "Client/Server OLTP," *Faulkner Technical Reports, Inc.*, August 1994, pp. 1–12.

Bartlett, Jeffrey, "Wired for Change," *Uniforum Monthly*, February 1995, pp. 26–31.

Baum, David, "Three Tiers For Client-Server," *Information Week*, May 29, 1995, pp. 42–52.

Beever, Stephen, "Mainframe-to-Unix Connectivity," *Advanced Systems*, March 1994, pp. 71–90.

Bennett, Keith, "Legacy Systems: Coping With Success," *IEEE Software*, January 1995, pp. 19–23.

Bower, Barry D., "Global, Mobile and Secure: Lessons from the Open Systems Front," *Uniforum Monthly*, January 1994, pp. 14–19.

Boyle, Brian, "Unix Takes on the OLTP Challenge," *UNIX Today*, September 16, 1991, pp. 43–50.

Brown, A.J., "What is a Data Warehouse?" *UNIX Review*, August 1995, pp. 39–44.

Bucken, Michael, "SAP Holds Early Lead in C/S Applications Market," *Software Magazine*, April 1995, pp. 104–109.

Burchfield, Barbara, "Cooperative Processing: A Home on the Midrange?" *Beyond Computing*, September/October 1993, pp. 49–50.

Cole, Richard, "Leading-Edge Communications Turn to Open Systems," *Uniform Monthly*, November 1994, pp. 14–18.

Datamation Advertising Section Articles, "Discover the Fountain of Youth," *Datamation*, March 1, 1995.

————, "Groupware and the Virtual Enterprise," *Datamation*, March 15, 1995.

Davydov, Mark M., "Big Database Under Unix: What Can Make it Fly?" *Database Programming & Design*, September 1994, pp. 37–45.

Dugdale, Don, "Open Systems Stock Goes Up," *Uniforum Monthly*, May 1994, pp. 24–28.

Edelstein, Herb, "Unraveling Client/Server Architectures," *DBMS*, May 1994, pp. 34–42.

Frye, Colleen, "Move to Workflow Provokes Business Process Scrutiny," *Software Magazine*, April 1994, pp. 77–89.

————, "EIS Evolution: From Executive to Everybody's Information System," *Client/Server Computing*, August 1994, pp. 38–47.

————, "Paper-Heavy Financials Position for Workflow Wave," *Software Magazine*, April 1995, pp. 81–88.

————, "Groupware Means Change," *Software Magazine*, May 1995, p. 28.

Fryer, Bronwyn, "Do You Really Need ...Three-Tier Client-Server Computing?" *Open Computing*, March 1995, pp. 70–71.

Gerber, Barry, "Front Ends for SQL Databases," *Network Computing*, March 1992, pp. 55–70.

————, "How Low Cost File Services Got the Job Done," *Network Computing*, July 1992, pp. 121–124.

Gill, Philip J., "Transaction Processing Without Fear," *Uniforum Monthly*, November 1994, pp. 20–26.

————, "Workflow Stands and Delivers," *Uniforum Monthly*, July 1995, pp. 20–25.

Goldberg, Beverly and John G. Sifonis, "Leveraging Your Legacy Systems," *Data Management Review*, January 1995, pp. 32–36.

Guglielmo, Connie, "Documenting Success," *Open Computing*, February 1995, pp. 57–62.

Hachtel, George, "A Best of Breed Approach to Client/Server," *Data Management Review*, January 1994, pp. 17–19.

Higgins, Kelly Jackson, "Transaction Processing Moves to Users," *Open Systems Today*, September 12, 1994, pp. 48–52.

Himmelstein, Marty, "Cooperative Database Processing," *Database Programming & Design*, October 1989, pp. 66–73.

Inmon, Bill, "The Data Warehouse: Managing the Infrastructure," *Data Management Review*, December 1994, pp. 9–13.

Inmon, W.H. and Chuck Kelley, "The 12 Rules of Data Warehouse for a Client/Server World," *Data Management Review*, May 1994, pp. 6–11.

Johnson, Jim, "C/S Developers Stepping up to Three-tiered Architecture," *Software Magazine*, May 1994, pp. 71–78.

Kay, Alan S., "The Business Case for Multimedia," *Datamation*, June 15, 1995, pp. 55–60.

King, Peggy, "In it for the Long Run," *Uniforum Monthly*, July 1994, pp. 24–27.

————, "Planning for Change by Looking for Flexibility (A Case Study: Brewers Retail)," *Uniforum Monthly*, October 1994, pp. 33–38.

————, "MIS Builds a Warehouse," *Uniforum Monthly*, February 1995, pp. 16–24.

Korzeniowski, Paul, "No Consensus on Line Dividing Client, Server," *Software Magazine*, June 1993, pp. 87–91.

————, "EIS Vendors Looking Beyond the Corner Office User," *Software Magazine*, November 1993, pp. 45–57.

Krill, Paul, "Groupware Should Leave Old Data Intact," *Open Systems Today*, February 7, 1994, pp. 32–39.

Knowles, Anne, "Just in Time," *RS/Magazine*, January 1994, pp. 41–43.

Liang, Ting-Peng and others, "When Client/Server Isn't Enough: Coordinating Multiple Distributed Tasks," *IEEE Computer*, May 1994, pp. 73–79.

Mayer, John H., "Easy Access Opens Door to Legacy Environments," *Client/Server Computing*, February 1994, p. 18.

Palmer, James D. et al., "Multigroup Decision-Support Systems in CSCW," *Computer*, May 1994, pp. 67–72.

Quinlan, Tim, "The Second Generation of Client/Server," *Database Programming & Design*, May 1995, pp. 31–39.

Potts, Colin et al., "Inquiry-Based Requirements Analysis," *IEEE Software*, March 1994, pp. 21–32.

Radding, Alan, "New Front End on the Block," "Data Integration Desktop DBMS," *Client/Server Computing*, December 1994, pp. 64–70.

———, "Support Decision Makers with a Data Warehouse," *Datamation*, March 15, 1995, pp. 53–56.

Rauch, Wendy, "Will Unix Build Your Next Whatever?" *UNIX/World*, November 1987, pp. 37–45.

Raven, Christopher, "The Army Reserve's War on Paper," *Uniforum Monthly*, April 1994, pp. 24–28.

Riggs, Brian, "Directing Traffic: TP Monitors Accept New Assignments," *Software Magazine*, May 1995, pp. 77–81.

Ruber, Peter, "EIS: Selling to the Top," *VARBusiness*, October 1994, pp. 89–97.

Schlack, Mark, "The KEY to Client/Server OLTP," *Datamation*, April 1, 1995, pp. 53–56.

Schreiber, Richard, "Workflow Imposes ORDER on Transaction Processing," *Datamation*, July 15, 1995, pp. 57–60.

Semich, J. William, "Client/Server Unchained: Finally, Hardware Independence," *Datamation*, June 15, 1995, pp. 40–45.

Stafford, Jan, "Helping Customers Live With Legacy Systems," *VARBusiness*, August 1994, pp. 89–98.

Tulloch, Gord, "Easy as E-D-I," *RS/Magazine*, January 1994, pp. 50–54.

Varhol, Peter D., "Three Routes to OLAP," *Datamation*, August 15, 1995, pp. 57–63.

Walker, Doug, "Challenges of Cooperative Processing," *Interact*, March 1992, pp. 90–98.

Watson, Todd L., "Workgroup Computing: The Evolution of Teamwork," *Software Quarterly*, Volume 2, Number 1, pp. 8–16.

Whiting, Rick, "The Go-Getters," *Client/Server Today*, January 1995, pp. 54–63.

Wood, Alan, "Predicting Client/Server Availability," *Computer*, April 1995, 41–48.

Chapter 4: Phase Three: Develop an Architectural Model

Department of Defense, "Technical Architecture Framework for Information Management (TAFIM)," Volume 3, *Architecture Concepts and Design Guidance*, Version 2.0, June 1994.

Foley, Mary Jo, "10 Architectures That Will Boost Your Business," *Systems Integration*, June 1990, pp. 26–42.

Hollyman, Burnes and Lyle Anderson, "Implementing an Open Systems Architecture," *CommUNIXations*, January 1991, pp. 23–29.

Marca, David A. and Clement L. McGowan, *SADT: Structured Analysis and Design Technique*, New York: McGraw-Hill, Inc., 1988.

Osmundsen, Sheila, "Blueprints for the 1990s," *Byte*, April 1990, pp. 237–248.

Reinhard, Walter and others, "CSCW Tools: Concepts and Architectures," *Computer*, May 1994, pp. 28–36.

Sowa, J.F. and J.A. Zachman, "Extending and Formalizing the Framework for Information Systems Architecture," *IBM Systems Journal*, Vol. 31 No. 3, Page 590.

Zachman, J.A., "A Framework for Information Systems Architecture," *IBM Systems Journal*, Vol. 26 No. 3, Page 276.

Chapter 5: Phase Four: Infrastructure Planning Tasks

Appleby, Chuck, "Taking Control of Documents," *Information Week*, January 9, 1995, pp. 53–61.

Azzara, Mike, "Client-Server's Not-So-Hidden Secret," *Open Systems Today*, May 10, 1993.

Batten, Nancy and Linda Kyrnitszke, "Adding Real Time to Unix," *UNIX World*, February 1988, pp. 75–78.

Carr, Jim, "Specifying Remote Access," *VARBusiness*, April 1, 1995, pp. 84–94.

Department of Defense, "Technical Architecture Framework for Information Management (TAFIM)," *DoD Standards-Based Architecture Planning Guide*, Volume 4, Version 2.0, June 1994.

Edelstein, Herb, "Relational vs. Object-Oriented," *DBMS*, November 1991, pp. 68–79.

IEEE, *P1003.0—Guide to the POSIX Open System Environment, Section 3*, New York: IEEE, (Available from IEEE, 345 E. 47th Street, New York, NY 10017), 1995.

Kador, John, "Searching for Text Retrieval," *Database Programming & Design*, November 1991, pp. 62–65.

Kramer, Mitch, "Developers Find Gains Outweight OO Learning Curve," *Software Magazine*, November 1993, pp. 23–33.

Krol, John, "The New Story for Storage," *Information Week*, January 23, 1995, p. 67.

Leinfuss, Emily, "Portability Priorities Drive Developer Picks," *Software Magazine*, October 1993, pp. 103–108.

McCusker, Tom, "Open Documents Across the Enterprise," *Datamation*, March 15, 1994, pp. 70–72.

McKie, Stewart, "A New Era of Document Management," *DBMS*, June 1995, pp. 62–70.

Morse, Stephen, "E-Mail and Messaging," *Network Computing*, December 1, 1994, pp. 122–124.

Orfali, Robert and Dan Harkey, "Client/Server with Distributed Objects," *Byte*, April 1995, pp. 151–162.

Quiat, Barry, "Document Shock!" *Network Computing*, January 15, 1994, pp. 82–92.

Radoff, David, "Toward a Global Operating Environment," *CommUNIXations*, August 1990, pp. 15–19.

Rauch, Wendy, "Unix Overcomes its Real-Time Limitations," *UNIX World*, November 1987, pp. 62–78.

———, "User Interfaces For Art's Sake?" *UNIX Today*, November 28, 1988, p. 19.

Richman, Dan, "Fixes For OLTP," *Open Systems Today*, July 20, 1992, pp. 24–26.

Rist, Richard, "Building a Data Warehousing Infrastructure," *Data Management Review*, February 1995, pp. 42–62.

Taylor, Dave, "International Unix," *Unix Review*, November 1990, pp. 48–54.

Tanenbaum, Andrew S., "Modern Operating Systems," Englewood Cliffs, NJ: Prentice-Hall, Inc., 1992.

———, "Distributed Operating Systems," Englewood Cliffs, NJ: Prentice-Hall, Inc., 1995.

Tannenbaum, Todd, "How to Play the Unix Network Name Services Game: DNS," *Network Computing*, March 1993, pp. 156–162.

Tristram, Claire, "Do You Really Need Version Control Software?" *Open Computing*, December 1994, pp. 75–78.

Ybarro, Dano, "Device Independence," *Workstation News*, November 1992, pp. 22–27.

Chapter 6: Standards Selection and Prioritization Tasks

Adler, Richard M., "Emerging Standards for Component Software," *Computer*, March 1995, pp. 68–77.

Akerley, John, "Overview of PCTE," *AIXpert*, May 1992, pp. 25–28.

Austen, Rebecca F., "The Common Desktop Environment," *AIXpert*, August 1994, pp. 32–37.

Baker, Steven, "Remote-Access Protocols," *Unix Review*, May 1995, pp. 19–26.

———, "Solaris 2 Revisited," *Unix Review*, June 1995, pp. 49–55.

Bartlett, Jeffrey, "X/Open Runs on a Faster Track," *Uniforum Monthly*, February 1994, pp. 24–30.

———, "Spec 1170 Explained and Analyzed," *Uniforum Monthly*, April 1994, pp. 19–23.

Belisle, Don J., "OMG Standards for Object-Oriented Programming," *AIXpert*, August 1993, pp. 38–42.

Benchener, Paul, "Asking the Right Questions About EDI," *Information Week*, March 29, 1993, p. 60.

Bowen, Barry D., "Go for the Globe," *Sun World*, June 1992, pp. 90–96.

Boyle, Brian, "When Software Goes International," *UNIX Today*, August 5, 1991, pp. 34–38.

———, "Applications: Thinking Globally," *UNIX Today*, August 19, 1991, pp. 48–52.

Bozman, Jean S., "Unix CDE Debuts With Revised Role," *Computer World*, March 27, 1995, pp. 39–40.

Butler, Janet, "Data, Data Everywhere, Looking for a Link," *Software Magaine*, September 1995, pp. 65–73.

Carl-Mitchell, Smoot, "The New Internet Protocol," *Unix Review*, June 1995, pp. 31–38.

Celko, Joe, "SQL2: The Sequel to SQL," *Unix Review*, March 1995, pp. 33–36.

Cole, Bernard C., "Multimedia: Interpreting the Standards Nightmare," *OEM Magazine*, February 1994, pp. 30–44.

———, "Coming to Grips With Compression," *OEM Magazine*, April 1994, pp. 28–36.

Cook, Rick, "The Power of OLE," *VARBusiness*, October 1992, pp. 45–51.

Defense Information Systems Agency (DISA), Center for Standards, "Information Technology Standards Guidance," Release 2.1, Sept. 1995.

Department of Defense, "Technical Architecture Framework for Information Management (TAFIM)," Volume 7, Adopted Information Technology Standards (AITS), Version 2.0, August 1994.

DePompa, Barbara, "Unification: An Open Question," *Information Week*, October 3, 1994, pp. 32–34.

Foley, John, "Unix Finds Common Ground," *Information Week*, July 31, 1995, p. 90.

Feibus, Andy, "A Look at Unicode 16-bit Set of Character Codes, Plus Portable Battery Standards," *Open Systems Today*, April 25, 1994, p. 28.

———, "WinSock Conformance Means Little Without a Test Suite," *Open Systems Today*, October 31, 1994, p. 20.

———, "Andy's Handy-Dandy Top 10 List of Future Standards," *Open Systems Today*, February 20, 1995, p. 40.

Fryer, Bronwyn, "Will the Open Systems Crowd Embrace OLE?" *Open Computing*, August 1995, pp. 54–55.

Funkenhauser, Mark, "Single UNIX Specification," *Unix Review*, June 1995, pp. 41–47.

Gallmeister, Bill O., "Real-Time POSIX," *Embedded Systems Programming*, October 1992, pp. 28–40.

Garfinkel, Simson L., "Special Report: The Internet," *Sun Expert Magazine*, May 1995, pp. 59–66.

Gill, Philip J., "The Curtain Rises on CDE," *Uniforum Monthly*, March 1995, pp. 26–32.

Hajagos, Lani, "Documents and SGML," *Unix Review*, Vol. 11 No. 3, pp. 39–41.

Hinge, Kathleen Conlon, *Electronic Data Interchange: From Understanding to Implementation*, New York: American Management Association, 1988.

Hudgins-Bonafield, Christine, "The Desktop Management Discontinuity," *Network Computing*, January 15, 1995, pp. 78–86.

IEEE, *P1003.0—Guide to the POSIX Open System Environment*, New York: IEEE, 1995.

Information Management Forum, "Data Compression: Too Much of a Good Thing?" *American Management Association*, April 1994.

Issak, Jim, "POSIX Is Only the First Step," *UNIX World*, June 1988, pp. 103–110.

Johnson, Lowell, "An Update on (PASC) Standards Relevant to USENIX Members," *login:* Vol. 20, No. 4.

———, "What the Process is at IEEE POSIX," *Open Systems Today*, October 12, 1992, pp. 58–62.

Joseph, Moses, "Is POSIX Appropriate for Embedded Systems?" *Embedded Systems Programming*, July 1995, pp. 90–101.

Kay, Emily, "Taming the Paper Jungle," *Information Week*, July 3, 1995, pp. 58–66.

Kennedy, Randall C., "Windows NT," *Unix Review*, April 1994, pp. 63–66.

Knight, Robert, "Standards Groups Attack Open Systems With Unified Front," *Software Magazine*, May 1994, pp. 85–89.

Krill, Paul, "Vendors, Users Back Shamrock Doc Spec," *Open Systems Today*, March 7, 1994, pp. 2–75.

Kunert, Del, "Real Time Systems: Now in the Standards Mainstream," *Computer Technology Review*, pp. 17–22.

Lamb, Chris, "You Really Can Make X.400 Work," *Network Computing*, May 1, 1994, pp. 176–178.

Lawton, Stephen, "Thanks to MIME, Businesses Can Talk," *Client/Server Today*, April 1994, p. 22.

Lebovitz, Gregg, "An Overview of the OSF DCE Distributed File System," *AIXpert*, February 1992, pp. 55–64.

Levitt, Jason, "Choosing Cross-Platform Network APIs," *Open Systems Today*, February 21, 1994, pp. 62–73.

Linthicum, David S., "Creating Compound Document Standards," *Open Computing*, January 1995, pp. 55–60.

———, "Common Request Broker Architecture?" *Open Computing*, February 1995, pp. 68–69.

———, "What UNIX Branding Means to You," *Datamation*, July 15, 1995, pp. 53–55.

Logan, Syd, "XIE: The New X Image Extension," *Unix Review*, August 1994, pp. 29–37.

Lynch, Clifford A., "The Z39.50 Information Retrieval Protocol," *Computer Communication Review*, Vol 21, No. 1, Jan. 1991.

Mamone, Salvatore, "The IEEE Standard for Software Maintenance," ACM SIGSOFT, Software Engineeering Notes Vol. 19, No. 1, Jan. 1994, Page 75–85.

Moore, Michael, "The CDE Libraries," *Unix Review*, March 1993, pp. 53–57.

Morris, Tom and Susan Yost, "Multimedia Standards for Unix," *Unix Review*, April 1995, pp. 55–61.

North, Ken, "Understanding OLE," *DBMS*, June 1995, pp. 50–91.

Orfali, Robert et al., "OLE vs. OpenDoc: Are All Parts Just Parts?" *Datamation*, November 15, 1994, pp. 38–46.

Peterson, Dave, "Open Systems Realities," *ComputerWorld*, March 27, 1995, p. 78.

Rauch, Wendy, "Standards 'Opera' Yields High Odds," *UNIX Today*, July 1988, pp. 19–20.

Reed, James, "X.500: Truly Global Directory Services," *Unix Review*, July 1995, pp. 53–59.

Richman, Dan, "Many Vendors of ODBC Drivers, But No Test Suite," *Open Systems Today*, Jan. 9, 1995, pp. 32–34.

Robertson, Bruce, "Shoot-Out at the Database API Corral: IDAPI vs. ODBC," *Network Computing*, August 1993, pp. 132–138.

Robertson, Bruce, "XDMCP Helps Orchestrate X Windows Environments," *Network Computing*, June 1992, pp. 126–134.

Schoffstall, Martin L. and Wengyik Yeong, "A Critique of Z39.50 Based on Implementation Experience," *Computer Communication Review*, Volume 20, No. 2, April 1990.

Scott, Karyl and Paul Krill, "New Grail: Universal Document Access," *Open Systems Today*, May 23, 1994.

Semich, J. William, "Bill Gates Explains WOSA," *Datamation*, July 15, 1992, pp. 38–40.

Sippl, Roger, "ODBC and Unix: Port No More?" *Unix Review*, August 1995, pp. 27–36.

Smith, Jeanne K., "XIE-Image Extension to X," *AIXpert*, August 1992, pp. 17–22.

Song, Cavin, "MIME: Multimedia on the Internet," *Unix Review*, April 1995, p. 43–52.

Starks, Cindy, "A Developer's Look at the COSE Desktop," *Unix Review*, March 1994, pp. 41–45.

Tristram, Claire, "Spec 1170 Unix?" *Open Computing*, March 1995, pp. 65–66.

Vacca, John R., "Unicode Breaks the ASCII Barrier," *Datamation*, August 1, 1991, pp. 55–56.

Vecchione, Anthony, "A New Standard of Freedom: SGML Promises to Ease Cross-Platform Document Sharing," *Information Week*, March 29, 1993, pp. 22–23.

Wagner, Mitch, "Avoiding Open Systems Pitfalls," *Open Systems Today*, September 14, 1992, pp. 48–52.

Walli, Stephen, "Open Systems, POSIX, and NT," *login:* Vol. 20, No. 6, pp. 43–47.

Whiting, Rick, "A New Push in the OLAP Software Arena," *Client/Server Today*, March 1995, pp. 22–23.

Chapter 7: Develop Implementable Profiles

CCTA, "Towards Open Systems: Open Systems Profile for UK Government Departments," February 1994. (Available from The GOSIP Project Office, Strategic Programmes Division, CCTA, Riverwalk House, 157–161 Millbank, London SW1P 4RT.)

Childs, Ronald G., "Seven Steps to Successful E-Mail," *Datamation*, September 15, 1991, pp. 56–58.

European Workshop for Open Systems (EWOS), "ETG nn Development and Use of OSE Profiles," EWOS, EG-OSE, May 5, 1995. (Available from Jeremy Tucker, Logica UK Limited, Stephenson House, 57 Hampstead Road, London NW1 2PL, England.)

European Workshop for Open Systems (EWOS), "Method for Defining Functional Profiles for Health Care," EWOS/TA/92/260. (Available from European Workshop for Open Systems, Rue de Stassart, 36, B-1050 Brussels, Belgium.)

IEEE, "P1003.0—Guide to the POSIX Open System Environment," Sections 6 and 7. (Available from IEEE, 345 East 47th Street, New York, NY, 10017.)

ISO/IEC, "TR-10000-1: General Principles and Documentation Framework," June 1995. (Available from ISO in Geneva, ANSI in the US, and Nederlands Normalisatie-Instituut, Netherlands.)

ISO/IEC, "TR-10000-2: Principles and Taxonomy for OSI Profiles," June 1995. (Available from ISO in Geneva, ANSI in the US, and Nederlands Normalisatie-Instituut, Netherlands.)

ISO/IEC, "TR-10000: Principles and Taxonomy for OSE Profiles," June 1995. (Available from ISO in Geneva, ANSI in the US, and Nederlands Normalisatie-Instituut, Netherlands.)

Mikulis, Marise J. B., *How You and Your Organization Can Benefit From the POSC Software Integration Platform Specification, Base Computer Standards, Version 2.0*, Houston, TX: Petrotechnical Open Software Corp., 1995.

Petrotechnical Open Software Corp. (POSC), Software Integration Platform Specification Profile "Base Computer Standards Version 2.0," Englewood Cliffs, NJ: Prentice-Hall, 1995.

Chapter 8: Planning for Deployment

Bennett, Matthew, "Development Tools: Finding a Match," Client/Server '94 Supplement to *Information Week*, pp. 36–39.

Bentley, Richard and others, "Architectural Support for Cooperative Multiuser Interfaces," *IEEE Computer*, May 1994, pp. 37–45.

Berst, Jesse, "Where the Mainframe Meets Client-Server," *Information Week*, May 10, 1993, p. 60.

Bray, Olin, and Michael M. Hess, "Reengineering a Configuration-Management System," *IEEE Software*, January 1955, pp. 55–63.

Burton, Tom, "Software Change and Configuration Management (CM) in Client/Server Environments," *Computing Solutions*, February 1994, pp. 37–39.

Business Process Re-Engineering, Supplement to *Federal Computer Week*, September 20, 1993.

Casey, Thomas and Robert Metcalf, "Providing Highly Available NFS Services With HACMP," *AIXpert*, May 1995, pp. 32–38.

Cole, Richard, "IS Changes Produce Smoother Ride, (Dunlop Tire)," *Uniforum Monthly*, January 1995, pp. 20–24.

Corcoran, Cate T., "Does Plug and Play Really Mean Buy All New Desktops?" *Datamation*, March 1, 1995, pp. 49–52.

Danielle, Diane, "The Physical Plant Successfully Negotiating an Enterprise Network," *Network Computing*, June 1992, pp. 98–111.

Dedene, Guido, "Realities of Off-Shore Reengineering," *IEEE Software*, January 1995, pp. 35–46.

DeLottinville, Paul, "Open OLTP: To Monitor or Not to Monitor," *Datamation*, November 1, 1994, pp. 59–61.

Dietzen, Scott, "Distributed Transaction Processing with Encina," *AIXpert*, November 1992, pp. 20–29.

Edelstein, Herb, "Seeking Solutions to DBMS Connectivity," *Open Systems Today*, February 7, 1994, pp. 62–67.

Edelstein, Herb and Janet Millenson, "Selecting End-User Data Access Tools," *Open Systems Today*, September 26, 1994, pp. 48–52.

Ettorre, Barbara, "Reengineering Tales From the Front," *Management Review*, January 1995, pp. 13–18.

Francett, Barbara, "Database Performance: Not Just OLTP Anymore," *Software Magazine*, September 1994, pp. 61–72.

Garry, Greg, "Linking up a Suitable E-Mail System: A Market Primer," *Client/Server Today*, October 1994, pp. 58–63.

———, "Client/Server Hits the Road," *Datamation*, August 1, 1995, pp. 43–45.

Gaskin, James E., "Unix NFS Software: A Ticket to Unix," *Network Computing*, May 1, 1994, p. 48.

Greenstein, Irwin, "Exploring Client/Server Operating Systems," *Networking Management*, December 1991, pp. 27–33.

Haapaniemi, Peter, "Beyond Reengineering," *Unisys*, Spring 1995, pp. 8–15.

Haight, Timothy, "The Varieties of Rightsizing," *Network Computing*, February 1993, pp. 86–97.

Hall, Eric, "Managing User Access: Choosing Cross-Platform Solutions," *Network Computing*, April 1, 1994, pp. 132–133.

Hammer, Michael, and James Champy, "What is Reengineering?" *Information Week*, May 5, 1992, pp. 10–24.

Hanna, Mary, "Reengineering Aims for Legacy Salvation," *Software Magazine*, September 1993, pp. 41–50.

Hindin, Harvey and Wendy Rauch, "IBM's AS/400 Openness Strategy," *Systems Management*, December 1994, pp. 54–60.

Hollar, Jeffrey D., "Connecting to Heterogeneous Data," *AIXpert*, May 1993, pp. 35–38.

Industry Forum, "Expert Answers Questions About Reengineering," *American Management Association*, NY. January 1994, pp. 1–2.

———, "Is There Life After Reengineering?" *American Management Association*, NY. April 1995, pp. 1–3.

Information Management Forum, "Reengineering as an Enabler of Information Technology," *American Management Association*, NY. December 1993, pp. 1–3.

Kaswin, Reuven, "Designing Client-Server Applications," *Unix Review*, December 1993, pp. 59–64.

Kawanami, Jim, "Process Engineering and BPR: Critical for Client/Server," *Data Management Review*, August 1994, pp. 6–11.

Kimball, Ralph and Kevin Strehlo, "Why Decision Support Fails and How To Fix It," *Datamation*, June 1, 1994, pp. 40–45.

King, Peggy, "Database Needs Drive High-End Server Decisions," *Open Systems Today*, September 20, 1993, pp. 62–64.

Kirzner, Rikki, "The Siren Call of Business Process Reengineering," *Uniforum Monthly*, January 1995, pp. 14–19.

Korzeniowski, Paul, "When Licensing C/S Software, One Size Does Not Fit All," *Software Magazine*, June 1994, pp. 73–77.

Linthicum, David S., "How to buy TP Monitors," *Open Computing*, July 1955, pp. 66–67.

Lorence, Mark J., "Avoid the Pitfalls of Distributed Development," *Datamation*, May 1, 1993, pp. 69–70.

Manganelli, Raymond and Mark K. Klein, "Should You Start From Scratch?" *Management Review*, July 1994, pp. 45–47.

———, "Your Reengineering Toolkit," *Management Review*, August 1994, pp. 26–39.

Manganelli, Raymond and Steven P. Raspa, "Why Reengineering has Failed," *Management Review*, July 1995, pp. 39–43.

Mason, D., Dean, "Distributed Programming," *Unix Review*, Vol. 11, No. 1, pp. 31–37.

MacKenzie, Jonathan, "Document Repositories," *Byte*, April 1995, pp. 131–138.

Mehta, Rahul and Claire Mann, "Selecting Data Warehouse End-User Access Tools," *Data Management Review*, July/August 1995, pp. 46–48.

Moad, Jeff, "Object Methods Tame Reengineering Madness," *Datamation*, May 15, 1995, pp. 43–48.

Morse, Stephen, "Rightsizing: Tailoring the Applications and the Platforms," *Network Computing*, February 1993, pp. 63–77.

Mullins, Craig S., "Client/Server Development Considerations," *Data Management Review*, September 1994, pp. 40–42.

Neely, Kris, "Where the AS/400 Fits Into Client/Server Systems," *Datamation*, May 15, 1995, pp. 57–59.

Olsen, Paul, "How To Design Applications that Cross Platforms," *Systems Management*, June 1995, pp. 20–26.

Orfali, Robert et al., "Intergalactic Client/Server Computing," *Byte*, April 1995, pp. 109–122.

Poe, Vidette, "Clear, Careful, and Realistic: Guidelines for Warehouse Development," *Database Program & Design*, September 1994, pp. 60–64.

Radding, Alan, "Repository Van Winkle," *Client/Server Computing*, August 1994, pp. 60–64.

Rasmus, Dan, "Reengineering, or Evolution Through Violent Overthrow," Sept. 1992, pp. 52–58.

Ranade, Jay, "Why the Mainframe Survives," *Open Computing*, April 1995, pp. 34–35.

Rauch, Wendy and Harvey Hindin, "IBM Makes More Openness Moves," *Systems Management*, January 1995, pp. 62–64.

Reichard, Kevin and Eric F. Johnson, "The CDE Applications Builder," *Unix Review*, September 1994, pp. 67–70.

Richter, Jane, "Distributing Data," *Byte*, June 1994, pp. 139–147.

Riggs, Brian, "Directing Traffic: TP Monitors Accept New Assignments," *Software Magazine*, May 1995, pp. 77–81.

Rosenblatt, Bill, "Unix RDBMS: Developing a Future," *Advanced Systems*, March 1994, pp. 94–102.

Russell, Lou, "Re-engineering Legacy Systems," *Data Management Review*, July 1994, pp. 20–22.

Saracco, C.M. and Charles J. Bontempo, "A Closer Look at DB2/6000 Version 2," *AIXtra*, Nov./Dec. 1994, pp. 57–61.

Schur, Stephen G., "Reengineering: Destination Workflow," *Database Programming & Design*, December 1994, pp. 52–58.

Sedore, Christopher, "Integrating Unix and Windows NT Using NFS," *Network Computing*, July 1, 1995, pp. 146–148.

Serlin, Omri, "Unix on a Mainframe? The Idea's Growing," *UNIX World*, May 1991, pp. 37–39.

Shelton, Robert E., "Business Objects & BPR," *Data Management Review*, November 1994, pp. 6–20.

———, "Data Warehouse Infrastructure," *Data Management Review*, July/August 1995, pp. 70–74.

Simpson, David, "Downsizing: Pull the Plug Slowly," *Datamation*, July 1, 1995, 34–37.

Sneed, Harry M., "Planning the Reengineering of Legacy Systems," *IEEE Software*, January, 1955, pp. 24–34.

Stapleton, Lisa, "Reverse Engineering Puzzles Out the Past," *Open Computing*, March 1994, pp. 77–82.

Stevens, Larry, "Mapping Your Business Processes," *Open Computing*, February 1995, pp. 73–78.

Storey, Tony, and John Knutson, "CICS/6000 Online Transaction Processing with AIX," *AIXpert*, November 1992, pp. 31–42.

Strom, David, "The Trials and Tribulations of Remote Access," *Network Computing*, March 1992, pp. 41–42.

Tait, Peter, "The Future of Partitioning," *Unix Review*, May 1995, pp. 41–44.

Teng, James T.C. and William J. Kettinger, "Business Process Redesign and Information Architecture: Exploring the Relationships," *Data Base Advances*, February 1995, pp. 30–40.

The', Lee, "Now You Can Automate BPR," *Datamation*, March 1, 1995, pp. 61–65.

———, "Need Groupware? Think Functions, Not Products," *Datamation*, July 15, 1995, pp. 67–74.

———, "Workflow Tackles the Productivity Paradox," *Datamation*, August 15, 1995, pp. 65–67.

Tucker, Michael Jay, "3 Rightsizing Recipes," *SunExpert Magazine*, September 1994, pp. 43–52.

Varhol, Peter D., "The Truth About Windows on Alternative Platforms." *Datamation*, July 1, 1994, pp. 43–45.

Wadhwa, Vivek, "Partitioning Apps: What are the Issues?" *Unix Review*, May 1995, pp. 35–38.

Weissman, Steven, "The Business End of Network Redesign," *Network World*, July 10, 1995, p. 47.

White, Colin, "Choosing the Right Client/Server Operating Environment," *DBMS*, August, 1995, pp. 50–58.

Whiting, Rick, "Cutting-Edge Tools for Client Server Development," *Client/Server Today*, April 1994, pp. 27–31.

Wilson, Jane R., "Strategies for Streamlining In-House Development," *Uniforum Monthly*, September 1994, pp. 32–36.

Wilson, Linda, "Devil in Your Data," *Information Week*, August 31, 1992, pp. 48–54.

Wong, Kenny et al., "Structural Redocumentation: A Case Study," *IEEE Software*, January, 1995, pp. 46–53.

Worobec, Bruace, "Enterprise Data One Step at a Time," *Database Programming & Design*, pp. 64–67.

Wreden, Nick, "Re-engineering: The Ultimate Test of Skill," *Beyond Computing*, May/June 1994, pp. 30–36.

Yevich, Richard, "Enterprise Data Modeling for the Client/Server World," *Data Management Review*, April 1994, pp. 36–37.

Chapter 9: Choosing Middleware

Adhikari, Richard, "Messaging and Transaction Management Step Into Middleware Spotlight," *Client/Server Computing*, September 1995, pp. 99–110.

Ananda, A. L. and B. H. Tay, "A Survey of Asynchronous Remote Procedure Calls," *Operating Systems Review*, Vol. 26. No. 2, pp. 92–109.

Blakely-Fogel, Debora, "Object-Oriented Programming with SOM/6000," *AIXpert*, June 1994, pp. 25–34.

Butler, Janet, "Data, Data Everywhere, Looking for a Link," *Software Magaine*, September 1995, pp. 65–73.

Dickman, Alan, "The RPC-vs.-Messaging-Debate: Under the Covers," *Open Systems Today*, August 15, 1994, pp. 58–59.

Dolgicer, Max, "Messaging Middleware: The Next Generation," *Data Communications*, July 1994, pp. 77–84.

Edelstein, Herb, "Distributed Databases," *DBMS*, September 1990, pp. 36–48.

———, "One Image From Many Databases," *Open Systems Today*, April 26, 1993, pp. 60–66.

Engler, Natalie, "Riding the Bleeding Edge of Distributed Computing," *Open Computing*, February 1995, pp. 35–44.

Finkelstein, Richard, "Client/Server Middleware: Making Connections Across the Enterprise," *DBMS*, Jan. 1993, pp. 46–54.

Finkelstein, Rich, "The New Middleware," *DBMS*, February 1995, pp. 50–58.

Gill, Philip J., "DCE Status Report," *Uniforum Monthly*, March 1995, pp. 54–58.

Gordon, Robert, "Middleware: Client/Server Bridge to Legacy Systems," *Data Management Review*, January 1995, pp. 26–29.

Hackathorn, Richard D. and Mark Schlack, "How to Pick Client/Server Middleware," *Datamation*, June 15, 1994, pp. 52–56.

Hayes, Frank, "Bridging the Object Gap," *Information Week*, August 14, 1995, p. 70.

Johnson Johna, T., "Client-Server's Magic Bullet?" *Data Communications*, August 1995, pp. 44–54.

King, Steven S., "Middleware!" *Data Communications*, March 1992, pp. 58–67.

Korzeniowski, Paul, "Distributed DBMS Vendors Turn to Replication to Eliminate Bottlenecks," *Client/Server Computing*, May 1994, pp. 77–81.

Kumar, Ram, "OSF's Distributed Computing Environment," *AIXpert*, Fall 1991, pp. 22–30.

Kramer, Mitch, "IS Managers Take the Middle Road," *Client/Server Computing*, April 1994, pp. 60–67.

Linthicum, David S., "Should You Standardize on Common Request Broker Architecture?" *Open Computing*, pp. 68–69.

Liszewski, Steven J., "Application Specific Gateways," *Data Management Review*, September 1994, pp. 5–9.

Majkiewicz, Jane, "Taking the Plunge into Objects," *RS Magazine*, July 1994, pp. 36–44.

Mason, Tony, "OSF's DCE," *Unix Review*, Vol. 10, No. 1, pp. 31–34.

Mattison, Rob, "Is an OODBMS for Me?" *Data Management Review*, March 1994, pp. 41–43.

Mattison, Rob and Michael J. Sipolt, "An Object Lesson in Management," *Datamation*, July 1, 1995, pp. 51–55.

Meade, Duane A., "Object Lessons," *Beyond Computing*, July/August 1995, pp. 41–42.

Moran, Brian, "Middleware & Cross-Platform Development," *Network Computing*, January 15, 1995, pp. 144–147.

Morrison, David, "With Middleware, Maybe You Can Get There From Here," *Beyond Computing*, May-June 1994, pp. 18–21.

Paone, Joe, "The Object is Interoperability," *Internetwork*, October 1994, pp. 33–34.

Rauch, Wendy, "True Distributed DBMSes Presage Big Dividends," *Mini-Micro Systems*, May 1987, pp. 65–73.

———, "Distributed Databases Clear Hurdles," *Mini-Micro Systems*, June 1987, pp. 61–79.

Rettig, Hillary, "Middleware: When Your Customer Wants You Everywhere," *VARBusiness*, August 1995, pp. 109–118.

Richman, Dan, "Many Databases, Multiple Apps: What to Do?" *Open Systems Today*, September 5, 1994, pp. 64–65.

Robertson, Bruce, "APIware vs. Middleware," *Network Computing*, December 1, 1994, pp. 120–121.

Russell, Bob, "DCE Performance Study," *AIXpert*, November 1994, pp. 48–58.

Schreiber, Richard, "Middleware Demystified," *Datamation*, April 1, 1995, pp. 41–45.

———, "Getting Distributed Apps to Communicate: Let's Talk Middleware," *Datamation*, July 1, 1995, pp. 57–60.

———, "Glue Enterprise Apps Together," *Datamation*, August 15, 1995, pp. 41–43.

Siegel, Jon, "Programming in the OMG Environment," *RS/Magazine*, March 1994, pp. 50–55.

Simpson, David, "Still Chasing the Interoperability Butterfly," *Client/Server Today*, pp. 28–34.

Spector, Alfred Z., and Jeffrey L. Eppinger, "RPC as Middleware," *RS/Magazine*, March 1994, 46–49.

Stahl, Stephanie et al., "Middleware," *Information Week*, November 1, 1993, pp. 62–68.

Sutherland, Jeff, "Business Objects Architecture: Key to Client/Server Development," *Data Management Review*, November 1994, pp. 46–50.

The', Lee, "Distribute Data Without Choking the Net," *Datamation*, January 7, 1994, pp. 35–38.

Tibbitts, Fred, "CORBA: A Common Touch for Distributed Applications," *Data Communications*, May 21, 1995, pp. 71–75.

Vaughan, Jack, "Amid Praise and Catcalls, DCE Comes Into the Open," *Software Magazine*, pp. 55–62.

Wade, Jim, "DCE With HACMP/6000," *AIXpert*, May 1994, pp. 43–46.

Whiting, Rick, "Getting on the Middleware Express," *Client/Server Today*, November 1994, pp. 70–93.

Yeamans, Les, "The Message is the Medium," *RS/Magazine*, March 1994, pp. 56–59.

Chapter 10: Managing the Open Client/Server Environment

Adhikari, Richard, "Unweaving the Tangled Web of Print Management," *Client/Server Computing*, December 1994, pp. 75–80.

Blakely-Fogel, Debora, "SMP Overview," *AIXpert*, November 1994, pp. 4–12.

Bowen, Barry D., "Living with Remote Possibilities," *Uniforum Monthly*, April 1994, pp. 30–32.

Bunch, Steve, "Security on Unix Systems," *Unix Review*, March 1992, pp. 39–48.

Burleson, Don, "Managing Security in a Distributed Database Environment," *DBMS*, May 1995, pp. 72–86.

Cashin, Jerry, "Open, Distributed Users Tightening Unix Security," *Software Magazine*, January 1994, pp. 81–91.

Danielle, Diane, "Network Management: Keeping Tabs on the Network's Vital Signs," *Network Computing*, September 1, 1994, pp. 177–178.

Dichter, Carl, "Easy Unix Security," *Unix Review*, Vol. 11, No. 4, pp. 43–48.

Dugdale, Don, "System Administration in an Age of Limited Resources," *Uniforum Monthly*, August 1994, pp. 15–25.

Durr, Michael, "Remote Site Management Tricks," *Datamation*, April 1, 1995, pp. 49–51.

Ellis, James and others, "Keeping Internet Intruders Away," *Unix Review*, September 1994, pp. 35–44.

Jander, Mary, "Management Frameworks," *Data Communications*, February 1994, pp. 58–68.

Faden, Mike, "X/Open Taps Tivoli's Technology," *Open Systems Today*, February 7, 1994, p. 76.

Feibus, Andy, "Desktop Management Interface: How the Spec Manages to Manage Everything," *Open Systems Today*, March 7, 1994, p. 17.

Feibus, Andy, "Desktop Management Interface: Standardizing the Dialog With System Components," *Open Systems Today*, March 21, 1994, p. 20.

Gerber, Barry, "Network Storage: A New Perspective," *Network Computing*, April 1993, pp. 84–98.

Hanna, Mary, "Dynamic Corporate Networks Have Managers on a Tightrope," *Software Magazine*, December 1994, pp. 45–53.

Girishankar, Saroja, "DCE Slated to Gain Mgm't Component," *Communications Week*, January 31, 1994, pp. 1–51.

Hindin, Harvey and Wendy Rauch, "Managing Disparate Systems," *Systems Management*, November 1994, pp. 78–90.

Huntington-Lee, Jill, "SNMP: The Wonder Years," *Lan Computing*, April 1994, pp. 27–31.

Jacobson, Holly, "Enterprising Print Management," *Distributed Computing Solutions*, Supplement to *Internetwork*, November 1994, pp. S10–S11.

Jilg, Jeff, "NetLS: The Key to Network Licensing," *AIXpert*, November 1993, 43–49.

Jones, Katherine, "Working Toward End-to-End Control in the Open Systems Enterprise," *Client/Server Computing*, December 1994, pp. 80–86.

Kay, Russell, "Distributed and Secure," *Byte*, June 1994, pp. 165–178.

Kolodziej, Stan, "Rightsizing Rewrites Rules for Managing Performance," *Software Magazine*, February 1994, pp. 51–57.

Korzeniowski, Paul, "SNMP Standard Enables Hub, Router Management Tool Integration," *Client/Server Computing*, March 1994, pp. 77–81.

———, "Backup Becomes a Beast When Data is Distributed," *Software Magazine*, December 1994, pp. 67–71.

———, "Distributed Discomfort? Prescription Includes Regular System Check-ups," *Software Magazine*, March 1995, pp. 52–63.

Lenatti, Chuck, "How to Buy System Management Software," *Open Computing*, September 1995, pp. 63–66.

Linthicum, David S., "Managing Networks," *Open Computing*, September 1995, pp. 49–50.

McNamara, George, "DMI Targets Open Desktop Management," *Computer Technology Review*, January 1994, pp. 6–8.

McNut, Dinah, "Who Are You (Kerberos)," *Unix Review*, November 1992, pp. 47–51.

Melford, Robert J., "Secure Unix for Enterprise Computing," *Datamation*, March 1, 1995, pp. 55–58.

Moeller, Mike, "Net Managers Struggle to Complete the Configuration Management Puzzle," *Client/Server Computing*, August 1994, pp. 65–71.

Nemeth, Evi and others, "UNIX System Administration Handbook," second edition. Englewood Cliffs, NJ: 1995. Prentice Hall.

Rauch, Wendy, "Can Your Systems Manage Themselves?" *Systems Management*, December 1994, pp. 29–35.

———, "Unix Tech Support: The Good, The Bad and the Ugly," *UNIX Today*, June 25, 1990, P. 65.

Sandberg, Russel, "Sybil, The Psychology of Network Management," *Unix Review*, Vo. , 8, No. 5, pp. 62–67.

Simpson, David, "DMI Promises PC, Peripherals Management," *Client/Server Today*, October 1994, pp. 24–29.

———, "Can SMS Play With the Big Boys?" *Client/Server Today*, March 1995, pp. 24–28.

———, "Can Sun Rise to the Systems Management Challenge?" *Client/Server Today*, March 1995, pp. 30–31.

Stallings, William, "Network Security With SNMPv2," *Unix Review*, February 1995, pp. 41–47.

Stephenson, Peter, "Securing Remote Access," *Network Computing*, February 1, 1995, pp. 130–134.

Sylvester, Tim, "DMTF Releases its Desktop Specification," *Client/Server Today*, May 1994, p. 32.

Taber, Mark, "Call Growing for Open Systems Management," *Software Magazine*, March 1992, pp. 51–59.

Tristram, Claire, "Looking for the Big Picture," *Uniforum Monthly*, February 1995, pp. 32–35.

———, "Simple Network Management Protocol?" *Open Computing*, May 1995, pp. 68–69.

———, "Microsoft SMS?" *Open Computing*, July 1995, pp. 62–63.

Vacca, John, "Networks Put Mainframe Security Tools to the Test," *Software Magazine*, January 1994, pp. 51–57.

Varhol, Peter D., "UPSIZING with SMP: Don't Ignore the OS," *Datamation*, January 15, 1995, pp. 59–61.

White, Daniel, "Taking Charge of Security," *Information Week*, November 28, 1994, p. 96.

Chapter 11: Migration Strategies

Adhikari, Richard, "New SMP, MPP Workhorses Spur Database Suppliers," *Software Magazine*, January 1995, pp. 58–63.

Baker, Steven, "Solving the PC Connectivity Puzzle," *Unix Review*, January 1995, pp. 29–36.

Bunch, Steve, "Security on Unix Systems," *Unix Review*, March 1992, pp. 39–48.

Clarke, Michele and Rick Boyd-Merritt, "Laying Siege to the Server," *OEM Magazine*, April 1995, pp. 52–60.

Clements, Brad, "Resolving Portability Problems," *UNIX Today*, August 6, 1990, pp. 42–46.

Dellecave, Tom, Jr., "Remote Aids for Win95," *Information Week*, August 28, 1995, p. 68.

Dichter, Carl R., "Overcoming Portability Problems," *UNIX Today*, April 29, 1991, pp. 50–56.

Edelstein, Herb, "Auditing the Auditors," *DBMS*, March 1990, pp. 46–50.

Fahey, Michael, "The PC-To-Unix Connection," *RS/Magazine*, July 1995, pp. 35–39.

Fordyce, Wayne, "Making the Leap to Unix SVR4," *Network Computing*, June 1, 1994, pp. 166–170.

Friscia, Tony, "Enterprise Integration Strategies," White Paper. *Computer World*, September 12, 1994, Special Advertising Supplement.

Fund, Glenn, "When Superservers are the Best Bet," *Datamation*, March 15, 1992, pp. 52–54.

Gage, Beth, "ATM Under the Covers," *Network World*, July 10, 1995, pp. 45–46.

Garry, Grey, "Migrating Data: What are Your Options?" *Client/Server Today*, January 1995, pp. 48–53.

Gasiewski, Donna, "End of the Line for Terminal Emulation," *DEC Professional*, August 1995, pp. 18–20.

Hebert, Thomas, "Don't Blame the Integrator," *Information Week*, May 30, 1994, p. 156.

Hindin, Harvey J., "Plants Try Own Solutions in Wait for Real-Time Unix," *Computer World*, October 31, 1988, p. 69.

Hobart, James, "Principles of Good GUI Design," *Unix Review*, September 1995, pp. 37–46.

Hamilton, Dennis, "Don't Let Client/Server Performance Gotchas Getcha," *Datamation*, November 1, 1994, pp. 39–40.

Larribeau, Bob, "ISDN Branches Out," *Network World*, July 10, 1995, pp. 41–43.

Marsh, Vivien, "Test Client/Server Apps Before They Bug You to Death," *Datamation*, August 1, 1995, pp. 32–35.

Mills, Brendon W., "Where to Turn for Network Bandwidth," *Unix Review*, July 1995, pp. 47–51.

Olson, Craig S., "Unplugging the I/O Bottleneck," *Workstation News*, July 1991, pp. 21–26.

Price, Josh, and Bharat Vijay, "The New Workgroup Servers," *DBMS*, September 1995, pp. 44–56.

Quinlan, Tim, "How to Predict Client/Server Performance," *Database Programming & Design*, December 1994, pp. 33–41.

Schneeman, Richard D., "Porting Multimedia Applications to the Open System Environment," *IEEE Software*, November 1992, pp. 39–47.

Stevens, Larry, "High-End Multiprocessing Servers," *Open Computing*, August 1995, pp. 67–69.

Strauss, Paul, "Plan Your 2001 Network Now," *Datamation*, August 1, 1994, pp. 32–37.

Thackray, John, "A Road Map for Migration," Client/Server '94 Supplement to *Information Week*, pp. 63–65.

Thompson, Don, "Migration Between Environments Made Easy With RPC," *Open Computing*, November 1994, pp. 21–26.

Tristram, Claire, "Do You Really Need License Management Software?" *Open Computing*, July 1995, p. 65.

———, "Stalking the Mega Outsourcing Deal," *Open Computing*, March 1995, pp. 33–40.

———, "Ten Things to Know About Migrating to Client-Server Accounting," *Open Computing*, Nov. 1994, pp. 75–76.

Tulk, Jon, "Making the Switch a Success," *Open Systems Today*, July 6, 1992, pp. 47–52.

Wittman, Art and James E. Drews, "Netware 4.1 Puts Novell in the Spotlight," *Network Computing*, Jan. 15, 1995, pp. 50–60.

Wong, Carolyn W.C., "12 Steps for Negotiating Interoperability," *Open Computing*, August 1994, pp. 57–59.

Chapter 12: How Much Will it Cost?

Atre, Shaku, "The Hidden Costs of Client/Server," *DBMS*, June 1995, pp. 71–74.

Bartlett, Jeffrey, "Making Open Systems Make Business Sense," *Uniforum Monthly*, September 1994, pp. 26–39.

Beaver, Jennifer, "The Hidden Costs of Downsizing," *Uniforum Monthly*, March 1994, pp. 48–50.

Carner, Rochelle, "Unsuportable Costs," *Open Computing*, February 1994, pp. 35–41.

Chabrow, Eric R., "The Training Payoff," *Information Week*, July 10, 1995, pp. 36–46.

Chisholm, John, "Enterprise Client-Server Costs," *Unix Review*, January 1994, pp. 9–12.

Cook, Rick, "Georgia Medical Care Foundation: Open Systems as the Low-Cost Option," *Uniforum Monthly*, February 1994, pp. 16–22.

Devers, Linda, "Uncovering the Hidden Costs of E-Mail," *Network Computing*, August 1,1994, pp. 142–145.

Dugdale, Don, "Getting a Handle on Cost," *Uniforum Monthly*, November 1994, pp. 32–35.

Economic Justification Workbook For Bar Code and Factory Data Collection Systems. (Tucson, AZ: Burr-Brown Corp., P.O. Box 11400, Tucson, AZ 85734). 1991.

Gill, Philip J., "The Challenges of Downsizing," *Open Systems Today*, March 2, 1992, pp. 70–78.

———, "When Technology Isn't the Issue," *Open Systems Today*, April 27, 1992, pp. 66–77.

Guteri, Fred, "IT Expands Despite Bargain Basement Budgets," *Datamation*, August 15, 1994, pp. 46–48.

Henderson, Tom, "Tough Questions to Ask a Client/Server Integrator," *Datamation*, August 15, 1995, pp. 59–61.

Hindin, Eric, "The Branch-Office Balancing Act: More Sites, More Networks, Same Budget," *Data Communications*, June 1994, pp. 60–66.

Hufnagel, Ellen, "The Hidden Costs of Client/Server," Client/Server '94 Supplement to *Information Week*, pp. 22–27.

Information Management Forum, *Analyzing Your Help Desk Needs*, American Management Association, 1994.

Kirwin, William, "Migration Plans," *CIO*, April 1, 1995, pp. 24–30.

Marketing Forum, *Texas Instruments' Company-Wide IMC Training*, New York: American Management Association, 1994.

Marx, Wendy, "The New High-Tech Training," *Management Review*, February 1995, pp. 57–60.

McPartlin, John P. and others, "The Hidden Costs of Downsizing," *Information Week*, November 18, 1991, pp. 35–38.

Moad, Jeff, "Calculting the Real Benefit of Training," *Datamation*, April 15, 1995, pp. 45–47.

Raynor, Darrel A., "Get the Most From Training Dollars," *Datamation*, April 15, 1995, pp. 47–49.

Scrupski, Susan, "How to Hire an Integrator," *Datamation*, August 15, 1994, p. 32.

Semich, J. William, "Can You Orchestrate Client/Server Computing?" *Datamation*, August 15, 1994, pp. 36–43.

Simpson, David, "Downsizing: Pull the Plug Slowly," *Datamation*, July 1, 1995, pp. 34–37.

Snell, Ned, "Client/Server Chaos Busters," *Datamation*, October 15, 1994, pp. 45–50.

Chapter 13: Implementation at Last

Eshom, Terry, "An MVS Systems Programmer in a Unix World," *Computing Solutions*, June 1994, pp. 28–29.

Johnson, Jim, "Migration Survivors: New Jobs for Old Pros," *Uniforum Monthly*, December 1994, pp. 22–25.

Index